Schriftenreihe des
EUROPA-KOLLEGS HAMBURG
zur Integrationsforschung

Herausgegeben von
Prof. Dr. Peter Behrens
Prof. Dr. Sigrid Boysen
Prof. Dr. Thomas Bruha
Prof. Dr. Thomas Eger
Prof. Dr. Armin Hatje
Prof. Dr. Markus Kotzur
Prof. Dr. Gert Nicolaysen †
Prof. Dr. Stefan Oeter
Prof. Dr. Jörg Philipp Terhechte
Prof. Dr. Wolf Schäfer †

Band 83

Annalisa Morticelli

Human Rights of Irregular Migrants in the European Union

Implementation of European Policy and Legislation for the Effective Protection of these Rights

Nomos

The Deutsche Nationalbibliothek lists this publication in the Deutsche Nationalbibliografie; detailed bibliographic data are available on the Internet at http://dnb.d-nb.de

ISBN 978-3-8487-8107-2 (Print)
978-3-7489-2525-5 (ePDF)

British Library Cataloguing-in-Publication Data
A catalogue record for this book is available from the British Library.

ISBN 978-3-8487-8107-2 (Print)
978-3-7489-2525-5 (ePDF)

Library of Congress Cataloging-in-Publication Data
Morticelli, Annalisa
Human Rights of Irregular Migrants in the European Union
Implementation of European Policy and Legislation
for the Effective Protection of these Rights
Annalisa Morticelli
357 pp.
Includes bibliographic references.

ISBN 978-3-8487-8107-2 (Print)
978-3-7489-2525-5 (ePDF)

Onlineversion
Nomos eLibrary

1st Edition 2021

Acknowledgements

This important work could not have come to light without the contribution of my supervisor, my family and my dear friends.

For this reasons first of all I would like to thank my supervisor, Prof. Dr. Markus Kotzur, who gave me the opportunity to undertake and complete this doctorate, who believed in this research project since the beginning, who dedicated time and attention to me every time I asked through his professional and moral support especially in the most difficult moments of this path. I thank him for his great competence and professionalism and for his enthusiasm in supporting international and multicultural projects.

I also would like to dedicate this work to my family who supported me with conviction and affection in all aspects so that I could achieve my goal. In particular, I thank my Dad, who encouraged me and accompanied me along the way from the beginning, supporting me in the most strenuous moments, certain that the result would come. To him I dedicate the result of this research and this enriching life journey with infinite love.

To my mom and my sister, my rocks, an infinite thanks for always being there with tenderness and wisdom.

Finally, I would like to thank all those whom I met along this path, they are many and all in my heart, who have shared moments of joy, sadness and difficulties without ever giving up their warmth and support. Today they are special friends without whose this experience and work would not have been the same.

Abstract

Human rights of irregular migrants in the European Union: implementation of European policy and legislation for the effective protection of these rights

In the current European legal framework there are many aspects that are very relevant subjects of investigation: the migration flows issue, the need of a common asylum system for all States, the protection of the human rights of vulnerable persons, the integration issue and so on[1].

Among these, one relevant theme in the current political and juridical European context and an area to which academic research can also make a contribution is the field of irregular migration: the movement of migrants who enter and/or stay in a Member States without legal status, namely against the national law of the Member State and European Union law[2].

These persons are particularly vulnerable to human rights abuses because of their position in the territory in contravention of the law of that State: they are in the middle of a strong tension between the security needs of the State that can be seen to be undermined by their illegal entry and/or residence, and the obligation of Member States to guarantee the protection of their human rights enshrined in several international and European Union conventions and laws.

Given the tensions at the European Union level, it is very important to achieve a balance and a coordinated system. In this context, the theme of protection of irregular migrants is considered a relevant topic in the legal framework of the European Union[3].

---

1 S. CASTELS & M.J. MILLER, *The age of migration: international population movements in the modern world* (4th ed.) New York: Guilford Press, 2004.

2 A. BLOCH, *Irregular Migrants: Policy, Politics, Motives and Everyday Lives*, London, Routledge, 2012; A. TRIANDAFYLLIDOU, *Irregular Migration in Europe: Myths and Realities*, Farnham, Surrey, Ashgate, 2010.

3 A. TRIANDAFYLLIDOU, *Irregular Migration in Europe: Myths and Realities*, Farnham, Surrey, Ashgate, 2010; M. TODINO, *The Legality of Intercepting Boat People Under Search and Rescue and Border Control Operations with Reference to Recent Italian Interventions in the Mediterranean Sea and the ECtHR Decision in the Hirsi Case*, in Journal of International Maritime Law, April 2012, Vol. 18, No. 1, pp. 59-74. at 62: "In the case of active resistance, the interception cannot fall within the SAR legal regime".

The main aim of this research is to try to outline the actual legal framework concerning the protection of human rights of irregular migrants at European level, to verify how the Member States implemented this law through a focus on two countries, Italy and Germany, to detect and analyze the critical points in the framework, and finally try to offer a contribution in terms of research to improve the critical aspects drawing on the comparison between the two Member States previously mentioned.

The analysis reported in the dissertation has been divided into three Chapters: the initial chapter deals with a classification of migration phenomena in general and the specific category of irregular migration in the European Union; the second has been dedicated to the analysis of the European legal tools for protecting the human rights of irregular migrants with a focus on first reception of this category of migrants in the European Union; finally, the third part of the thesis addresses a comparison between the two Member States, Italy and Germany, to understand how these Member States implemented European legislation on the protection of human rights of irregular migrants in the entry phase, analyzing the specific national law.

The methodology used for each Chapter consisted of collecting legal materials, laws and jurisprudence, and international literature on the topic, adding also material from international organization recognized as experts who conduct empirical work in this field, as for instance the Agencies of United Nations. The material has been organized to give a detailed overview of the subject of each chapter and to highlight what the main literature concludes in order to then be able to proceed to a critical analysis. The update of the thesis regarding the part of analysis on the Italian system excludes the last legislative changes starting from decree law of 4 October 2018, n. 113, coordinated with the conversion law of 1 December 2018, n. 132, containing "Urgent provisions on international protection and immigration, public safety, as well as measures for the functionality of the Ministry of the Interior and the organization and functioning of the National Agency for the administration and destination of seized and confiscated property to organized crime"[4].

Returning to the contents of the individual Chapters, in the first one the broader category of migration is explored including irregular migration in the European Union context. The migration category has been analyzed with the goal to understand the phenomenon of migration in general from a sociological point of view: what are the reasons underpinning the move-

4 Italian Official Journal 3 December 2018, n. 281.

ment? The chapter analyses this phenomenon in several Member States that have known large flows of migration in their history, (such as Germany, France, United Kingdom, Italy and Spain). After this description, the focus is on the birth of the concept of irregular migration in the European Union analyzing this category specifically in some Member States where the irregular status of migrants has been a significant phenomenon.

After that the focus moves to explore exactly who irregular migrants are from a legal point of view in the European Union regulation. There is not an exact definition of irregular migrants or the status of irregularity at the European Union level. However, the legislation, such as the Schengen Code and Directive 2008/115/EC through the definition of "illegal stay", identify the requirements necessary for legal entrance and residence in the European Union territory. Consequently in the absence of these requirements a foreigner is irregularly in the European Union territory[5].

Finally, the last part of the first Chapter focusses on the terminology used to define this category: initially, the term used in the literature and by European Union institutions was "illegal". This analysis highlights how that is not correct, starting from the assumption that a person, from a legal point of view, cannot be illegal. Indeed only their actions and behaviors can be defined as illegal. The correct terminology, currently recognized at academic level, is irregular because it is more neutral. Also used are undocumented, *sans papier* or clandestine[6].

In the second Chapter the protection of human rights of irregular migrants is explored on two levels: international law and in the context of the European Union. Firstly, the focus is on the content of the International Conventions, such as the European Convention of Human Rights, and then in particular in the context of the European Union, the European Union Charter of Fundamental Rights. That allows and understanding of the tools which guarantee protection for irregular migrants.

Thereafter the illustration of the European Union framework for the protection of human rights of irregular migrants in relation to the entry phase into Member States will be analysed. In particular it will be explored

---

5 Schengen borders Code, Regulation (EU) 2016/399 of the European Parliament and of the Council of 9 March 2016 on a Union Code on the rules governing the movement of persons across borders OJ L 77, 23.3.2016, p. 1–52; Directive 2008/115/EC of the European Parliament and of the Council of 16 December 2008 on common standards and procedures in Member States for returning illegally staying third-country nationals OJ L 348, 24.12.2008, p. 98–107.

6 A. TRIANDAFYLLIDOU, *Irregular Migration in Europe: Myths and Realities*, Farnham, Surrey, Ashgate, 2010.

in depth, what kind of guarantee of human rights is provided in the context of the high seas and hot spots and during detention and return procedures.

The migrants in an irregular situation are more likely to face discrimination, exclusion, exploitation and abuse at all stages of the migration process. They often face prolonged detention or ill-treatment and, in some cases, enslavement, rape or murder. They are more likely to be targeted by xenophobes and racists, victimized by unscrupulous employers and sexual predators, and can easily fall prey to criminal traffickers and smugglers[7]. Rendered vulnerable by their irregular status, these men, women and children are often afraid or unable to seek protection and relief from the authorities in countries of origin, transit or destination. Clearly, the irregular situation in which international migrants may find themselves should not deprive them either of their humanity or of their human rights. International human rights law provides that everyone, without discrimination, must have access to the fundamental rights provided in the international bill of human rights.

Moreover, the whole first reception phase is particularly interesting for the aim this research project because it is a delicate phase in which the protection of the human rights of irregular migrants risks being subject to violations because of the lack of balance between the need for security of the State and the protection of the fundamental rights of these migrants Member States are obligated to guarantee.

The third Chapter of this thesis is dedicated to analysing how the European law described is implemented in the Member States: the aim of the Chapter is to try to understand the major criticisms in the implementation of the European regulation and international and European conventions by the Member States in the first reception phase. The chapter also considers the national law, and, through the comparison between two legal frameworks on the topic, explores what can be improved in the legislation at European Union level. The countries chosen are Italy and Germany: these are different States but, as the research makes clear, it is useful to understand how the European Union legislation can be implemented in both

7 V. T. REITANO, L. ADAL, M. SHAW, *Smuggled Futures: The Dangerous Path of the Migrant from Africa to Europe, The Global Initiative against Transnational Organized Crime*, Geneva, 2014, available online; D. WEISSBRODT, *The Protection of Non-Citizens in International Human Rights Law*, in R. CHOLEWINSKY, R. PERRUCHOUD and E. MACDONALD (eds.), *International Migration Law: Developing Paradigms and Key Challenges*, T.C.M. Asser Press.,The Hague 2007, pp. 228-232.

situations. It is interesting to see how these two countries have implemented the same European Union legislation in different ways and to explore what each system can learn from the other. This then leads to inspiration for more efficient legal framework at European Union level.

It possible to anticipate that in both States the violations of human rights of irregular migrants arise from the already mentioned tension between the need of the country to guarantee the security of its borders and the obligation to protect human rights.

Both countries, as will be illustrated, adopted restrictive law towards irregular foreigners, for instance they both provide the crime of clandestinity and limit the application of migrants' rights. In Germany in the specific case of *duldung,* which relates to foreigners who have to be returned and do not have any legal status, but, for various reasons, such as administrative ones, are subject to a formal suspension of enforcement action, migrants see the right to health and to education for example limited.

Although the phenomenon of irregular migration presents different characteristics in the two States, both countries are restrictive in the respect of the human rights of irregular foreigners committing many violations in particular concerning the phase of deportation and return.

Italy was transformed from an emigrant country to a country of destination as many studies underline[8]. In recent years, especially with the increase of the democratic instability of the Mediterranean region, as shown by the "Arab Spring"[9] and the tragic wars which are characterizing the Middle East[10], the number of persons who flee from their countries to reach the European shores has been growing, Italy has developed an articulated legal, political and diplomatic instrument for controlling sea migration over the last few years, especially with a view to combating clandestine migration.

In Germany the phenomenon of irregular migration has a smaller dimension than in Italy. With respect to the subject of this analysis, namely

8 For a detailed reconstruction under an historical point of view of the Italian immigration policy, see L. EINAUDI, *"Le Politiche dell' Immigrazione in Italia dall 'Unita' ad oggi* ", Laterza, 2007.

9 Wave of pro-democracy protests and uprisings that took place in the Middle East and North Africa beginning in 2010 and 2011, challenging some of the region's entrenched authoritarian regimes (Jasmine Revolution in Tunisia 2010, Egypt Uprising of 2011, Yemen Uprising of 2011–12, Libya Revolt of 2011, and Syria Uprising of 2011–12.)

10 For instance: Egyptian Revolution 2011; Lybian war 2011; Syrian Civil war 2011-2018; Turk-Syrian Kurd Conflict 2018.

the protection of fundamental rights of this category of migrants, most of the violations are related to the procedure of return.

The violations of human rights seem to be the result of a lack of good management and organisation in the German territory and related more to the structure than a policy aimed to restrict the fundamental rights of this category of migrants. This is a difference with the Italian policy that tries to restrict the human rights of these migrants using more severe legislation. Although, in the German scenario a similar normative framework is in force in relation to *duldung*, mentioned above.

In general terms, the comparison showed that the recognition of important human rights, such as the right to work, right to health or the right to education is limited for irregular migrants during the time they have to stay in the European territory before being returned.

In conclusion the main themes emerging from this research project are: there is poor protection of the rights of irregular migrants when they remain in the territory, albeit irregularly, and the issue of repatriations is in addition problematic.

As it falls within the competence of the Member States, the matter of immigration, is managed with too much diversity between the them and the European legislation which regulates some aspect of the matter, allows too much discretion in its application by them. This is so for several reasons analysed in the research, like the lack of clarity and ambiguity of some directives. There is also a lack of specific legislation at European level, there are mainly references to international legislation, which in turn guarantee protection without providing strictly specific rules on this category of migrants. As long as the issue of immigration is not within the competence of the European Union, there will not be more precise and effective legislation or a common regulatory framework in all member states.

The repatriation issue represents one of the most critical moments in relation to violations of human rights, and must be addressed by the European Union in all its aspects, including the stipulation of agreements with third countries with the EU and the identification of the precise procedure that limits the most common violations of human rights. Within this framework the system of voluntary repatriation should be further developed. It should be managed according to precise and binding procedures. Member States should be called to adequately promote this instrument. The European Union should have more initiative in signing agreements with the countries of origin in order to facilitate voluntary repatriations.

Table of Contents

Introduction

The migration phenomenon is currently a very relevant topic in the European Union and within each of its Member States. Indeed, the migration issue affects the political, sociological and economical debate in all Member States and at the European level[11].

The constant high flows of migrants who arrive in Europe in particular from the African continent and Middle East, does not seem likely to stop or decrease given the difficult conditions in which, very often, the countries of origin or transit are in: wars, lack of democracy, low or absent protection of human rights, lack of work, etc[12].

The European Union institutions as well as the majority of Member States continue to face criticism in management of the flows and in creating an efficient common system of regulation in relation with the migration phenomenon in general, as for instance in the asylum field. The will of the States to reach common legislation is still far from being achieved[13].

In the current European legal framework there are many aspects that are very relevant subjects of investigation: the migration flows issue, the need of a common asylum system for all States, the protection of the human rights of vulnerable persons, the integration issue and so on[14].

Among these, one relevant theme in the current political and juridical European context and an area to which academic research can also make a contribution is the field of irregular migration: the movement of migrants

---

11 L. MASERA, G. SAVIO, *La "prima" accoglienza*, in M., Savino, La crisi migratoria tra Italia e Unione Europea: diagnosi e prospettive, Editoriale Scientifica, Napoli, 2017.

12 M. BORRACCETTI, La prima assistenza ai migranti in arrivo tra diritti fondamentali e zone franche, in Dir. Imm. Citt., 2014, No 2, 13; G. CAMPESI, L'Italia e il controllo delle frontiere marittime, in M. SAVINO, La crisi migratoria tra Italia e Unione Europea: diagnosi e prospettive, Editoriale Scientifica, Napoli, 2017.

13 G. VERMEULEN, E. DESMET, *Essential text on European and International Asylum and Migration Law and Policy,* Maklu, Antwerpen-Apeldoorn-Portland, 2017.

14 S. CASTELS & M.J. MILLER, *The age of migration: international population movements in the modern world* (4th ed.) New York: Guilford Press, 2004.

who enter and/or stay in a Member States without any legal status, namely against the national law of the Member State and European Union law[15].

This subject is particularly delicate in relation to the protection of human rights. Indeed, there are many decisions by the European Union Courts which condemned Member States for human rights violations of irregular migrants. These persons are particularly vulnerable to human rights abuses because of their position in the territory in contravention of the law of that State: they are in the middle of a strong tension between the security needs of the territory of the State that can be undermined from their illegal entry and/or residence, and the obligation of Member States to guarantee the protection of their human rights enshrined in several international and European Union conventions and laws.

Given the tensions at the European Union level, it is very important to achieve a balance and coordinated system. Otherwise, the integration project will be at risk. For the reasons illustrated above the theme of protection of irregular migrants is considered a relevant topic in the legal framework of the European Union[16].

The main aim of this research is to try to rebuild the actual legal framework concerning the protection of human rights of irregular migrants at European level, to verify how the Member States implemented this law through a focus on two countries, Italy and Germany, to detect and analyze the critical points in the framework, the reasons why, and finally try to offer a contribution in terms of research to improve the critical aspects also by the comparison between the two Member States previously mentioned.

The analysis reported in the dissertation has been divided in three Chapters: the initial chapter deals with a classification of migration phenomena in general and the specific category of irregular migration in the European Union; the second one has been dedicated to the analysis of the European legal tools for protecting the human rights of irregular migrants with a fo-

---

15 A. BLOCH, *Irregular Migrants: Policy, Politics, Motives and Everyday Lives*, London, Routledge, 2012; A. TRIANDAFYLLIDOU, *Irregular Migration in Europe: Myths and Realities*, Farnham, Surrey, Ashgate, 2010.

16 A. TRIANDAFYLLIDOU, *Irregular Migration in Europe: Myths and Realities*, Farnham, Surrey, Ashgate, 2010; M. TODINO, *The Legality of Intercepting Boat People Under Search and Rescue and Border Control Operations with Reference to Recent Italian Interventions in the Mediterranean Sea and the ECtHR Decision in the Hirsi Case*, in Journal of International Maritime Law, April 2012, Vol. 18, No. 1, pp. 59-74. at 62: "In the case of active resistance, the interception cannot fall within the SAR legal regime".

cus on first reception of this category of migrants in the European Union; finally, the third part of the thesis addresses a comparison between two Member States (the reasons why the two countries have been selected will be explained later), Italy and Germany, to understand how these Member States implemented the European legislation on the protection of human rights of irregular migrants in the phase of entrance, analyzing also the specific national law.

The methodology used for each Chapter consisted of collecting legal materials, laws and jurisprudence, and international literature on the topic, adding also material from international organization recognized as experts who conduct empirical work in this field, as for instance the Agencies of United Nations. The material has been organized to give a detailed overview of the subject of each chapter and to highlight what the main literature concludes in order to then be able to proceed to a critical analysis.

Returning to the contents of the individual Chapters, in the first one the broader category of migration is explored including irregular migration in the European Union context. The migration category has been analyzed with the goal to understand the phenomenon of migration in general from a sociological point of view: what are the reasons underpinning the movement? The chapter analyzes this phenomenon in several Member States that have known a huge flow of migration in their history, such as Germany, France, United Kingdom, Italy and Spain.

After this description, the focus will be on the birth of the concept of irregular migration in the European Union analyzing this category specifically in some Member States where the irregular status of migrants has been a significant phenomenon: Austria, Czech Republic, Greece, France, Germany, Italy, Netherlands, Poland, Spain, United Kingdom.

A distinction within the category of irregular migrants is outlined referring to the classification proposed by Professor Frank Düvell: quasi-legal illegal and total illegal migrants. This distinction has consequences in terms of protection of fundamental rights of the migrants[17]. Further, the Chapter is dedicated to understanding the relationship between the irregular and regular status and how the immigration categories of documented and undocumented immigrants are not static.

Following the analysis on the phenomenon of migration in general and then irregular migration from a mainly sociological perspective, the focus moves to explore exactly who are irregular migrants from a legal point of

17 F. DÜVELL, *Illegal immigration in Europe beyond control?*, Palgrave Macmillan, 2006.

view in the European Union regulation. As it has been explained, there is not an exact definition of irregular migrants or the status of irregularity at the European Union level. However, the legislation, such as the Schengen Code and Directive 2008/115/EC through the definition of "illegal stay", identify the requirements necessary for legal entrance and residence in the European Union territory. Consequently in absence of these requirements a foreigner is irregular in the European Union territory[18].

Finally, after outlining the normative framework of who can be defined as an irregular migrant, the last part of the first Chapter focusses on the terminology used to define this category: initially, the term used in the literature and by European Union institutions was "illegal" . This analysis highlights how that is not correct starting from the assumption that a person, from a legal point of view, cannot be illegal. Indeed only their actions and behaviors can be defined as illegal. The correct terminology, currently recognized at academic level, is irregular because it is more neutral. Also used are undocumented, *sans papier* or clandestine[19].

After having delineated in general the migration phenomenon in European Union and defined who are irregular migrants according to the European Union law, in the second Chapter the focus is on the protection of human rights of irregular migrants. *In primis* an analysis of the international and EU legal tools that are implemented by the European Union and consequently by the Member States, with the aim to protect the human rights of irregular migrants has been conducted. As it will be shown, there are several important conventions that provide protection of the fundamental rights of everyone without any distinction based on the status of the person. Therefore, the irregular migrants are also covered by these conventions: as the European Convention of Human Rights in which is enshrined the protection to all persons regardless their status according to Art. 1 thus including irregular immigrants; or the Universal Declaration of Human Rights that protects *without distinction of any kind, such as race,*

---

18 Schengen borders Code, Regulation (EU) 2016/399 of the European Parliament and of the Council of 9 March 2016 on a Union Code on the rules governing the movement of persons across borders OJ L 77, 23.3.2016, p. 1–52; Directive 2008/115/EC of the European Parliament and of the Council of 16 December 2008 on common standards and procedures in Member States for returning illegally staying third-country nationals OJ L 348, 24.12.2008, p. 98–107.

19 A. TRIANDAFYLLIDOU, *Irregular Migration in Europe: Myths and Realities*, Farnham, Surrey, Ashgate, 2010.

colour, sex, language, religion, political or other opinion, national or social origin, property birth or other status[20].

The analysis continues with a focus on the protection of human rights of irregular migrants in the specific phase of first reception of these migrants, namely the phase of entrance. This phase includes different subphases: high sea; hotspots and the phase of procedure of detention and return to the country of origin or transit. The whole first reception phase is particularly interesting for the aim this research project because it is a delicate phase in which the protection of the human rights of irregular migrants risks being subject to violations because of the balance the Member States have to guarantee.

Indeed, for the European Union and for the Member States, to find a balance between the protection of human rights of irregular migrants and to guarantee the security of the European Union borders from irregular entrance, represents a challenge in which most of the violations of the fundamental rights of the category of migrants under analysis occur.

The three aforementioned subphases are those in which the irregular foreigners are more exposed to not seeing the correct application of their rights. In particular, the high sea is a critical phase due the complex juridical framework of international legislation on sea law, refugee law, European Union law and the Convention on Human Rights which are crucial for the control activity and that must be applied simultaneously. The issue is very complicated considering the complex framework and the large number of actors who are involved in the control of maritime borders. Most of the violations are to the right to life, collective expulsion and violation of the principle of *non-refoulment.*

Another critical phase for the protection of human rights of irregular migrants related to the hotspot: as will be explained, the hotspot is a section of external borders characterized by the arrival of huge migration flows. In these areas a proper team composed by European Union Agencies (FRONTEX, EASO, Eurojust and Europol that will be analyzed subsequently) and personnel from Member States that collaborate in order to accomplish the first reception. These hotspots arose in particular in Greece and Italy where the pressure of irregular migration flows is more relevant. Very often violations of fundamental rights occurred as for instance to the right of information concerning the rights the migrants have once on the

20 Art. 2(1) of the Universal Declaration of Human Rights, UN General Assembly Resolution A/RES/217 (III) of 10 December 1948.

territory of the European Union or of violations during the identification procedures in the hotspot[21].

Finally, when the irregular migrant does not have, or does not have anymore, any legal status to stay in the territory of the Member States, he or she has to be returned to the country of origin or transit, and during these procedures violations of personal freedom frequently occur in several Member States, especially due the prolonged detention over the terms provided by the European legislation.

Having concluded a terminological analysis on irregular migration, a general overview on irregular migration in the European Union, after the exact detecting of whom can be defined irregular in the European territory, and subsequently to the deepening of the protection of human rights of this category of migrants specifically in the most critical phase, first reception one, the third Chapter of this thesis is dedicated to analyzing how the European law described is implemented in the Member States. The aim of the Chapter is to try to understand the major criticisms in the implementation of the European regulation and international and European conventions by the Member States in the first reception phase. The chapter considers also the national law, and, through the comparison between two legal frameworks on the topic, Italian and German, explores what can be improved in the legislation at European Union level.

The countries chosen are Italy and Germany: these are different States but, as will be better explained in this part of the research, it is useful to understand how the European Union legislation can be implemented in both situations. It could be interesting to see how these two countries have implemented the same European Union legislation noting the differences and to see if there are legal elements presented in one legislation that can be integrated by the other one in order to improve the own system. That could be also an inspiration for more efficient legislation at European Union level.

It possible to anticipate that in both States the violations of the human rights of the irregular migrants arise from the already mentioned tension between the need of the country to guarantee the security of its borders and the obligation of the protection of human rights.

Both countries, as it will be illustrated, adopted restrictive law towards irregular foreigners, for instance they both provide the crime of clandestin-

---

21 F. CASOLARI, *The EU's Hotspot Approach to Managing the Migration Crisis: A Blind Spot for International Responsibility?*, in The Italian Yearbook of International Law, 2015, Vol. 25.

ity and limit the application of migrants rights,. In Germany in the specific case of *duldung*, which relates to foreigners who have to be returned, do not have any legal status, but, for different reasons, such as administrative ones results in a formal suspension of enforcement action. The figure of *duldung* sees for instance the right to health and to education limited.

Although the phenomenon of irregular migration presents different characteristics in the two States, both countries are restrictive in the respect of the human rights of the irregular foreigners committing many violations in particular both concerning the phase of deportation and return.

CHAPTER I: The phenomenon of irregular migration in the European Union: historical developments and preliminary questions of terminology

1. Theories of migration: an overview

Ernest Georg Ravenstein, a German-born geographer who worked for the Royal Geographical Society in London, gave the first major contribution to a theory of migration at the end of nineteenth century[22]. William Farr[23], a contemporary scholar who stated that the phenomenon of migration occurred basically at random, prompted him to theorize about the structured features of migratory movement.

Ravenstein tried to articulate a series of laws that could be used to both explain and predict migratory movements, relevant to migrations within and outside of national borders. It is possible to summarize the main "laws" (understood as guidelines) as follows[24]:

- *migration and distance:* most migrants travel short distances, while those who do travel long distances prefermajor commercial and industrial centers;
- *migration by stages:* a current of migration occurs when commercial and industrial centers absorb large numbers of migrants; the closest rural dwellers move to cities, thereby leaving gaps that are filled by the rural population from more remote areas; and the process of dispersion is the reverse of that of absorption;
- *stream and counter stream:* mainstreams of migration produce a counter stream;
- *urban/rural differences in propensity to migrate:* rural dwellers are more likely to migrate than the natives of cities;

---

22 T. FAIST, P. KIVISTO, *Beyond a Border: The Causes and Consequences of Contemporary Immigration*, Thousand Oaks, CA: SAGE/Pine Forge Press, 2010.

23 T. FAIST, P. KIVISTO, *Beyond a Border: The Causes and Consequences of Contemporary Immigration*, Thousand Oaks, CA: SAGE/Pine Forge Press, 2010.

24 Using Everett Lee's grouping of Ravenstein's conclusion. E. LEE, *A Theory of migration*, *Demography*, 1966, 3(1), 47-57.

- *predominance of females among short distance movers:* more women make short-distance migrations, particularly within national borders, than males;
- *technology and migration:* improvements in transportation networks and the expansion of industrialization lead to increased levels of migration;
- *centrality of economic factors:* while levels of migration can be influenced by state actions (e.g. laws, tax policies), climate and geographic factors, they not only are not nearly as consequential aseconomic considerations, but are often actually intervening obstacles that can sometimes be eliminated and permitting economic forces to operate in an essentially unimpeded way[25].

The most fundamental accusations leveled against Ravenstein´s work was that he had failed to articulate what would generally be construed as theory. Instead, some authors like Petersen[26] consider that it does not add up to a theory or, in his terminology, to "laws". Nevertheless, Ravenstein's work influenced two subsequent currents of migration theorizing, which will be detailed below: the push-pull model and an economic model based on neoclassical economic presuppositions.

The push-pull model is attributed to Everett Lee, although he did not use the term in describing his "theory of migration"[27]. Lee distilled a model that is based on the assumption that the volume, that he called the "stream", and the selection of those who fall within the stream, are structured by four factors. He identifies these factors as: point of origin, those with the destination, intervening obstacles and the personal characteristics of potential migrants. There are three types of factors which are operative at both the origin and destination, those that promote migration, those that deter or prevent it, and those that have no bearing on it[28].

---

25 T. FAIST, P. KIVISTO, *Beyond a Border: The Causes and Consequences of Contemporary Immigration*, Thousand Oaks, CA: SAGE/Pine Forge Press, 2010.

26 W. PETERSEN, *A General Typology of migration*, in *American Sociological Review*, 1958, 23(3), 256-266.

27 H. DE HASS, *Engaging diasporas: How governments and development agencies can support diaspora*
involvement in the development of origin countries, A study for Oxfam Novib, Oxford: International Migration Institute, James Martin 21st Century School. New York: University of Oxford, 2006, p. 9.

28 T. FAIST, P. KIVISTO, Beyond a Border: The Causes and Consequences of Contemporary Immigration, Thousand Oaks, CA: SAGE/Pine Forge Press, 2010.

This model offers a remarkably intuitive and parsimonious account of the process, indeed a major part of the task at hand in accounting for migrations is to provide a cost-benefit calculus[29].

The assumption is that migrations occur as a consequence of two complementary processes:

1) they commence when the weight of the factors pushing people out of one place are more powerful than those keeping them there. Among the most important push factors are rapid population growth, poverty and a lack of economic opportunity, and political repression. In various combination, these and other factors contribute to the migratory push[30];

2) it occurs when the weight of factors pulling people into another area are powerful than those deterring entry. Among the key factors that pull people to a society are job opportunities, more wages than in the homeland, the possibility of acquiring land, and political and cultural freedom. The respective intensity of these forces contributes to the volume and defines the particular nature of the stream, moving from A to B rather than to C.

Moreover, Lee considers that two other factors need to be factored into the equation: "natural inertia" that refers to the fact people are by nature stayers rather than movers. Therefore, migrations are not persistent features of the modern world, being triggered only in extraordinary times. Other factors shaping migrations are the "intervening obstacles" like distance. They are linked to the state of existing transportation systems. Physical barriers, such as the fence that has been built along section of the U.S.-Mexican border, represent another obstacle, as do legal barriers.

Lee is clear that some people are more likely to migrate than others. Migrations are selective, thus young people are more likely to migrate than older ones because they are more adequate candidates for the receiving society's labor market. However, those with certain types of human capital (such as educational credentials, employment skills) are far more likely to migrate than those with human capital deficits[31].

---

29 E. LEE, *A Theory of migration. Demography*, 1966, 3(1), 47-57; H. DE HASS, (2006). *Engaging diasporas: How governments and development agencies can support diaspora involvement in the development of origin countries*, A study for Oxfam Novib, Oxford: International Migration Institute, James Martin 21st Century School. New York, University of Oxford, 2006.

30 Among the most important push factors are rapid population growth, poverty and a lack of economic opportunity, and political repression.

31 T. FAIST, P. KIVISTO, *Beyond a Border: The Causes and Consequences of Contemporary Immigration*, Thousand Oaks, CA: SAGE/Pine Forge Press, 2010.

With regards to the neoclassical economics model[32] of migration this theory, with a more recent approach, is preferred to the push-pull model[33]. In part, this is because one variant of the push-pull model is frequently taken to be representative of the model as a whole, an economic theory known as the neoclassical equilibrium perspective[34]. It portrays migration as a consequence of the interplay between the size of the labor supply and wages are consequently reduced in one place, a segment of the surplus population is attracted to a destination characterized by labor shortages and, due to the demand for labor, higher wages.

The earliest articulations of this model were intended for internal migrations within developing nations, specifically the mass movements of workers from rural to urban settings[35], but it has also been used to explain international migration[36].

For both kinds of migration, the internal and the international, this model assumes that the volume of migration is determined by the relative differences in the supply of and demand for labor in different geographical locations. When the differences are significant, the volume will be high; viceversa when the differences are low, the volume will be low. It must be emphasized that the migrants need to factor into the equation the cost of migration and potential problems they might encounter before gaining entrance into the destination countries with a higher wage labor market.

In the case of undocumented migrants, on whom this research is focused, the potential costs associated with arrest and deportation must also

---

32 T. FAIST, P. KIVISTO, *Beyond a Border: The Causes and Consequences of Contemporary Immigration*, Thousand Oaks, CA: SAGE/Pine Forge Press, 2010.

33 This theory has been developed in particular from Douglas Massey and colleagues (D. MASSEY, S. ARANGO, J. HUGO, G. KOUAOUCI, A. PELLEGRINO & T.J. EDWARD, *An evaluation of international migration theory: The North American case*, in *Population and Development Review*, 1994, 20(4), 699-751; D. MASSEY, & J.E. TAYLOR, (Eds), *International migration: prospects and policies in a global market*. New York: Oxford University Press, 2004.

34 T. FAIST, P. KIVISTO, *Beyond a Border: The Causes and Consequences of Contemporary Immigration*, Thousand Oaks, CA: SAGE/Pine Forge Press, 2010.

35 J.R. HARRIS & M.P. TODARO, *Migration, unemployment, and development: A two-sector analysis*, in *American Economic Review*, 1970, 60(2), 126-142; M.P. TODARO, A model of labor migration and urban unemployment in low-developed countries, in American Economic Review, 1969, 59(1), 138-148; M.P. TODARO, Internal Migration in developing countries, Geneva: International Labor Office, 1976.

36 G. BORJAS, Economic theory and international migration, in International Migration Review, 1989, 23(3), 457-485; G. BORJAS, Friends or strangers: the impact of immigrants on the U.S. economy. New York: Basic Books, 1990.

be factored in[37]. Massey and colleagues, summarize the essence of neoclassical economics in the following way: *"The difference between incomes expected at origin and destination, when summed and discounted over some time horizon and added to the negative costs of movement, yields the expected net gain from movement, which if positive promotes migration"*[38].

The reason that migrations are not considered to be perpetual or a constant state is that as more migrants enter a high-demand, higher-wage area, over time their presence reduces demand and wages. However, from the point of view of the place of origin, migrants can be seen as surplus labor. Their departure signals a decline in the surplus, which over time will increase the demand for labor, which in turn leads to increases in prevailing wages. In this way, a new equilibrium is achieved and the migratory wave comes to end as the incentives to migrate evaporate.

Massey and colleagues conclude that *"the accumulated evidence generally supports neoclassical theory's fundamental proposition that immigration is tied to international differences in wage rates"*[39]. Although it has had a decided impact on both the ways the public thinks about the cause of immigration and has played a role in shaping immigration policy, there are limitations to its utility. The critique is that due to its singular focus on the individual, neoclassical equilibrium theory is not in itself sufficient to provide a compelling explanation of immigration. One might also note that the theory is only applicable to voluntary migratory flows with high degrees of freedom.

A theory which complemented the model mentioned above, is the "new economics of migration", which is associated with economist Oded Stark[40]. His approach did not seek to reject completely the neoclassical theory, but to amend it chiefly by complementing its insights with a more empirically grounded theoretical framework. The new economics approach calls into question the assumption that migration is a phenomenon pursued by individuals. Ignored by the neoclassical perspective is the fact

37 M.P. TODARO, & L. MARUSZKU, Illegal immigration and U.S. immigration reform: a conceptual framework, in Population and Development Review, 1987, 13(1), 104-114.

38 D. MASSEY, S. ARANGO, J. HUGO, G. KOUAOUCI, A. PELLEGRINO & T.J. EDWARD, An evaluation of international migration theory: the North American case, in Population and Development Review, 1994, 20(4), 699-751.

39 In the review of the literature that has attempted to the test the neoclassical equilibrium model in accounting for post 1945 immigration to the United States from elsewhere in the Western Hemisphere, 1994, p. 710.

40 O. STARK, *The Migration of Labour*, Oxford, Blackwell, 1991.

immigrants are embedded in what Simmel[41] called "webs of group affiliations".

Stark's position concentrated on the role of families. Building on this insight, Massey melded the new economics of migration to sociology by introducing network theory. Simmel's loosely conceived idea of webs takes on analytical rigor a "networks", which he and his associates (Massey et al. 1994, p. 728)[42] define in the following way: "*Migrant networks are sets of interpersonal ties that connect migrants, former migrants, and non migrants in origin and destination areas through ties of kinship, friendship, and shared community origin. The existence of these ties is hypothesized to increase the likelihood of emigration by lowering the costs, raising the benefits, and mitigating the risks of international movements. Network connections constitute a valuable form of social capital that people draw upon to gain access to foreign employment and high wages*".

Historians of immigration have long been aware of what was once called the "friends and relatives effect" or "chain migration" in creating and sustaining immigration streams[43].

Another geographer, Robert C. Ostergren[44], in 1998, with regards to the last great migratory wave in the United States, described the process as one in which "*the first emigrants from Europe community commonly went to some place about which they possessed information. They in turn sent additional information home once they had reached their destination. As new emigrants followed in their footsteps, certain "axes of information" developed between places on either side of the Atlantic. Once the migrant stream began moving along these axes, it became self-reinforcing, ultimately taking on all the attributes of a chain migration*".

The social ties served to link individual immigrants both to those who remained in the homeland and those who were fellow immigrants. The

---

41 G. SIMME, *Exkurs über den Fremend*, in G. SIMMEL, *Soziologie: Untersuchungen über die Formen der* Vergesellschaftung, 1908/1992, vol. 11, Frankfurt, Suhrkamp.

42 D. MASSEY, S. ARANGO, J. HUGO, G.KOUAUOCI, A. PELLEGRINO & T.J. EDWARD, *An evaluation of international migration theory: the North American case*, in *Population and Development Review*, 1994, 20(4).

43 D.E. BAINES, *Emigration from Europe, 1815-1930.* Cambridge, UK: Cambridge University, 1995, pp. 33-38; T.J. HATTON & J.G. WILLIAMSON, *The age of mass migration: causes and economic impact.* New York: Oxford University Press, 1998, p. 14; J. G. WILLIAMSON, *Migration to the new world: long term influences and impact. Explorations in Economic History*, 1974, II, 357-390.

44 R. C. OSTERGREN, *A community transplanted: The trans-Atlantic experience of a Swedish immigrant settlement in the Upper Middle West, 1835-1915*, Madison: University of Wisconsin Press, 1988.

journey was the result of the economic calculations of a family or other intimates and not made simply by an isolated individual. The significance of prepaid tickets purchased for potential migrants by friends or family is an indication of the collective nature of the migration decision-making process[45]. The ongoing sharing of information between origin and destination about such matters as whether or not economic and other conditions were conducive to additional immigration was also part of the equation. At the same time, the creation of ethnic enclaves in both urban and rural setting indicates the significance immigrants attached to the maintenance of ethnic connections in the new world[46].

The model in question, contrary to the neoclassical equilibrium theory, treats migration as a phenomenon that involves both economic and non-economic factors. In a significant departure from neoclassical economics, the new economics model does not assume that migrations inevitably occur in a wave that ends with the return to wage equilibrium. The advocates of the new economics model contend that whatever sets in motion the initial impetus to migrate, the establishment of migratory networks serves to perpetuate migration because "*they lower the costs and risks of movement and increase the expected net returns to migration*"[47].

Charles Tilly[48] contends that "networks migrate", by which he means that the network rather than the individual is the proper unit of analysis. In conclusion, the network can suggest that migration should either be declining or cease altogether.

Massey and associates[49] reinforce the idea that once underway, contemporary migrations tend to become self-perpetuating. Among the explicit economic factors that contribute to cumulative causation are changes in

---

45 T. FAIST, P. KIVISTO, *Beyond a border: the causes and consequences of contemporary immigration*. Thousand Oaks, CA: SAGE/Pine Forge Press, 2010.

46 T. FAIST, P. KIVISTO, *Beyond a border: the causes and consequences of contemporary immigration*. Thousand Oaks, CA: SAGE/Pine Forge Press, 2010.

47 D. MASSEY, S. ARANGO, J. HUGO, G. KOUAOUCI, A. PELLEGRINO & T. J. EDWARD, *Theories of i*nternational migration: a review and appraisal, in Population and Development Review, 1993, 19(3), 431-466, p. 448.

48 C. TILLY, Transplanted networks, in V. YANS-MCLAUGHLIN (Ed.), Immigration reconsidered: history, sociology and politics, 1990, New York: Oxford University Press, p. 84.

49 D. Massey, S. ARANGO, J. HUGO, G. KOUAOUCI, A. PELLEGRINO & T.J. EDWARD, Theories of
International migration: a review and appraisal, in Population and Development Review, 199319(3), 431-466, pp.451-454; D. MASSEY, S. ARANGO, J. HUGO, G. KOUAOUCI, A., PELLEGRINO & T.J. EDWARD, An evaluation of internation-

income distribution, changes in land distribution, and changes in the organization of agricultural production. Fundamental element to changes in income distribution patterns at the point of origin is the role played by remittances sent to relatives from migrants. When household incomes rise as a result, those households not receiving remittances suffer from growing deprivation, thereby increasing the motive to migrate.

Migrants often purchase land back home, which impacts land distribution because it is thought they are less inclined to put such land into agricultural production, instead maintaining it as a place for retirement.

When they do work the land productively, they tend to do so in a more capital-intensive way than local owners, thus reducing the number of available agricultural jobs; in either event, the result is added incentive to migrate[50].

There are three other factors that contribute to cumulative causation: a culture of migration, the regional distribution of human capital, and social labeling[51]. The first of these factors refers to the fact that as migration changes the point of origin, those embedded in the migratory network come to see migration as one of a number of viable options. In some places, over time an expectation arises that young men will migrate, if only for a time and if only to test the waters. Due to the selective character of migration, those with human capital deemed valuable at the receiving location will come first, thereby increasing the level of human capital there while reducing it at the point of origin. Over time, this contributes to economic decline in the sending community, thereby ratcheting up the inducement to migrate[52].

Finally, social labeling refers to the stereotypical matching of immigrants to certain job categories. This is certainly the case with those jobs described as dirty, dangerous, and difficult but it also applies to those "brain drain" immigrants who are perceived to possess educational credentials in short supply[53].

---

al migration theory: the North American case, in Population and Development Review, 1994, 20(4). pp. 733-738.

50 T. FAIST, P. KIVISTO, *Beyond a border: the causes and consequences of contemporary immigration*. Thousand Oaks, CA: SAGE/Pine Forge Press, 2010.

51 T. FAIST, P. KIVISTO, *Beyond a border: the causes and consequences of contemporary immigration*, Thousand Oaks, CA: SAGE/Pine Forge Press, 2010.

52 T. FAIST, P. KIVISTO, *Beyond a border: the causes and consequences of contemporary immigration*. Thousand Oaks, CA: SAGE/Pine Forge Press, 2010.

53 Indian case in Silicon Valley are a case in point.

Although there are parallels to be drawn, each nation has its own immigration dynamic: a brief overview within the context of the European Union is useful at this point before the field of irregular migration in the EU is explored.

2. The phenomenon of migration in the Member States

What follows is an analysis of what are the specific immigration flow characteristic of the five countries in the European Union with the largest numbers of immigrants and the main reasons for these flows.

Germany

From the division of the nation by the Cold War powers until reunification in 1990, the situation differed in the capitalist Federal Republic of Germany (West Germany) and the Soviet-bloc German Democratic Republic (East Germany). While the former experienced a post-war economic boom that made it the "economic miracle" of Western Europe and necessitated the import of foreign labor in order to make development possible, its communist counterpart lagged behind economically and created a fortress like border system that made immigration difficult and unattractive for western Europeans. That being said, during the 1980s there were several hundred thousand contract workers in the German Democratic Republic, mainly from Cuba, Mozambique, Angola and Vietnam. Thus, for most of the second half of the 20th century, immigration to Germany meant immigration to the Federal Republic.

During the early years of the Cold War, many individuals from the Soviet Union and elsewhere in the Warsaw Pact nations moved to Germany: the largest contingent came from Poland, followed by Romania and the Soviet Union. However, communist governments soon restricted this movement. So, the vast majority of immigrants during this period did not come from eastern Europe, but from southern and southeastern Europe, and did not have German ancestry, and therefore were officially categorized as *Gastarbeiter*[54] or guest workers.

54 It refers to foreign or migrant workers, particularly those who had moved to West Germany mainly in the 1950s, 60s and early 70s, seeking work as part of a formal guest worker program (*Gastarbeiterprogramm*).

Immigration during the second half of the 20th century occurred in two waves: the first began in the late 1950s and ended in 1975, shortly after the impact of the oil crisis began to be felt and economic restructuring from an industrial to a postindustrial system began to change the dynamics of labor demand. During this quarter of a century, more than 12 million left again, leaving a total stock that remained at 3.6 million. The German Federal Labor Office played an activist role in recruitment efforts, negotiating guest worker agreements with a number of countries, beginning in 1955 with neighboring Italy[55].

Over time, the numbers immigrating to Germany from European countries decreased while the numbers from Turkey increased. The expectation that workers would return home and the government's general opposition to family reunification decreased over time, with the result being that the temporary workers began to look like permanent residents. Indeed, the rotation principle, repatriation built into the guest workers system, was abolished very early. As early as the 1960s, the government ceased to enforce it at the request of employers who wanted to keep their migrant workers. In the wake of OPEC[56] crisis, with a decline in the demand for labor, public opinion made clear that Germans were opposed to the future settlement of additional workers from Yugoslavia and Turkey[57].

At the same time, the government hesitated to repatriate guest workers already in the country, seeking instead to find ways to improve their social rights. There was an effort on the part of the workers to return to their nations of origin, however the plan failed.

In the decade that followed, immigration levels dropped considerably, and in fact during the first half of the 1980s, Germany was actually a nation of emigration rather than immigration. The second wave began in 1985, between then and the end of the century, 5.5 million immigrants settled in Germany, this include immigrants from Eastern block nations who began to arrive when travel restrictions were relaxed prior to the end of communism and continued to arrive after the fall of the Iron Curtain[58]. It also included asylum seekers and refugees, the latter including refugees

---

55 P. KIVISTO & T: FAIST, *Citizenship: Discourses, theory, and transnational prospects*, Malden, MA: Blackwell, 2007.

56 Organization of the Petroleum Exporting Countries.

57 P. ODMALM, Migration policies and political participation, Basingstoke, UK: Palgrave Macmillan, 2005, p. 29.

58 Iron Curtain is a term used in the West to indicate the boundary line that divided Europe into two separate zones of political influence, from the end of the Second World War to the end of the Cold War. During this period, Eastern Europe was

from Bosnia-Herzegovina who were forced into exile as a result of the ethnic conflict that arose in the aftermath of the collapse of a unified Yugoslavia[59].

The number peaked by the mid-1990s, after which the rate of immigration reduced. In part, this decline was due to the passage of a more restrictive asylum law, one that reflected the institutionalization of a fortress Europe approach to reducing the number of foreigners from outside the European Union. At the same time, the European Union's labor policies called for the free movement of workers from among the Member States. This meant, for example, that not only could workers from the less developed nations of the European Union freely enter Germany to seek employment, but so could workers from the more developed ones. Thus, when a decline in the construction industry in Britain led to increased levels of unemployment in that sector of the economy, many British workers took their construction skills to Germany, plying their trade there while awaiting a turnaround in the situation back home[60].

France

France has long been viewed as *le creuset francaise,* the French melting pot, a nation open to all newcomers prepared to embrace the ideals of the republic and in the process to forsake any allegiance to their pasts[61].

France has, in contrast to Germany, long been a nation of immigration. The French state, due to demographic factors, had, since the 18th century, a longstanding policy of encouraging immigration. During the 19th century it was the most significant immigrant-receiving nation in Europe. The immigrants during this era were overwhelmingly from European points of origin, with Italy providing the greatest numbers, followed by Spain, Portugal, and Poland. Although since the French Revolution the nation has tended to view itself as being particularly open to those seeking political

---

under the political control and / or influence of the Soviet Union, while Western Europe fell under the influence of the United States.

59 Yugoslavia was one state existed between 1929 and 2003, passing through different institutional arrangements, which administered the territory of the Western Balkan Peninsula during the twentieth century.

60 T. FAIST, P. KIVISTO, *Beyond a border: the causes and consequences of contemporary immigration.* Thousand Oaks, CA: SAGE/Pine Forge Press, 2010.

61 T. FAIST, P. KIVISTO, *Beyond a border: the causes and consequences of contemporary immigration*. Thousand Oaks, CA: SAGE/Pine Forge Press, 2010.

asylum, in fact the vast majority of those entering the nation did so as conventional labor migrants. Prior to World War I, the overall percentage of immigrants remained consistent but relatively low, amounting to no more than 3% of the total population. Thus, in general the immigrants were accepted, though during periods of economic distress, anti-immigration sentiments would rise, at times leading to violence. The labor shortage created by World War I led to a liberalization of immigration laws and as a consequence, during the 1920s the percentage of the population that was foreign born rose to a historic high of 6.6 %[62].

Immigration levels would continue to decline throughout World War II, but by the middle of the 20th century, when the nation began to rebuild, the demand for labor again grew. The quarter century beginning in 1950 proved to be the peak point in the history of immigration to France.

A steady rise during the first half of the 1950s continued to increase, peaking in the first years of the 1970s and then, in the wake of the OPEC oil crisis, dropping precipitously. Italy did not prove to be the major source of the new immigration, with Portugal supplying about three times more workers than Spain. In both instances, these nations were economic laggards in western Europe, and remained so until the respective long-term dictatorship of Salazar and Franco finally ended in the 1970s and democracy took root. Nevertheless, the Iberian Peninsula did not in itself meet France's labor needs[63]. The other major source of immigrants was, for the first time in the nation's history, from outside of Europe.

Three nations in the North African Maghreb region emerged as major sources of workers, from the largest to the smallest these were Algeria, Morocco, and Tunisia. Algerian migrants were not simply labor migrants: their move was motivated in part by political events in Algeria leading to independence in 1962. These migrants included *pied-noirs*, French nationals who lived in the former colony and what were knows as *harkis* (indigenous Algerians who had sided with the French during the independence struggle). After independence, the French and Algerian governments entered into the Evian Agreement, which was designed to establish a formal mechanism for structuring labor recruitment. By 1970, there were nearly a

62 G. NORIEL, *The French melting pot: immigration, citizenship, and national identity*, Minneapolis: University of Minnesota Press, 1996, p. 64.

63 T. FAIST, P. KIVISTO, *Beyond a border: the causes and consequences of contemporary immigration.* Thousand Oaks, CA: SAGE/Pine Forge Press, 2010.

half million Algerians in France, at which time the French government increasingly raised concerns about the need to limit immigration levels[64].

Moroccans and Tunisians began to arrive somewhat later than Algerians. The former found employment in the automotive and coal industries, two sectors that since the 1970s have experienced significant deindustrialization. Thus, by the mid-1970s, unemployment levels for Moroccans increased. Tunisians found work in the construction industry and as unskilled laborers in various settings[65]. In addition to the Maghreb, 340,000 post-colonials arrived from Departments d'Outre-Mer and Territories d'Outre-Mer (DOM-TOM), including the Caribbean nations of Guadeloupe, Martinique, and French Guyana, the island of Reunion in the Indian Ocean, Vietnam, and former colonies in sub-Saharan Africa and finally, Turks also arrived.

By the early 1970s, as part of a trend occurring throughout EU nations, the French government sought to bring an end to mass immigration. In 1974, it ended its labor migration agreements with other countries, and in a preemptive effort to combat the prospect of rising levels of irregular immigration, it passed legislation imposing sanctions on employers hiring such migrants. Financial incentives to repatriate were offered but while immigrants from the Iberian Peninsula were attracted, immigrants from elsewhere were not. Rather, their numbers increased as they took advantage of family reunification provisions in the law. From the 1990s to the present[66], French policies have fluctuated, based on whether right-of-center or left-of-center governments were in power. While the former have attempted, in the end unsuccessfully, to put in place what Interior Minister Charles Pasqua[67] calls a "zero immigration" policy, the left's platform on immigration has been guided by recognition of the fact that the nation needs immigrants, particularly highly skilled ones[68].

---

64 K. HAMITON, P. SIMON & C: VENIARD, *The challenge of French diversity*, Migration Information Source. Retrieved February 8, 2006.

65 A. HARGREAVES, *Immigration, "race", and ethnicity in contemporary France*. London: Routledge, 1995, p. 79.

66 President of the Republic Francois Mitterand, 1981-1995, from socialist party; President of the Republic Jacques Chirac, 1995–2007, from liberal democracy and union for a popular movement party; President of the Republic Nicolas Sarkozy, 2007–2012, from union for a popular movement party; President of the Republic François Hollande, 2012 2017, from socialist party; President of the Republic Emmanuel Macron 2017 – from republican party.

67 He was Minister of Interior from 1993 until 1995.

68 K. HAMITON, P. SIMON & C. VENIARD, *The Challenge of French diversity*, Migration Information Source, Retrieved February 8, 2006. p.2.

The situation during the last quarter of the past century and the first decade of the current one was shaped by a more restrictive climate for labor migrants. At the same time, the number of asylum seekers has increased and in part this is due to the constriction of the flow of labor migrants. As Schuster[69] has pointed out, the increase in asylum seekers in western Europe, including France, has yielded new policies aimed at excluding immigrants.

United Kingdom

Since the 19th century, British immigration has been defined to a significant degree but not entirely by its colonial legacy[70]. This is also true of emigration, which prior to the middle of the 20th century was considerably higher than levels of immigration[71].

The wave of immigration that commenced after World War II would continue to include Europeans, but what made this a novel migratory wave was the presence of large numbers of people from former colonies, immigrants who as people of color would change the racial composition of the British Isles. This migratory movement's symbolic beginning occurred in 1948, when the *Empire Windrush* arrived in Britain with nearly 500 Jamaicans on board. These passengers, like those who would follow, held British passports because their nations of origin were part of the British Commonwealth nations[72].

These newcomers arrived from three major points of origin: the British Caribbean, the Indian subcontinent, and various nations in sub-Saharan Africa. English-speaking Caribbean often opted for the United States, given its geographical proximity and expanding postwar economy, but provi-

---

69 L. SCHUSTER, *The exclusion of asylum seekers in Europe*, Center on Migration, Policy, and Society Working Paper No. 1, Wp-04-01. Oxford: University of Oxford, 2004.

70 From its colonial empire: from India, Australia, Africa and America.

71 One of the most significant destinations of British emigrants was the United States; other significant destinations included Australia, Canada, New Zealand, and South Africa. The largest immigrant group to Britain during the late 19th and early 20th centuries came from its first colony, Ireland. Immigrants came from European continental origins as well, including a sizable number from Italy.

72 Sociologist Paul Gilroy and colleagues at the Centre for Contemporary Cultural Studies in 1992 have studied this phenomenon and depicted this movement in tongue-in-cheek fashion as "the empire strikes back".

sions in the 1952 McCarran-Walter Act served to close the door to such would be immigrants. Thus, Britain soon became the destination of choice. This was true for Jamaicans, who came to constitute about half, and thus the largest contingent, of immigrants from the Caribbean, but it also was true for migrants from other Commonwealth nations in the region[73].

During the 1950s, labor recruiters seeking to address acute labor shortages in Britain set their sights on these immigrants. At the same time, despite the fact that they spoke English and were familiar with British culture, these newcomers were forced to confront the reality of unvarnished racism. For many, being British and being white was seen as synonymous, and thus the prospect of blacks integrating into British society was seen as impossible[74]. Despite racist animosity, Caribbean continued to enter the country. During the 1950s, they constituted by far the largest of the non-white groups entering the nation, their numbers rising to a half million by 1990 and to over three quarters of a million by the end of the past century, though in recent years the numbers have tapered off.

The Indian subcontinent also became the major source of what became know in the United Kingdom as Asians. The largest numbers arrived from India, with substantial flows entering the nation from Pakistan and somewhat later Bangladesh and in smaller numbers from Sri Lanka. This migratory stream was religiously diverse, including Hindus, Muslims, and Sikhs. While many of the earliest arrivals were young men destined for the unskilled sector of the labor market, over time the migrants became more diverse in terms of human capital levels, including more highly educated professionals and businesspersons. Moreover, family reunification led to the establishment of internally complex ethnic communities in major cities such as London[75].

The third source of post-colonial immigrants was sub-Saharan Africa. This migratory stream included Indians forced out of various locales in Africa due to policies that called for the "Africanization" of local economies. As middleman minorities in nations such as Kenya and Ugan-

73 Including Antigua, Barbados, Belize, Dominica, Grenada, St. Kitts, St. Lucia and Trinidad and Tobago.

74 T. FAIST, P. KIVISTO, *Beyond a Border: The Causes and Consequences of Contemporary Immigration*.
Thousand Oaks, CA: SAGE/Pine Forge Press, 2010.

75 T. FAIST, P. KIVISTO, *Beyond a Border: The Causes and Consequences of Contemporary Immigration*.
Thousand Oaks, CA: SAGE/Pine Forge Press, 2010.

da, they were targeted by nationalists and forced out of the countries, becoming in effect "twice migrants". While some returned to their homeland, many ended up in the United Kingdom. Added to this exodus, Africans from former British colonies also joined the migratory stream, adding numerically to the size of what became known as the Afro-Caribbean population[76].

The combined impact of these three migratory sources was that the UK became considerably more diverse in terms of race and religion. Yet, however significant this transformation was, in terms of sheer numbers, the largest single nationality of immigrants throughout the second half of the 20th century up to the present derived from nearby Ireland. As the nation's first colony, Ireland had long been a source of labor migrants. As an economically struggling nation for most of this period, conditions in Ireland were conducive for emigration and given both the proximity and the intertwined histories of the UK and Ireland, it is not surprising that many emigrants simply crossed the Irish Sea.

In contrast to the Irish, some of the new EU member states have taken advantage of the ability to move freely across borders in order to access labor markets in the wealthier nations in the Union. When several new central and eastern European countries joined the European Union, several of the wealthier Member States placed restrictions on the flow of workers from these countries. The UK resisted pressures to act similarly, in part because in contrast to some of those nations, it enjoyed a growing economy and a low unemployment level[77]. It did, however, limit the ability of migrants from the new Member States to have ready or complete access to the nation's package of social benefits, in an effort to address what was referred to as "benefits tourism"[78].

In addition to legal migrants, the numbers of undocumented migrants have risen in recent years, which includes evidence of human trafficking, smuggling, and forced labor. Of particular concern to authorities are undocumented people entering from either China or various points in eastern Europe. While it is also difficult to determine with any precision the origins of the undocumented migrants, based on evidence obtained from

---

76 H. GOULBOURNE, *Race relations in Britain since 1945*, London: Macmillan, 1988.

77 T. FAIST, P. KIVISTO, *Beyond a Border: The Causes and Consequences of Contemporary Immigration*, Thousand Oaks, CA: SAGE/Pine Forge Press, 2010.

78 D. SRISKANDARAJAH & F. H. ROAD, 2005, Road, United Kingdom: Rising numbers, rising anxieties. Migration Information Source. Retrieved February 9, 2006.

people the authorities have detained, the largest percentage originated in Africa, followed by Asia, Europe, the Americas and the Middle East[79].

In this regard, the UK is no different from the rest of the wealthy countries of Western Europe: estimates of undocumented migrants in Germany, for instance, are higher than estimates of those in the UK. For that reason, the undocumented migrants have become a policy priority not only for the nations involved but within the European Union itself[80].

In terms of Asylum seekers, the 1990s witnessed an increase in the number of applications, peaking at about 40,000 applicants per year, and with it, growing public sentiment that this constituted a problem[81].

The Blair administration in 2004 responded to this growing chorus by instituting policies intended to reduce the number of applicants, streamline the process, and enhance the ability to deport unsuccessful applicants[82]. The detention of asylum seeker has become more common since the beginning of the new century. This shift in policy was intended to make it more difficult for asylum seekers to have their applications approved.

Italy and Spain

While mass immigration to Germany, France, and the United Kingdom has been occurring for half a century, this is not true of the other two major immigrant-receiving nations in western Europe, Italy and Spain. Both of them have until relatively recently been predominantly nations of emigration rather than of immigration.

This has changed during the past two decades: in the case of Italy, its geographic location defines it as the closest point of entry for immigrants from both North Africa and eastern Europe. This accounts for the distinctive nature of the migratory streams that have emerged in recent decades. Four such streams have been identified. The first one is the oldest, with

79 T. FAIST, P. KIVISTO, *Beyond a Border: The Causes and Consequences of Contemporary Immigration*, Thousand Oaks, CA: SAGE/Pine Forge Press, 2010.

80 T. FAIST, P. KIVISTO, *Beyond a Border: The Causes and Consequences of Contemporary Immigration*, Thousand Oaks, CA: SAGE/Pine Forge Press, 2010.

81 T. FAIST, P. KIVISTO, *Beyond a border: the causes and consequences of contemporary immigration*. Thousand Oaks, CA: SAGE/Pine Forge Press, 2010.

82 L. SCHUSTER, The exclusion of asylum seekers in Europe, Centre on Migration, Policy, and Society Working Paper No. 1, Wp-04-01). Oxford: University of Oxford, 2004.

roots dating to as early as the 1960s[83]. It linked migrants from Tunisia to Sicily and involved Italian merchants living in Tunisia who returned to Italy because of nationalization policies implemented in that country. Many of these migrants found employment opportunities awaiting them in the fishing and agricultural sectors. While this stream reflected the connection across the Mediterranean between Italy and Africa, the second one involved a similar connection between both sides of the Adriatic[84]. After a devastating earthquake in Friuli in 1976, the demand for construction workers was met in part by laborers from Yugoslavia[85].

The third stream was defined by Italy's colonial past, as immigrants arrived from Eritrea, Ethiopia and Somalia who have settled in Milan and Rome, where they found work in the unskilled sector and in the ethnic enclave economy. In terms of the latter, they became a visible presence as street peddlers. The fourth migratory stream differs from the previous three insofar as the immigrants in it did not originate in places close to Italy. Rather, it involved people in countries that had experienced a history of Catholic missions in which Italian priests, nuns, and monks had played a prominent role. Thus, this stream included migrants from places such as Cape Verde and Philippines[86].

Ahead of Italy numerically was Spain: the end of the Franco dictatorship and the rapid economic modernization of Spain resulted in a dramatic reduction of Spaniards emigrating, whether it be to western Europe or elsewhere. By the 1990s, Spain had became an immigrant-receiving state. At first, immigrants often treated Spain as a jumping-off point for a subsequent move to somewhere else in Europe. This changed by the mid-1980s, a time when those other ultimate destinations became more restrictive and

---

83 T. CAPONIA, *(Im)Migration research in Italy: A European comparative perspective*, in *The Sociological Quarterly*, 2008, 49(3) 445-464; G. SCIORTINO, A. COLOMBO, *The Flows and the Flood: Public Discourse on Immigration in Italy*, 1969-2001, in *Journal of Modern Italian Studies*, 2004, 9(1): 94-113.

84 T. CAPONIA, *(Im)Migration research in Italy: A European comparative perspective*, in *The Sociological Quarterly*, 2008, 49(3) 445-464; G. SCIORTINO, A. COLOMBO, *The Flows and the Flood: Public Discourse on Immigration in Italy, 1969-2001,* in Journal of Modern Italian Studies, 2004, 9(1): 94-113.

85 T. CAPONIA, *(Im)Migration research in Italy: A European comparative perspective*, in *The Sociological Quarterly*, 2008, 49(3) 445-464; G. SCIORTINO, A. COLOMBO, *The Flows and the Flood: Public Discourse on Immigration in Italy,* 1969-2001, in *Journal of Modern Italian Studies*, 2004, 9(1): 94-113.

86 G. SCIORTINO, A. COLOMBO, *The Flows and Flood: Public Discourse on Immigration in Italy*, 1969-2001, in *Journal of Modern Italian Studies*, 2004, 9 (1), 94-113.

ended guest worker programs that had been created shortly after World War II[87].

Given both Spain's proximity to the Maghreb and historic ties to the countries of the region, this area became one of its major sources of immigrants, with Morocco constituting the largest immigrant group from that region; indeed, as the largest contributor, but also including sizeable contingents from Peru, Colombia, Cuba, Argentina, and the Dominican Republic. These are largely labor migrants heavily concentrated in the service sector and agriculture[88].

As with Italy, Spain is wrestling with policies aimed at immigration control. Given the increase in undocumented migrants, many of whom enter Spain after treacherous journeys across the Mediterranean, controlling the border has become a matter of public concern. Thus, the focus of both legislators and the public has been on legislation regulating immigration flows.

Due to the relative newness of mass immigration, Spain is only beginning to consider matters related to immigrant incorporation. Founded in 1994, the National Integration Forum has been charged with responsibility for formulating policy regarding immigrant integration.[89]

3. The birth of the concept of irregular migration in the European Union

There are two fundamental aspects of contemporary migration policy: one is how to respond to those individuals who wish to try to migrate and this contains the question of immigration policies, migration management and border controls, and the ethical issues of admittance and exclusion; the other question is how to respond to those who are already in a host country and are undocumented. This last situation includes questions of voluntary return, deportation or regularization, and equally ethical matters of justice.

---

87 T. FAIST, P. KIVISTO, *Beyond a Border: The Causes and Consequences of Contemporary Immigration*, Thousand Oaks, CA: SAGE/Pine Forge Press, 2010.

88 N. O. PEREZ, Spain: forging an immigration policy, Migration Information Source, retrieved April 10, 2005.

89 Its most current effort is the „Strategic Plan on Citizenship and Integration, 2007-2010“.

Before analyzing, within this first Chapter, the concept of irregular migrants, it is useful to try to define what is irregular migration in the European context as phenomenon in general.

The "Europeanization" of migration policies has been triggered by external factors, namely spill-over effects from the completion of the internal market, the internationalization of European economies, and the increased migration pressure since the late 1980s. Irregular migration came for the first time into discussion at an EU level in 1976, when the European Commission presented a proposal for a directive on the harmonization of laws in EU Member States in order to combat irregular migration and illegal employment.

Irregular migration as a phenomenon, was neglected by the literature until the 1990s. As highlighted by Portes and De Genova[90], irregular migration has, for a long time, been approached as a problem, leading research to adopt a policy perspective and envisage solutions. Since the 1990s, researchers have tried to adopt a more comprehensive perspective.

It is necessary to start trying to understand what are the roots at the base of this phenomenon: the tensions between individual desires, market forces and political goals provoke the emergence of informal networks, and within them undocumented movements. Part of the problem with undocumented immigrants is that they are, for the most part, invisible in the daily life of the receiving country, as they can only be recognized by checks of identity documents. The unintended negative effects of undocumented migration are various: state authority is weakened; democratic control over migration issue is partially lost; criminal activities (smuggling, survival crimes) may be generated; the chance to tax migrant labour is missed; migrants are deskilled and thereby resources wasted; the immigrant workers themselves suffer from the consequences of exclusion; and social cohesion is undermined. These contradictions, failures and shortcomings lead to a "migration dilemma", that involves anthropological, economic and political concerns[91].

---

90 A. PORTES, *Illegal immigration and the international system: lessons from recent legal Mexican immigrants* to the United States, in Social Problems, 1979, 26 (4), p. 425-443.

91 This "dilemma" has been as the result of the coincidence of "unstoppable migration flows", strong incentives, "porous borders" and the fact that "enforcement to keep out all illegal immigrants is impractical" as supported by S. JOHNSON, S.J. FITZGERALD, The United States and Mexico: Partners in Reforms, Backgrounder, 2003; M. KETTLE, 2004, The Migration Dilemma, in The Guardian, 25 February 2004. Additionally identifies "liberal dilemmas about solidarity and

Until the second third of the nineteenth century, the history of migration was, by and large, an unregulated process with few political interventions and no systematic form of management. Only in occasional circumstances was the movement of humans restricted: feudal laws bound people to landlords, access to cities was often limited, and some colonial powers restricted movements to and within their overseas territories. Political forces sometimes moved humans forcibly, such as undesired populations, who were expelled, criminals, who were deported to overseas colonies, or slaves, who were abducted. The first modern and lasting immigration restrictions were issued around the late nineteenth century[92].

Most of these were not directed against migration in general but against specific groups: morally undesirable individuals, such as single mothers, unmarried couples, prostitutes and vagrants; political undesired individu-

---

diversity" and links this with the discussion about whether or not freedom of movement should be granted to the citizens of the new EU Member States. P. TARAN, Migration Today: the Global Challenge, in People and the Planet, 1994, vol. 3. no. 4, http://www.oneworld.org/patp/pap_migration.htlm, accessed 10 March 2004 concentrates on the seemingly contradictory phenomenon of forced migration being met with increasingly closed borders. The exclusion of immigrants seems, paradoxically, to undermine the otherwise expansionary logic of democracy. It characterizes a situation of fundamental conflicts between the sedentary and the mobile populations. Related public choice theories explore what is rational for individuals and minorities and what is rational for the group as a whole. Looked at in this fashion, the optimal outcome may not necessarily be the maximal outcome, but one that satisfies both groups.

Applied to undocumented migrations, the gains seem mediocre: some employers improve their wins, some migrants meet their expectations, and some sections of society profit from cheap services and products. Equally, the assumed gains from restrictions have to equilibrate against rising enforcement budgets, possible labour market bottlenecks and ethical shortcomings. However, most countries have opted instead for a strategy of conflict and have taken a biased stand in favor of the sedentary population. Countries seems to be prepared to close ranks around the agreed idea that international migration requires common international migration policies to control and restrict migration. Besides the obvious motives of keeping peace and promoting economic growth, the European integration process is driven not least by the national interest of each member state to take on the global migration challenge in a common international manner.

92 E.g. the 1849 Netherlands Alien Act; the 1882 Chinese Exclusion Act in the USA, and similar anti-Chinese
restrictions in Canada (1885, followed by a general Immigration Act in 1906; and Australia around 1890; the 1905 Aliens Restrictions Act in Great Britain; restrictions were also introduced in France in 1849, in Prussia in 1885, and in German Kaisseraich in 1892).

als such as labour militants, communists and anarchists; socially undesired individuals who were suspected of becoming "liable to public charge".

It is relevant to underline that only when States were in a position to formulate rules governing the entry and residence of foreigners and to enforce them that contravention of those rules, and consequently the concept of irregular immigration, became possible. This has not always been applied in legal or political discourses.

Many historical sources do not apply the expression, simply because it was not in use at the time[93]. The European historians often discover the use of the terms "nuisance foreigners" and "unwanted migration" for the period from 1880 to 1960[94].

Arendt (1968), analyzing the major displacement processes that took place during and after the First World War and the subsequent formation of modern nation-states, describes the concept of statelessness as another expression for those who had been refused immigration status.

Historical sources up to the 1920s thus seem to lack the very term "illegal immigrants". One reason for this may be that the rules had not been accompanied by techniques to enforce them and it was only with the invention of passports and deportation procedures after the First World War that governments were able to put immigration restrictions into practice, therefore, historians agree that the concept of "illegal aliens" was only created during the 1920s.[95] However in Europe, very few examples of immigrants being labeled "illegal" can be identified prior to the founding of the State of Israel (1920-47). In Belgium instead, following the 1920 Immigra-

93 In the Netherlands, which was among the first countries to issue immigration restrictions, illegal entry was legally, but nevertheless vaguely, defined since the late nineteenth century but such immigrants were labeled "stowaways", "paid off" or "deserted" seamen and not "illegals". Equally, neither in France nor in Belgium was there a readily available term for those who had neither a work permit nor a residence permit, as required by law. Instead, Dutch historical literature refers to "undesired aliens" as does French historical research.

94 M. MARRUS, The unwanted: European refugees in the twentieth century, Oxford University Press,1985; H. KLEINSCHMITT, Menschen in Bewegung. Inhalte und Ziele historischer Migrationsforschung, Gottingen, Vandenhoeck und Ruprecht, 2002; D. HOERDER, Cultures in contact: World Migrations in the Second Millennium, Durham and London, Duke University Press 2002.

95 F. CAESTECKER, *Alien policy in Belgium, 1840-1940: the creation of guest workers, refugees and illegal aliens*, New York, Berghahn, 2000; *Illegal aliens and alien citizens: United States immigration policy and racial formation*, 1924-1945. Ann Arbor: UNI dissertation service, 1999.

tion Act, the idea of "unwanted immigrants" was legally formalized into the concept of "illegal entry".

Nevertheless, most migrants up until the late 1930s, were appreciated and therefore admitted as "colonial workers" for example[96]. They were tolerated, and could easily regularize their status by registering with the local administration and, before 1925, there was no consistent policy of exclusion which would lead to undocumented entry[97].

The birth of the idea of " illegal immigrants", the focus of this paragraph, can be associated with the emergence of the post-First World War modern nation-state. Thus, it was determined less by increasing migration than by the political processes of nation building as shown in the case of Belgium. These processes defined the extent of the state's territory, its national borders, national space, and so nationality and membership were reconstructed and deserving and undeserving individuals defined and members created. Immigration controls became a tool of demarcation, and enforcement its crucial means. Following the earlier era of free trade, the "illegal immigrants" are also closely related to the inter-war era of economic protectionism[98].

During the post-Second World War growth period in Europe, which also was an era of great labour market demand and major recruitment schemes (1960-1970), those migrating on their own initiative were initially treated as "spontaneous migrants"[99]. Usually, such movements occurred outside active recruitment schemes, and because entry was legal and residence not intended, they were not actively organized by governments. However, in Germany and the Netherlands, for instance, immigrants, after having found an employer, could easily regularize their status and obtain a

---

96 F. CAESTECKER, *Alien policy in Belgium, 1840-1940: the creation of guest workers, refugees and illegal aliens*, New York, Berghahn, 2000.

97 F. CAESTECKER, *Alien policy in Belgium, 1840-1940: the creation of guest workers, refugees and illegal aliens*, New York, Berghahn, 2000.

98 M. NGAI, *The strange career of the illegal alien: immigration restriction and deportation policy in the US, 1921-1965*, in *Law and History Review*, 2003, 21(1), 69-107; F. CAESTECKERC, *Alien policy in Belgium, 1840-1940: the creation of guest workers, refugees and illegal aliens*, New York, Berghahn, 2000; J. CAPLAN, J. TORPEY, J. (eds), Documenting Individual Identities, Princeton University Press, 2000.

99 F. DÜVELL, *Illegal immigration in Europe beyond control?*, Palgrave Macmillan, 2006.

resident permit[100]. In France, in 1945 a *carte de sèjour* (work permit) was introduced and anybody working without such a document effectively was a *sans papier* (without papers). Such a "clandestine" situation, however, was not particularly problematic and anybody who could provide a payslip could regularize his or her position *a posteriori*[101]. It was not until 1972 that two regulations were issued- the *circulaire* Marcellin and another of Fontanet, named after the ministers for social affairs, penalizing immigrants working undeclared, thus finally transforming irregular work into illegal work. In the UK, until 1968 even clandestine entry did not lead to an illegal status, because after twenty-four hours in the country, an immigrant could no longer be refused admission. In the same context, African Indians, expelled from Uganda and entering by "jumping the queue", as it was called, were finally resettled[102].

The first references to "illegal immigrants" can be found in the 1969s and in Germany, the term "illegal sojourners" was first used in 1970. Though such terms were coined during the first third of the twentieth century, their post-war use was limited to some exceptional instances and did not enter widely into public culture. That would only change with the introduction of new legislation, sophisticated technologies and further immigration restrictions[103].

In the wake of the recessions in the 1970s and 1980s, almost all industrialized countries first abandoned their recruitment schemes, and then followed this up by introducing generally more restrictive immigration policies. At first, in order to clear up the existing immigration situation, to make a fresh start, or simply to bow to the force of reality, those who, at the time, resided without any status, or who were *de facto* residents, were often regularized *post hoc*[104].

In a similar manner, coinciding with the post-Cold War situation and the asylum crisis, another series of immigration restrictions (in Germany

100 N. CYRUS, D. VOGEL, *Immigration as a side-effect of other policies: principles and consequences of the German non-immigration policy*. IAPASIS, first report. Oldenburg: University of Oldenburg, 2000.

101 J. SIṂEANT, *La cause de sans papiers*, Paris, Presses de Sciences Po, 1998.

102 MADMADAMI, *Meanwhile, in Australia, queue jumper has become another synonym for irregular immigrant*, 1973.

103 N. CYRUS, D. VOEGEL, *Immigration as a side-effect of other policies: principles and consequences of the German Non-immigration Policy*. IAPASIS, first report. Oldenburg: University of Oldenburg, 2000.

104 In the UK in 1974 and 1978; in France in 1981; in the Netherlands in 1980; and in the US in 1986.

1991) and regularization schemes ensued (in Spain 1991). Throughout the 1980s and 1990s, visa regulations were imposed by all OECD[105] countries and successively extended into an increasing number of countries, "reducing freedom of movement" but preparing the ground for what became undocumented immigration.

Thereafter, rules have been added successively to most countries' immigration legislation declaring irregular immigration an offence, to be dealt with by either administrative or criminal procedures. These are, for example, in the UK the 1971 Immigration Act (illegal immigration), and the 1996 Immigration Act (illegal employment); in France, the Pasqua Laws from 1986 and 1993; in Spain, the 1985 Organ Law. In Germany, post-war immigration was basically left to administrative practice, but in 1982 a "Law to Combat Illegal Employment" was passed, and enforcement agencies were set up. As late as 1991, a comprehensive Foreigners Act came into force. In the US, the 1986 Immigration Reform and Control Act included a section making it illegal to employ undocumented immigrants[106].

Meanwhile, "illegal stay" and work are criminal offences. In Italy, as will be subsequently explored, where the first immigration legislation was introduced as late as 1986 and 1989 (Martelli law)[107], specific immigrant strategies have became offences through a series of emergency ordinances in 1995, 1996 and in 2002 with the Bossi-Fini law[108].

The Greek government issued a new Immigration Act (number 1975) in 1991[109]. It regularized many of those already in the country, but aimed to

105 OECD, 1990, SOEPEMI. Trends in International Migration. Annual Report 1989, Paris: OECD.

106 The Immigration Reform and Control Act (IRCA), Pub. L. 99–603, 100 Stat. 3445, enacted November 6, 1986, signed into law by Ronald Reagan on November 6, 1986, is an Act of Congress which reformed United States immigration law.

107 Conversion into Law No. 39 29 February 1990, with amendments, of the decree-law of 30 December 1989, n. 416, containing urgent regulations on the subject of political asylum, entry and stay of non-EU citizens and regularization of non-EU citizens and stateless persons already present in the territory of the State. Provisions on asylum. Official Journal 49 of 28-02-1990.

108 The law of 30 July 2002, No. 189, better known as the Bossi-Fini law, is a regulation of the Italian Republic that regulates immigration, thus dictated by the first signatories Gianfranco Fini and Umberto Bossi who in the Berlusconi II government respectively held the positions of vice-president of the Council of Ministers and Minister for Institutional Reforms and Devolution. Official Journal General Series n.199 of 26-08-2002 – Ordinary Supplement No. 173.

109 Until 1991 the basic piece of legislation regulating the status of alien immigrants in Greece was Law 4310 of 1929.

deter and expel those who continued to be irregular. Consequently, the category of "illegal immigrants" was introduced and illegal stay penalized. In Portugal, staying or working without permission, or hiring such a person, has been subject to harsh sanctions since 2001 (Decree law no. 4, 2001)[110].

On the European Community level, "illegal immigration" was declared a topic in 1985, and this was reaffirmed in 1989[111]. Therefore, the deepening integration process, aiming at the abolishment of internal borders and free movement of legal residents has had, as its precondition, efficient external borders. Further stages have been the Schengen process, in operation since 1985, and Tampere (presidency conclusions) and Amsterdam (Treaty) processes, which have speeded up policies on "illegal immigration"[112]. Nevertheless, the relationship between EU policy-making and national policy-making is two -fold. On the one hand, national governments act as pacemakers for EU processes, such as the initial Schengen states

---

110 A particularly enlightening analysis is presented by Couper, and Santamaria, (K. COUPER and U. SANTAMARIA, *An Elusive Concept: the Changing Definition of Illegal Immigrant in the Practice of Immigration Control in the United Kingdom*, in *International Migration Review*, 1984, 18 (3): 437-52) which, by taking the case of the UK, shows how the initially very narrow definition of what constitutes illegal immigration in the early twentieth century has been extended on the further groups and migration strategies throughout the century. From "undesirable aliens" being portrayed as "fugitive offenders, the mad, the destitute, and "continental agitators", this concept was later generalized as aliens, whose deportation was "conducive to the public good", and it was applied to "commonwealth citizens" in 1962 and addressed to their families in 1971. However, only in 1962 that the offense of overstaying visa limits was introduced, and a 1965 White Paper referred to "evasion from control", which in 1971 finally and legally became "illegal entry". By constantly refining the definition of "undesired aliens" and including new groups, such as, first, commonwealth citizens, and thereafter their families, and successively developing the concept of "illegal entry", the number of people considered as "illegal entrants" increased ten-fold in the decade between 1970 and 1980. A similar process is reflected in the treatment of tourist who work. Until the early 1970s, most OECD countries did not have any negative regulations for this group. But in the wake of the recruitment stop, all countries, one by one, introduced employment restrictions for tourist. During the 1980s, as illustrated above, most countries also added administrative or criminal penalties. Thus, previously liberal practices have been successively abandoned and replaced by increasingly severe restrictions.

111 Commission of the European Communities, 1985; Council of the European Community 1989.

112 See Commission of the European Union, 2001.

(Germany, France, Benelux); on the other hand, the EU pressurises national governments towards more restrictive measures[113].

These developments have been underscored by the trend towards a common visa regime in Europe, and moreover, the introduction of carrier sanctions in the US and in Europe has been interpreted as a general process of criminalization[114], "irregularising"[115] or "illegalising" migration

Hence, even the United Nations Special Rapporteur on Human Rights "note[s] with concern that criminalization of irregular migration is increasingly being used by Governments to discourage it"[116].

The increasing popularity of the idea of illegal migration, and its history, correlates with this emergence of immigration restrictions and, in particular, the criminalization of entry, stay and employment. During the 1970s, the immigration discourse began to apply the concept of "illegal immigration" occasionally, such as in the UK, after the first effective immigration restrictions had been imposed, but its use only peaked during the 1990s "asylum crisis"[117]. In France, the concept became endemic after the introduction of a series of immigration restrictions in 1968[118].

---

113 As Kreienbrink has illustrated in the Spanish case, 2003 (A. KREIENBRINK, *Spanische Einwanderungspolitik im* Spannungsfeld von europäischen Anforderungen und nationalem Interessen, in Materialen zur Bevölkerungswissenschaft, 2003, 107: 49-76) and Triandafyllidou has shown for Greece 2000 (A. TRIANDAFYLLIDOU, The political discourse on immigration in Southern Europe: a critical analysis, in Journal of Community and Applied Social Psychology, 2000, 10 (5): 373-89).

114 L. GIACOMO, Migration Policies in Europe and the United States, Dordrecht, Klumer Academic Publishers, 1993; V. GUIRADON, Controlling the EU Border by Proxy? The Delegation of Migration Control in Practice, Paper presented at the 13th International Conference of Europeanists, 14-16 March, 2002, Chicago.

115 G. ENGBERSEN, Panopticum Europe and the Criminalisation of Undocumented Immigrants, paper presented to the 6th International Metropolis Conference, Rotterdam, 26-30 November 2001.

116 United Nations, 2002, Specific Groups and Individuals: Migrant Worker. Report of the Special Rapporteur, Gabriel Rodriguez Pizarro, submitted pursuant to Commission on Human Rights resolution 2002/62. E/CN.4/2003/85. Geneva: UN.

117 F. DÜVELL, Undocumented Migrant Workers in the UK: Historical Background, State of Research and Thesis, research report No.1, Exeter, University of Exeter, 1998.

118 U. HOLM, The Implication of the Concept of the French State-Nation and "Patrei" for French Discourses on (Algerian) Immigration. Columbia International Affairs Online (CIAO). Working Paper, New York, Columbia University Press, 2003.

In the Netherlands, the concept dates back to 1969, when new immigration restrictions were introduced[119] and in the US it has gained in relevance after the 1986 Immigration Act[120].

In Germany, after the 1973 recruitment stop, "illegal employment for foreigners" became a matter of some public interest[121].

Nevertheless[122], in assessing the available historical sources, it must be concluded that "*all in all the subject of illegal employment of foreigners did not raise much attention*"[123]. Instead, migrations as such caused public concerns, and these were usually versions of legal migration, such as family reunification. Hoerder[124] pinpoints the concept of illegal migration to the late 1970s. The final increase in the use of this term is closely related to the collapse of the Iron Curtain, the flux of new migration in the early 1990s.

In Italy, for instance, up until the early 1980s, migrants were generally labeled "foreigners". The term "immigrants" only came into use after the mid-1980s in the wake of the first immigration legislation in 1986.

And the expression "clandestini" appeared only following the 1990 implementation of the Martelli Act, and its use has become endemic only since 1995[125].

In the last decade of the twenty century, the topic of undocumented migration also entered on to the international stage. For the OECD region, for example, the SOPEMI[126] reports until 1976 referred to "uncontrolled

119 G. ENGBERSEN, J. V.D. LEUN and R. STARING, Illegal immigrants in the Netherlands, Sopemi-Report 2002, Paris, OECD.

120 L. MARTIN, L. PHILIP, *Illegal Immigration and the Colonization of the American Labour Market*, CIS Paper, No.1, Washington DC: Center for Immigration Studies, 1986.

121 M. DIAMANT, *Die Illegalen*, Der Gewerkschafter, 1973, 12: 474-5; B. HUBER, *Illegal Ausländerbeschäftigung und ökonomische Krise*, in *Demokratie und Recht*, 1993, vol. 4, 370-3.

122 N. CYRUS and D. VOGEL 2000, *Immigration as a Side-effect of Other Policies: Principles and Consequences of* the German Non-immigration Policy, IAPASIS, first report. Oldenburg: University of Oldenburg, 2000.

123 N. CYRUS, D. VOEGEL, *Ausländerdiskriminierung durch Außenkontrollen im Arbeitsmarkt? Fallstudienbefunde – Herausforderungen – Gestaltungsoptionen, Mitteilungen aus der Arbeitsmarkt und Gerusforschung*, 2000, 35(2), 254-70.

124 D. HOERDER, *Cultures in Contact: World Migrations in the Second Millennium,*, Durham and London: Duke University Press, 2000.

125 G. SCIORTINO, A. COLOMBO, *The Flows and the Flood: Public Discourse on Immigration in Italy*, 1969 2001, in *Journal of Modern Italian Studies*, 2004, 9 (1): 94-113.

126 OECD. 1977. *SOPEMI.* Trends in International Migration. Annual Report 1976. Paris: OECD.

flows". One year later there is a single referral to "clandestine immigration", and only in 1980 can the first referral to "illegal immigration" be found. However, it was only as late as 1986 that the label "illegal immigration" made it to the headlines. During these years this expression was used alternatively with "irregular status immigrants", "illegal alien residents", "illegal residents", and at the end of the 1980s, during a period of economic growth, such migrants became "new foreign workers", a term emphasizing the positive economic aspects rather than their legally precarious character[127]. A change took place in the early 1990s, when the first references to policies to "combat illegal immigration" were made, hence against "illegal immigrants". In fact, only since 1998 has "illegal immigration" become a permanent column in SOPEMI reports, which have recently redefined it "undocumented immigration". However, these definitions will be explored in depth later on in this chapter[128].

In Europe, on the political stage, this has been reflected through the so-called "Berlin process", whereby West and East European states have acknowledged that "illegal migration", is a major political topic to be addressed through a joint effort[129]. Meanwhile, there are hardly any European development aid, reconstruction, trade or technical cooperation negotiations or agreements with African, Asian or South American states that do not also include a paragraph on "illegal migration" and readmission policies[130].

Moreover, during the 1990s, the concept of "illegal" or "irregular" immigration has been frequently confused with refugees and asylum seekers. To better understand the reasons of confusion, it is useful outline who are refugees, asylum seeker and person eligible for subsidiary protection. Ac-

---

127 OECD, 1989: *SOPEMI*. Trends in International Migration. Annual Report 1988 20.

128 Chapter I, paragraph 7.1., p. 41.

129 F. DÜVELL, *Illegal immigration in Europe beyond control?*, Palgrave Macmillan, 2006.

130 Three examples: the 1995 EU Mediterranean development conference, held in Barcelona, agreed to contain future unwanted migration and to return undocumented immigrants; in 1991, the International Labour Organization, the International Organization for Migration and several governments held an "International Symposium on Migration: Towards Regional Cooperation on Irregular/Undocumented Migration" in Bangkok, which aimed to tackle undocumented migration on an intergovernmental level; in 2002, the Asian-European Meeting (ASEM) agreed to jointly tackle migration flows and to combat undocumented migration.

cording to the Article 2, paragraph c) of Directive 2011/95/EU[131] "refugees" are "*...a third country national who, owing to a well-founded fear of being persecuted for reasons of race, religion, nationality, political opinion or membership of a particular social group, is outside the country of nationality and is unable or, owing to such fear, is unwilling to avail himself or herself of the protection of that country, or a stateless person, who, being outside of the country of former habitual residence for the same reasons as mentioned above, is unable or, owing to such fear, unwilling to return to it, and to whom Article 12 does not apply*"; according to same Article but paragraph e) 'person eligible for subsidiary protection' are "*...a third country national or a stateless person who does not qualify as a refugee but in respect of whom substantial grounds have been shown for believing that the person concerned, if returned to his or her country of origin, or in the case of a stateless person, to his or her country of former habitual residence, would face a real risk of suffering serious harm as defined in Article 15, and to whom Article 17(1) and (2) do not apply, and is unable, or, owing to such risk, unwilling to avail himself or herself of the protection of that country*"; "asylum seeker (applicant) means a third-country national or a stateless person who has made an application for international protection in respect of which a final decision has not yet been taken[132].

As shown, the concept of "irregular migration" is a legal, political and social construct of the twentieth century, which has only gained prominence during the latter third of that century. It is a blurred concept, it is loaded with ideological import and it is highly politicized[133].

---

131 Directive 2011/95 / EU of the European Parliament and of the Council of 13 December 2011 laying down rules on the allocation to third-country nationals or stateless persons of the status of beneficiary of international protection, on a uniform status for refugees or for persons eligible for subsidiary protection and on the content of the recognized protection. OJ L 337, 20.12.2011, p. 9–26.

132 For example, an IOM report on "Irregular Migration in Central Europe" discussed how and why Afghan refugees come to Hungary. The reason behind such confusions are multiple: refugees do not usually have a visa when they appear at the point of entry, and because they have no visa they cannot enter legally and therefore often find access through illegal means. Moreover, because states have more or less closed their front doors, this has left only the asylum path open to would-be migrants. Also, undocumented migrants, when they have been apprehended, have often applied for asylum in order to prevent immediate deportation. Finally, post-Cold War refugees and asylum seekers have generally been perceived as a burden and are not much desired in Europe, which has prompted a general scapegoating and stereotyping.

133 F. DÜVELL, *Illegal immigration in Europe. Beyond control?*, Palgrave Macmillan, 2006.

After this analysis of the birth of irregular migration in EU context and before exploring the problematic of the status of the irregular migrants in EU in more detail, an analysis of the phenomenon in some of the Member States of EU will be conducted in the next section.

4. Irregular immigration into Member States of European Union

In the following the phenomenon of irregular migration in some Member States of the European Union will be briefly analyzed in order to explore the extent of this phenomenon in the European Union.

Austria

In Austria, irregular migration became an issue of public and policy debates only in the 1990s. During the wake of the breakdown of the communist regimes in the early 1990s, the disintegration of ex-Yugoslavia, and hence the massive increase of migration, in particularly asylum related migration, as well as the increasing politicization of migration, the policy framework governing migration and dating from the "guest-worker" period was completely overhauled. The reform shifted the emphasis from control over migrants access to the labour market to control of entry and residence of migrants. These changes in the regulation of migration can be largely credited for producing irregular migration, both as a discursive space and as an empirical phenomenon. Irregular migrant work has consistently been another major issue of public debates and for a considerably longer period of time[134]. Irregular workers are non-citizens employed in regular jobs without authorization to work, such as foreigners who cross borders without detection and go to work without work authorization or with false documents. Some foreigners reside legally in a country and become irregular workers because their visas allow residence but not employment, as with foreigners who violate tourist visas by going to work.

In contrast to illegal entry and residence, which continues to be largely associated with asylum and hence with migrants from major asylum sending countries, irregular work has been largely associated with migrants outside the asylum nexus and mostly with migrants from Eastern Europe.

---

134 A. TRIANDAFYLLIDOU, *Irregular Migration in Europe: Myths and Realities*, Farnham, Surrey, Ashgate, 2010.

All available evidence suggests that both flows and stocks or irregular staying migrants have considerably decreased since about 2002, as a consequence of the decrease of asylum applications and as a result of the successive EU enlargements.

The same cannot be said in regard to irregular employment where the reverse might be true. However, the majority of persons irregularly employed is not strictly speaking illegally staying and includes a large number of citizens from new EU Member States who do not yet have formal access to the labour market but will in the future.

Czech Republic

Legal migrants and, even more importantly, irregular migrants, supply the secondary labour market. Irregular migrants have come mostly from economically less developed countries, particularly Ukraine. The most crucial reason for the presence of irregular migrant workers is a large demand on the labour market, the demand for a cheap and flexible labour force[135].

The demand and supply side are effectively connected by formal and informal networks of middlemen. The size of irregular migrant population remains unknown, though various estimates indicate that it could be as high as several hundred thousand[136].

Greece

Irregular migration became an relevant factor in Greek public and political discourse in the 1990s. Initially this was strongly connected with the immigration waves from Albania.

In view of European Presidency of Greece in the first half of 2014, Samaras, the Greek Prime Minister, has initiated a discussion among Italy, Malta and Greece, to figure out a path for a common approach regards the problem of irregular migration[137].

---

135 A. TRIADAFYLLIDOU, *Irregular migration in Europe: myths and realities*, Farnham, Surrey, Ashgate, 2010.

136 F. DÜVELL, *Illegal immigration in Europe beyond control?*, Palgrave Macmillan, 2006.

137 F. DÜVELL, *Illegal immigration in Europe beyond control?*, Palgrave Macmillan, 2006.

Experience related to managing irregular migratory flows to Greece over the years 2008-2012 suggests that it is difficult to estimate the cost of managing irregular migration flows and to assess their effectiveness[138]. With regard to the wave of migration, in March 2016, the Bank of Greece published data suggesting that in 2016 alone, the cost of managing the migration crisis will exceed EUR 600 million[139]. The financial crisis had an impact on the management of the migration crisis and on the irregular flows. Given the fact that the number of migrants increased, the cost rose. Since the beginning of 2015, emergency assistance of EUR 181 million has been awarded by the European Commission to Greek authorities, international organizations and NGOs involved in managing the migration crisis in Greece. This emergency assistance comes on top of EUR 509 million already allocated to Greece under the national programs for 2014-2020.[140] It is unclear how much of the sums allocated will be actually disbursed.

France

France is an old immigration country, the oldest one in Europe as it has received immigrants since the mid-19th century. However, it is an immigration country which does not appear to recognize itself as such. For a long time, number of foreigners in France has been stable, at 3.5 million[141] because the foreign entries into country are roughly equal to the number of those who become French citizens by naturalization, marriage or birth[142].

---

138 D. ANGELI, A. TRIANDAFYLLIDOU, A. DIMITRIADI, Assessing the Cost-effectiveness of Irregular Migration Control Policies in Greece, MIDAS Policy Paper, ELIAMEP, 2014.

139 Kathimerini (Greek journal) reported by Greek Central Bank on 13 March 2016 that migrant costs to exceed 600 million euros.

140 European Commission, on 12 April 2016, Managing the Refugee Crisis: EU Financial Support to Greece, Fact Sheet, Migration and Home Affairs.

141 A. TRIANDAFYLLIDOU, *Irregular Migration in Europe: Myths and realities*, Farnham, Surrey, Ashgate, 2010.

142 Children born in France acquire citizenship if at least one of the parents was born in France. Children of foreign parents acquire citizenship: at age 18 if they have resided in the country for at least 5 years since they were 11; between 16 and 18 years if they have resided continuously in the country since they were 8. Foreign adults can apply for it through naturalization after having resided in France for 5 years. In case of marriage you have to wait 4 years.

The largest foreign group present are the Maghrebian[143]. Due to the globalization of migration, new nationalities and groups have appeared, from countries which had few previous links with France (Sri Lankans, Chechens, Iraqis, Kurds, Afghans, and Chinese. Sub-Saharan Africans are also present in the French territory, due to the links of historical link. French, introduced in the African continent with the colonization by France and Belgium, is often a second language for the local population but in some regions and contexts has become a mother tongue, replacing the local languages in all the communicative functions.

Indeed, even where local languages survive in everyday life, French is the main language of education, media (television, radio and press) and formal and international communications.

In spite of this long experience in migration management and migrant integration, in recent times, border control has progressively acquired a central place in the French migration policy agenda. This development is mainly related to pressure from extreme right-wing parties[144].

After a period where legislation on immigration was absent, the country has seen an inflation of legislative proceedings and the pressure of EU rules is a factor that has led to criminalization of irregular migration[145].

Germany

Germany is a country famous for its government's attitude in favor of strict migration control. In spite of its political rhetoric, this State hosts also irregular migrants. It must be stressed that the rhetoric has also changed during the last years based also on the migration crisis that has affected the EU in these recent years. In particular the Syrian war that caused Germany to open a privileged channel for asylum seekers coming from that country. The Federal Foreign Office and its missions abroad provide information locally about the dangers of fleeing and irregular migration, as well as about the actual and legal conditions for refugees and migrants in Germany.

143 The Algerians, Moroccans and Tunisians.

144 As for instance *Front National*.

145 For instance the so called "Return Directive", Directive 2008/115 / EC of the European Parliament and of the Council of 16 December 2008 on common rules and procedures in Member States for returning illegally staying third-country nationals, OJ L 348, 24.12.2008, p. 98–107.

The phenomenon of irregular immigration in Germany will be discussed in depth subsequently.

Italy

The most salient feature of the Italian experience is the persistently high level of undocumented migration. This phenomenon has translated on the policy level into frequent general amnesties, five since 1986, granting legal status to about 1.5 million migrants, which is roughly half of the current stock of resident migrants. As with the section on Germany, the analysis of the phenomenon of irregular immigration in Italy will be expanded upon in a following chapter of this research project[146].

Netherlands

The Netherlands is one of the countries which, since the 1990s, is actively dealing with the issue of irregular migration[147]. The Dutch policies toward irregular immigrants have become much more restrictive over time, with an emphasis on protecting public services against what is perceived as their abuse by irregular immigrants. Even if internal controls have been fine-tuned over the years within the county's extensive and highly-regulated welfare state, irregular migration is still present.

Poland

Poland's migration regime is fairly strict, in large part because of the requirements it needed to meet for EU accession and for entering the Schengen zone[148]. Together, its migration policy and relatively poor economy, as compared to other Member States of the EU, has not allowed for the creation of massive groups of clandestine migrants. As of yet, the only signifi-

---

146 Chapter III, p. 122.

147 A. TRIANDAFYLLIDOU, *Irregular migration in Europe: myths and realities*, Farnham, Surrey, Ashgate, 2010.

148 Entry into force of the Schengen Convention in Poland is on May 1st, 2004. The Schengen Convention (officially the Convention implementing the Schengen Agreement) is an international treaty that regulates the opening of borders between the signatory countries.

cant irregular migrant group, in quantitative terms, drifts from Eastern neighbouring countries. However, their irregularity has resulted from the fact that they pursue illegal work on the basis of valid tourist visas.

The Ukrainian migrants represent the most significant nationality in terms of legal immigrants and irregular foreign workers in Poland. It is evident that the trend of illegal work, on the basis of legal residence visas and documents, it was the most characteristics feature of the Ukrainian immigrant group since the enlargement of the Schengen zone.

Spain

Typically immigrants arrive to Spain as tourists, overstay their visa, and some years later regularize their situation. During the period of irregular stay, immigrants find a job in those sectors where informal procedures for recruitment are usual such as construction, domestic service, catering, hotels, agriculture or retail trade, and the shortage of labour controls contribute to facilitate their stay and work.

Regularization, extraordinary or ordinary, have become the main instrument used in the management of migration flows, and irregularity has been implicitly accepted by successive governments despite the dominant rhetoric of a "struggle against irregular immigration"[149]. A liberal market approach has dominated and given priority to the demands of the job market over the orderly management of the migratory flows. Yet this balance between the demands of the job market and the arrival of immigrants could have been reached in a more orderly fashion and much of the irregularity been prevented[150].

149 A. TRIANDAFYLLIDOU, *Irregular migration in Europe: myths and realities*, Farnham, Surrey, Ashgate, 2010.

150 F. DÜVELL, *Illegal immigration in Europe beyond control?*, Palgrave Macmillan, 2006.

United Kingdom

On the whole, the general migration policy in the UK was seemingly haunted by the myth of an "unknown number" of irregular migrants in the country or potentially entering the country[151].

The problematic state of available data, made any rigorous attempt to estimate the scope of the irregular migrant population scientifically unsatisfying or a matter of highly politicized forces[152]. It was found that a paradoxical development has grown over the years, resulting in a traditional political culture of avoiding a quantification of the phenomenon and proving a certain sensitive awareness of the subject matter, while at the same time an increasing trend of measures towards enhanced control and surveillance has taken place. This development stood for a shift in the UK's tradition of rather liberal values in this particular policy domain.

After analyzing briefly irregular migration as a concrete reality in the Member State, the next section will start to study irregular migrants themselves.

5. Different typologies of migrants

In the following an analysis will be conducted of the typologies of migrants in relation to their legal or irregular status.

First of all, it is useful to outline the several categories, as suggested by Frank Düvell, in which irregular migrants can be included.[153]. Below is submitted an identification of a range of migration patterns:

- some move only once or a very few times. These are occasional migrants;
- others frequently commute between two countries. These represent a typical transnational strategy;
- one group chose their destinations throughout Europe and even beyond, wherever there is an opportunity. Thereare continentally or even globally mobile;

151 A. TRIANDAFYLLIDOU, *Irregular migration in Europe: myths and realities*, Farnham, Surrey, Ashgate, 2010.

152 A. TRIANDAFYLLIDOU, *Irregular migration in Europe: myths and realities*, Farnham, Surrey, Ashgate, 2010.

153 F. DÜVELL, *Illegal immigration in Europe: beyond control?*, Palgrave Macmillan, 2006.

- another group may come only once, but stay as long as possible. They are medium-term immigrants;
- and some may prolong their stay indefinitely and become long-term residents, sometimes undocumented, but usually acquiring a legal status[154].

It must be emphasized that a complex interrelation of immigration legislation, social boundaries and racism determine the legal and social status of immigrants; immigration legislation varies with respect to the nationality of immigrants and according to each country's regulations[155].

Hence, the *de facto* status thereby depends on, first, the visa policy of a country, and second, on the linkages between different system, and whether or not there are systems of data exchange in place. A comparative study enables one to identify different levels of integration of irregular immigrants, from quasi-legal illegal, and semi-legal illegal, to totally illegal immigrants.

Immigrants from countries that do not require a visa, usually enter legally, as visitors, tourist, students or *au pairs*; but immigrants from countries requiring a visa either have to apply for a visa showing the usual restriction on duration and employment or enter clandestinely. Nationals from visa-free countries or visa holders stay legally, but, because employment is restricted, work illegally; immigrants from countries which need a visa both stay and work illegally. This means that, for instance, an undocumented Polish national in any EU Member State who is caught in an immigration check-up cannot easily be identified as an over-stayer, because his or her passport does not show a visa with a date of entry. He or she can usually only be detected when caught whilst working undocumented. In contrast, an Albanian, who has entered clandestinity and who is caught in an immigration check-up, must show an entry clearance, but will not able to provide it, and so will be immediately identified as an illegal immigrant.

Quasi-legal illegal

Countries with weak internal controls, provide some opportunities for undocumented immigrants. In case where immigration status is not checked

154 F: DÜVELL, *Illegal immigration in Europe, beyond control?*, Palgrave Macmillan, 2006.

155 F. DÜVELL, *Illegal immigration in Europe, beyond control?*, Palgrave Macmillan, 2006.

at the point of access to a social system, or in cases where personal data is required but not cross-checked with data held by immigration authorities, an undocumented immigrant may access some social services, as subsequently analyzed. These could be the health system, education, and public services, but also the labour market. Such immigrants do not have an immigration status but pay taxes and make contributions to national insurance schemes. They are, at the same time, both illicit members of a political community, and legal members of often several, if not all, of the internal social system, such as the club of taxpayers or insurance schemes. They could be defined as quasi-legal illegal[156];

Totally illegal

Countries with tight control such as Germany, Sweden and Netherlands, make such forms of illegal stay, by and large, impossible[157]. There are strict internal, which combine immigration tests and data exchange between social services and enforcement services, an undocumented immigrant would be immediately detected.

Even within illegality exist different rights, resulting in a hierarchy of rights and thereby a hierarchy of illegality[158].

6. The relationship between a regular and an irregular status

The immigration categories of documented and undocumented immigrants are not static: several patterns can be identified. As mentioned above, migrants enter legally as tourists, students, *au pairs* or workers, over -stay, as said before, change their activities and become undocumented. Undocumented residence can be regularized through appropriate schemes or by applying to alternative provisions, such as business-visa or marriage, etc. Those once regularized can fall back to an irregular status, once the

---

156 F. DÜVELL, *Illegal immigration in Europe, beyond control?*, Palgrave Macmillan, 2006; P. KIVISTO & T. FAIST, *Citizenship: discourses, theory, and trasnational prospects*, Malden, MA: Blackwell, 2007.

157 F. DÜVELL, *Illegal immigration in Europe, beyond control?*, Palgrave Macmillan, 2006.

158 Semi-legal and economically more successful immigrants may leave sooner, after having met their targets, whilst totally and therefore economically less successful migrants may instead have to stay longer to fulfil their aspirations.

limits have expired or the legal preconditions are no longer given. Or else they originally come to work illegally and then apply for a visa when they come again, perhaps because they have in the meantime learned about legal alternatives or because their circumstances have changed and they qualify for a legal immigration category. Or, still, they have been working undocumented in one country and at a later stage legally work in another country which offers such opportunities.

Therefore, it is not a surprise that documented and undocumented immigrants have some characteristics in common, first of all, the aim to migrate as mentioned above; as it is caused by opportunity restraints in the countries of origin, migration is a positive life-project[159] to enhance the prospects of an individual, a family or an entire community, and will be realized by any means necessary. Some accomplish it within the legally available opportunities, though even in cases where there are provisions, these may be dismissed if they are perceived to be too cumbersome. The secondary aim for most of them seems to be to regularize their position, indeed where there are such opportunities they are keen to apply.

Although a regular position is preferred, in cases where this is not possible, immigrants are unlikely to leave, therefore in countries which do not have any such provision, undocumented migrants rather laconically accept their position, even reject the idea of regularization[160].

Another group favor the advantages of an undocumented status and does not wish to regularize its position. This is for reasons of competition with the regular workforce, or for additional reasons such as tax evasion or their general "claiming and working" strategy.

The typical reasoning is "I came here to work and for nothing else", indeed migrants are attracted by the employment and earning opportunities, and interpret signals from either employers or acquaintance as a call to come to try. The chances to do so legally entirely depend on the immigration opportunities. Those who fall under existing provisions, such as those in scarce professions, under sectoral recruitment schemes or special bilateral opportunities, migrate legally; but those whose skills, professions or nationalities do not match such criteria try their luck illegally. Migrants of

159 F. DÜVELL, *Illegal immigration in Europe, beyond control?*, Palgrave Macmillan, 2006.

160 N. CYRUS, (2001), *Schattenwirtschaft und Migration in Berlin. Ethnologische Annäherungen an ein offenes Geheimnis, in Frank Gesemann* (ed), Migration und Integration in Berlin, Wissenschaftliche und Politische Perspektiven. Opladen, Leske und Budrich, 2001, pp. 209-32.

both categories also often wish to improve their human capital, either by learning a foreign language or by gaining some work experience.

It is possible to identify different types of migrants: young people of learning age and mature and experienced workforce. Often, a considerable proportion of undocumented immigrants fall exactly in between both groups: they are old enough to have finished their education but too young to have gained any work experience[161]. That points to a gap within the legal provisions for migrants between both groups, because there are very few temporary immigration statuses that combine the working and learning aspects. It is possible to conclude, as Düvell mentioned in his book[162], that some undocumented migration derives from this lack of legal opportunities for an age group which is also the most mobile.

Furthermore, the learning strategy is often initially related to return intentions: improving one's human capital with the aim of increasing one's competitiveness in the home labour markets. Migrants who succeed may return sooner, but migrants who fail may stay longer[163]. The undocumented immigrants often do not succeed in acquiring new skills; they are usually situated in niches where they are separated from society. Indeed, languages are not learned, nor is the regular market world experienced, no references are acquired and many times they have neither the time nor money to attend language or other courses. Migrants explain that this is because irregular work is usually low-skilled, low-paid and exhausting. Such conditions are not suitable for the satisfaction of the learning strategy, and they thereby slow down return considerably. Some of these mechanisms are unintended side-effects of immigration restrictions[164].

Another unwanted side-effect of immigration restriction is that when immigrants are restricted from entering a country, they tend to stay as long

---

161 F. DÜVELL, *Illegal immigration in Europe: beyond control?*, Palgrave Macmillan, 2006.

162 F. DÜVELL, *Illegal immigration in Europe: beyond control?*, Palgrave Macmillan, 2006.

163 N. CYRUS, (2001), *Schattenwirtschaft und Migration in Berlin. Ethnologische Annäherungen an ein offenes Geheimnis*, in F. GESEMANNF (ed), Migration und Integration in Berlin. Wissenschaftliche und Politische Perspektiven. Opladen, Leske und Budrich, 2001, pp. 209-32; F. DÜVELL, *Illegal Immigration in Europe: Beyond Control?*, Palgrave Macmillan, 2006.

164 F. DÜVELL, *Illegal immigration in Europe: beyond control?*, Palgrave Macmillan, 2006; G. ENGBERSEN, Panopticum Europe and Criminalisation of Undocumented Immigrants. Paper presented to the 6th International Metropolis Conference, Rotterdam, 26-30 November 2001.

as possible once they get in, whilst immigrants from, for instance, visa-free countries may come repeatedly but also leave again voluntarily.

After analyzing the relationship between the regular and irregular status above, the following paragraphs offer some general considerations on the specific phenomenon of irregular immigration. There are additional factors that precipitate irregular migration and irregularity: these include the children of irregular migrants who are born into irregularity and the partners of irregular migrants asylum seekers who have had their cases rejected, visa over-stayers (student, holiday and work) as well as those who enter clandestinely. As detected by several authors[165], this diversity highlights that irregularity can be a process and/or migration strategy and is, among other factors, related to increased difficulty of migrating legally to EU Member States.

In a globalized era, demand for both high-and low-skilled migrant workers in northern economies has grown[166], however alongside the need for labour, immigration controls have been developed at national-state and supra-national levels, creating a disjuncture between economic and political interests regarding immigration, in what Hollifield[167] calls the "liberal paradox" of open markets and closed political communities. This intensified attempt to manage migration, including with technological tools, obliges individuals to use different and sometimes fluid immigration statuses and strategies. In short, legal immigration has become more difficult and is increasingly limited to the privileged few[168].

While, in the 1970s, irregular migration was more of a phenomenon in the wealthier countries of the global north and west, it is now globally prevalent, as most irregular migration takes place between countries in the developing world[169]. For a lot of countries irregular migration is seen as a "problem" to be solved. This can be explained by the fact that irregular mi-

165 A. BLOCH, *Irregular Migrants: Policy, Politics, Motives and Everyday Lives*, London, Routledge, 2012, et al. B. JORDAN and F. DÜVELL, *Irregular migration: the dilemmas of transnational mobility*, Cheltenham: Edward Elgar, 2002.

166 S. CASTEL & M.J. MILLER, *The age of migration: international population movements in the modern world* (4th ed.) New York: Guilford Press, 2004.

167 J.F. HOLLIFIELD, *Immigrants, market and states: the political economy of postwar Europe*, Cambridge, MA: Harvard University Press, 1992.

168 A. BLOCH, *Irregular migrants: policy, politics, motives and everyday lives*, London, Routledge, 2012.

169 K. KOSER, Irregular Migration, State Security and Human Security. A paper prepared for the Policy Analysis and Research Programme of the Global Commission on International Migration. Global Commission on International Migration, available, 2005.

gration is intrinsically related to immigration policy, border controls and definitions of citizenship by nation-states. It is not surprising, therefore, that the notion of "clandestine migration" appeared for the first time in the nineteenth century when nation-states concretized and provided the legal tools to define legal and illegal mobility[170].

The debates on this issue show that nation-states still aim to protect a juridical membership and their territorial sovereignty. However, despite attempts to prevent irregular migration, it persists, and consequently a growing criminalization of phenomenon can be observed [171].

Increased immigration controls and greater surveillance and the overview of irregular migration policy shows that states tend to adopt a pragmatic perspective, focusing on employers, criminals, migrant smugglers and agents and newcomers instead of promoting the continuous mass deportation of irregular migrants workers[172]. This pragmatism, highlights on the one hand the inability of governments to control immigration flows and on the other hand the human rights that nation-states are obliged to provide to any human beings independently of their status, such as healthcare and education.

Another relevant key, has been the form that irregular migration takes, which has altered in a number of ways since the 1970s: irregular migration flows are no longer just related to labour migration[173].

Irregular migrants were mainly from close by countries: from Latin America to the US and from Eastern or Southern Europe to Northern and Western Europe; in the European context, the expansion of the EU means

---

170 M. CVAJNER, G. SCIORTINO, *Theorizing irregular migration: the control of spatial mobility in differentiated societies,* in *European Journal of Social Theory*, 2010, vol. 13, no. 3, pp. 389-404; M. NGAI, (2004), *Impossible subject: illegal aliens and the making of modern America*, Princeton, NJ, and Oxford, Princeton University Press, 2004.

171 M. NGAI, *Impossible subject: illegal aliens and the making of modern America*, Princeton, NJ, and Oxford,
Princeton University Press, 2004.

172 W. A. CORNELIUS, *Controlling "unwanted" immigration: lessons from the United States 1993-2004,* in *Journal of Ethnic and Migration Studies*, 2005, vol. 31, no. 4, pp. 775-94; S. CASTELS, *Why migration policies fail, ethnic and racial studies*, 2004, vol. 27, no.2; J. GUIRAUDON, *De-nationalizing control: analysis state responses to restraints on migration control*, in V. GUIRAUDON and C. JOPPKE (eds), *Controlling a new migration world*, London, Routledge, 2001; C. JOPPKE, *Why liberal states accept unwanted immigration*, in *World Politics*, 1998, vol. 50, no.2, pp.266-93.

173 A. BLOCH, *Irregular Migrants: policy, politics, motives and everyday life*, London, Routledge, 2012.

that people from traditional migrant-sending countries from the south and east of Europe are now able to move freely within the EU zone and, if previously irregular, have been able to regularize their situation.

The migration is longer, more expensive, can entail greater risks and for many necessitates the use of agents and smugglers for border crossing and documentation[174]. The conclusion reached is that repressive policies have not prevented irregular migration, but have diversified its characteristics and modes of illegality, these aspects will be explored in depth in the subsequent chapters. This diversification means that most countries, even non-traditional countries for immigration, are affected by irregular migration[175].

Anderson and Rush[176] argue that irregularity may be "a consequence of shifting state policies or individual choices and opportunities". For this reason the conceptualization of irregularity goes beyond the illegal/legal divide and instead represents a range of situations on a continuum between two ideal types. At one end of the spectrum are those who combine all types of irregularity (irregular entry, residence, work and illegal practices) while at the other end is the perfect citizen[177].

7. Irregular migration by European Union legislations: questions of definition

It is relevant when talking about irregular migrants at European level, to classify these migrants according to the EU legislation. For that reason, this section analyzes whether and in which officials documents of European Union, it is possible to find a definition of irregular migrants that outlines what are the requirements which characterize these citizens. Anticipating

174 I. VAN LIEMPT, *Navigating Borders: Inside Perspectives on the Process of Human Smuggling into the Netherlands*, Amsterdam: Amsterdam University Press, 2007; K. KOSER, *Irregular Migration, State Security and Human Security, paper prepared for the policy analysis and research programme of the Global Commission for International Migration*, September 2005.

175 A. TRIANDAFYLLIDOU, *Irregular migration in Europe: myths and realities*, Farnham, Surrey, Ashgate, 2010; A. BLOCH, *Irregular migrants: policy, politics, motives and everyday lives*, 2012.

176 B. ANDERSON, M. RUSH, *Guest editorial: researching illegality and lobour migration*, in *Population, Space and Place*, 2010, vol. 16, no. 3, pp. 175-9.

177 F. DÜVELL, *Clandestine migration in Europe*, in *Social Science Information*, 2008, vol. 47, No. 4, pp. 479-97.

the result of this specific analysis, there is a lack of a precise definition of irregular migrants or the status of irregularity at European Union level. There is just a definition of "illegal stay" provided by the Directive 2008/115/EC, better known as the Return Directive.

First of all, in the Treaty on the functioning of the European Union in the Article 20, 1 paragraph (ex Article 17 of TEC) states that "...*Every person holding the nationality of a Member State shall be a citizen of the Union. Citizenship of the Union shall be additional to and not replace national citizenship*".

In the Schengen Code in Article 2, (5) outlines who are persons enjoying the Union right of free movement: "*(a) Union citizens within the meaning of Article 20(1) TFEU, and third-country nationals who are members of the family of a Union citizen exercising his or her right to free movement to whom Directive 2004/38/EC of the European Parliament and of the Council*[178] *applies; (b) third-country nationals and their family members, whatever their nationality, who, under agreements between the Union and its Member States, on the one hand, and those third countries, on the other hand, enjoy rights of free movement equivalent to those of Union citizens*"[179].

For completeness, in the Schengen Code, in paragraph 6 of Article 2, there is a definition of third-country national: "'*third-country national' means any person who is not a Union citizen within the meaning of Article 20(1) TFEU and who is not covered by point 5 of this Article*".

Moreover, paragraph 7 outlines '*persons for whom an alert has been issued for the purposes of refusing entry' means any third-country national for whom an alert has been issued in the Schengen Information System (SIS) in accordance with and for the purposes laid down in Articles 24 and 26 of Regulation (EC) No 1987/2006 of the European Parliament and of the Council*"[180], "*persons for whom an alert has been issued for the purposes of refusing entry*" as any third-

178 Directive 2004/38/EC of the European Parliament and of the Council of 29 April 2004 on the right of citizens of the Union and their family members to move and reside freely within the territory of the Member States amending Regulation (EEC) No 1612/68 and repealing Directives 64/221/EEC, 68/360/EEC, 72/194/EEC, 73/148/EEC, 75/34/EEC, 75/35/EEC, 90/364/EEC, 90/365/EEC and 93/96/EEC (OJ L 158, 30.4.2004, p. 77).

179 Regulation (EU) 2016/399 of the European Parliament and of the Council of 9 March 2016 on a Union Code on the Rules governing the movement of persons across borders (Schengen Borders Code), OJ L 77, 23.3.2016, p. 1–52 (which repealed and replaced the Regulation (EC) No 562/2006).

180 Regulation (EC) No 1987/2006 of the European Parliament and of the Council of 20 December 2006 on the establishment, operation and use of the second generation Schengen Information System (SIS II) (OJ L 381, 28.12.2006, p. 4).

country national for whom an alert has been issued in the Schengen Information System (SIS) in accordance with and for the purposes laid down in Article 96 of the Schengen Convention.

Finally, Directive 2008/115/EC[181] on common standards and procedures in Member States for returning illegally staying third-country nationals, offers a positive definition of "illegal stay": "...means the presence on the territory of a Member State, of a third-country national who does not fulfil, or no longer fulfils the conditions of entry as set out in Article 5 of the Schengen Borders Code or other conditions for entry, stay or residence in that Member State".

Following up these general considerations, not only legal, on the phenomenon of irregular migration the next section will explore the several terminologies attributed to irregular migrants, highlighting the reasons for them and try to outline which, according to this research project, is more correct.

As shown above, the phenomenon of "irregular migration" is a legal, political and social terminology of the twentieth century, which has only gained prominence recently and which is loaded with ideological import and is highly politicized.

Anticipating what this section will try to analyze and referencing Düvell[182], irregular migration has become an issue to be found worldwide in policies as diverse as trade agreements, development policies, military strategies and international relations; sometimes, the only reasons for the usage of this terminology is because it raises attention, sells well, and has entered commonly used language. While legal systems and most public discourses usually adopt the concept of illegality in referring to this phenomenon, employing such terms as "illegal immigrants" or, in shorter form "illegal", the social sciences prefer to refer "undocumented" or "irregular" immigrants. This is done to avoid any discriminatory connotation, to prevent further criminalization and to emphasize that it is not the immigrant as a human being who is illegal but his or her mode of entry and stay or work.

As already mentioned previously, irregular migration has become a priority issue for EU migration policy during the last ten years. Often, govern-

181 Directive 2008/115/EC of the European Parliament and of the Council of 16 December 2008 on common standards and procedures in Member States for returning illegally staying third-country nationals.

182 F. DÜVELL, *Illegal immigration in Europe: beyond control?*, Palgrave Macmillan, 20006.

ments of Member States have accused one another for their lax policy in dealing with irregular migrants and right wing politicians have struck a chord with EU electorates with regard to security issues and irregular migration. Nevertheless, the size and main features of the irregular migrant population of the EU as a whole and of each specific member state remains under-researched.

In any studies of this field, irregular migration, it is possible to note that there are many forms and types of "irregularity" or "illegality" related to entry, stay or work of foreign citizens in a third country. There are a number of terms and expressions used for persons who enter a country illegally, over stay their terms of legal residence, live in a country without a resident permit and/or break immigration rules in a way that makes them liable to expulsion.

There are many adjectives "irregular", "illegal", "undocumented", "unauthorized" or "clandestine" which are combined with the nouns "migrants", "immigrants", "aliens" or "foreign nationals"; while expressions like "sans-papiers" and "clandestinos" have acquired an international use[183].

In a largest sense, the term "illegal migration", connotes an act of migration that is carried out against legal provisions of entry and residence; as mentioned before, the European Union attributes this meaning to this term.

Scholars, such as Sciortino[184], have argued the lack of neutrality of the term "illegal" and have pointed out that the adverb associates this type of migration with criminal behavior and should therefore be avoided.

Subsequently, indeed, the derived expression "illegal migrants" is considered demeaning and discriminatory by human rights advocates, since "no human being is illegal". Technically, the term in question designates the act of entering a country in violation to national law and is confined to illegal border crossing, referring only to a flow and not to a stock of persons.

"It's notable that the countries that most pride themselves on their commitment to equality, human rights, and democracy (like the United States and the western European countries) are precisely those that, in the late

183 The discussion of terminology is based on the CLANDESTINO Project Research: Report on Methodological Issues, edited by A. KRALER and D. VOGEL and prepared by M. JANDL, D. VOGEL and K. IGLICKA, in November 2008.

184 G. SCIORTINO, *Between phantoms and necessary evils. Some critical points in the study of irregular migrations to Western Europe*, IMIS-Beitrage, 2004, 24, p. 17-43.

twentieth century, invented a new status ('illegal') in order to deprive some of their residents of access to equality, human rights, and democracy. When we use the term "illegal" in this way, we are implicitly accepting the idea that all people are not created equal, that all people do not deserve equal rights, and that the law should treat people differently depending on the category they are assigned to."[185]

However, in recent years, the term "illegal migration" in is broadest sense, has been increasingly replaced with the term "irregular migration". This expression denotes a form of migration that is "not regular" or is "unlawful" because of its violation of migration rules, without necessarily being "illegal" or "criminal". Therefore, an "irregular migrant" is a migrant, who at some point in his migration, has contravened the rules of entry or residence. The term "irregular" is widely understood as a very broad concept and can refer to both stocks and flows of migrants[186].

Another term frequently used with the meaning of "irregular migrant" described above, is "undocumented migrant". It has the implicit meaning of a migrant who is not in possession of the required residence papers. It refers to people who enter or stay in a country without legal authorization. Of course, not everyone residing in a state that is not his own needs explicit authorization to do so as, for example, in the case of an EU national who has free movement rights within the EU, and it is necessary to interpret "unauthorized" as not authorized according to the law[187].

There are certain groups of people that have shifted status during the last few years, as well as some people who are in possession of residence documents but not of the correct documents justifying their stay[188].

EU citizens may move and reside freely in other Member States for reasons of study or leisure if they can prove they have the financial means to support themselves, and for reasons of work if they can prove they have a work offer or contract. They can take advantage of the welfare system of

185 A. CHOMSKY, *Undocumented: how immigration became illegal*, Boston, Beacon Press, 2015.

186 A. TRYANDAFYLLIDOU, *Irregular migration in Europe: myths and realities*, Farnham, Surrey, Ashgate, 2010; K. KOSER, Irregular Migration, State Security and Human Security, paper prepared for the policy analysis and research programme of the Global Commission for International Migration, September 2005.

187 A. TRIANDAFYLLIDOU, *Irregular migration in Europe: myths and realities*, Farnham, Surrey, Ashgate, 2010.

188 A. TRIANDAFYLLIDOU, *Irregular migration in Europe: myths and realities*, Farnham, Surrey, Ashgate, 2010.

another Member State only after they have acquired residence rights in that state and thus the full protection offered under EU freedom of movement rights legislation.[189]

Irregular migrants are non EU-citizens who have no residence status at all, and/or people whose activities would make them liable to expulsion if detected. The latter particularly concerns persons who conduct irregular work on a tourist visa or during visa-free tourism (working tourists). In some countries, "working tourists" are assumed to be the majority of irregular migrants, while in others irregular migrants usually do not have any residence status. Migrants with a temporary or conditional work permit, such as seasonal and contract workers, may be liable to expulsion if they violate their terms of employment by working for longer periods than foreseen in their papers or in labor market sectors other than those foreseen in their permits[190].

Thus, there is a migrant working population in the EU that is "documented" but may be irregular because of various violations by migrants of the conditions in their papers. In many countries, whether these persons are included in the concept of irregular migration or not plays a crucial role in the concept of irregular migration and in the regularization process. Usually, foreign nationals with a regular residence status who conduct informal work are not referred to as "irregular migrants"[191]. Currently, it is reasonable to restrict the term "irregular foreign resident" to "person without any residence status" and to "working tourists"[192].

Thus, we can conclude, that there are people with legal residence status who work in violation of the conditions of regular status; people who have no documented status at all, lack of legal residence and work status; people who are regular and allowed to work but do so in an informal labour market because they are unable to find a job with a proper contract in line with the national labour law.

The chances of immigrants on the labour and housing markets, as well as their chances to improve their position, are also determined through the

---

189 Directive 2004/38/EC of the European Parliament and of the Council of 29 April 2004 on the right of citizens of the Union and their family members to move and reside freely within the territory of the Member States.

190 A. TRIANDAFYLLIDOU, *Irregular migration in Europe: myths and realities*, Farnham, Surrey, Ashgate, 2010.

191 A. TRIANDAFYLLIDOU, Irregular migration in Europe: myths and realities, Farnham, Surrey, Ashgate, 2010.

192 A. TRIANDAFYLLIDOU, Irregular migration in Europe: myths and realities, Farnham, Surrey, Ashgate, 2010.

construction of social and cultural boundaries, and are reflected in identity-construction processes[193].

Lack of immigration status combined with discrimination leads to an inferior labour market rank, so migrants are confined to low-status jobs.

The category of irregular migrants includes not only undocumented people but also people who are in possession of forged papers or people who have assumed false identities with real papers. They may live the life of a regular migrants unless they are discovered by the authorities[194].

It is interesting to note the categories that Tapinos[195] detects on this issue, distinguishing between clandestine entrants, clandestine workers and clandestine residents and identifying six precise groups, similar to what has just been outlined:

-migrants who have entered the country legally with a legal residence permit, but who are working illegally either because the job is not declared or because their residence permit does not allow them to work[196];

migrants who have entered the country legally but are living in the country illegally[197], and who are working illegally. It is assumed that a migrant without a residence permit cannot work legally under the legislation in force[198];

- the same category as above, but covering inactive migrants from an economically point of view[199];

---

193 A. TRIANDAFYLLIDOU, *Irregular migration in Europe: myths and realities*, Farnham, Surrey, Ashgate, 2010.

194 In the Netherlands, persons without a residence status working in regular taxpaying jobs are called "white illegal". Their life may be very similar to the life of legal residents and citizens, involving regular jobs and free movement in the public sphere, or it can be similar to the life of migrants without any status. If the quality of the papers is so poor that the migrant does not dare to show them anywhere, these papers are not much different from having no papers at all.

195 G. TAPINOS, Irregular Immigration: Economic and Political Issues,, in OECD, Combating the Illegal Employment of Foreign Workers. Paris: OECD, pp. 13-43, 2000.

196 This includes tourists, family members without a work permit, students and au pair with employment restrictions, and also asylum seekers with employment restrictions.

197 Either because their work permits are invalid or expired or because they do not have residence permits.

198 This corresponds with visa overstayers, who can be tourists, workers, students, au pairs, rejected asylum seekers or divorcees who, because of a divorce, lost their immigration status.

199 These may be either family members of the above group or family members of legal residents refused or not eligible for family reunification.

- migrants who have entered the country clandestinely, who have no residence permit, and who are working illegally[200];
- the same category as above but covering inactive migrants;
- migrants who have entered the country clandestinely, who have a residence permit, e.g. following regularization or by variation in their status through marriage and are working illegally.

An additional category which ought to be mentioned are children born to irregular immigrants, who are irregular themselves without ever having crossed an international border.

In Europe, because of its efficient external border controls, it is generally assumed that most irregular immigrants fall into the first category; they had legally entered the country and then either violated employment restrictions or overstayed their visa time limit. They are an integral, though comparably small part of the legitimate global flow of people for reasons of tourism, business or employment[201].

It is rare to come across a country which does not report some sort of "illegal immigrants". Illegal migration has become an inherent aspect of global migration. It would appear to be impossible to ascertain the exact size of the phenomenon and so any figures must be treated with the utmost caution.

So far the division of migrants in categories proposed by a specific author has been noted, however, it is possible to detect other categories. In this regard, another category of uncertainty, quite common in Southern Europe, is that of people under review in the course of a regularization program. These are Third Country Nationals who were previously undocumented who applied to legalize their status and are still waiting for their permits to be issued. As this process may take from a few months up to a year, during this time these people live more or less the life of a regular migrant[202]. While technically they are irregular and do not appear in state databases on legal migrants.

Finally, the category of irregular migrants crosses with the category of asylum seekers, who enter a country without documents and then file an asylum application and have an uncertain legal status until their applica-

---

200 These can be workers, family members or refugees who did not make an asylum claim.

201 A. TRIANDAFYLLIDOU, *Irregular migration in Europe: myths and realities*, Farnham, Surrey, Ashgate, 2010.

202 Since authorities are instructed not to arrest nor deport them if they are in possession of a slip that certifies they have submitted a complete application for the issuing/renewal database on legal migrants.

tion is processed. There are asylum seekers whose application is pending for several years and whose residence status is uncertain even if technically legal, because they have to renew their short-term permits at regular intervals.

Moreover, there are rejected asylum seekers, notably people who have exhausted all means for obtaining asylum, whose applications have not been accepted but who are, nonetheless, unable to leave the country and hence remain without residence status, yet with the knowledge and toleration of the authorities.

This status may involve a formal suspension of enforcement action for a specific period of time as in the case of Duldung in Germany which is, in the form of a formal document, communicated to the tolerated person or an administrative suspension of enforcement action for practical reasons (as, for example, limited capacity to organize deportation, unwillingness of the country of origin to issue required travel documents; questionable citizenship status, etc.), whether or not enforcement is suspended for a specific time period or indefinitely. The main characteristic is that tolerated persons do not posses documents proving the suspension of enforcement action. Finally this status of "toleration" may also be due to the simple inaction of authorities rather than a specific decision to suspend enforcement. Whereas one can expect administrative statistics on the first type of toleration, statistics are usually not kept for the second type; in the third type, authorities may not be able to identify the number of persons who are thus informally tolerated.

In technically terms, toleration, both formal and informal, is only a suspension of an expulsion order and not in itself a legal status: toleration does not have a legalizing effect and does not change the unlawful presence of the tolerated alien. It is necessary to note, that there is a little practical difference between formal toleration, the formal suspension of an expulsion order for a specific period of time documented by some sort of permit, and comparable legal statuses such as those related to humanitarian stay or subsidiary protection.

It is possible also to identify some sub-category of irregular migrants, indeed irregular migration is by nature a non-registered phenomenon and hence most data available do not actually refer to irregular migrants but rather to people who, while being irregular migrants, have been identified by the authorities for one reason or another.

Thus, a sub-category of irregular migrants are aliens apprehended at the border or within the territory of a country. Such data are available in all countries studied but in most cases refer to apprehensions rather than individuals[203].

Moreover, it is in many cases difficult to distinguish data on apprehensions in the interior and at the border. People who are apprehended far from the geographical borders may have been residing in the country for a few days, weeks, months or several years. Thus, it is unclear whether they have to consider them newcomers or not.

The second sub-category of irregular migrants are people who are registered with health or other social service providers that serve irregular migrants[204].

In attempts to quantify the phenomenon of irregular migration, experts, politician and policymakers have been mostly interested in geographical flows. They are interested to know more about the countries of origin and in particular the countries of transit, especially if these border on the European Union. They thus attempt to identify the geographical routes of irregular migration from, for instance, Asia or Africa to Europe.

Third country nationals mostly enter the EU with legal papers, they may enter with a tourist visa, without a visa (where they are not required to have one), with forged papers, with a visa for a third country, with a study visa or with some other type of legal document that allows them to enter and temporarily stay in the EU[205].

They may then overstay and abuse the term of their residence. Therefore, what in scientific jargon is called "status-related flows" appear to be as important and actually even more important than geographical flows; the expression "status-flows" refers not only to legal entry and overstay but also to other types of paths into or out of irregular status.

---

203 If a Pakistani citizen, for example, attempts to cross the Greek-Turkish border several times within the same year and is caught and sent back several times, he will appear registered as many times as he was apprehended and not just once.

204 An example of this case is a special program in France that targets undocumented migrants so as to provide them with medical assistance. Data from this program refer not to the totality of irregular migrant residents in France but rather to irregular migrants who have used this specific health assistance program. Actually, the databases of non governmental organizations active in the field of migrant support often provide useful information concerning the share of the irregular population within the total migrant populations. The same limitations regard irregular migrant workers, they are by definition a non-registered group that only becomes visible when caught by labour inspection or police authorities.

205 A. TRIANDAFYLLIDOU, *Irregular migration in Europe: myths and realities*, Farnham, Surrey, Ashgate, 2010.

Analyzing the pathways into irregular status, we note a special case of "befallen illegality"[206], as they have been termed in Southern Europe. This refers to the case of irregular migrants who have managed to legalize their status temporarily through an amnesty program, but who shift back to irregular status because they are unable to fulfil the conditions for renewing their permits (for example because they could not prove legal employment).

The ultimate rejection of asylum seeking applications, or withdrawal of toleration status are other important types of "status flows" into irregular status, without this entry into the irregular migrant stock implying an actual geographical movement, or any action on the migrant's part.

Status flows are also related to changes in migration policy. When legal migration provisions become particularly restrictive and the legal residence status of migrants particularly uncertain, it is logical to expect that more legal migrants may fall into irregular status. Whether permits are issued for short term periods and constantly require proof of legal employment for renewal, if there are no provisions for unemployment support for migrant workers who are temporarily out of work, if the migrant's permit is connected to his employer, then in all these cases the slightest change in the migrant's working conditions may result in the loss of legal status.

The special character of irregular migration is by nature non-registered phenomenon and the role of both status and geographical flows needs to always be taken into account when attempting to quantify and explain the phenomenon.

---

206 A. TRIANDAFYLLIDOU, *Irregular migration in Europe: myths and realities*, Farnham, Surrey, Ashgate, 2010.

CHAPTER II: The protection of human rights of irregular migrants in the legal framework of European Union

Introduction

In this Chapter the protection of human rights of irregular migrants will be explored on two levels: international law and in the context of the European Union. Firstly, a focus will be on the content of the International Conventions, such as the European Convention of Human Rights, and then in particular in the context of the European Union, the European Union Charter of Fundamental Rights. That will allow and understanding of the tools which guarantee protection of irregular migrants.

Thereafter the illustration of the European Union framework for the protection of human rights of irregular migrants in relation to the entry into Member States phase will be analysed.

In particular it will be explored in depth, what kind of guarantee of human rights is provided in the context of the high seas, hot spot and during the detention and return procedures.

A. Human rights and irregular migrants at international level

1. Preliminary observations on international human rights law

International human rights law is a set of international rules, established by treaty or custom, on the basis of which individuals and groups can expect and/or claim certain entitlements or benefits from governments[207].

The following is a list of the Conventions and other relevant instruments created at international level to protect human rights.

207 C.OVEY and R.A.W. HITE, *The European Convention on Human Rights*, 4th end. Oxford University Press, Oxford 2006, pp. 419-429; S.GRANT, *International Migration and Human Rights*, Global Commission on International Migration, 2005, p. 16.

International Bills of Human Rights:
- Universal Declaration of Human Rights (1948) – UDHR;
- International Covenant on Civil and Political Rights (1966) – ICCPR;
- International Covenant on Economic, Social and Cultural Rights (1966) – ICESCR.

Other Core Human Rights Instruments (Thematic or Protecting Specific Groups):
- International Convention on the Elimination of All Forms of Racial Discrimination (1965) – ICERD;
- Convention on the Elimination of All Forms of Discrimination Against Women (1979) – CEDAW;
- Convention Against Torture and Other Cruel, Inhuman or Degrading Treatment or Punishment (1984)-CAT;
- Convention on the Rights of the Child (1989) – CRC;
- International Convention on the Protection of the Rights of All Migrant Workers and Members of Their Families (1990) – ICRMW.

Human rights are inherent entitlements which belong to every person as a consequence of being human[208]. International human rights law is composed, as shown in the list above, of the Universal Declaration of Human Rights (UDHR)[209] and the seven United Nations (UN) human rights treaties[210]. Together these instruments represent international standards for the respect and promotion of human rights.

The Universal Declaration of Human Rights (UDHR) is the basic document of all UN human rights conventions. The declaration consists of 30 articles which outline the view of the United Nations on the human rights that are guaranteed to all people. Even though the UDHR is a declaration

---

208 D. WEISSRODT, *The Protection of Non-Citizens in International Human Rights Law* in R. CHOLEWINSKY, R. PERRUCHOUD and E. MACDONALD (eds.), *International Migration Law: Developing Paradigms and Key Challenges*, T.C.M. Asser Press.,The Hague 2007, pp. 228-232.

209 the Declaration was proclaimed by the United Nations General Assembly in Paris on 10 December 1948 (General Assembly resolution 217 A.

210 International Convention on the Elimination of All Forms of Racial Discrimination (ICERD) 1965; International Covenant on Civil and Political Rights (ICCPR) 1966; International Covenant on Economic, Social and Cultural Rights (ICESCR) 1966; Convention on the Elimination of All Forms of Discrimination against Women (CEDAW) 1979; Convention against Torture and Other Cruel, Inhuman or Degrading Treatment or Punishment (CAT)1984; Convention on the Rights of the Child (CRC) 1989; International Convention on Protection of the Rights of All Migrant Workers and Members of Their Families (ICMRW) 1990.

and is not binding on states, in 1968 the United Nations International Conference on Human Rights decided that it *"constitutes an obligation for the members of the international community"* for all persons[211].

The seven UN human rights conventions establish the UN treaty body system which sets international standards for the protection and promotion of human rights. These conventions are not part of customary law but states can subscribe to them by becoming a party to each treaty. Each state party has an obligation to take steps to ensure that everyone in the state can enjoy the rights set out in the treaty.

All of the Member States of the European Union have ratified all of the treaties with the notable exception of the International Convention on the Protection of the Rights of All Migrants Workers and Members of Their Families[212]. Therefore the provisions granted in each of the human rights

---

211 The International Conference on Human Righ, having met at Teheran from April 22 to May 13, 1968 to review the progress made in the twenty years since the adoption of the Universal Declaration of Human Rights and to formulate a programme for the future. In that occasion has been solemnly proclaimed that: "*The Universal Declaration of Human Rights states a common understanding of the peoples of the world concerning the inalienable and inviolable rights of all members of the human family and constitutes an obligation for the members of the international community;*", Proclamation of Teheran, Final Act of the International Conference on Human Rights, Teheran, 22 April to 13 May 1968, U.N. Doc. A/CONF. 32/41 at 3 (1968). Nowadays the UDHR is considered to be part of customary international law and is thus intended to be binding on states.

212 Since the beginning of the drafting process of International Convention on the Protection of the Rights of All Migrants Workers and Members of Their Families (ICRMW), there have been many objections to ratification raised especially by so-called "receiving" countries. Since the ICRMW entered into force in 2003, no EU member state, the United States, Canada nor Australia – all major so-called immigrant "receiving" countries – have ratified the convention. Nonetheless, the number of countries that have ratified the ICRMW is constantly increasing and is starting to include not only "sending" countries but also receiving ones such as Turkey or Libya. Furthermore, policy makers on different levels of government in EU member states have started to debate on the opportunity to ratify the ICRMW, (See the European Economic and Social Committee, Opinion of the European Economic and Social Committee on the International Convention on Migrants, Brussels, 30 June 2004, OJ C 302, 7.12.2004, p. 49–52, and the Parliamentary Assembly of the Council of Europe, Resolution 1509 (2006) on Human rights of irregular migrants (Assembly debate on 27 June 2006 (18th Sitting: see Doc. 10924, report of the Committee on Migration, Refugees and Population, rapporteur: Mr van Thijn, text adopted by the Assembly on 27 June 2006, 18th Sitting). Calls for the ratification of the ICRMW have been recently raised from various European institutions such as for example the

conventions must be considered to be binding for all of the Member States that make up the European Union.

Each of the seven core human rights treaties has established a treaty monitoring body, whose purpose is to ensure the implementation of the treaty provisions of the state parties[213]. State parties are obliged to report to the treaty monitoring bodies on the implementation of the treaty into national law and practice and the treaty monitoring bodies then assist the state parties in the implementation of the treaties.

Furthermore the treaty monitoring bodies publish general comments/ general recommendations on each treaty, which consist of the treaty monitoring body's interpretation of the content of the human rights provisions. The treaty monitoring bodies can also consider individual complaints from individuals alleging that their rights have been violated by a state party[214].

European Economic and Social Committee and the Parliamentary Assembly of the Council of Europe.13 An exhaustive list of the positions taken by EU member states as well as various EU institutions and different stakeholders on the local, regional, national and European levels can be found in a study by the organization December 18, The U.N. Migrant Workers Convention: Steps Towards Ratification in Europe (See A. GUILBERT, R. PLAETEVOET, The U.N. Migrant Workers Convention: Steps towards Ratification in Europe, European Platform for Migrant Workers' Rights, March 2007, (http://www.december18.net/web/docpapers/doc5096.pdf).

213 The human rights treaty bodies are committees of independent experts that monitor implementation of the core international human rights treaties. Each State party to a treaty has an obligation to take steps to ensure that everyone in the State can enjoy the rights set out in the treaty. There are ten human rights treaty bodies composed of independent experts of recognized competence in human rights, who are nominated and elected for fixed renewable terms of four years by State parties. The Office of the High Commissioner for Human Rights (OHCHR) works to offer the best expertise and support to the different human rights monitoring mechanisms in the United Nations system: UN Charter-based bodies, including the Human Rights Council, and bodies created under the international human rights treaties and made up of independent experts mandated to monitor State parties' compliance with their treaty obligations. Most of these bodies receive secretariat support from the Human Rights Council and Treaties Division of the Office of the High Commissioner for Human Rights (OHCHR).

214 There are nine core international human rights treaties. Each of these treaties has established a "treaty body" (Committee) of experts to monitor implementation of the treaty provisions by its States parties. Treaty bodies (CCPR, CERD, CAT, CEDAW, CRPD, CED, CMW, CESCR and CRC) may, under certain conditions, consider individual complaints or communications from individuals.

There are three main procedures for bringing complaints of violations of the provisions of the human rights treaties before the human rights treaties bodies:

1. Individual communications (complaints or communications set forth by individuals);
2. State-to-state complaints (one state party may complain about alleged violations of the treaty by another state party);
3. Inquiries (CAT and CEDAW may initiate inquiries if they have received reliable information containing wellfounded indications of serious or systematic violations of the conventions in a state party)[215].

2. The protection of migrants within an international scenario: the issue of irregular migration

"The body of international human rights law has opened a new chapter in international affairs in that it does not concern the traditional function of international law, that of regulating relations between sovereign states, but rather seeks to regulate the relationship between the state and individuals within its territory and jurisdiction"[216]

The migrants in an irregular situation are more likely to face discrimination, exclusion, exploitation and abuse at all stages of the migration process. They often face prolonged detention or ill-treatment and, in some cases, enslavement, rape or murder. They are more likely to be targeted by xenophobes and racists, victimized by unscrupulous employers and sexual predators, and can easily fall prey to criminal traffickers and smugglers[217]. Rendered vulnerable by their irregular status, these men, women and children are often afraid or unable to seek protection and relief from the authorities in countries of origin, transit or destination. Clearly, the irregular

---

215 For a general overview of the Treaty Bodies System, see OHCHR, (http://www.ohchr.org/english/bodies/treaty/index.htm), accessed on 10 January 2007.

216 S. GRANT, International Migration and Human Rights, Global Commission on International Migration, 2005, p. 16.

217 V. T. REITANO, L. ADAL, M. SHAW, *Smuggled Futures: The Dangerous Path of the Migrant from Africa to Europe, The Global Initiative against Transnational Organized Crime*, Geneva, 2014, available online; D. WEISSBRODT, *The Protection of Non-Citizens in International Human Rights Law*, in R. CHOLEWINSKY, R. PERRUCHOUD and E. MACDONALD (eds.), *International Migration Law: Developing Paradigms and Key Challenges*, T.C.M. Asser Press.,The Hague 2007, pp. 228-232.

situation in which international migrants may find themselves should not deprive them either of their humanity or of their human rights.

International human rights law provides that everyone, without discrimination, must have access to the fundamental rights provided in the international bill of human rights.

Where differential treatment is contemplated, between citizens and non-citizens or between different groups of non-citizens, this must be consistent with international human rights obligations, undertaken for a legitimate objective, and the course of action taken to achieve this objective must be proportionate and reasonable.

Governments have an interest in promoting and protecting the human rights of all migrants, including irregular migrants, because no society can develop to its true potential when legal, social or political barriers prevent entire sectors of that society from contributing to it. Indeed, the irregular immigrants tend to work in sectors that are dirty and dangerous, often doing jobs that local workers are unwilling to do[218].

2.1. Human rights protection of irregular migrants under the United Nation treaties

The United Nations have among their purposes the promotion of the universal respect for and the observance of human rights and fundamental freedoms for all, without distinction as to race, sex, language, or religion, for the achievement of which the state parties and the organization shall take action[219].

Human rights are universal, inalienable, egalitarian and indivisible. The Universal Declaration of Human Rights (UDHR) defines human rights as *"basic rights and freedoms that all human beings are entitled to, without distinction of any kind, such as race, colour, sex, language, religion, political or other opinion, national or social origin, property birth or other status"*.[220]

In 1948, the UDHR was adopted by the UN General Assembley. It was drafted in the aftermath of World War II as the first international human

218 A. TRIANDAFYLLIDOU, *Irregular Migration in Europe: Myths and Realities*, Farnham, Surrey, Ashgate, 2010.

219 Arts. 55 and 56 of the Charter of the United Nations, 1 UNTS XVI, signed on 26 June 1945.

220 Art. 2(1) of the Universal Declaration of Humanr Rights, UN General Assembly Resolution A/RES/217 (III) of 10 December 1948.

rights treaty for the benefit of mankind composed of a catalogue of rights. One of the most important principle set out is the principle of non-discrimination which is central to all important international human rights treaties and an exception to non-discrimination is only permissible if the differential treatment at stake pursues a legitimate aim, can objectively be justified and is proportionate to the aims sought to be achieved[221].

There are other human rights instruments which are more precise in their application as regards the distinction between citizens and non-citizens. The International Covenant on Civil and Political Rights[222] (ICCPR) of 1966 sets out certain rights that cannot be deviated from: most rights contained in the Covenant must be guaranteed, regardless of the nationality of a person, as the Human Rights Committee made clear in its General Comment No 15[223] on the position of aliens under the ICCPR. In particular, the Committee highlighted especially that Article 2(1) requires each State Party to ensure that the rights in the Covenant apply to "*all individuals within its territory and subject to its jurisdiction*", irrespective of reciprocity, nationality or statelessness[224].

---

221 J. FITZPATRICK, *The Human Rights of Migrants*, in T.A. ALEINIKOFF and V. CHETAIL (eds.), *Migration and International Legal Norms*,T.M.C. Asser Press, The Hague 2003, pp. 171-172.

222 UN General Assembly Resolution 2200A (XXI) of 16 December 1966.

223 General Comment No. 15: The position of aliens under the Covenant of 11 April 1986.

224 J. FITZPATRICK in *The Human Rights of Migrants,* in T.A. ALEINIKOFF and V. CHETAIL (eds.), *Migration and International Legal Norms*,T.M.C. Asser Press, The Hague 2003, pp. 171-172. He classifies the rights set out in the ICCPR in view of migrants into five categories: 1) rights that must be guaranteed in equal measure to nationals and migrants, such as the right to life (Article 6 ICCPR); equality before the law and a fair trial (Article 14 ICCPR); the prohibition of any advocacy of national, racial or religious hatred that constitutes incitement to discrimination, hostility or violence (Article 20(2) ICCPR (this first category of rights includes Arts. 6, 7, 8, 10, 11, 12(2), 14, 15, 16, 18, 19(1), 20(2), 23, 24, 27 ICCPR of which some are non-derogable rights in line with Art. 4 ICCPR; see General comment No. 15: The position of aliens under the Convenant of 11 April 1986, para. 7); 2) arbitrary state action is prohibited by some provisions, which may allow for a narrow differentiation between nationals and migrants; for instance, immigration detention does not fall under the prohibition on arbitrary arrest and detention, but migrants may not be treated differently in criminal proceedings; 3) discriminatory treatment of migrants may be justified on the basis of national security or public order, if the state objective is legitimate and the action undertaken proportionate (this case relate for example to the freedom of expression, Article 18 ICCPR); 4) certain political rights are reserved for nationals, including the right to vote and to be elected (Article 25 ICCPR);

Although there is no general codification of rights of aliens[225], one has to take into account that the UN Migrant Worker Convention, which entered into force in 2003, applies to any person who is to be engaged, is engaged or has been engaged in a remunerated activity in a state of which he or she is not a national. This extended definition of a migrant worker includes those who have an irregular status in the country of employment[226]. Just as the UN Migrant Worker Convention, the Convention on the Elimination of All Forms of Discrimination Against Women of 1979, as well as the Convention on the Rights of the Child of 1989 envisage the provision of protection for specifically vulnerable groups of society[227].

The UN also provided the protection of human rights for irregular migrants, indeed, in 1999, the Commission on Human Rights created the post of the UN Special Rapporteur on the Human Rights of Migrants who has the task to examine ways and means to overcome the obstacles to the full and effective protection of the human rights of this vulnerable group, including obstacles and difficulties for the return of migrants who are undocumented or in an irregular situation[228]. The conclusion of this Special Rapporteur has been "*all persons should by virtue of their essential humanity enjoy all human rights unless exceptional distinctions, for example, between citizens and non-citizens, serve a legitimate State objective and are proportional to the achievement of that objective*"[229]. Moreover, a large gap has been indicated between the rights that international human rights law guarantees to

5) some rights aim at the protection of all migrants, such as the special rules on expulsion (Article 13 ICCPR), other rules exclusively protect nationals and migrants having a legal status, such as the right to liberty of movement within a state's territory (Article 12(1) ICCPR.

225 J. FITZPATRICK, *The Human Rights of Migrants*, in T.A. ALEINIKOF and V. CHETAIL (eds.), *Migration and International Legal Norms*, T.M.C. Asser Press, The Hague 2003, pp. 171-172.

226 Art. 2(1) of the UN Migration Worker Convention: UN General Assembley Resolution A/RES/45/158 on International Convention on the Protection of the Rights of all Migrant Workers and Members of Their Families of 18 December 2006, 69th Plenary Meeting.

227 Convention on the Elimination of All Forms of Discrimnation Against Women, UN General Assembley Resolution 34/180 of 18 December 1979; Convention on the Rights of the Child, UN General Assembley Resolution 44/25 of 20 November 1989.

228 Commission on Human Rights Resolution 1999/44 on the Human Rights of Migrants of 26 April 1999, 55th session.

229 The mandate of the Special Rapporteur on the Human Rights of Migrants was created in 1999 by the Commission on Human Rights, pursuant to resolution 1999/44.

non-citizens and the realities they must face as, in many countries, there are still institutional and endemic problems confronting non-citizens[230]: D. Weissbrodt, in this role as Special Rapporteur affirms that xenophobia and racism, abuse and harassment continue to exacerbate the everyday lives of non-citizens in host countries, despite clear international human rights standards that are either not enforced, or actively disgregarded and infringed by discriminating legal rules[231].

2.2. Irregular migrants under the ILO Conventions No. 97 and No. 143

The ILO[232] Conventions No 97 and No 143 are the most significant treaties providing for the protection of migrant workers and their families which were drafted under the patronage of the ILO[233]. Undocumented migrants do not fall under the scope of application of the Convention No 97[234] as clarified in Article 11(1) but they do fall within the scope of No 143.

---

230 D. WEISSBRODT, *The Protection of Non-Citizens in International Human Rights Law*, in R. CHOLEWINSKY, R. PERRUCHOUD and E. MACDONALD (eds.), *International Migration Law: Developing Paradigms and Key Challenges*, T.C.M. Asser Press.,The Hague 2007, pp. 228-232.

231 UN Sub-Commission on the Promotion and Protection of Human Rights, rights of non-citizens; Final report of the Special Rapporteur, Mr. David Weissbrodt, submitted in accordance with Sub-Commission decision 2000/103,Commission resolution 2000/104 and Economic and SocialCouncil decision 2000/283AddendumExamples of practices in regard to non-citizens, 26 May 2003, E/CN.4/Sub.2/2003/23/Add.3.

232 International Labour Organization.

233 ILO Convention No. 97 concerning Migration for Employment of 1 July 1949; ILO Convention No. 143 concerning Migrations in Abusive Conditions and the Promotion of Equality of Opportunity and Treatment of Migrant Workers of 24 June 1975.

234 ILO Convention No 97 regarding Migration for Employment was prepared in the wake of World War II and adopted in 1949. Post-war reconstruction efforts and the huge number of refugees and internally-displaced persons in Europe prompted the formulation of immigration and emigration policies, as well as resettlement schemes. The drafting of Convention No 97 responded to the call for migrant labour by providing a flexible tool covering the migration circle from entry and recruitment to return. Article 6 of Convention No 97 enshrines the non-discrimination for lawfully resident migrant workers compared to national workers in the respect of remuneration and employment conditions, membership of trade unions, accommodation, social security, employment taxes and legal proceedings.

ILO Convention No 143, adopted in 1975, supplements Convention No 97 in that has a broader scope of application than its precedessor[235]. The political climate in 1975 was tense as *"clandestine migration, discrimination and xenophobia moved to the forefront of public concern"*[236] and the Convention was designed at a time of economic downturn caused by the oil crisis at the beginning of the 1970s which led to unemployment and, subsequently, to the closing up of borders for labour migration[237]. The Convention has the focus on the prevention of clandestine migration and associated illicit employment and promotes equality of opportunity and treatment.

R. Cholewinsky, referring to Recitals 3 and 4 of the Preamble, remarked that the document recognises the link between a lack of economic opportunity in the countries of origin and existence of irregular migration movements connected to the search of employment[238].

The Convention No 143 applies to all migrant workers, including irregular migrants. Article 1 states that *"each member for which this Convention is in force undertakes to respect the basic human rights of all migrant workers"*. The integration of migrants that have an irregular status in the state of employment is reflected, moreover, in Article 9 of the Convention No 143 which specifies equality of treatment for undocumented migrant workers with regular migrants in respect of rights arising out of past employment, as regards remuneration, social security and other benfits. However, this concession is restricted insofar as Part II of Convention No 143 on Equality of Opportunity and Treatment sets out rules that are only applicable to migrant workers who have been regularly admitted in accordance with article 11(1).

State parties shall determine the scope of clandestine migration in their territories and take appropriate measures to suppress clandestine movements and to prevent people smuggling and illegal employment. These

---

235 ILO Convention No. 143 concerning Migrations in Abusive Conditions and the Promotion of Equality of Opportunity and Treatment of Migrant Workers of 24 June 1975; R. CHOLEWINSKY, *The Human and Labor Rights of Migrants: Visions of Equality*, in 22 *Georgetown Immigration Law Journal*, 2008, 177, p. 189.

236 M. HASENAU, *ILO Standards on Migrant Workers: The Fundamentals of the UN Convention and their Genesis*, 25 *International Migration Review*, 1991, 687, p. 695.

237 K. BADE, *Migration in European History*, Blackwell Publishing, Oxford 2003, p. 228.

238 R. CHOLEWINSKY, *Migrant workers in International Human Rights Law: Their Protection Countries of employment*, Clarendon Press, Oxford 1997, p. 96.

measures include administrative, civil and penal sanctions[239]. Futhermore, state parties shall ensure systematic contact and mutual information exchange on the subject-matter[240].

2.3. Irregular migrants under the UN Migrant Worker Convention

The UN General Assembley approved the UN International Convention on the Protection of the Rights of Migrant Workers and their Families (UN Migrant Worker Convention, ICMW), in December of 1990[241].

The ICMW entered into force on 1 July 2003[242] and it was drafted with the objective to provide a comprehensive legal framework for the protection of migrant workers and their family members[243]. The Preamble indicates the need to strengthen the position of migrant workers and their families on the one hand and to prevent irregular migration while recognising and assuring the protection of fundamental human rights on the other[244].

Concerning the Preamble, as R. Cholewinsky pointed out, not all the rationales for the IMCW are stated in the Preambe, e.g. "*the ICMW constitutes a delicate balance between the protection of migrants' rights and the principle of state soverignity*"[245].

239 K. EISELE, *The External Dimention of the EU's Migration Policy. Different Legal Position of Third-Country Nationals, in the EU: A Comparative Perspective, in Immigration and Asylum Law and Policy in Europe*, 2014, Vol. 34, Jan Niessen and Espelth Guild.

240 Arts. 2 to 6 ILO Convention No. 143.

241 UN General Assembley Resolution A/RES/45/158 on Internationl Convention on the Protection of the Rights of all Migrant Workers and Members of Their Families of 18 December 2006, 69th Plenary Meeting.

242 Art. 87(1) ICMW stipulates that the Convention enters into force on the first day of the month following a period of three months after the date of the deposit of the twentieth instrument of ratification or accession.

243 M. HASENAU, *ILO Standards on Migrant Workers: The Fundamentals of the UN Convention and their Genesis*, 25 *International Migration Review*, 1991, 687, p. 695; R. CHOLEWNSKY, *The Rights of Migrant workers*, in R. CHOLEWINSKY, R. PERRUCHOUD and E. MACDONALD (eds.), *International Migration Law: Developing Paradigms and Key Challenges*, T.M.C. Asser Press, The Hague 2007, p. 259.

244 Vienna Convention on the Law of Treaties Art. 31 represents the legal importance of Preamble to Public International law treaties.

245 R. CHOLEWINSKY, *Migrant Workers in International Human Rights Law: Their Protection in Countries of Employment*, Clarendon Press, Oxford 1997, p. 146.

This Convention is characterized by inclusiveness, indeed it applies to migrants to have a legal status in the country of residence, as well as migrants who are undocumented. The first category of migrants, those with a regular situation are granted more extensive rights, which are laid down in Part IV of the ICMW. The broad definition of who is considered to be a migrant worker in Article 1 of the ICMW makes this international treaty an ambitious and important contribution in mitigating the precarious conditions that irregular migrants have to face[246]. With a view to ensuring the application of the Convention to all migrant workers, Article 88 of the ICMW expressly prohibits state parties from excluding any category of migrant workers from its scope of application; this is an innovative element of the ICMW seeing that, by way of comparison, the ILO Convention No 143 and the European Social Charter do allow for such derogations[247].

Although the state parties may notify reservations to the UN Secretary-general, these reservations may not be incompatible with the object and the purpose of the ICMW in accordance with Article 91(2)[248]. The ICMW was adopted under the auspices of the UN after disagreements with the ILO which had a keen interest in drafting and shaping the specialised agency, and it was stressed that it was inevitable that the ICMW draws heavily on, and sometimes duplicates, standards set out in the ILO Conventions[249]. The ICMW is structured in nine parts, including scope and definitions: non-discrimination with respect to human rights is one of these.

With the objective to discourage irregular migration as set out in Recital 15 of the Preamble to the ICMW, documented migrants are granted additional rights in Part IV. They concern the right to be informed about admission and employment conditions (Article 37); the right to liberty of movement in the territory of the state of employment (Article 39); the

---

246 L.S. BOSNIAK, *Human Rights, State Sovereignty and the Protection of Undocumented Migrants under the International Migrant Workers convention*, 25 *International Migration Review*, 1991, 737, p. 740.

247 As pointed out by R. CHOLEWINSKY, *Migrant Workers in International Human Rights Law: their Protection in Countries of Employment,* Clarendon Press, Oxford 1997, p. 148.

248 K. EISELE, *The External Dimention of the EU's Migration Policy. Different Legal Position of Third-Country Nationals, in the EU: A Comparative Perspective*, in *Immigration and Asylum Law and Policy in Europe*, 2014, Vol. 34, Jan Niessen and Espelth Guild.

249 R. BOHNING, *The ILO and the New UN Convention on Migrant Workers: The Past and Future*, in *International Migration Review*, 1991, 698.

right to form association and trade unions (Article 40); the right to participate in public affairs of the state of origin (Article 41); the right to equal treatment with regard to access to education, vocational guidance and training, housing, social and health services and cultural life (Article 43 and 45); protection of family unity (Article 44); freedom to choose a remunerated activity (52); equal treatment in respect to dismissal, unemployment benefits, access to public work schemes intended to combat unemployment (Article 54). Part V the ICMW specifies particular categories of migrant workers, such as frontier and seasonal workers, project-tied workers and specified-employment workers (all defined in article 2). Part VI of the ICMW provides cooperation and consultation mechanisms for state parties so as to promote that the international migration of workers takes place under sound, equitable, humane and lawful conditions.

These procedures of the ICMW – the Convention that has been labelled as one of the most comprehensive human rights instruments with 93 provisions – allow for mutual information exchange and collaboration fighting irregular migration by *inter alia* introducing employer and trafficker sanctions. In this regard, the ICMW actively promotes the prevention and abolition of all forms of irregular migration and does away with the "myth" that the Convention would encourage undocumented human[250] mobility[251].

In 2006, at the United Nations Economic and Social Council, EOSOC High-Level Segment that took place in Geneva, J. Somavia, Director General of the International Labour Office, claimed that *"gains from migration*

250 The signature and ratification process has been criticised as rather slow. Although, to date, 45 states – for the most part sending and developing countries – have ratified the ICMW (as of 21 September 2011). The ICMW has not been high on the agenda of governments and UN institutions, the ICMW because the Convention was considered as "impractical", "too ambitious" and "unrealisable" (see P.A. TARAN, *Human Rights of Migrants: Challenges of the New Decade*, 38 *International Migration*, 2001, 7, pp. 18-19). R. Cholewinsky stressed that the protection that the ICMW offers is incomplete owing to the changing forms of labour migration entailing dynamics that ICMW does not account for, such as the feminisation of migrant labour, temporary labour movements and an increasing number of irregular migrants (R. CHOLEWINSKY, *The Rights of Migrant Workers*, in R. CHOLEWINSKY, R. PERRUCHOUD, and E. MACDONALD (eds.), *International Migration Law: Developing Paradigms and Key Challenges*, T.M.C. Asser Press, The Hague 2007, pp. 259-260.

251 R. CHOLEWINSKY, *The Rights of Migrant workers*, in R. CHOLEWINSKY, R. PERRCHOUD and E. MACDONALD (eds.), *International Migration Law: Developing Paradigms and Key Challenges*, T.M.C. Asser Press, The Hague 2007, p. 259.

and protection of migrant rights are indeed inseparable. Migrant workers can make their best contribution to host and source countries when they enjoy decent working conditions and when their fundamental human and labour rights are respected"[252]. The statement underlines the key role of migrants′ rights, also for promoting development processes. Among these migrants have to be included also the irregular category[253].

3. The rights of migrants in the international migration discourse

First held on 9 to 11 July 2007 in Brussels, the Global Forum on Migration and Development (GFMD) is an initiative that resulted directly from the 2006 UN High-Level Dialogue because of the UN Member States′ strong interest in continuing the debates on "*how to make migration work for development*". The Global Forum is an informal platform for dialogue led by governments and founded with the objective to share experiences and practices, to discuss policies and to enhance the consultation process among stakeholders[254] related to the migration-development nexus. The actors involved are meant to benefit from concrete and action-oriented output of the Global Forum, such as the setup of partnerships and the formulation of policy recommendations.

Since the Brussels GFMD, the event has been conducted annually, each time with one meeting for civil society actors and one for policy makers. The 2011 GFMD was held in Geneva, from 29 November to 2nd December 2011, with more than 120 representatives of 100 states and 20 observers.

The civil society days took place under the central topic "Taking Action on Labour Migration, Development and the Protection of Migrant Work-

252 J. SOMAVIA, *Statement of the Director-General of the International Labour* Office, ECOSOC High-Level Segment, Geneva, 5 July 2006.

253 Annan professed that "for the full benefits of international migration to be realised, the rights of migrants must be respected. States have the obligation to protect the fundamental rights of all persons in their territory and they must take effective action to protect migrants against all forms of human rights violations and abuse. They must also combat all forms of discrimination, xenophobia, ethnocentrism and racism" (K. ANNAN, UN Secretary-General Report on International Migration and Development, UN/GA A/60/871 of 18 May 2006, para 77).

254 K. EISELE, *The External Dimention of the EU′s Migration Policy. Different Legal Position of Third-Country Nationals*, in *The EU: A Comparative Perspective, in Immigration and Asylum Law and Policy in Europe*, 2014, Vol. 34, Jan Niessen and Espelth Guild.

ers and their Families". Two subsessions were relevant taking into consideration[255] that they concern the legal protection of migrants: one session concerned rights-based policy-making for the benefit of migrant workers and their families, and the other one addressed protection of migrants working or moving in irregular circumstances.

Special emphasis was put first on the ILO's Multilateral Framework on Labour Migration of 2005, which underscored that "*The human rights of all migrant workers, regardless of their status, should be promoted and protected*" and that "*the contribution of labour migration to employment, economic growth, development and the alleviation of poverty should be recognised and maximised for the benefit of both origin and destination countries*"[256]. It reiterated the appeal to states of previous GFMD's meeting to ratify the ICMW. Moreover, the ILO Convention Concerning Decent Work for Domestic Workers adopted in June 2011 was put in the spotlight stressing its potential to provide protection to a large and vulnerable group of migrant domestic workers from explotation and abuse[257].

B. *Human rights and irregular migrants at European Union level*

1. The general principles of EU Law and human rights

In *Nold* the Court confirmed its view that fundamental rights form an integral part of the general principles of Community law and it has been stated that, in safeguarding these rights, it is bound to draw inspiration from the Member States' constitutional traditions and from international human rights treaties to which the Member States are signatories[258]. The general principles of Community law comprise thus two distinct elements: the constitutional traditions as exist in the Member States' national legal systems and international human rights conventions according to the Court. In the past, far more references were made, however, to international

255 2011 Programme GFMD Civil Society Days.

256 ILO Multilateral Framework on Labour Migration: Non-binding Principles and Guidelines for a Rights-Based Approach to Labour Migration (International Labour Office, Geneva 2006), pp. 15 and 29.

257 ILO Convention PR No. 15a concerning Decent Work for Domestic Workers of 16 June 2011.

258 Case 4/73 Nold (1974) ECR 491, para.13; the Court has affirmed this approach in Case 44/79 Hauer (1979) ECR 3727, para. 15. Literature reference: E. MASSA, *Human Rights Law*, Fourth Edition, Oxford University Press, 2011.

treaties than to national constitutional traditions. This imbalance was regarded as "obviuos" considering the difficulty faced by the Court to ascertain a tradition in the form of a common right in casea certain right is not reflected in every single Member State constitution[259].

In respect of international human rights treaties, the Court has granted the ECHR a special status as a source of the general principles of Union Law[260]. This is mirrored within the ambit of the Treaty of Lisbon. Article 6(3) of the Treaty on European Union (TEU) determines that fundamental rights, as guaranteed by the ECHR and as they result from the constitutional traditions common to the Member States, constitute general principles of the Union's law. The Court has alluded to other international human rights standards to a lesser extent; these include the International Covenant on Civil and Political Rights (ICCPR)[261], the European Social Charter[262], the International Convention on the Rights of the Child[263], the 1951 UN convention relating to the Status of Refugees[264], but also the principle of *ius cogens*[265].

The legal bases of some general principles of EU law can be found directly in the Treaties, such as the principle of subsidiarity and the principle of proportionality stipulated in Article 5 TEU, both already mentioned previously.

---

259 P. CRAIG and G. DE BURCA, *EU Law: Text, Cases, and Materials*, 4th edn. Oxford University Press, Oxford 2008, p. 386; Case 6/64 Costa v. ENEL, 1964, ECR 585.

260 Case 36/75 Rutili (1975) ECR 1291, para. 32; Case 222/84 Jhonston (1986) ECHR 1651, para. 18; many other cases followed that contained a reference to the ECHR, see Part III, Section 2.1 on the ECHR. K. EISELE, *The External Dimention of the EU's Migration Policy. Different Legal Position of Third-Country Nationals, in the EU: A Comparative Perspective, in Immigration and Asylum Law and Policy in Europe*, 2014, Vol. 34, Jan Niessen and Espelth Guild.

261 Case C-374/87 Orken (1989) ECR 3283, para. 31; case C-249/96 Grant (1998) ECR I-621, para. 44.

262 Case 199/77 Defrenne (1978) ECR 1365, para. 28; see also Opinion of AG Stix-Hackl in Case C-459/99 MRAX (2002) ECR I-6591, para. 26.

263 Case 199/77 Defrenne (1978) ECR 1365, para. 28; see also Opinion of AG Stix-Hackl in Case C-459/99 MRAX (2002) ECR I-6591, para. 26.

264 Joined Cases C-95/99 to C-98/95 Khali and Others and C-180/99 Addou (2001) ECR I-7413, para. 44; according to S. Peers, the UN Refugee Convention and its New York Protocol also constitute a source of the general principles of EU law, see S. PEERS, *Human Rights, Asylum and European Community Law*, 24 Refugee Survey Quartely, 2005, 24, p. 29.

265 See Case T-315/01 Kadi (2005) ECR II-3649, paras. 221-226.

Another general principle of EU law is the principle of legal certainty which demands that EU legislation must be clear and predictable[266]. Related to the principle of legal certainty is the principle of legitimate expectations that sets strict limitations on the retroactive application of EU law: it has been pointed out that *"Legal certainty requires the rules which apply at a given time to be clear and precise for the benefit of the individual, whereas protection of legitimate expectations requires public authorities to exercise their powers over a period of time in such as a away as to ensure that situations and relationships lawfully created under Community law, are not affected in a manner which could not have been foreseen by a diligent person"*[267].

Concerning the matter of irregular migration, two general principles are relevant in the EU legal framework. In the management of the phenomenon of irregular migration it is important to guarantee the protection of the security of the borders of the European Union from illegal entries on the one hand, and on the other it is important to guarantee the protection of the human rights of these migrants, although their status is irregular. The greatest difficulty for the Europea Union is finding the right balance between the two principles[268].

---

266 Joined Cases 212-217/80 Salumi (1981) ECR 2735, para. 10.

267 T. TRIDIMAS, *The General Principles of EU Law*, 2nd edn. Oxford University Press, Oxford, 2006, p. 262 referring to Case C-63/93 Duff and Others, 1996, ECR I-569; see also J. RAITIO, *The General Principle of Legal Certainty as a General Principle of EU Law*, in U. BERNITZ, J. NERGELIUS and C. CARDNER (eds), *General Principles of EC Law in a Process of Development*, Kluwer Law International, Alphen aan den Rijn, 2008, pp. 47-73.

268 The EU has adopted some major pieces of legislation to manage the phenomenon of irregular immigration considering the security of th borders and the protection of human rights of the irregular migrants (all legislations and their references will be better treated in this current Chater): the so-called 'Facilitation Package' comprises Council Directive 2002/90/EC (OJ L 328, 5.12.2002, p. 17–18), setting out a common definition of the crime of facilitating unauthorised entry, transit and residence, and Framework Decision 2002/946/JHA (OJ L 328, 5.12.2002, p. 1–3), establishing criminal sanctions for this conduct. The package is complemented by Council Directive 2004/81/EC (OJ L 261, 6.8.2004, p. 19–23), providing for the granting of a residence permit to trafficked or smuggled persons who cooperate with the competent authorities (on trafficking, see also fact sheet on 'Judicial cooperation in criminal matters' 4.2.6). In May 2015, the Commission adopted the EU Action Plan against migrant smuggling (COM (2015)285 final). The 'Return Directive', 2008/115/EC (OJ L 348, 24.12.2008, p. 98–107), sets out common EU standards and procedures for returning irregularly resident third-country nationals. The first report on its implementation was adopted in March 2014. In September 2015, the Commission published the EU action plan on return, which was followed by the adoption,

2. The issue of irregular migration of the European Union level: overview

This paragraph is dedicated to a brief introductory overview of the EU context concerning the tools used for dealing with irregular migration before analysing in detail the human rights legislation in the EU.

The European Commission in November 2001 stated that the prevention of and the fight against irregular movement of persons to the EU constituted a cornerstone of a comprehensive European migration and asylum policy, and specified in a Communication[269] which are the principles, targets, required action to deal with the phenomenon of unauthorised migration. To this end, it emphasised the need to carry out analyses and research concerning the patterns of unauthorised residence, organised crime geared towards human trafficking and the irregular movements from countries of origin via transit countries to countries of destination. In the Commission's Communication it was important to send clear signals to potential criminals and to reinforce the existing rules. Consequently severe sanctions for serious crimes, such as people smuggling, were adopted. Action plans in different fields, including visa policy, readmission and return and border management, were proposed.

The following year, a Commission Communication followed on a Community return policy on irregular residents which demonstrated the determination with which the Community pursued the goal to reduce irregular migration[270]. The Hague Programme put a special emphasis on this sub-

---

in October 2015, of the Council conclusions on the future of the return policy. In March 2017, the Commission adopted a renewed action plan on a more effective return policy in the EU, and in September 2017, it published its updated 'Return Handbook' (OJ L 348, 24.12.2008, p. 98–107). The Directive 2009/52/EC (OJ L 168, 30.6.2009, p. 24-32) specifies sanctions and measures to be applied in Member States against employers of illegally resident third-country nationals. The first report on the implementation of the directive was submitted on 22 May 2014 (COM (2014)286 final). At the same time, the EU is negotiating and concluding readmission agreements with countries of origin and transit with a view to returning irregular migrants and cooperating in the fight against trafficking in human beings. These agreements include reciprocal cooperation commitments between the EU and its third-country partners. For these agreements mentioned see p.79 footnote 221 of the Chapter II.

269 Communication from the Commission to the Council and the European Parliament on a common policy on illegal immigration.COM (2001) 672 final, 15 November 2001.

270 European Commission Communication, COM(2002) 564, 14 October 2002.

ject matter and put illegal employment, return and readmission and border security on the agenda.[271].

Moreover the management of the EU's external borders was said to be closely linked to the fight against irregular migration. The border control agency FRONTEX, was established in 2004 with the aim of the coordination of operational cooperation between the Member States in view of border security[272].

To counteract the irregular migration another tool created by the EU was the immigration liaison officers' network. The underlying idea of the network is the deployment of Member States' representatives (ILOs) to a third country where the officer is in contact with the local authorities in order to gather and exchange information on the flows and routes of unauthorised migrants, the smuggling of migrants, the falsification of identity documents and return options[273].

The Commission in 2006, proposed another initiative to address the phenomenon of irregular migration, such as cooperation with third countries and the conclusion of readmission agreements[274]. The EU readmission agreements are bilateral agreements between the Union and a third country, which lay down reciprocal obligations and administrative and operational procedures to facilitate the return and transit of persons who do not, or no longer, fulfil the conditions for entry into, presence in or residence in the requesting state[275].

As regards return, thepreviously mentioned Council Directive 2008/115/EC which lays down common standards and procedures in Member States for returning irregularly staying third-country nationals is

271 Council of the European Union: "The Hague Programme: strengthening freedom, security and justice in the European Union", document number 16054/04 JAI 559 of 13 December 2004.

272 FRONTEX also provides training for border guards, assistance to Member States in need of technical and operational support at the EU's external borders and it cooperates with the law enforcement agencies in third countries (Council Regulation (EC) No 2007/2004 of 26 October 2004 establishing a European Agency for the Management of Operational Cooperation at the External Borders of the Member States of the European Union).

273 Council Regulation (EC) No 377/2004 of 19 February 2004 on the creation of immigration liaison officer's network.

274 European Commission Communication, COM(2006) 402, 19 July2006.

275 European Commission Communication, COM(2002) 564, 14 October 2002, p. 26. Moreover, See III Session General Part, paragraph 1.4. "Recent Legislative Developments" for more details on readmission agreements.

important as a tool to deal with irregular migration[276]. This will be explained in more detail later. In 2009 the EU institutions adopted the employer sanctions′ Directive which set out the measures and sanctions against employers of third-country nationals residing without authorization[277].

The Commission also suggested cooperation to establish a European External Border Surveillance System, EUROSUR, within the framework of the European Neighbourdhood Policy and collaboration with the main countries of origin and transit among other things under the Cotonou Agreement[278].

The European Union Agenda on Migration presented by the European Commission on May 13th, 2015[279], shows some innovative aspects, however ambiguities prevail on relevant aspects. Indeed, for instance, it is possible to still detect a closing off of legal immigration into the EU for economic reasons, forcing the potential migrant to choose irregular channels of entrance or to request international protection, with negative effects on the European asylum system. The Agenda is built upon four pillars and to the scope of current research, those interesting are the following:

- reducing the incentives for irregular migration: the focus is on addressing the root causes behind irregular migration in non EU countries, dismalting smuggling and trafficking networks and defining actions for the better application of return policies;
- saving lives and securing the external borders: this involves better management of the external border, in particular through solidarity towards those Member States that are located at the external border crossing;
- developing a new policy on legal migration: in view of the future demographic challenges the EU is facing, the new policy need to focus on attracting workers that the EU economy needs, particularly by facilitating entry and the recognition of qualifications.

---

276 Council Directive 2008/115/EC of 16 December 2008 on common standards and procedures in the Member States for returning illegally staying third- country nationals.

277 Council Directive 2009/52/EC of 18 June 2009 providing for minimum standards on sanctions and measures against employers of illegally staying third-country nationals.

278 COM(2008) 611, on Strengthening the global approach to migration: increase coordination, consistency and synergies, 8 October 2008.

279 COM (2015) 240 final,on European Agenda on Migration, 13 May 2015.

Within the Agenda some tools are proposed in order to reduce the incentives for irregular migration.

a) Addressing the root causes of irregular and forced displacement in third countries:

Civil war, persecution, poverty, and climate change all impact directly and immediately on migration, so the prevention and mitigation of these threats is of primary importance for the migration debate[280].

Partnerships with countries of origin and transit is crucial and there are a series of established bilateral and regional cooperation frameworks on migration in place[281].

These will be enriched by stepping up the role of migration for EU delegations in key countries. Delegations will in particular report on major migratory related developments in the host countries, contribute to mainstream migration issues related to development cooperation and reach out to host countries to ensure coordinated action. European migration liaison officers will be detached in EU delegations in key third countries, in close cooperation with the Immigration Liaison Officers Network and with local authorities and civil society, with the purpose of gathering, exchanging and analysing information[282].

With a budget allocation of EUR 96.8 billion for the 2014-2020 period[283], EU external cooperation assistance, and in particular development cooperation, plays an important role in tackling global issues like poverty, insecurity, inequality and unemployment which are among the main root

280 Concerning the scope of the measures which already apply and/or will be proposed, under Title V TFEU, to implement the Agenda, see footnote 3 on the "opt-in" rights concerning the United Kingdom and Ireland and the "opt-out" status concerning Denmark.

281 Rabat Process, Khartoum Process, the Budapest Process, the Prague Process, the EU-Africa Migration and Mobility Dialogue.

282 A good example of where there is much to be gained from stepping up cooperation is Turkey. Since the beginning of 2014, Turkey has received EUR 79 million to contribute to its efforts to deal with the pressure on its refugee management system and to help prevent hazardous journeys in the Eastern Mediterranean. Deploying a dedicated Frontex liaison officer in Turkey will take cooperation one step further.

283 Communication from the Commission to the European Parliament, the Council, the European Economic and Social Committee and the Committee of the Regions a European Agenda on Migration. COM/2015/0240 final.

causes of irregular and forced migration. This includes support in regions of Africa, Asia and Eastern Europe where most of the migrants reaching Europe originate from[284].

b) The fight against smugglers and traffickers

Action to fight criminal networks of smugglers and traffickers is first and foremost a way to prevent the exploitation of migrants by criminal networks[285]. It will also act as a disincentive to irregular migration. The goal must be to transform smuggling networks from '"low risk, high return" operations for criminals into "high risk, low return" ones. Cooperation with third countries is of critical importance. Most of the smugglers are not based in Europe, and those who are arrested on the boats in the Mediterranean are normally the last link in the chain. Cooperation to crack down on the local and international criminal groups that control smuggling routes will be a major focus of the intensified cooperation set out above. EU Agencies can also assist Member States' authorities in intensifying their action against criminal networks of smugglers.

Agencies help to identify smugglers, investigate them, prosecute them, freeze and confiscate their assets. Action will build on immediate efforts to identify, capture and destroy vessels before they are used by criminal networks. Proactive financial investigations, aiming at seizures and recovery of criminal assets, and actions against money laundering connected to migrant smuggling will be supported through enhanced cooperation with Financial Intelligence Units on financial flows and new cooperation with financial institutions, such as banks, international money transfer services,

284 Delegate handbook Canterboury model European Union 2015 " The EUresponse to migration & refugees in the Mediterraean in 2015" University of Canterboury, Christchuch 3-4, September 2015.

285 These efforts will also be pursued under the European Agenda for Security and the Maritime Security Strategy. Migrants smuggling and trafficking are two diverse yet interlinked criminal activities perpetrated by criminal networks. The difference between the two is that in the former, migrants willingly engage in the irregular migration process by paying for the services of a smuggler in order to cross an international border, while in the latter they are the victims, coerced into severe exploitation which may or may not be linked to the crossing of a border. In reality, the two phenomena are not easy to disentangle as persons who start their journeys in a voluntary manner are also vulnerable to networks of labour or sexual exploitation.

and credit card issuers. This will also draw on the improved information-sharing set out in the European Agenda on Security.

In order to strengthen the instruments available to prosecutors to address smuggling networks, the Commission will improve the existing EU legal framework to tackle migrant smuggling and those who profit from it[286]. In order to take specific action against traffickers' networks and provide assistance to victims of trafficking, the Commission will also complete the initiatives suggested in the current strategy against Trafficking in Human Beings. Another potential source of exploitation comes from employers inside the EU.

Whilst promoting better integration into the labour market of legal migrants, the Commission will step up action against illegal employment of third country nationals, *inter alia* through better enforcement and application of the Employers Sanctions Directive[287], which prohibits the employment of third-country nationals who have no right to stay in the EU. It will also prioritise infringement procedures relating to this Directive.

---

286 Some of the measures adopted by the Union prior to 1 December 2009 with regard to police cooperation and judicial cooperation in criminal matters no longer apply to the United Kingdom since 1 December 2014, on the basis of Articles 9 and 10 of Protocol 36 to the Treaties, which set out a specific "block opt-out" and "opt-back-in" procedure (see decisions adopted by the Commission and the Council on the measures notified by the United Kingdom, OJ L 345, 1.12.2012, p. 1 and OJ C 430, 1.12.2014, p. 1). In 2002, the EU adopted rules to crack down on migrant smuggling: Directive 2002/90/EC establishing a common definition of the offense of facilitation of unauthorised entry, transit and residence (OJ L 328, 5.12.2002, p. 17) and Framework Decision 2002/946/JHA on the strengthening of the penal framework to prevent the facilitation of unauthorised entry, transit and residence (OJ L 328, 5.12.2002, p. 1). The United Kingdom and Ireland "opted in" both the Directive and the Framework decision. Nevertheless, for the United Kingdom, the Framework decision no longer applies by virtue of the block opt-out provided for in Protocol 36 referred to above. The United Kingdom may however still decide to "opt-in" to this Framework Decision.

287 Directive 2009/52/EC of the European Parliament and of the Council of 18 June 2009 providing for minimum standards on sanctions and measures against employers of illegally staying third-country nationals, OJ L 168, 30.6.2009, p. 24–32. The United Kingdom and Ireland did not "opt-in" to this Directive and are therefore not bound by it or subject to its application.

c) Return

One of the incentives for irregular migrants is the knowledge that the EU's return system – which is meant to return irregular migrants or those whose asylum applications are refused – works imperfectly[288]. Smuggling networks take advantage of the fact that few return decisions are enforced – only 39.2% of return decisions issued in 2013 were effectively enforced. To increase the enforcement rate, we first need to ensure that third countries fulfil their international obligation to take back their own nationals residing irregularly in Europe[289]. The EU should be ready to use all leverage and incentives at its disposal. The agreed Pilot Project on Return to Pakistan and Bangladesh offers an important practical demonstration of the way forward[290]. The EU will help third countries to meet their obligations by offering support such as capacity building for the management of returns, information and awareness campaigns, and support for reintegration measures. The Commission will also revise its approach to readmission agreements[291], prioritising the main countries of origin of irregular migrants.

In parallel, Member States have to apply the Return Directive[292]. The Commission will give priority to monitoring implementation of the Direc-

---

288 G. VERMEULEN, E. DESMET, *Essential text on European and International Asylum and Migration Law and Policy*, Maklu, Antwerpen-Apeldoorn-Portland, 2017.

289 A specific obligation exists in the Cotonou Agreement with the ACP countries. In accordance with Article 13 of the Cotonou Agreement, each Member State of the European Union shall accept the return of and readmission of any of its nationals who are illegally present on the territory of an ACP State, at that State's request, without further formalities; and each of the ACP States shall accept the return of and readmission of any of its nationals who are illegally present on the territory of a Member State of the European Union, at that Member State's request and without further formalities.

290 Council Conclusions on EU Return Policy adopted at the Justice and Home Affairs Council meeting of 5 and 6 June 2014.

291 A readmission agreement facilitates the return of third-country nationals. Contracting parties will readmit to their territory without any formality persons with the nationality of that country who are residing without authorisation in the other country or who have crossed its frontier illegally.

292 Directive 2008/115/EC, of 16 December 2008, on common standards and procedures in Member States for returning illegally staying third-country nationals, OJ L 348 98, 24.12.2008, p. 98–107. The United Kingdom and Ireland did not "opt-in" to this Directive and are therefore not bound by it and not subject to its application.

tive, with a more swift return system going hand-in-hand with the respect of the procedures and standards that allow Europe to ensure a humane and dignified treatment of returnees and a proportionate use of coercive measures, in line with fundamental rights and the principle of non-refoulement[293]. The implementation of the EU rules on the return of irregular migrants is now being assessed thoroughly in the framework of the Schengen Evaluation Mechanism, and a "Return Handbook" supports Member States with common guidelines, best practice and recommendations. While the EU has common rules on return, it lacks effective operational cooperation. Frontex is currently offering considerable support to Member States, but its mandate has been reinforced to increase its capacity to provide comprehensive operational assistance by the new European Border and Coast Guard[294] which will be examined in more detail below.

The recent recommendation contained in the European Agenda to adopt new guidelines which facilitate regular entries preventing irregular ones and providing greater measures of social cohesion in order to preclude the expansion of xenophobia, which is certainly positive, is also of relevance[295].

Decisions on the volume of admissions of third country nationals coming to seek work will remain the exclusive competence of Member States. But there is a specific role for the EU. Over the next seven years, European programmes such as Horizon 2020 and Erasmus+ will attract talented individuals to the EU. The Directive on Students and Researchers, now under negotiation by the co-legislators, aims to give these groups new mobility and job-seeking opportunities. The swift adoption of the legislation would

293 Non-refoulement is a principle of international law, endorsed by the Charter of fundamental rights, according to which a person must not be returned to a place where there is a serious risk of death penalty, torture or inhuman or degrading treatment.

294 The European Border and Coast Guard Agency, also known as Frontex[3] (from French: Frontières extérieures for "external borders"), is an agency of the European Union headquartered in Warsaw, Poland, tasked with border control of the European Schengen Area, in coordination with the border and coast guards of Schengen Area member states. Regulation (EU) 2016/1624 of the European Parliament and of the Council of 14 September 2016 on the European Border and Coast Guard and amending Regulation (EU) 2016/399 of the European Parliament and of the Council and repealing Regulation (EC) No 863/2007 of the European Parliament and of the Council, Council Regulation (EC) No 2007/2004 and Council Decision 2005/267/EC.

295 COM(2015) 240 final, European Agenda on Migration, on 13 May 2015.

allow these strategically important groups to see the EU as a welcoming environment for their work[296].

Another tool for attracting legal migrants is a EU-wide scheme for highly qualified third-country nationals. The Blue Card Directive[297] already provides such a scheme, but in its first two years, only 16,000 Blue Cards were issued and 13,000 were issued by a single Member State[298]. Another sector with important economic impact is services[299].

The services sector includes well trained, highly-skilled foreign professionals who need to travel to the EU for short periods in order to provide services to businesses or governments. The Commission will assess possible ways to provide legal certainty to these categories of people, which would also strengthen the EU's position to demand reciprocities when negotiating Free Trade Agreements (FTAs)[300]. Member States' role in these decisions calls for a more direct and open dialogue to build common thinking and policy approaches and exchange best practice at European level. The Commission will support Member States in promoting a permanent dialogue and peer evaluation at the European level on issues such as labour market gaps, regularization and integration – issues where decisions by one Member State have an impact on others. The Commission will also establish a platform of dialogue to include input from business, the trade unions, and other social partners, to maximise the benefits of migration for the European economy and the migrants themselves. The EU needs the tools to identify those economic sectors and occupations that face, or will face, recruitment difficulties or skill gaps. Existing tools already provide some information, but a more complete picture is needed[301]. Existing web portals, such as the EU Migration portal and Europe's Job Mobility Portal (EURES) can also play an important role in facilitating job matching for third country nationals already in the EU. In matching migrants' skills, a

---

296 COM/2013/0151 final. Concerning the scope of this proposal see also footnote 3.

297 Directive 2009/50/EC of 25 May 2009 on the conditions of entry and residence of third-country nationals for the purposes of highly qualified employment, OJ L 155, 18.6.2009, p. 17–29. The United Kingdom and Ireland did not "opt-in" to this Directive and are not bound by or subject to its application.

298 A review has been provided looking at issues of scope such as covering entrepreneurs who are willing to invest in Europe, or improving the possibilities for intra EU mobility for Blue Card holders.

299 COM(2015) 240 final, European Agenda on Migration, on 13 May 2015.

300 COM(2015) 240 final, European Agenda on Migration, on 13 May 2015.

301 Such as the Skills Panorama and the Skills Alliances.

particular problem is the lack of recognition of qualifications acquired by migrants in their home country. The EU can help to improve understanding of qualifications gained outside the EU[302].

The efforts to develop the new legal migration policy mirror the modernisation of visa policy[303]. In 2014, the Commission tabled a revision of the Visa Code and proposed the establishment of a new type of visa: the Touring Visa[304]. The adoption of these proposals provided the EU with more flexible visa policy tools, aiming to maximise the positive economic impact of attracting more tourists, and visitors on personal or professional grounds while minimising the risks of irregular migration and to security.

d) Effective integration

Although the competence lies primarily with Member States, the European Union can support actions by national governments, local authorities and civil society engaged in the complex and long term process of fostering integration and mutual trust[305]. Funding is provided by the Asylum Migration and Integration Fund (AMIF)[306]. But the European Regional

302 For example through the European Qualification Framework and in the context of the upcoming revision of the EUROPASS system.

303 The common visa policy mainly provided for in the Visa Code (Regulation 810/2009) sets out the rules for the issuing of short stay visas to third country nationals travelling for the purpose of e.g. tourism, business, private visits family/friends, cultural and sport events. It is part of the Schengen acquis in which Ireland and the United Kingdom do not participate. In 2014, the Schengen States issued approximately 15.8 million visa which represents an increase of approximately 60% compared to 2009.

304 It is a new type of visa both for visa-exempt and visa requiring third-country nationals with a legitimate interest in travelling around the Schengen area for more than 90 days in any 180-day period (COM(2014)163). This proposal builds on the part of the Schengen acquis in which Ireland and the United Kingdom do not participate.

305 COM/2015/0240 final, Communication on European Agenda on Migration.

306 Regulation (EU) No 516/2014 of the European Parliament and of the Council of 16 April 2014 establishing the Asylum, Migration and Integration Fund, amending Council Decision 2008/381/EC and repealing Decisions No 573/2007/EC and No 575/2007/EC of the European Parliament and of the Council and Council Decision 2007/435/EC.

Development Fund (ERDF)[307] and the European Social Fund (ESF)[308] can also be of particular importance[309]. For the period (2014-20), at least 20% of ESF resources will contribute to social inclusion, which includes measures for the integration of migrants with a particular focus on those seeking asylum and refugees as well as on children. The funds can support targeted initiatives to improve language and professional skills, improve access to services, promote access to the labour market, inclusive education foster inter-cultural exchanges and promote awareness campaigns targeting both host communities and migrants[310].

e) Maximising the development benefits for countries of origin:

The EU's legal migration policy should also support the development of countries of origin[311]. The EU has continued to actively support migration-related targets as part of the final overall framework, and to emphasise the importance of harnessing the positive effects of migration as a horizontal means of implementation for the post-2015 development agenda. This complemented the work of the EU's Mobility Partnerships[312] and the ef-

307 Regulation (EU) No 1301/2013 of the European Parliament and of the Council of 17 December 2013 on the European Regional Development Fund and on specific provisions concerning the Investment for growth and jobs goal and repealing Regulation (EC) No 1080/2006 laying down tasks, scope, aims, thematic and investment priorities and output indicators for regional development. The ERDF aims to strengthen economic and social cohesion in the European Union by correcting imbalances between its regions.

308 Regulation (EU) No 1304/2013 of the European Parliament and of the Council of 17 December 2013 on the European Social Fund and repealing Council Regulation (EC) No 1081/2006.

309 The implementation of these measures will be assessed by the end of 2015 to see whether Member States have met their objectives and whether any reprogramming of ESF resources is required.

310 COM/2015/0240 final, Communication on European Agenda on Migration.

311 Commission Communication: "Maximising the Development Impact of Migration" (COM(2013)292 final); Council Conclusions on Migration in EU development cooperation of 12 December 2014.

312 The Commission Communication: "The Global Approach to Migration and Mobility" (COM/2011/743 final). These are the most elaborated bilateral cooperation frameworks in the field of migration. They offer a political framework for comprehensive, enhanced and tailor-made dialogue and cooperation with partner countries, including a set of targets and commitments as well as a package of specific support measures offered by the EU and interested Member

forts to mainstream migration issues into key development sectors. The Commission made provisions in the Agenda to make available at least EUR 30 million to support partners with capacity building on effective management of labour migration, focusing on empowering migrant workers and tackling exploitation. To mirror the success of Europe in establishing a single market underpinned by labour mobility, the EU has also launched a EUR 24 million initiative to support free movement in the Economic Community of West African States. Regional labour mobility schemes encouraging South-South mobility can bring an important contribution to local development. The Commission also promoted ethical recruitment in sectors suffering from a lack of qualified workers in countries of origin by supporting international initiatives in this field.

However, concrete measures indicated in the Agenda appear overly vague and lack innovation. It is necessary and urgent to adopt a new realistic approach that overcomes the rigidity and the current barriers to allow an easy and convenient access of regular entry channels. In this context it is necessary:

a) to exclude any verifications of the unavailability of nationals and EU workers or of foreign workers already residents before issuing new working permits;

b) to promote projects of temporary migration which will not hinder but foster migration individual programs where you can alternate between periods of work and professional experiences in the EU with periods of return to the country of origin. To do this the establishment, even on an experimental basis, of agreements on free movement of people (for example EU agreements with the Community of West African States) is necessary;

c) to introduce the possibility of regular entries for job research, under established conditions which take into account the migration movements preventing migrants from using criminal organizations dealing with human trafficking (smuggling);

d) to expand and simplify the regulation of entry and stay of foreigners, which means abandoning the EU Blue Card for highly skilled workers. In implementing migration policies, it is necessary to avoid policies applying a logic of selective immigration and brain appropriation which would deprive States of origin of high skilled staff;

States. They include the negotiation of visa facilitation and readmission agreements.

e) to fully implement the measures provided for in Directive 2009/52/EC in order to protect more effectively the foreign workers employed illegally and to combat situations of exploitation;

f) to allow the conversion of short term stays for work permits giving a real possibility for migrants to establish a viable employment relationship at the end of the short term work permit;

g) to introduce in the various EU Member States, legislation which allows the establishment of residency in case of illegal entry or the possibility to recover the previous condition of regularity, often lost because of economic difficulties, especially where there is a clear right to family reunification or where migrants have real working opportunities;

h) to effectively implement the directive on people trafficking, including the proper identification of victims of trafficking and the issuance of a residence permit on humanitarian grounds to the victims;

i) to establish the European touring visa proposed by the European Commission in 2014, so that the visa can be released in the country of origin or in transit by European representation offices on site and, when agreed, allow the issuing of such visa for job searching;

j) to strengthen programmes and cultural initiatives to support social cohesion and counteract the hostile propaganda against migrants and hatred or incitement to racist or xenophobic activities[313].

The growing emphasis on strict measures against irregular immigration at ports, airports and inland border crossings, where large resources are injected, is likely to have an effect on the deterioration of the current dramatic situation of violence and subjugation faced by migrants from criminal organizations, as opposed to the fight against organized crime. Criminal organizations must be fought in the field of legislative policy choices where efforts should be directed at increasing the possibilities for legal access to the EU territory[314].

The increasing criminalization of all types of travel from irregular migrants appears unacceptable without distinguishing the conduct of those who, for a variety of reasons (for example the existence of family ties or friendship) and notfor profit directly or indirectly facilitate the journey of an irregular migrant or even that of a refugee from the phenomena of hu-

313 G. VERMEULEN, E. DESMET, *Essential text on European and International Asylum and Migration Law and Policy*, Maklu, Antwerpen-Apeldoorn-Portland, 2017.

314 Report by the European Union Agency for Fundamental Rights, 2014, Luxemburg: publications office oft he European Union.

man smuggling and trafficking run by organized crime. Increasing criminalization has the effect of inhibiting or otherwise obstructing (often through the use of explicit or veiled threats of criminal prosecution) the completion of initiatives of solidarity and rescue operations for migrants that where put in place by individuals, associations and institutions whose ethical impulse to act in favour of the weakest should, on the contrary, be valued as an authentic expression of the fundamental values of the European Union.

3. Human rights of irregular migrants and their protection in EU

The EU has transformed into a supranational organization that "*is founded on the values of respect for human dignity, freedom, democracy, equality, the rule of law and respect for human rights …*"[315]. As regards the issue of whether the EU could be regarded as a human rights organitation, A. von Bogdandy considered that "*human rights, though important, should not be understood as the raison d´etre of the Union*" [316]. S. Peers indicated three principal sources of human rights protection in the EU legal framework: the European Convention on Human Rights (ECHR), the EU Charter and the general principles of EU law [317].

3.1. The European Convention on Human Rights and irregular migrants

The Council of Europe was founded in 1949 as an international organisation with the aim to promote human rights, democracy, the rule of law, as well as cultural identity in Europe. It advocated its mission by composing norms and standards and opened them for signature to its members, and it became a major regional institution committed to fighting human rights

315 A. VON BOGDANDY, *The European Union as a Human Rights Organization? Human Rights and the Core of the European Union*, 37 Common Market Law Review, 2000, 1307, p. 1338.

316 A. von BOGDANDY, *The European Union as a Human Rights Organization? Human Rights and the Core of the European Union*, 37 Common Market Law Review, 2000, 1307, p. 1338.

317 S. PEERS, *EU Justice and Home Affairs Law 3rd end*, Oxford University Press, Oxford, 2011, p. 96.

violations. Among these, the most pivotal instrument is the ECHR[318]. The ECHR was signed in Rome on 4 November 1950 with the objective to protect human rights and fundamental freedoms and entered into force on 3 September 1953. The signatory states of the Convention are 47[319], including all 28 Member States of European Union. It was drafted within the Council of Europe some years after the end of World War II (between 1949 and 1950), when Europe was engaged in a laborious work of reconstruction, both in its economy and material infrastructures and the lives of its people. In this period, when European countries where healing the still open wounds deriving from the war, "human rights" became the object of strong interest and study throughout the world.

Thus, shortly after that the United Nations (recently established for the main purpose of maintaining and promoting international peace and security) had adopted the "Universal Declaration on Human Rights" of 1948, in the "old continent" the movement for European integration was becoming stronger and stronger and, with it, also the will to create a common "charter" for the protection of human rights and liberties[320].

---

318 European Convention for the Protection of Human Rights and Fundamental Freedoms, 4 November 1950, CETS No 5.

319 As indicated in http://conventions.coe.int/treaty/Commun/CherchSig.asp?NT=005&CM=&DF=&CL=ENG (accessed on 1 November 2013), as of 1November 2013 the Member States were: Albania, Andorra, Armenia, Austria, Azerbaijan, Belgium, Bosnia and Herzgovina, Bulgaria, Croatia, Cyprus, Czech Republic, Denmark, Estonia, Finland, France, Georgia, Germany, Greece, Hungary, Iceland, Ireland, Italy, Latvia, Liechtenstein, Lithuania, Luxembourg, Malta, Moldova, Monaco, Montenegro, Netherlands, Norway, Poland, Portugal, Romania, Russia, San Marino, Serbia, Slovak Republik, Slovenia, Spain, Sweden, Switzerland, the former Yugoslav Republic of Macedonia, Turkey, Ukraine and the United Kingdom.

320 The seed of the principles sets forth in the European Convention on Human Rights, as well as the concept itself of "human rights protection", is to be found much earlier in time, probably already in 1215, when the Magna Carta was sealed by King John (on 15 June 1215) granting "all free men" for his Kingdom a number of rights and liberties including what is believed to be archetype of the "right to fair trial".King John was forced by the feudal barons – who wanted to limit the King′s power and to protect their privileges – to accept Magna Carta, and indeed soon after he withdrew from it. However, its principles remained alive and, with several amendemends, were included it following editions of the Charter. See, ex multis, A. PALLISTER, *Magna Carta: the Heritage of Liberty*, Oxford: Oxford University Press, 1971; A.D. BOYER, (edited by), Essays by T. GARDEN BARNES, *Shaping the Common Law: from Glanvill to Hale, 1188-1688*, Standford University Press, 2008, 27; G. SLAPPER & D. KLLY, *Sourcebook on the English Legal System*, London: Cavendish Publishing Limited, 2001, 487.

The high number of states which ratified the ECHR, has proven that this tool is one of the most effective regional human rights laws for the protection of human rights, particularly thanks to the activity of its judicial body.

The European Convention was not, *per se*, exceptional and innovative, as it was in many aspects similar to other international instruments on human rights but what was "extraordinary" was its "enforcement machinery"[321], which allowed its effective implementation through the possibility, granted either to a State or an individual, to file a petition with the European Commission of Human Rights[322], and with the subsequent establishment of an effective judicial authority of the European Court of Human Rights to adjudicate the cases brought before it[323].

This important tool has as scope of application to include *all persons within the jurisdiction* of the contracting parties, thus the Convention covers citizens and non-citizens alike[324]. Closer scrutiny of the Convention has proven that only a limited set of basic rights is guaranteed to everyone under the convention, notwithstanding the impression that the ECHR conveys of being an inclusive and all-embrancing agreement. A. Drzemczewski[325] said "*in reality is must be admitted that the classical approach of distinguishing between aliens and nationals continues to exist...after all, it is not difficult to draft provisions, which are noble, objective and non-discriminatory in purpose and yet whose practical effect is at times quite marginal*". The non-derogable rights relate *inter alia* to the right of life (Article 2 ECHR), as well as the prohibition of torture, slavery and servitude (Articles 3 and 4(1) ECHR)[326]. Some provisions explicity concern non-nationals: for instance, concerning irregular migrants, state parties may derogate from the right to liberty in cases where the lawful arrest or detention shall either prevent

321 See, in these terms, M. W. JANIS, R.S. KAY & A.W. BRADLEY, *European Rights Law, Text and Materials*, Third Edition, Oxford.

322 The Commission was given the right to hear complaints submitted by individuals in 1955, with the consent of the interested State.

323 With Protocol No. 11 to the Convention, a permanent European Court of Human Rights was established.

324 See Art. 1 ECHR on the notion of "jurisdiction" under Art. 1 ECHR, see M. GONDEK, *Extraterritorial Application of The European Convention on Human Rights: Territorial Focus in the Age of Globalization?*, 52 *Netherlands International Law Review*, 2005, 3.

325 A. DRZEMCEWSKI, *The Position of Aliens in Relation to the European Convention of Human Rights: a General Survey*, in: Council of Europe (ed.), *Human Rights of Aliens in Europe*, Martinus Nijhoff Publishers, Dordrecht 1985, pp. 351-399.

326 See Art. 15 ECHR on derogation in time of emergency.

unauthorised entry into the country, or shall ensure the capture of a person against whom action is being taken with a view to deportation or extradition[327].

Moreover, Article 1 of Protocol No 7 determines procedural safeguards relating to the expulsion of legally staying aliens, and Article 4 of Protocol No 4 prohibits the collective expulsion of aliens. Article 16 ECHR expressly permits the contracting parties to impose restrictions on the political activity of aliens; nothing in Article 10, 11 and 14 ECHR shall be interpreted otherwise in this respect[328].

The European Court of Human Rights (ECtHR) is in charge of monitoring the adherence of the contracting parties to the ECHR. The ECtHR initially left the state parties wide discretionary powers in controlling and regulating immigration[329]. In parallel, the Court of Justice of European Union has generated constructive principles as it started to interpret free movement rights with reference to Article 8 ECHR[330].

Wiesbork argued that the most important rights of the ECHR concerning the treatment of foreigners are Article 8 on the right to family life, Article 9 on the freedom of thought, conscience and religion and Article 14 on the principle of non-discrimination[331]. These rights are related to fundamental aspects of the life of the person: and they are very important for a

327 Art. 5(1)(f) ECHR.

328 K. EISELE, *The External Dimention of the EU's Migration Policy. Different Legal Position of Third-Country Nationals, in the EU: A Comparative Perspective, in Immigration and Asylum Law and Policy in Europe*, 2014, Vol. 34, Jan Niessen and Espelth Guild.

329 It was only when the Strasbourg Court handed down the precedent in *Abdulaziz Cabales and Balkandali v. The United Kingdom* in 1985 that it became clear that the right to respect for family life also applies to national immigration legislation (Abdulaziz Cabales and Balkandali v. The United Kingdom (Application No. 9214/80; 9473/81; 9474/81) Judjment of 28 May 1985, 7 EHRR 471). Incrementally, the ECtHR has developed clearer guidelines on how the right to family life interacts with immigration policy on the basis of its case law.

330 N. ROGERS, *Immigration and the Convention on Human Rights: Are New Principles Emerging?*, in *European Human Rights Law Review*, 2003, 53, p. 54.

331 A. WIESBROK, 2010, *Legal Migration to the European Union*, Martinus Nijhoff Publishers, Leiden, 2010, pp. 209-210; as right of potential relevance for migrants the author indicates: the freedom to move within a state (Art. 2(1) of Protocol No 4); the freedom to leave a state (Art. 2(2) of Protocol No 4); the prohibition of expulsion of nationals (Art. 3(1) of Protocol No 4); the right to enter the territory of one's own state (Art. 3(2) of Protocol No 4); the procedural rights for lawful residents as regards expulsion (Art. 1 of Protocol No 7).

foreigner because their correct exercice contributes significantly to the integration of the person in the new country.

Concerning the latter Article mentioned above, Article 14, it provides one of the most relevant principles in the issue of protection of human rights of irregular migrants: the prohibition of discrimination. The Article, specifically, provides that "*the enjoyment of the rights and freedoms set forth in this Convention shall be secured without discrimination on any ground such as sex, race, colour, language, religion, political or other opinion, national or social origin, association with a national minority, property, birth or other status*". This provision is not a free standing provision in that it cannot be invoked alone but applies only in combination with other rights protected under the Convention. However, it does not presuppose the breach of such rights[332].

Article 14 ECHR is supplemented by Protocol No 12 which has created a general and independent right of non-discrimination to remedy the shortcomings of the protection under Article 14 ECHR, taking into account that the principles of equality and non-discrimination are fundamental elements of international human rights law.

The Protocol No 12 covers the same, non-exhaustive, grounds as listed in Article 14 ECHR in respect of the enjoyment of any right set forth by law. The expression "any right set forth by law" relates to any legal right recognized in domestic or international law and to the acts or omissions of public authorities[333]. Thus, Protocol No 12 provides greater protection than Article 14 ECHR which aims to ensure equal treatment within the ambit of rights contained in the Convention only.

The notion of discrimination has consistently been interpreted in the case law of the Court namely that a difference of treatment is discriminatory if it has no objective and reasonable justification, that is if it does not pursue a legitimate aim or if there is not a reasonable relationship of proportionality between the means employed and the aim sought to be realised[334].

---

332 *Van Raalte v. The Netherlands*, Application No. 20060/92, Judgment of 2 February 1997, 24 EHRR 503, para 33.

333 G. MOON, *The Draft Discrimination Protocol to the European Convention on Human Rights: A progress Report*, in European Human Rights Law Review, 2000, 49, pp. 51-52.

334 Explanatory Report to Protocol No 12 to the Convention for the Protection of Human Rights and Fundamental Freedoms, para. 18.

In order to test whether or not differential treatment or practice is justified under Article 14 ECHR, the Court examines the following questions according to C. Ovey and R.A.W. White[335]:

- Does the discrimination at hand fall within the scope of a protected right?
- Is there a violation of the substantive provision?
- Is there different treatment?
- Does the treatment pursue a legitimate aim?
- Are the means employed proportionate to the legitimate aim?
- Does the differential treatment go beyond a state´s margin of appreciation?

The ECtHR has adopted an extensive reading for determing whether the facts of a case relate to rights that are protected under the ECHR and made clear that the scope of the ECHR extends beyond the actual letter of the rights guaranteed[336].

3.2. The EU and the ECHR: interpretation and accession

Despite the fact that the EU is not yet a party to the ECtHR, the Court of Justice in Luxembourg has repeatedly referred to this human rights treaty in the past, stating that the ECHR has special significance as regards fundamental rights protection in the Community framework[337]. In the *Nold* case[338], 1974, the Court of Justice held that fundamental rights form an in-

---

335 C. OVEY and R.A.W. WHITE, *The European Convention on Human Rights*, 4th end. Oxford University Press, Oxford, 2006, pp. 419-429.

336 EU Agency for Fundamental Rights, European Court of Human Rights and Council of Europe, Handbook on European Non-Discrimination Law (Vienna/ Strasbourg 2011), pp. 61-63. Moreover, with regard to the appraisal as to whether there is violation of a substantive provision, the Court explained in *Chassagnou and Others v. France* that "Where a substantive Article of the Convention has been invoked both on its own and together with Article 14 and a separate breach has been found of the substantive Article, it is not generally necessary for the Court to consider the case under Article 14 also, though the position is otherwise if a clear inequality of treatment in the enjoyment of the right in question is a fundamental aspect of the case" (Chassagnou and Others v. France, (Application Nos. 25088/94; 28331/95; 28443/95) Judgment of 29 April 1999, 29 EHRR 615, para.89.

337 Case C-299/95 Kremzow (1997) ECR I-2629, para. 14.

338 Case 4/73 *Nold* (1974) ECR 491, para. 13; later confirmed in Case 44/79 *Hauer* (1979) ECR 3727, para. 15; see also Joint Declaration by the European Parlia-

tegral part of the the general principles of law and that *"international treaties for the protection of human rights on which the Member States have collaborated or of which they are signatories can supply guidelines (for the protection of fundamental rights, next to constitutional traditions common to the Member States)"*.

It was pointed out that *"in the absence of any catalogue of actual rights, the ECHR was, in practice, the only realistic point of reference. The occasional references made by the Court to inspiration from national constitutions were, in reality, perfunctory rather than scientific and were in any event incomplete"*[339]. The judgment in *Nold* must be considered against the backdrop of the Rome Treaty that did not intrinsically protect fundamental rights, apart from the four freedoms and the prohibition of discrimination[340]. Moreover, the protection of fundamental rights by the Court was endorsed by the Member States in successive treaty amendments: a first reference to human rights was integrated into the SEA of 1986; the Preamble to the Maastricht Treaty confirms the respect for human rights, and Article F TEU first specifically referred to the respect of fundamental rights as guaranteed by the ECHR[341]; the Treaty of Lisbon has created a legal basis for the EU to accede to the ECHR to provide a sound fundamental rights protection in the EU framework, together with the legally binding EU Charter[342].

3.3. The EU Charter of Fundamental Rights and irregular migrants

In 2009 the European Union recognised, under the Treaty of Lisbon, the rights, freedoms and principles set out in the EU Charter of Fundamental Rights (EU Charter) which considerably adds to the fundamental rights protection in the EU[343]. The EU Charter acknowledges that the Union is

---

ment, the Council and the Commission "Concerning the Protection of Fundamental Rights and the European Convention for the Protection of Human Rights and Fundamental Freedoms", OJ C 103, 27 April 1977, p. 1.

339 N. FENNELLY, *Pillar Talk: Fundamental Rights Protection in the European Union*, in *Judicial Studies Institute Journal*, 2008, 95, p. 100.

340 J.L. MURRAY, *Fundamental Rights in the European Communuty Legal Order*, 32 *Fordham International Law Journal*, 2008, 531, p. 534.

341 Art. F. TEU under the Treaty of Maastricht was, however, not enforceable by the Court of Justice, see Art. L TEU.

342 See Art. 6(2) TEU as amended by the Treaty of Lisbon; Protocol No 8 to the Treaty of Lisbon; Art. 17 of Protocol No 14 to the ECHR.

343 Charter of Fundamental Rights of the European Union, *OJ C* 83, 30 March 2010, p. 389.

founded on the indivisible, universal values of human dignity, freedom, equality and solidarity and that it is based on the principles of democracy and the rule of law[344]. The Preamble of the Charter moreover sets forth its principle aim: *"This Charter reaffirms...the rights as they result, in particular, from the constitutional traditions and international obligations common to the Member States, the European Convention for the Protection of Human Rights and Fundamental Freedoms, the Social Charters adopted by the Union and by Council of Europe and the case law of the Court of Justice of the European Union and of the European Court of Human Rights"*[345].

Two relevant aspects of this Charter are: first, it reaffirms existing rights resulting from traditions and obligations and consequently it does not create any new rights; second, the legal sources of the Charter are listed, that is to say, the national constitutions of the Member States, the ECHR, the case law of the Court of Justice and the ECtHR.

In Article 6(1) of TEU is laid down the legal effect of the EU Charter, *"the same legal value of the Treaties"*.

But even before the entry into force of the Lisbon regime, the Court and the Court of First Instance, now the General Court, referred to the Charter for interpretative purposes[346]. In many instances the Court of Justice has made references to the Charter after it became legally binding in December of 2009[347].

The Charter was proclaimed in Nice on 7 December 2000. It is subdivided into seven Titles, including Title I on dignity (Articles 1 to 5); Title II on freedoms (Articles 6 to 19); Title III on equality (Articles 20 to 26); Title IV on solidarity (Articles 27 to 38); Title V on citizen's rights (Articles 39 to 46); Title VI on justice (Articles 47 to 50); and Title VII on general provisions governing the interpretation and application of the migrants as its scope of application relates to, except for Title V and some other provisions that are reserved for Union citizens, everyone covering third-coutry nationals and Union citizens alike. Thus, it affirms the universal nature of

---

344 See Recital 2 of the Preamble to the EU Charter.

345 See Recital 5 of the Preamble to the EU Charter, Case C-540/03 *EP v. Council* (2006) I 5769, para. 38.

346 See Case C-540/03 EP v. Council (2006) I-5769, para. 58; Case C-438/05 *Viking* (2007) ECR I-10779, paras. 43-44; Case T-77/01 Territorio Historico de Alava (2002) ECR II-81, para. 35; Case T-54/99 max.mobil Telecommunication (2002) ECR II-313, para. 48.

347 See for instance Case C-555/07 *Kücükdecevi* (2010) ECR I-00365, para. 22; Case C-578/08 *Chrackoun* (2010) ECR I-01839, para. 44; Case C-571/07 *Blanco Perez* (2010) ECR I-04629, para. 65.

rights accorded to everyone regardless of nationality or place of residence, thus also to undocumented migrants. The specific provisions that are of importance for migrants are discussed in Parts V to VII of the Charter.

Article 51(1) of the Charter provides that the provisions of the document are addressed to the institutions, bodies, offices and agencies of the Union with due regard for the principle of subsidiarity and to the Member States only when they are implementing Union law. Article 51(2) of the Charter stipulates that the Charter does not extend the field of application of EU law beyond the powers of the Union, and it does not establish any new power or task for the Union, or modify powers and tasks as defined in the Treaties. The Court of Justice emphasised, in this respect, that it is called upon to interpret, in the light of the Charter, the law of the EU within the limits of the powers conferred on it[348].

Article 52 of the EU Charter specifies the scope and interpretation of the rights and principles. It determines that:

- any limitation on the exercise of the rights and freedoms recognised by this Charter must be provided for by law and respect the essence of those rights and freedoms. Subject to the principle of proportionality, limitations may be made only if they are necessary and genuinely meet objectives of general interest recognised by the Union or the need to protect the rights and freedoms of others (Article 52(1) EU Charter);
- rights recognised by this Charter for which provision is made in the Treaties shall be exercised under the conditions and within the limits defined by those Treaties (Article 52(2) EU Charter).
- As regards the interpretation of the EU Charter, it is laid down that:
- in so far as this Charter contains rights which correspond to rights guaranteed by the ECHR, the meaning and scope of those rights shall be the same as those laid down in the said Convention. This provision shall not prevent Union law providing more extensive protection (Article 52(4) EU Charter);
- in so far as this Charter recognises fundamental rights as they result from the constitutional traditions common to the Member States, those rights shall be interpreted in harmony with those traditions (Article 52(4) EU Charter).

Article 53 of the Charter makes clear that the existent level of protection with respect to human rights and fundamental freedoms as guaranteed by

---

348 Case C-400/10 PPU McB (2010) ECR I-08965, para. 51; see also Joined Cases C-483/90 and C-1/10 Gueye and Salomeron Sanchez (2011) Judgment of 15 September 2011, not yet reported, para. 69.

other relevant legal sources, in their respective fields of application, shall be upheld in the sense that nothing in the Charter shall be interpreted as restricting adverserly affecting such rights and freedoms. These sources comprise EU law, international law, international agreements to which the Union or all the Member States are party, including the ECHR and the Member States′ constitutions. The Court of Justice dealt with the correlation of the EU Charter and the ECHR in *Dereci and Others*[349] in which it instructed the national court to decide whether the situation was covered by EU law, which would entail the application of the Charter, or whether the situation fall outside the scope of EU law, which would imply the application of the ECHR[350].

3.4. The European Social Charter and irregular migrants

The European Social Charter (ESC) was drafted in 1961 under the auspices of the Council of Europe as a counterpart to the International Covenant on Economic, Social and Cultural Rights (ICESCR) of the UN framework to guarantee social and economic human rights in Europe and it entered

349 Case C-265/11 *Dereci and Others* (2011) Judgment of 15 November 2011, not yet reported, paras. 72-73; the case concerned the right of residence of third-country family members of Union citizens.

350 The British and the Polish governments′ position as regards the EU Charter are laid down in Protocol No 30 to the Treaty of Lisbon (Protocol to the Treaty of Lisbon No 30 to the application of the Charter of Fundamental Rights to the European Union to Poland and to the United Kingdom). Article 1(1) of Protocol No 30 states that the Charter does not extend the ability of the Court of Justice, or any court of Poland or of the UK, to find that the laws, regulations or administrative provisions, practices or actions of Poland or of the UK are inconsistent with the fundamental rights, freedoms and principles that it reaffirms. Article 1(1) of Protocol No 30 further specifies that, for the avoidance of doubt, nothing in Title IV of the Charter creates justiciable rights applicable to Poland or the UK, except in so far as Poland or the UK has provided for such rights in its national law. Finally, Article 2 of Protocol No 30 clarifies that, to the extent that a provision of the Charter refers to national laws and practices, it shall only apply to Poland or the UK to the extent that the rights or principles that it contains are recognised in the law or practices of the Charter shall not extend, in any way, the competences of the Union as defined in the Treaties (See Article 6(1) TEU and Art. 51(2) of the EU Charter).

into force in 1965[351]. The ILO standards are reflected in the document[352]. Despite "exensive jurisprudence" on the ESC, the latter treaty has led "a twilight existence" as *"various factors have conspired to prevent the Charter realising its full potential result from a lack of political will"*[353].

The Amending Protocol provides for oral hearings and the inclusion of observers of employers′ and trade union organisations in the Governmental Committee; furthermore, under the Amending Protocol it is the Committee of Independent Experts only that is competent to interpret the Charter and decide on questions of compliance. In order to become effective, all contracting states have to ratify the Amending Protocol[354].

Importantly, the revised ESC introduced a general prohibition of discrimination in its Article E laying down that *"The enjoyment of the rights set forth in this Charter shall be secured without discrimination on any ground such as race, colour, sex, language, religion, political or other opinion, national extraction or social origin, health, association with a national minority, birth or other status"*. It means that the Charter is valid also for irregular migrants.

However, the ESC′s most significant contribution to protecting irregular migrants derives from its vibrant case law. For instance, in the *IFHR (International Federation of Human Rights) vs France* (complaint No. 14/2003, decision of 8 September 2004) the European Committee on Social Rights held *"that legislation or practice which denies entitlement to medical assistance to foreign nationals, within the territory of a State Party, even if they are there illegally, is contrary to the Charter"*.

The decision of this case represents the importance of the correct application of this right and its application which must be guaranteed to everybody independently from their status.

---

351 European Social Charter CETS No 035 of 18 October 1961/CETS No 163 of 3 May 1995 (revised); D. HARRIS, *A Fresh Impetus for the European Social Charter*, 41 *International and Comparative Law Quarterly* (1992), 659.

352 ILO, The European Social Charter and International Labour Standards, 84 International Labour Review (1961), 354.

353 D. HARRIS, *A Fresh Impetus for the European Social Charter, 41 International and Comparative Law Quarterly*, 1992, 659, p. 659.

354 See Protocol Amending the European Social Charter; for its entry into force, all contracting states have to ratify the Amending Protocol in accordance with its Art. 8; D. HARRIS, *A Fresh Impetus for the European Social Charter*, 41 *International and Comparative Law Quartely*, 1992, 659, pp. 662-672; the absence of a tripartist structure within the ambit of the ESC was pointed out by B. HAPPLE, *European Social Charter*, 17 *Industrial Law Journal* 1988, 124, p. 125.

In view of the fact that various other rights under the Charter are closely linked to the notion of human dignity, one cannot exclude further dynamic interpretations[355].

3.5. The European Code of Social Security a well as the European Convention on Social Security and irregular migrants

The European Code of Social Security, together with an annexed Protocol, has been open for signature since 1964 and came into force four years later, in 1968[356]. The Code sets out minimum standards for national social security system which are higher than those embodied in ILO Convention No 102 concerning Minimum Standards of Social Security[357]. The Code has been described as a "menu" from which states can pick and choose the rules they wish to adhere to[358]. The detailed provisions of the Code concern a broad range of benefits covering *inter alia* medical care, as well as sickness, unemployment and old-age benefits.

The Code and its Protocol contain norms of a more technical nature and irregular migrants are surely excluded from the scope of the Code. However, Shoukens cites Art. 73 of the Code, and states that as both "foreigners" and "migrants" are not specified in the given article, one might include irregular labour migrants under these terms. Art. 73 reads as follow: *"the contracting parties shall endeavour to conclude a special instruments governing questions relating to social security for foreigners and migrants, particularly with regard to equality of treatment with their own nationals and to the mainteinance of acquired rights and rights in course of acquisition"*[359]. In 1990 the Code was revised, however the changes did not effect the parts dealing with the rights of foreign workers[360].

355 CoE Parliamentary Assembley (2006) Para 35.

356 European Code of Social Security CETS No. 048 of 16 16 April 1964 and the Protocol to the European Code of Social Security; as of 16 November 2011, the European Code of Social Security has 21 ratifications.

357 ILO Convention No. 102 concerning Minimum Standards of Social Security of 28 June 1952.

358 J. NICKLESS, *European Code of Social Security: A Short Guide*, Council of Europe Publishing, Strasbourg 2003, p. 11.

359 P. SCHOUKENS, *Exploratory report on the access to social protection for illegal labour migrants, International Social Security Association – European Regional Meeting: Migrants and Social Protection,* Oslo, 21–23 April 2004, ISSA/EUR/OSLO/04.

360 The revised European Code of Social Security updates and improves the provisions of the European Code of Social Security. Rome, 06/11/1990 – Treaty open

3.6. The European Convention on the Legal Status of Migrant Workers and irregular migrants

In 1977, the Council of Europe adopted the first multilateral treaty that expressly envisaged the protection of migrants: the European Convention on the Legal Status of Migrant Workers (ECMW), which came into force in 1983[361]. The Convention is open for signature of Member States of the European Council.

The Convention can only be applied to migrants coming from countries which themselves have ratified the Convention and who are officially allowed to take up employment in the host state.

3.7. The European Convention for the Prevention of Torture and Inhuman or Degrading Treatment or Punishment and irregular migrants

The European Convention for the Prevention of torture and inhuman or degrading treatment or punishment (ETS 126) is applicable to irregular migrants in some contexts (especially in terms of their detention on arrival, during their stay or in preparation for their expulsion from the country) and The Convention on Action against Trafficking in Human Beings (ETS 197) makes an important contribution to the protection of a particularly vulnerable group of irregular migrants as well.

As regards some more measures of the Council of Europe, the Committee of Minister has declared the foundations for promoting the rights of irregular migrants in Recommendation No (2000) 3 to Member States on the Right to the Satisfaction of Basic Material Needs of Persons in Situations of Extreme Hardship. The Committee of Ministers recognises that certain rights should be open to all citizens and foreigners, whatever their status[362].

The Parliamentary Assembly of the Council of Europe has expressed the basics of its attitude towards employers hiring irregular migrants in its Recommendation 1211 (1993) on clandestine migration – traffickers and

---

for signature by the member States and for accession by non-member States and by the EU.

361 European Convention on the Legal Status of Migrant Workers CETS No 093 of 24 November 1977.

362 CoE Parliamentary Assembly (2006) Para 39.

employers of clandestine migrants: "*Employers thus save a large proportion of the cost of declared labour, since the clandestine migrant is not in a position to contest the proffered wage. This wage is very often lower than the legal wage, for long and irregular hours of work. The employment of clandestine migrants results in economic distortions which jeopardise the national economy as a whole.*" (Para 5.). The Parliamentary Assembly has also adopted a charter of intent on clandestine migration, which refers to the need to protect the basic rights of irregular migrants [Recommendation 1577 (2002)].

As regards social rights, the Parliamentary Assembly declared in its recent Report from 2006[363] that the following minimum rights should, *inter alia*, apply to irregular migrants as well:

- adequate housing and shelter guaranteeing human dignity (13.1.);
- emergency healthcare (13.2.);
- social protection through social security where it is necessary to alleviate poverty and preserve human dignity (children are in a particularly vulnerable situation and they should be entitled to social protection which they should enjoy on the same footing as national children) (13.3.);
- irregular migrants who have made social security contributions should be able to benefit from these contributions or be reimbursed, for example if expelled from the country (13.4.);
- in relation to irregular migrants in work, they should be entitled to fair wages, reasonable working conditions, compensation for accidents, access to the courts to defend their rights and also freedom to form and to join a trade union. Any employer failing to comply with these terms should be rigorously pursued by the relevant authorities in member states (13.5.) etc.

From the perspective of employers' liability, the last point is the most notable.

4. Some concluding consideration on the protection of human rights of irregular migrants at the European and International law level

The international legal framework consists, as described, of international declarations (soft law) and treaties that are open for signature for all states. On the other hand, regional instruments were created setting out human and migrants′ rights protection in countries on the European continent.

363 CoE Parliamentary Assembly (2006) Para 13.

Meanwhile, the UN and the ILO as specialised agencies have taken a leading role in drafting, advancing and disseminating international standards, and the Council of Europe assumed such a key role for the European conventions. It is relevant that some human rights standards, such as most of the UDHR, have, from the point of view of interational lawyers, become customary international law in the course of time. It is remarkable that membership of the Council of Europe and the associated adherence to the ECHR enjoys great popularity among European countries, whereas other conventions have only a very limited number of ratifying states[364].

The ECHR and the jurisprudence of the ECtHR have had a major impact on the human rights protection within the EU legal order.

The Court of Justice in Luxembourg was ready to interpret EU law in the light of and with explicit reference to the case law of the Court in Strasbourg. Once the EU has acceded to the ECHR, there is no doubt that not only the EU Member States but the EU itself must observe the ECHR as a party.

Moreover, concerning specifically the protection of human rights of irregular migrants, from the analisys conducted thus far, it possible to affirm that, the protection provided by several Conventions, covers the category of irregular migrants in some cases. However, very often not a complete extention of the tools to protect the human rights of these persons is provided and very often in order to try to guarantee this extention, new interpretations are necessary. Given the lack of a specific status as a category of vulnerable individuals at international and European level, there is no specific legislation to protect the human rights of these migrants.

C. Human Rights and Irregular Migrants in the Entry Phase at European Union Level: General overview

The irregular migrants in all aspects of their life, as human beings, have the right to see their fundamental rights protected. However, as already explained, because of the lack of a legal status recognized by States, they have serious difficulties asserting their rights and in particular this is evident in the phase of entry into a State.

---

364 K. EISELE, *The External Dimention of the EU´s Migration Policy. Different Legal Position of Third-Country Nationals, in the EU: A Comparative Perspective, in Immigration and Asylum Law and Policy in Europe*, 2014, Vol. 34, J. Niesse and E. GUILD.

Indeed, this is a very delicate and difficult phase in which their rights often collide with the interests and policies of the European Union States of destination. The analysis of the level and effectiveness of protection of this category of migrants in this phase is very relevant and currently also widely discussed at European Union level as result of serious incidents of violation of human rights[365].

This is the reason why this section of the Chapter will be dedicated to the analysis of the correlation of protection of human rights in this phase in the EU in general, and then with a particular look at the high sea, hot spot and detention facilities contexts.

1. An overview on EU migration policies: irregular migration

A brief analysis of the general framework on the policy of the EU towards immigration matters follows before a specific analysis of EU legislation on irregular migration in the entry phase is presented.

A forward-looking and comprehensive European immigration policy, based on solidarity, is a key objective for the European Union. Immigration policy is intended to establish a balanced approach to dealing with both regular and irregular immigration.

Articles 79 and 80 of the Treaty on the Functioning of the European Union (TFEU)[366] are the legal basis of this policy.

The competences in general of the European Union in the field are the following four points:

- *regular immigration* for which the EU is competent to lay down the conditions governing entry into and legal residence in a Member State, including for the purposes of family reunification, for third-country nationals. Member States retain the right to determine admission rates for people coming from third countries to seek work;

365 M. SAVINO, *La crisi migratoria tra Italia e Unione Europea: diagnosi e prospettive*, Editoriale Scientifica, 2017; N. KLEIN, *Maritime Security and the Law of the Sea*, Oxford University Press, Oxford, 2011, p. 75; Y. TANAKA, *The International Law of the Sea*, Cambridge University Press, Cambridge, 2012, p. 85; P. MONZINI, *Il Traffico di Migranti per via marittima*, cit, p. 45; A. FISCHER-LESCANO, L. TILLMAN, T. TOHIDIPUR, *Border Controls at Sea: Requirements under International Human Rights and Refugee Law*, in *International Journal of Refugee Law*, 21, 2009, p. 290.

366 Consolidated version of the Treaty on the Functioning of the European Union, OJ C 326, 26.10.2012, p. 47–390.

- *integration* on which the EU may provide incentives and support for measures taken by Member States to promote the integration of legally resident third-country nationals; EU law makes no provision for the harmonisation of national laws and regulations, however;
- *combating irregular immigration*, a relevant point for the object under investigation for this thesis, on which the European Union is required to prevent and reduce irregular immigration, in particular by means of an effective return policy, in a manner entirely consistent with fundamental rights;
- *readmission agreements* on which the European Union is competent to conclude agreements with third countries for the readmission to their country of origin or transit of third-country nationals who do not or no longer fulfil the conditions for entry into or presence or residence in a Member State.
- The EU aims to set up a balanced approach to dealing with regular immigration and combating irregular immigration. Proper management of migration flows entails ensuring fair treatment of third-country nationals residing legally in Member States, enhancing measures to combat irregular immigration and promoting closer cooperation with non-member countries in all fields. It is the EU's aim to establish a uniform level of rights and obligations for regular immigrants, comparable with that for EU citizens. Improving and increasing regular flows also represents a tool to reduce irregular flows.

Under the Lisbon Treaty immigration policies are to be governed by the principle of solidarity (Article 80 TFEU), and fair sharing of responsibility, including its financial implications, among the Member States. The Treaty, which entered into force in December 2009, introduced co-decision and qualified majority voting on regular immigration and a new legal basis for integration measures. The ordinary legislative procedure now applies to policies on both irregular and regular immigration, making Parliament a co-legislator on an equal footing with the Council[367]. The provisional measures to be taken in the event of a sudden inflow of third-country nationals

367 Lisbon maintains the principle of double majority voting (citizens and Member States). However, the previous arrangements remained in place until November 2014; since 1 November 2014, the new rules apply but the use of previous voting weights can be requested by any Member State until 31 March 2017.
A qualified majority is reached when 55 % of members of the Council, comprising at least 65 % of the population, support a proposal (Article 16(4) TEU). When the Council is not acting on a proposal from the Commission or the VP/HR, the necessary majority of Member States increases to 72 % (Article

are adopted by the Council alone, however, after consulting Parliament (Article 78(3) TFEU).

The Lisbon Treaty also made it clear that the EU shares competence in this field with the Member States, in particular as regards the number of migrants allowed to enter a Member State to seek work (Article 79(5) TFEU). Finally, the Court of Justice[368] now has full jurisdiction in the field of immigration and asylum.

1.1. Recent policy developments: the "Global Approach to Migration and Mobility"

The 'Global Approach to Migration and Mobility' (GAMM)[369], a comprehensive migration policy based on common political principles and solidarity, adopted by the Commission in 2011 establishes a general framework for the EU's relations with third countries in the field of migration. It is based on four pillars: regular immigration and mobility, irregular immigration and trafficking in human beings, international protection and asylum policy, and maximising the impact of migration and mobility on development. The human rights of migrants are a cross-cutting issue in the context of this migration policy.

238(2) TFEU). To block legislation, at least four Member States have to vote against a proposal. A new scheme inspired by the 'Ioannina compromise' will allow 75 % (55 % from 1 April 2017) of the Member States necessary for the blocking minority to ask for reconsideration of a proposal during a 'reasonable time period' (Declaration 7).
The Council meets in public when it deliberates and votes on a draft legislative act. To this end, each Council meeting is divided into two parts, dealing respectively with legislative acts and non-legislative activities. The Council Presidency continues to rotate on a six-month basis, but there are 18-month group presidencies of three Member States in order to ensure better continuity of work. As an exception, the Foreign Affairs Council is continuously chaired by the VP/HR.

368 The jurisdiction of the Court is extended to all activities of the Union with the exception of the CFSP. The number of Advocates-General can be increased from eight to eleven. Specialised courts can be set up with the consent of Parliament. Access to the Court is facilitated for individuals. A European Public Prosecutor's Office should be set up in order to investigate, prosecute and bring to judgment offences against the Union's financial interests.

369 COM/2011/0743 final on Global Approach to Migration and Mobility, on 18 November 2011.

The migration policy suggested by GAMM focuses on regional and bilateral dialogue between countries of origin, transit and destination. One of the main instruments of the Global Approach are the "mobility partnerships"[370] which can be concluded with third countries. These partnerships incorporate not only readmission agreements, but a whole set of measures, ranging from development aid to temporary entry visa facilitation, measures on circular migration, and among these measures also those combating irregular immigration.

1.2. The June 2014 strategic guidelines

The Stockholm Programme[371] ("An open and secure Europe serving and protecting citizens"), adopted in December 2009 as a successor to the multiannual programmes adopted at Tampere (1999) and The Hague (2004), expired in December 2014. In March 2014, the Commission published a new communication setting out its vision on the future agenda for home affairs, entitled "An open and secure Europe: making it happen"[372], so that the European Council and Parliament could debate the strategic guidelines in June 2014.

In accordance with Article 68 TFEU, in its conclusions of 26 and 27 June 2014 the European Council then defined the strategic guidelines for legislative and operational planning within the area of freedom, security and justice for the period 2014-2020[373]. These guidelines focused on the objective of transposing, implementing and consolidating the existing legal instruments and measures. The guidelines stress the need to adopt a holistic approach to migration, making the best possible use of regular migration, affording protection to those who need it, combating irregular migration and managing borders effectively.

---

370 These partnerships are the most complete framework for bilateral cooperation between the EU and its partners, based on mutual offers of commitments and project initiatives covering mobility, migration and asylum issues, within the Global Approach to Migration and Mobility.

371 The Stockholm Programme-an open and secure Europe serving and protecting citizens (2010/C 115/01).

372 An open and secure Europe: making it happen COM(2014) 154 final European Commission.

373 European Council 26/27 June 2014, EUCO 79/14.

1.3. The European Agenda on Migration

On the basis of a Commission proposal (10-point action plan)[374], on 23 April 2015 the Member States undertook (see European Council statement) to take swift action to save lives and step up the EU's action in the field of migration. A European Parliament resolution was adopted a few days later, on 29 April 2015[375].

More details on European Agenda on Migration are in the Part II paragraph 2 "Irregular Migrant Issue at EU Level: Overview"[376].

1.4. Recent legislative developments

Since 2008, a number of significant directives on immigration have been adopted and some other relevant directives are due to be revised in the near future.

a) Irregular immigration

The EU has adopted two major pieces of legislation to combat irregular immigration:

the "Return Directive" (2008/115/EC)[377], briefely analysed previously, which sets out common EU standards and procedures for returning irregularly resident third-country nationals. Member States were called upon to transpose the directive by 24 December 2010. The first report on its implementation was adopted in March 2014[378]. The main areas for further action include ensuring its proper implementation, promoting consistent, fundamental rights-compatible practices, and improving cooperation between Member States. One of the main tasks of the teams supporting na-

374 COM(2015) 240 final, European Agenda on Migratio, on 13 May 2015.

375 Resolution on the latest tragedies in the Mediterranean and EU migration and asylum policies, 2015/2660(RSP).

376 P.108 of Chapter II.

377 See pg. 96, paragraph 1, Special Part, Part VI.

378 Communication from the Commission to the Council and the European Parliament on EU Return Policy, COM(2014) 199 final.

tional authorities at hotspots[379] in Italy and Greece is to ensure that people actually return to their country of origin. On 9 September 2015, the Commission published an European Union Action Plan on Return[380] which was endorsed by the Council the following October.

Directive 2009/52/EC[381] specifies sanctions and measures to be applied in Member States against employers who infringe the ban on employing illegally resident third-country nationals. Member States were required to transpose the directive by 20 July 2011. The first report on the implementation of the directive was submitted on 22 May 2014[382].

At the same time, the EU is negotiating and concluding readmission agreements with countries of origin and transit with a view to returning irregular migrants and cooperating in the fight against trafficking in human beings. These agreements include reciprocal cooperation commitments between the EU and its third-country partners[383]. In February 2014, Parliament approved the conclusion of a readmission agreement with

379 The European Asylum Support Office (EASO), EU Border Agency (Frontex) EU Police Cooperation Agency (Europol) and EU Judicial Cooperation Agency (Eurojust) will work on the ground with the authorities of the frontline Member State to help to fulfil their obligations under EU law and swiftly identify, register and fingerprint incoming migrants. The work of the agencies will be complementary to one another. See more on pg. 101, b) Hot Spot, Special Part, Part IV, of the current Chapter II.

380 COM(2015)0453 final, on EU action plan on return, on 9 September 2015.

381 Directive 2009/52 / EC of the European Parliament and of the Council of 18 June 2009 introducing minimum rules on penalties and measures against employers employing illegally staying third-country nationals OJ L 168, 30.6.2009, p. 24–32.

382 The application of Directive 2009/52/EC of 18 June 2009 providing for minimum standards on sanctions and measures against employers of illegally staying third country nationals, COM(2014) 286 final.

383 The negotiations completed with the following countries resulted in the entry into force of such agreements: Hong Kong (OJ L 17, 24.1.2004, p. 25–39), Macao (OJ L 143, 30.4.2004, p. 99–115), Sri Lanka (OJ L 124, 17.5.2005, p. 43–60), Albania (OJ L 124, 17.5.2005, p. 22–40), Russia (OJ L 129, 17.5.2007, p. 40–60), Ukraine (OJ L 332, 18.12.2007, p. 48–65), Bosnia and Herzegovina (OJ L 334, 19.12.2007, p. 66–83), the Former Yugoslav Republic of Macedonia (OJ L 334, 19.12.2007, p. 7–24), Montenegro (OJ L 334, 19.12.2007, p. 26–44), Pakistan (OJ L 287, 4.11.2010, p. 52–67), Serbia (OJ L 334, 19.12.2007, p. 46–64), Moldova (OJ L 334, 19.12.2007, p. 149–167), Georgia (OJ L 52, 25.2.2011, p. 47–65), Armenia (OJ L 289, 31.10.2013, p. 13–29), Azerbaijan (OJ L 128, 30.4.2014, p. 17–42) and Cape Verde (OJ L 282, 24.10.2013, p. 15–34).

Turkey, which was finally signed on 16 December 2014[384]. On 18 March 2016, a new agreement was signed between the EU and Turkey, which included plans to repatriate to Turkey all irregular immigrants arriving in Greece from 20 March 2016 onwards and a resettlement agreement for Syrians[385].

b) Role of the European Parliament

Parliament actively supports the introduction of a European immigration policy. On the admission of third-country nationals, it has called for the development of legal instruments, and, in particular, measures to reduce incentives for irregular immigration[386].

In the resolution on the Stockholm Programme adopted on 25 November 2009, Parliament urged that integration, immigration and asylum policies be built on full respect for fundamental rights[387].

Since the entry into force of the Lisbon Treaty, Parliament has been actively involved in the adoption of new legislation dealing with immigration. For instance, it played a pivotal role in the drafting and adoption of the 'Return' and 'Single Permit' Directives[388].

In response to the arrival of increasing numbers of migrants on the Union's Mediterranean coasts and the growing number of shipwrecks since the end of 2013, on 17 December 2014 Parliament adopted a resolution on the situation in the Mediterranean and the need for a holistic EU

384 Agreement between the European Union and the Republic of Turkey on the readmission of persons residing without authorisation, OJ L 134, 7.5.2014, p. 3–27.

385 First Report on the progress made in the implementation of the EU-Turkey Statement COM/2016/0231 final.

386 A., WIESBROK (2010), Legal Migration to the European Union, Martinus Nijhoff Publishers.

387 2013/2024(INI) Mid-term review of the Stockholm Programme.

388 Directive 2011/98/EU of the European Parliament and of the Council of 13 December 2011 on a single application procedure for a single permit for third-country nationals to reside and work in the territory of a Member State and on a common set of rights for third-country workers legally residing in a Member State, OJ L 343, 23.12.2011, p. 1–9.

approach to migration, which authorised its Committee on Civil Liberties, Justice and Home Affairs (LIBE) to draft an own-initiative report[389].

Parliament adopted the draft report on 12 April 2016: the report, which deals with an increasingly topical subject, provides the European Parliament with a general framework for its future positions in this field, particularly for the two packages which the Commission published in 2016 on asylum and economic migration [390].

I. High Sea

There are various migratory routes into Europe: the main ones are Eastern Mediterranean, Western Mediterranean and Central Mediterranean. The individual migratory routes are used for different reasons and trends change constantly.

In its analysis of the Eastern Mediterranean route, FRONTEX noted that people smuggling has become an important industry in Turkey, with networks active around Istanbul, Izmir, Edirne and Ankara[391]. The vast majority of migrants on this route arrived in the EU at one of the Greek islands in the Aegean. The nationalities of facilitators vary, though they frequently mirror the nationality of their customers. The Central Mediterranean route is used by smuggler networks established in Libya, from where they cross the Mediterranean Sea[392]. The sea is usually crossed in old, often unseaworthy fishing boats or small rubber dinghies, usually with insufficient fuel and without proper navigation systems. In 2015 there were various fatal accidents resulting in considerable loss of life[393]. The destination on this particular route is usually Malta or Italy (Lampedusa or Sicily). The

389 European Parliament resolution of 17 December 2014 on the situation in the Mediterranean and the need for a holistic EU approach to migration (2014/2907(RSP)).

390 On the situation in the Mediterranean and the need for a holistic EU approach to migration (2015/2095(INI)).

391 European Parliament, Briefing, Implementation Appraisal, (2016), Combatting migrant smuggling into the EU. This briefing is one in a series of 'Implementation Appraisals' on the operation of existing EU legislation in practice.

392 European Parliament, Briefing, Implementation Appraisal, (2016), Combatting migrant smuggling into the EU. This briefing is one in a series of 'Implementation Appraisals' on the operation of existing EU legislation in practice.

393 European Parliament, Briefing, Implementation Appraisal, (2016), Combatting migrant smuggling into the EU. This briefing is one in a series of 'Implementation Appraisals' on the operation of existing EU legislation in practice.

Western African route is, according to FRONTEX, one of the least developed migration/smuggling routes[394]. It runs from Northern/Western Africa to the Canary Islands. FRONTEX noted that on the Western Mediterranean route sea passages are more often done on an individual basis and less often as part of organised networks[395]. Smuggling of migrants is not a priority on this route, as drug smuggling is easier and more lucrative. It should be noted, however, that given the nature of irregular entry, figures can only be estimates.

In some cases, not all entrants will have been detected, while in others, double counting may occur, i.e. *"a large number of the people who were counted when they arrived in Greece were again reported when entering the EU for the second time through Hungary or Croatia"*[396].

Given the high number of migrants attempting to reach Europe, the death toll has also risen to over 3770 migrants lost at sea in 2015[397].

In fact, the Mediterranean generally has the deadliest borders in the world with the International Organization for Migration (IOM) estimating that in 2014, 75% of all border-related fatalities worldwide occurred there[398]. An IOM study estimates that between 2000 and 2014, 22400 people died trying to reach Europe via the Mediterranean[399].

This migration by the sea is quite logical from a numerical point of view: indeed only via sea it is possible to gather relatively large groups of people, this is more difficult for movements by air or on the ground. Indeed, the capacity for receiving irregular migrants on board an airplane became reduced as organized air travel aimed at irregular migration presents serious risks.

Crossing land borders in more or less numerous groups in less supervised areas is substantial, but the statistics of irregular migration by trucks for transport to the Western Europe has become modest: indeed these op-

394 European Parliament, Briefing, Implementation Appraisal, (2016), Combatting migrant smuggling into the EU. This briefing is one in a series of 'Implementation Appraisals' on the operation of existing EU legislation in practice.

395 European Parliament, Briefing, Implementation Appraisal, (2016), Combatting migrant smuggling into the EU. This briefing is one in a series of 'Implementation Appraisals' on the operation of existing EU legislation in practice.

396 Disclaimer, Frontex News October 2015.

397 Ibid.

398 European Parliament, Briefing, Implementation Appraisal, (2016), Combatting migrant smuggling into the EU. This briefing is one in a series of 'Implementation Appraisals' on the operation of existing EU legislation in practice.

399 International Organization for Migration, study: Fatal journeys, tracking life lost during migration, 2014.

erations involve risks both under criminal law and the police and to the migrants' life The risks at the sea are perceived as less serious.

However, transport by sea to be carried at costs migrants can afford, it is often organized on boats which have a very low levels of seaworthiness and security and then end up posing a considerable risk to the survival of the transported, or at least for the conclusion of the operation in terms of modality, time and planned destination.

Indeed, the boats used are often old, outdated, usually too small and they move slowly: for these reasons the are particularly exposed to the atmospheric conditions of the sea.

1. Initiative of some Member States to counteract the irregular migration flow

Italy, because of its geographical position, is one of the Member States most hit by the irregular flow from the sea and in order to counteract the irregular flow of migrants it has implemented a number of initiatives.

Italy's first goal was to establish appropriate measures to safeguard human life at sea in the practices associated with the illegal transport of migrants by sea[400]. On December 1998, the Committee of the International Maritime Organization (IMO) Maritime Safety Agency, to which Italy had turned, promulgated a circular having the nature and effectiveness of a recommendation to Member States of the IMO (Circular MSC/896 of December 16th, 1998)[401].

The subject of the surveillance and control measures provided by circular are vessels in the broad sense, including all vessels suitable for trans-

400 See B. CONFORTI, I. Carta, *Immigrazione, Frontiere Esterne e Diritti Umani*, Teseo Editore, Roma, 2009.

401 The main character of the international act "recommendation", which can be not issued only by organs but also by international conferences, is to not bind the states that it is addressed, albeit with different arguments the doctrine has tried to identify the circumstances and factors they could make it binding acts. In this case, given the magnitude of the majority by which became been adopted by the IMO the Circular in exam, it is possible to attribute considerable importance to the authorization to hold the indicated behaviors, this anyway to put the states of reception of irregular migrants away from protests from most of the states of origin of contrast object flows. It should however be noted that the adoption of the Protocol Against the Smuggling of Migrants has turned into hard law the entire operating device provided by the Circular.

portation by water, even non-displacement crafts or seaplanes used as a means of transport on water[402] (Art. 2.1).

The Circular, addressed to all Member States of the IMO, recommended primarily the compliance with the SOLAS[403] standards of 1974, as amended; secondly invited States to notify the Secretary of the IMO of incidents of use of ships or dangerous practices associated with the trafficking and transport of migrants of which they become aware, and to adopt towards the commanders, officers and crew of these ships, any measure aiming to prevent these persons becoming re-involved in dangerous practices; thirdly the Circular invites them to prevent ships already used for a dangerous practice to again be engaged in such a practice and if those ships are in port to prevent them from sailing (Art. 4).

At the operational level the need to ensure an effective degree of cooperation between States in the enforcement of traffic or transport measures targeting irregular migrants was underlined (Art. 8).

The Circular also introduces a number of measures that aim to combat the threat to human life at sea represented by measures connected with trafficking or the transportation of immigrants. Whenever a coastal state has reasonable suspicion to believe that a ship operating under its own flag or not having a nationality or pretending to operate under a foreign flag when in reality being registered in that State is involved in the type of activities indicated in the Circular, the State can perform the appropriate coercive measures, and can also get the assistance of the other states in order to stop such a ship from carryng out its illegal actions.

Any action implemented by public vessels of the coastal state will have to be proportionate to ensure the safety of human life at sea[404].

402 Except they are only public ships and naval units used for a non-commercial service by the state of belonging. While only warships or military aircraft are entitled to enforcement actions, or other naval or air units identifiable as united in government service authorized to that effect.

403 International Convention for the Safety of Life at Sea and its successive forms is generally regarded as the most important of all international treaties concerning the safety of merchant ships. The first version was adopted in 1914, in response to the Titanic disaster, the second in 1929, the third in 1948, and the fourth in 1960. The 1974 version includes the tacit acceptance procedure – which provides that an amendment shall enter into force on a specified date unless, before that date, objections to the amendment are received from an agreed number of Parties.

404 M. SAVINO, *La crisi migratoria tra Italia e Unione Europea: diagnosi e prospettive*, Editoriale Scientifica, 2017.

The outcome of an investigation into vessels involved in a dangerous activity connected with irregular migration is that the authorities of the coastal state and of the flag state of the ship will reach an agreement on the necessary measures to be implemented. The Member States of the IMO have to prepare a report on the action taken based on the Circular to allow for the identification of gaps in the Circular and to provide improvements (Art. 23 and 24).

2. Protocol against the Smuggling of Migrant by Land, Air and Sea Supplementing the UN Convention against Transnational Organized Crime

It is important to underline the existence of the Protocol against smuggling of migrants by land, air and sea[405] attached to the United Nations Convention against trasnational organized crime[406]. Indeed, another relevant aspect related to irregular migrantion is that, more and more often, the migrant transport organization from the country of origin to the one of the Member State, or from a transit country to the Member States, is run by criminal organizations. Thus, the fight against irregular migration often has the characteristics of the fight against the organized crime[407]. Migrants become subjects of exchange for these organizations and therefore can be considered as victims of organized criminal activity.

For this reason integration of the content of the IMO Circular which considered, from one side, the criminal profiles of the repression of smuggling of migrants, for the reference of the entrance, and also for to the presence of the migrant on the territory of the host country has been necessary. On the other side, reassert strongly the clear necessity for the applicability of humanitarian rules of high level to the migrant, victim (also if voluntary and conscious) of the organization.

To counteract the situation, with reference not only to the maritime transport but also to eventual entrance by land and air, international UN Convention was created.

---

405 The Protocol was approved on behalf of the EU by Council. Decision 2006/616 and by Council Decision 2006/617.

406 See B. CONFORTI, I. *Carta, Immigrazione, Frontiere Esterne e Diritti Umani*, Teseo Editore, Roma, 2009.

407 E. MITZMAN, Il rimpatrio dei migranti irregolari, in M. SAVINO, La crisi migratoria tra Italia e Unione Europea: diagnosi e prospettive, Editoriale Scientifica, Napoli, 2017.

Therefore a Protocol scheme was prepared that could usefully complement the main Convention on international cooperation against transnational organized crime[408].

Within the Protocol, transnational organized crime is considered as the organizer of the regular smuggling and even accomplices who are not integrated into the structure of the criminal organization are subject to criminal prosecution[409].

The acts intended to organize or give instructions to people in sight and for the realization of a human smuggling, are to be evaluated as a criminal law case (Art. 6, par.1 and 2). The norms briefily described until here do not have self-executive character but they need to be implemented by the Member States of the Protocol[410].

The Article 5 contrasts logically and functionally the incriminating norms, which excludes the prosecution of migrants for having turned to a criminal organization and moved illegally in another country, to have benefited from the offered transportation, to have requested the production of identity documents or falsified transport and illegal entry in the territory of another state. Viceversa, the use of false documents in the country of arrival and possession in the time after the arrival by irregular migrants can not be considered covered by the provision of Article 5.

---

408 The originally Italian initiative, then became the Italian-Austrian, was inserted into a negotiated already underway in Vienna, after deliberation of the General Assembly of the United Nations, through the ECOSOC, and in the context of the Commission for the prevention of the crime and criminal justice. The Protocol signed in Palermo during the days 12-15 December 2000 and then in the UN headquarters of New York till December 12, 2002, pursuant to Article 22 became entered into force on 28 January 2004; December 31, 2007 is binding on 108 States. It's been approved by the EU Decision 2006/617 / EC of 24 July 2006, in which (Article 2). It's clear that, in the context of EU law, it applies to the extent that its provisions fall in the scope of Part III, title IV, of the TCE on the profile of comunitary interest (I pillar) and of the European Union Law (III pillar), see S. PASQUETTI, *L´azione della UE nel campo della immigrazione legale: principi e obiettivi*, in *Le Migrazioni*, by U. Leanza, cit. 309 ss.

409 Protocol against the Smuggling of Migrants by Land, Sea and Air, supplementing the United Nations Convention against Transnational Organized Crime, United Nation, New York 2004.

410 Anything (e.g., a document or legislation) that is effective immediately without the need of intervening court action, ancillary legislation, or other type of implementing action. In the case of study, it means these hipotesys of crime need to be implemented into domestic criminal law and the process could be long and the result partially different base on the national law.

This provision is definitely more ambitious than IMO Circular. This latest established only an obligation of mutual information from the authorities to exercice the contrast by sea. Instead the Protocol imposes more far reaching obligations (Art. 10), because it has for object all practices connected to the irregular migration, also previous to the transport, with particular attention to the methods to use in order to recognize false documents of travel of identity.

Other important provisions, to the aim of this research, are those ones which guarantee protection of the migrants. They are intended to guarantee their life and the right not to be subjected to torture in the country of destination but also prohibit the subjected to any cruel, inhuman or degrading treatment, and ensure adequate protection each shape of violence (Art. 16, parr. 1, 2, 3 and 5). Special mention has made for the special needs of children and women (Art. 16, par. 4).

The Protocol provides also norms on the irregular migrants (Art. 18). The obligation of receiving the irregular migrant is of the country of origin or of the state where the migrant has title to reside permanently.

The States of origin allow the state of receiving to return the migrant: for the realization of that they are obliged to guarantee all information on the identity of the migrant and issue the travel documents and the transport necessary to consent the return on their territory[411].

The dispositions of the Protocol do not have a self-executive character, as it is evident from the complexity of the return agreement which contains several obligations with instrumental character aimed to make the return of the migrant easier. The intention is define a kind of *minimum standard* on the matter[412].

The mechanism of contrast of irregular flow by sea above mentioned has had an important impact, under the profile of protection of human life into the sea and humanitarian protection of irregular migrants. It made heavier the risks run by the criminal organization determining major caution respect with the action of contrast to the unites in public services which act into the sea.

---

411 Protocol against the Smuggling of Migrants by Land, Sea and Air, supplementing the United Nations Convention against Transnational Organized Crime, United Nation, New York 2004.

412 Protocol against the Smuggling of Migrants by Land, Sea and Air, supplementing the United Nations Convention against Transnational Organized Crime, United Nation, New York 2004.

3. EU policies against smuggling

Due to the unprecedented number migrants arriving in 2015, the European Union and the Member States alike are facing various challenges which test their migration policies and their ability to cooperate internally, as well as with third countries. The prolonged conflict in Syria has increased the number of asylum seekers and led to people being smuggled across borders. There are various negative consequences that can stem from migrant smuggling. Those being smuggled often face a risk of serious harm or exploitation.

The EU as a whole also faces related challenges, including security and safety concerns as well as socio-economic impacts. According to Europol, over 90% of the more than one million irregular migrants entering the EU in 2015 used some form of "facilitation service" which was generally provided by smuggling networks[413]. Often, migrants are forced to work illegally throughout their journey to pay off their debts to the smugglers[414].

It is important, before continuing, to distinguish between migrant smuggling and human trafficking which is not the same. The concepts are relatively similar and often interconnected as, for instance, a smuggled person can become a trafficked person.

Smuggling of migrants facilitates irregular migration and can be defined as: intentionally assisting a person who is not a national of a Member States to enter, or transit across, the territory of a Member States in breach of the laws of the State concerned on the entry or transit of aliens or intentionally assisting a person who is not a national of a Member States, for financial gain, to reside within the territory of a Member States in breach of the laws of the State concerned on the residence of aliens[415].

Human trafficking consists of: the recruitment, transportation, transfer, harbouring or reception of persons, including the exchange or transfer of control over those persons, by means of the threat or use of force or other forms of coercion, of abduction, of fraud, of deception, of the abuse of power or of a position of vulnerability or of the giving or receiving of pay-

413 EUROPOL, study: Migrant Smuggling in the EU, February 2016.

414 J. O′ CONNEL DAVIDSON, *Troubling freedom: Migration, debt, and modern slavery*, in *Migration Studies*, 1 July 2013, Vol. 1, Issue 2, Pages 176–195.

415 Council Directive 2002/90/EC of 28 November 2002 defining the facilitation of unauthorised entry, transit and residence, OJ L 328, 5.12.2002, p. 17–18.

ments or benefits to achieve the consent of a person having control over another person, for the purpose of exploitation[416].

As a follow-up to the European Council meeting and based on Council Decision 2015/778 in 2015, the EU launched a European Union Military operation in the Southern Central Mediterranean – EUNAVFOR MED[417]. The operation was to undertake systematic efforts to identify, capture and dispose of vessels, as well as enabling confiscation of assets used or suspected of being used by migrant smugglers or traffickers[418].

Apart from this operation, various European agencies, namely Europol and FRONTEX, actively take part in the fight against smuggling. For instance, in March 2015 Europol launched operation JOT (Joint Operational Team) Mare, which focused on combatting the organised crime groups involved in migrant smuggling by boat across the Mediterranean and further into the EU[419]. In February 2016, the JOT Mare operation was integrated into the new European Migrant Smuggling Centre[420]. FRONTEX also launched various operations linked to combatting migrant smuggling, for instance, Lynx (2008)[421] – an operation to decrease migrant smuggling via the eastern border; Poseidon (2010)[422] – an operation tackling smuggling in the Mediterranean; and Triton (2014)[423] – an operation fighting people smuggling in the Mediterranean.

The European Commission is tackling smuggling through various policies. The Communication on the European Agenda on Security[424], published in April 2015, covered terrorism, cybercrime and organised cross

416 Directive 2011/36/EU of the European Parliament and of the Council of 5 April 2011 on preventing and combating trafficking in human beings and protecting its victims, and replacing Council Framework Decision 2002/629/JHA, OJ L 101, 15.4.2011, p. 1–11.

417 Council Decision (CFSP) 2016/2314 of 19 December 2016 amending Decision (CFSP) 2015/778 on a European Union military operation in the Southern Central Mediterranean (EUNAVFOR MED operation SOPHIA), OJ L 345, 20.12.2016, p. 62–64.

418 Factsheet on EUNAVFOR MED Mission, EEAS, February 2016.

419 EU Action Plan against migrant smuggling (2015 – 2020), COM/2015/0285 final.

420 The goal of the Centre is to proactively support EU Member States in dismantling criminal networks involved in organised migrant smuggling. The Centre will focus on geographical criminal hotspots, and will build a better capability across the European Union to fight people smuggling networks.

421 FRONTEX website, https://frontex.europa.eu/.

422 FRONTEX website, https://frontex.europa.eu/.

423 FONTEX website, https://frontex.europa.eu/.

424 COM(2015) 185 final on the European Agenda on Security, on 28 April 2015.

border crime including smuggling. The European Agenda on Migration[425], mentioned above, listed saving lives at sea and tackling criminal smuggling networks as key short-term priorities, while cooperation between enforcement agencies and with non-EU countries, as well as addressing the root causes of migration, were seen as important long-term goals. The European Action Plan against Migrant Smuggling[426] set out these commitments in more detail, including revising smuggling legislation, destroying smuggler vessels and stepping up the seizure and recovery of criminal assets. Other actions included strengthening the JOT MARE operation, developing guidance on migrant smuggling and strengthening bilateral and regional cooperation frameworks and financial support for non-EU countries to tackle smuggling in their territories.

Current European legislation includes two main legal documents relating to migrant smuggling, namely Council Directive 2002/90 establishing a common definition of the offence of facilitation of unauthorised entry, transit and residence, and Council Framework Decision 2002/946/JHA on the strengthening of the penal framework to prevent the facilitation of unauthorised entry, transit and residence. These two documents create what is known as the "facilitators package"[427].

The Directive presents one of the measures to combat aiding irregular immigration[428]. Its purpose is *"'to provide a definition of the facilitation of irregular immigration and to allow effective implementation of Framework Decision 2002/946/JHA"*[429].

The Directive requires that every Member State adopts appropriate sanctions for all persons who intentionally assist non-nationals of the Member States to enter, transit through or reside in the territory of the Member States. The Member States must sanction every incidence of instigation, participation and attempt to aid irregular migration. The Directive does not provide a list of specific sanctions, but only generally requires that the Member States adopt, with regard to this behaviour, their own effective, proportionate and dissuasive sanctions. There is an exception from a gener-

---

425 COM(2015) 240 final, on European Agenda on Migration, on 13 May 2015.

426 COM(2015) 285 final, on EU Action Plan against migrant smuggling (2015 – 2020), on 27 May 2015.

427 EU legal framework against facilitation of unauthorised entry, transit and residence: the Facilitators Package (Directive 2002/90/EC and Framework Decision 2002/946/JHA), SWD(2017) 117 final.

428 Denmark has not taken part in the adoption of this Directive and is not bound by it or subject to its application.

429 Recital 4, Council Directive 2002/90.

al requirement to sanction all the persons assisting the migrants, known as the "humanitarian clause", included in Article 1(2) of the Directive. According to this exception, the Member States may decide not to impose these sanctions in cases where the aim of the behaviour is to provide humanitarian assistance to the person concerned, for example, emergency shelter. This provision thus allows the Member States to "decriminalise" the humanitarian actions of NGOs or individuals. However, this exception clause applies only to facilitation of illegal entry and illegal transit, not to the facilitation of residence[430].

As the decision is intended to strengthen the penal framework for preventing the facilitation of irregular immigration, it requires that the Member States take measures that would punish the conduct defined by Directive 2002/90 with effective, proportionate and dissuasive criminal penalties which may include extradition. The criminal penalties can be accompanied by confiscation of the means of transport used to commit the offence, which is a prohibition on practising the occupational activity in the exercise of which the offence was committed. Acts committed for financial gain should be punished by custodial sentences.

Additionally, legal entities can be held responsible for this conduct. Together, the directive and the decision constitute the Facilitation Package. It is a regulatory plexus adopted nearly fifteen years ago in a context of migration flows, on both the Mediterranean and the "Balkan route" which was significantly different compared to today's reality in at least two aspects: the volume of the flows directed to EU countries, and the serious risk to the safety of migrants in countries of origin, transit and destination.

Unlike the laws around trafficking of human beings[431], the legal framework here has not been updated and remains inadequate to manage the complexities or migration to Europe as we are currently witnessing. The

430 European Parliament, Briefing, Implementation Appraisal, 2016, Combatting migrant smuggling into the EU. This briefing is one in a series of 'Implementation Appraisals' on the operation of existing EU legislation in practice.

431 Directive 2011/36 / EU of the European Parliament and of the Council of 5 April 2011 on preventing and combating trafficking in human beings and protecting victims, replacing Framework Decision 2002/629/JHA, OJ L 101 / 1, 15.4.2011. For a thorough examination of the innovations contained in the Directive, especially in terms of the protection of trafficking victims, v. C. AMALFITANO, *the European Union and protection of victims of trafficking in human beings*, in G. CAGGIANO (eds), *The legal pathways for integration. Migrants and beneficiaries of international protection between EU law and Italian law*, Turin, 2014, p. 753 ss.

framework should be considered as dealing with a structural phenomenon rather than an emergency situation.

The tragic events we are witnessing, unfortunately almost every day in the Mediterranean, with the loss of human lives at sea, are calling for a new reflections on the seriousness of the offence and highlight the need to do more to protect the lives and the rights of migrants.

It may be indicative in this respect to consider the significant proportion of migrants entering irregularly, often thanks to the action of the traffickers[432] rather than entering the Union through regular channels within the quota system, under state jurisdiction according to the Union Treaties and European Institution residual action[433]. It has been estimated that about 80% of the mixed flows across the Mediterranean is the work of traffickers[434].

The presence in the Mediterranean of mixed flows, where a significant proportion of trafficked migrants are refugees fleeing areas of armed conflict, requires consideration of the alternatives that are offered to migrants once criminal organizations that offer the unlawful "journeys of hope"are dismantled: the perspective is often that the migrants themselves are left in war zones where the risk to their lives is higher than that during the crossing of the Mediterranean, and that this explains why, despite the risks, migrants avail themselves of the services of traffickers.

Moreover, the method by which these trips are performed, are often accompanied by exploitation, extortion, violence and inhuman and degrading treatment against migrants, who are forced to perform of all kinds of activities and labour in order to pay for the trip, or a part of it[435]. All of

---

432 In 2015, 1,046,599 migrants have travelled direct to the European border through various routes: the African, the Asian and the Middle East. From January 2016 are already 301,757 people, following the same routes, have undertaken such a journey in an irregular manner often thanks to the action of the traffickers (IOM source). According to the latest Eurostat figures, which date back to 2014 but during 2015 have not undergone an appreciable change in percent, it was estimated the amount of 1.900.00 direct immigrants to the 28 states of the Union from non-EU member countries (available online).

433 Article. 79, par. 5, TFEU provides for the right "of the Member States to determine the volumes of admission to their territory of third-country nationals coming from third countries, in order to seek an employee or self-employment.".

434 V. T. REITANO, L. ADAL, M. SHAW, *Smuggled Futures: The Dangerous Path of the Migrant from Africa to Europe, The Global Initiative against Transnational Organized Crime*, Geneva, 2014, available online.

435 Model Law against the Smuggling of Migrants, United Nation Office on Drugs and Crime, 2010, New York.

these unique factors of the Mediterranean reality puts into question some of the typical elements that characterize the smuggling offence: first, consent.

One of the distinguishing features between smuggling and trafficking consists of the subjective element in trafficking which sees the migrant voluntarily contact the trafficker, to receive a benefit such as the crossing of the border, which offers the same on payment of a fee or of another material benefit[436]. Now, in the presence of migrants fleeing from war zones or armed conflict and crossing the Mediterranean, facing serious risks to their lives and safety, believing that the consent and the will to turn to traffickers happens without any element of coercion or physical or mental violence can influence the validity, is a *fictio iuris*.

Actually turning to traffickers and paying them handsomely cannot be the result of free choice when the alternative is to meet a greater risk, staying in countries ravaged by conflicts thus severely endangering their lives and that of their families. This element is well known and present to traffickers so they can impose any conditions for migrants, being well aware that there are no real alternatives to the trips offered by them.

Second, the manner by which it is realized the conduct of traffickers in the Mediterranean increasingly make similar and overlapping behaviors of which they are victims in the migrant smuggling and trafficking. As pointed out, in addition to the documents cited by the European institutions, also in the UNHCR report dedicated to the routes of African traffickers to Europe, *"risks of human trafficking, abduction and abuse are widely reported along the routes taken by refugees and migrants alike"* [437]. So the consensus of the migrants, even in those cases where it is initially lent validly, during the stages of the journey due to the various forms of exploitation[438] to which migrants are subjected often turns into a relationship of subordina-

436 In the case of trafficking as it is known, there is no consensus or consent is extorted by coercion, deception, threat or use of force and therefore is not validly given.

437 UNHCR, Smuggling and Trafficking from the East and Horn of Africa, Progress Report, October 2014, p. 2.

438 For an example of how the journey can be transformed into opportunity to practice forms of exploitation of each type on migrant v. M. VAN REISEN, C. RIJKEN, *Sinai Trafficking: Origin and Definition of a New Form of Human Trafficking*, in *Social Inclusion*, 2015, p. 113 ss. Among the forms of exploitation include prostitution, sexual servitude, forced labor, the transplantation of organs, slavery and other similar practices.

tion and dependence of the migrant by the trafficker with a relationship far removed from that position "equal".

In the Protocol on the smuggling scheme aggravating circumstances Art. 6 establishes, the fact of endangering, or risk putting in danger the lives and safety of the migrants involved, having them subjected to inhuman or degrading treatment, including exploitation. It seems difficult to distinguish, when the conduct of aiding you consume along with aggravating circumstances described, the smuggling from trafficking given that, for example, the exploitation is an essential element of trafficking.

The reforms of the Facilitation Package announced by the European Union should therefore not ignore those elements of smuggling in the Mediterranean representing an insult and an injury also to the rights of the individual, and thus restate, according to the protection of those rights, at least under the current framework the following profiles. First it expressly provides for the compulsory humanitarian clause that should stop to be considered optional. In the documents of the European institutions is examined in a generic calls for a reform aimed at the non-criminalization of those who provide humanitarian assistance, but does not explicitly indicate the mandatory nature. More generally, however, this option may not be the most effective to "distinguish" the behavior of those who in various ways offer assistance to migrants. In fact in the reform it seems essential to this end to introduce the reference to the profit for the perfecting of aiding and abetting illegal entry, this circumscribes clearly the scope of application of the offense.

Second, it is desirable to insert a provision devoted to regulating the criminal responsibility not only to those who provide humanitarian assistance, but also of trafficked migrants. In the EU legislation, unlike the Protocol, there is no reference to the criminalization of trafficked migrants. The arrangement should express the overcoming of the conception is the busiest migrant as an accomplice of the trafficker, because the consensus that in the circumstances described can not be considered validly given[439]. Such an approach would be difficult to reconcile with the criminalization of trafficked migrants as provided under various legal systems. From the point of terminology and vocabulary that would mean to use to qualify the subjective condition of trafficked migrants, always to the conditions in the Mediterranean today, the term "victims" and to acknowledge that as a real subjectivity as for trafficking. To account in terms of regulation of this change of perspective rather than reform the existing European legislation

439 Conception to which adheres the Facilitation Package.

to a "neutral" solution compared to the criminalization of migrants, the preferred model seems to be that provided for by art. 8 of the Directive is, when requiring Member States not to prosecute or impose penalties on victims of trafficking in human beings for their involvement in criminal activities they have been compelled to commit as a direct result of an act that constitutes the crime of trafficking.

It is appropriate, in addition, the amendment of Directive 2004/81/EC on the residence permit. The current legislation[440] establishes the obligation for Member States to regulate the release of the residence permit, for those who cooperate with the competent judicial authorities, only to victims of crimes related to the trafficking of human beings, even if they have illegally entered the territory of Member States. For third-country nationals involved in irregular immigration, action is instead simply provided the possibility for Member States to introduce a similar tool in their legal system. A revision of that scheme, making it mandatory also for smuggling the preparation of discipline in the granting of a residence permit, is certainly desirable and would find its foundation both the need to counter the danger of the migrant smuggling networks, both in the substantial equalization that occurs in some cases, as we have seen, between the exploitation position in which they are the victims of trafficking with respect to trafficked migrants; elements which make it difficult to justify the continued existence of differences in the Directive. On the occasion of the reform of the directive should be accommodated in the new text the possibility of issuing residence permits even in the presence of various types of needs, such as those related to condition of particular vulnerability in which you can find trafficked migrants.

Finally it is necessary the expansion of the use of aggravating circumstances, as currently provided by the Framework Decision 2002/946/JHA. Within the framework of penalties for traffickers the aggravating circumstance established by the Framework Decision 2002/946 / JHA operate only when the offense endangers the lives of people who are the victims[441]

---

440 As seen is art. 3 dedicated to the scope of the directive which differentiates the regime applicable to trafficking victims by those who instead are involved in aiding and abetting irregular immigration, when it establishes that: "1. Member States shall apply this Directive to third-country nationals who are or have been victims of offenses related to trafficking in human beings, even if they have illegally entered the territory of Member States. 2. Member States may apply this Directive to third-country nationals who have been involved in an action to facilitate irregular immigration ".

441 Art. 1, par. 3 of the Framework Decision.

and not when, as it frequently happens, the migrants are the subject of exploitative, inhuman or degrading treatment, deception, physical or psychological violence. The inclusion of this additional aggravating circumstance, as also required by the Protocol[442], seems particularly appropriate because of the mode, as described above, through which we realize the smuggling of migrants in the Mediterranean.

Ultimately the protection logic is now subordinate to that of the repression and the priority that is assigned to criminal prosecution in combating the phenomenon, this approach facilitated by the use of a single legal instrument adopted with the main objective to combat irregular immigration.

4. The Mediterranean task force

After the tragedy off the Italian island of Lampedusa on 3 October 2013, the EU's most important response was the establishment of a Mediterranean Task Force by the European Commission which on 4 December 2013 suggested several ways to prevent further loss of life[443]. These included reinforcing border surveillance and maritime inter-agency civilian and military cooperation in the operations of FRONTEX. Moreover, EUROSURbecame operational in December 2013 and is used by FRONTEX is an information-exchange system designed to improve the management of the EU external borders[444].

The increasing militarisation of the issue of irregular migration was underscored in December 2013, when the European Council called for the establishment of an EU Maritime Security Strategy by June 2014 as well as for increased synergies between CSDP (the EU's Common Security and Defence Policy) and freedom/security/justice actors to tackle irregular mi-

442 Art. 6 par. 3, letter. b) of the Protocol which refers, in addition to putting in danger, or risk putting in danger the lives and safety of the migrants, inhuman or degrading treatment, including exploitation, of such migrants.

443 On the work of the Task Force Mediterranean, COM(2013) 869 final.

444 The Task Force Mediterranean brought together experts from the Member States of the South of EU, the European Commission, the European External Action Service, EASO, FRONTEX, Europol, FRA and the European Maritime Safety Agency (EMSA). European Commission (2013), Communication from the Commission to the European Parliament and the Council on the work of the Task Force Mediterranean, COM (2013) 869 final. http://ec.europa.eu/dgs/home-affairs/what-isnew/news/news/docs/20131204.

gration[445]. The Council also encouraged the use of CSDP to support third states in border management. The Greek presidency of the Council made irregular migration and maritime security priorities for the first half of 2014[446], which the subsequent Italian presidency then also adopted[447].

The creation of Schengen[448] allows that one Member State controls its section of the external borders on behalf of all the others. Due to their geographical location, and the patterns of travel flows and migratory routes, Member States face different situations.

However, based on the principle of solidarity, the EU needs to provide support to member states to compensate for these differences. There are individual operations carried out by member states[449] as well as Joint Operations which deploy from the EU through FRONTEX [450].

---

445 EUCO 217/13, European Council 19/20 December 2013 Conclusion.

446 Governing Irregular Migration and Asylum at the Borders of Europe: Between Efficiency and Protection Imagining Europe (6), Istituto Affari Internazionali Criminal Justice, Borders and Citizenship Research Paper No. 2602712.

447 Governing Irregular Migration and Asylum at the Borders of Europe: Between Efficiency and Protection Imagining Europe (6), Istituto Affari Internazionali Criminal Justice, Borders and Citizenship Research Paper No. 2602712.

448 The Schengen Agreement, incorporated into EU legislation, focuses on free movement inside the Schengen Area through the creation of a single external border. Checks at the internal borders are abolished, and controls at the external borders are tightened in accordance with a common set of rules, such as how checks are to be carried out, the types of visas needed, and the conditions of entry for third-country nationals. The Schengen Area covers: (a) EU member states except the United Kingdom and Ireland (both have opted out and have a separate arrangement, the Common Travel Area, but take part in some capacity, notably in the Schengen Information System (SIS)), Bulgaria and Romania (in the process of joining, having covered EU requirements according to a European Parliament vote in 2011), Cyprus and Croatia; (b) Several non EU States: Iceland and Norway (both belong to the Nordic Passport Union together with 3 EU member states), Switzerland and Liechtenstein. Additionally, Andorra and San Marino (not part of Schengen) no longer conduct checks at their borders. Schengen signatories may reinstate border controls at its internal borders in the case of serious threat to public policy or internal security, for a period of no more than 30 days or for the reseeable duration of the serious threat if its duration exceeds this. They can do so immediately if there is urgency, and then inform the other members without delay.

449 For example MARE NOSTRUM, an humanitarian and military Italian operation, it will be depth in the text, or XENIOS ZEUS or ASPIDA, two operations conducted by the Greek government.

450 Source from European Commission, www.europa.eu. .

Some relevant and recent examples of Joint Operations[451], useful for the following reflections, are:

- RABIT (Rapid Border Intervention Teams), November 2010-March 2011, created after Greece called for European solidarity and for further European assistance in the field of border operational cooperation. This call resulted from the exceptional pressure of the large number of persons crossing the border irregularly every day. During the operational period, every week close to 200 well-trained guest officers from 26 Member States assisted their Greek colleagues in controlling the border areas as well as in identifying the apprehended irregular immigrants. The deployment of the RABIT at the Greek-Turkish border has established a gradual decrease in the flow of irregular entries at the relevant border sections between Greece and Turkey[452].
- POSEIDON SEA[453], 2010, was carried out at the maritime borders in the Aegean Sea while POSEIDON LAND[454], 2011, was launched right after the RABIT operation for controlling the Greek-Turkish border, as well as in preventing irregular immigration in the Eastern Mediterranean region.
- HERMES[455], February – August 2011, launched by Italy and FRONTEX after the agency received a formal request for assistance from the Italian Ministry of Interior for the extraordinary migratory situation in the Pelagic Islands. The Italian Government requested assistance in strengthening the surveillance of the EU's external borders, assisting the Italian authorities in managing the inflow of migrants from North Africa, particularly arrivals from Tunisia, on the island of Lampedusa[456].

---

451 Source for all JO by FRONTEX, www.fronte.europa.

452 In October, prior to the operation, there were a total of 7 607 persons detected at the Greek-Turkish land border. In November, the operation reported a total of 4 616 detected entries and for the month of December, these detections had fallen further to 3 413. Subsequently, they decreased to 2 266 in January 2011 and to 1 632 in February 2011. Since the deployment of the RABIT operation, the numbers of irregular crossings have dropped by approximately 75 %. See Frontex Annual Risk Analysis 2010.

453 Frontex website, https://frontex.europa.eu/.

454 Frontex website, https://frontex.europa.eu/.

455 Frontex website, https://frontex.europa.eu/.

456 P. FARGUES, C. FANDRICH, 2012, Migration after the Arab Spring, Research Report, MPC Research Report 2012/09, Migration Policy Centre (MPC).

- AENEA, 2012, FRONTEX coordinatedthis operation with Italy as host state[457]. This operation mainly focused on migratory flows from Egypt and Turkey (via Greece) to Italy.
- MOS MAIORUM[458], October 2014, a Joint Police Operation launched by the Italian Presidency of the Council of the European Union. The coordinating authority is the Italian Ministry of Interior. Its purpose was to tackle the illegal trafficking of migrants, also by "apprehending" undocumented migrants and gathering relevant information to fight human trafficking. The operation has been concluded.
- TRITON[459], November 2014, was launched on 1 November 2014 by Italy and FRONTEX after the request of Italy for a significant EU intervention to deal with the exceptional inflows of migrant coming mainly from Syria.

In October 2013 Italyestablished a military and humanitarian operation MARE NOSTRUM[460] to tackle the dramatic increase of migratory flows and consequent tragic ship wreckages off the island of Lampedusa during the second half of the year. The operation, terminated with the start of TRITON[461], existed to improve maritime security, patrol sea lanes, combat illegal activities, especially human trafficking, and tackle the Mediterranean humanitarian emergency in the Sicily Straits. This operation had two official aims: to guarantee the safety of migrants' life at sea and to arrest and prosecute smugglers. It involved personnel, naval and aerial equipment of the Military Navy, Air Force, Army, Coast Guard, Carabinieri, Guardia di Finanza and Military Red Cross, as well as personnel of the Ministry of the Interior, Department of Public Security –Directorate for Immigration and Border Police.

Moreover, the operation MARE NOSTRUM covered a wide area in the Straits of Sicily about 70,000 sq. km, three times Region Sicily. When a migrant boat was detected, the migrants were all rescued and transhipped on military ships; they were provided medical assistance and were brought to an Italian port in Sicily or in other regions in Southern Italy, where they were disembarked[462].

---

457 Frontex website, https://frontex.europa.eu/.
458 Frontex website, https://frontex.europa.eu/.
459 Frontex website, https://frontex.europa.eu/.
460 Italian Ministry of Defense, www.marina.difesa.it.
461 The operation Mare Nostrum was too expensive for the Italian state that needed support for this kind of operation. The EU received the request for help with the Joint Operation Triton.
462 Italian Ministry of Interior, www.interno.gov.it.

Compared to the previous phase actions, there were two remarkable differences. Firstly, in 2011, unless a SAR[463] event was declared an operation at sea started only once the migrant boat entered the contiguous zone (closer than 24 nautical miles from the Italian coast) under the coordination of the Guardia di Finanza[464]; secondly, if the migrant boat was fit to continue its journey, migrants were not transported to Italian vessels, but escorted to the closest Italian port (mainly Lampedusa)[465]. If needed, members of the Italian crew took control of the migrant boat to lead it safely into the port.

In terms of results, MARE NOSTRUM was successful in preventing further shipwrecks and deaths at sea, as well as in identifying and arresting smugglers, as widely acknowledged at national, European and international level. However, its costs, which were almost entirely covered by Italy (available EU funds are limited compared to operational costs) represented a contentious issue and have fuelled a fierce debate on European contribution (or lack thereof) to the operation[466].

Indeed, the costs of the operation and the difficulty to manage the massive number of landings, has brought Italy to request others to share in the managing of the emergency. In this way the new Joint Operation TRITON was born, for which details have been agreed on between FRONTEX and Italy[467]. The operation merged and expanded the HERMES and AENEA operations and the sea area covered is close to the EU shores. The main aim of the operation is the surveillance of the borders and not search and rescue as with MARE NOSTRUM. However, the international law of the

463 SAR, International Convention on Maritime Search and Rescue. It has been adopted in 1979 and entered in force in 1985. http://www.imo.org/About/Pages/ContactUs.aspx.

464 Italian Ministry of Interior, www.interno.gov.it.

465 Italian Ministry of Interior, www.interno.gov.it.

466 A further controversial aspect of MARE NOSTRUM is related to its transparency. While in 2011 rather detailed
information was available about how operations at sea were carried out by the Guardia di Finanza and Coast Guard, the personnel's rules of conduct and the operational procedures of MARE NOSTRUM have never been disclosed. Although the Navy offers a constant update on the ongoing operations through its Twitter account; transparency on procedural elements of the operation is crucial, in particular with regard to possible on-board identification and screening procedures, as it is not clear whether they take place and with what modalities.

467 Council conclusions on "Taking action to better manage migratory flows" Justice and Home Affairs Council meeting
Luxembourg, 10 October 2014.

sea continues to be applied, meaning that the vessels which find persons in danger at sea have the obligation to rescue them[468].

4.1. The lack of protection of human rights in the joint operations

The main problematic aspect in the framework described above on the EU maritime operations, seems to be the lack of protection of human rights of the migrants, who are mostly irregular, within the operations. Indeed, these operations are deployed with a security approach which has as its main purposethe surveying of borders and detecting irregular entry. After detection, these citizens are returned to their country of origin[469].

In 2012 to combat the lack of human rights protection, the independent position of FRO (FRONTEX Fundamental Rights Officer) was created. The FRO' s role is to monitor, assess and make recommendations on the protection and guarantees of fundamental rights in all FRONTEX activi-

468 The duty to render assistance at sea is set out by Article 98 of the LOSC (United Nations Convention on the Law of the Sea). This duty is also regulated by the 1974 Convention for the Safety of Life at Sea (SOLAS Convention), the 1979 Search and Rescue Convention (SAR Convention), and the 1989 International Convention on Salvage. Because of its repetition in treaty and domestic law, and in the light of state practice, even if it is not always uniform, the duty to render assistance is today recognised as a principle of customary law.

469 F. PASTORE, E. ROMAN, *Implementing selective Protection: Comparative Review of the Implementation of Asylum Policies at National Level Focusing on the Treatment of Mixed Migration Flows at EU's Southern Maritime Borders*, FIERI working paper commissioned by the Sachverständigenrat deutscher Stiftungen für Integration und Migration, 2014, www.svr-migration.de. This paper focus on the EU Joint Operation, consequently the critic aspects analyzed here are related to these operations. However, it is necessary stressed on this regard that also the national operations, as the Greek XENIOS ZEUS operation, have been criticized for the violations of human rights. For example, the XENION ZEUS operation mentioned, which had the goal according to the Greek Police to seal the borders; return undocumented immigrants to their countries of origin; and "reinstate the rule of law" in the centre of Athens, has been heavily criticized as a discriminatory practice, among others by ECRE, Amnesty International, Human Rights Watch and the Greek Council for Refugees. Moreover, this kind of operation, as showed by a Greek project (Midas project, Assessing the cost-effectiveness of irregular migration control policies in Greece, by Danay Angeli, Anna Triandafillydou, Angeliki Dimitriadi) does not have a good cost-effective political tool: as more than 90% of resources are spent on checks that did not lead to the detection of irregular. Additionally, forced return via charter flight is the most expensive type of return, both in terms of cost and human resources.

ties and operations. On a similar note, the European Ombudsman, Emily O'Reilly, announced on 22 October 2014 that her office has opened an investigation into how FRONTEX ensures respect of fundamental rights in the context of forced returns under the agency's joint return operations (JROs).

The inquiry also looks at FRONTEX's cooperation with national monitoring bodies as per Article 9(1b) of the FRONTEX Regulation[470] and Article 8(6) of the Return Directive[471]. Ms O'Reilly highlighted that *"by their very nature, forced return operations have the potential to involve serious violations of fundamental rights. Through this investigation, I want to find out how FRONTEX is equipped to deal with potential violations and how it minimises the risk of such violations."*[472]

Both currently and in the past, there has been much criticism, in particular from NGO's, on several operations for the stigmatization of irregular migrants as criminal. This criminalization contributed to the lack ofeffective protection of human rights.

A debate on this issue was developed following the creation of the MOS MAIORUM and TRITON operations[473].

The most relevant criticism of the MOS MAIORUM operation concerned its use of mass identification. With the EU facing a demand for a more speedy return policy, the EU implemented a probable mass identification of people. This policy has shown to be very similar to round-ups as it has a very low chance of success in identifying refugees.

4.2. The lack of search and rescue joint operations

The main criticism of the TRITON operation was that there was no search and rescue for migrants making the trip across the sea. The vessels used by the smugglers are not able to survive a trip across the sea when they leave their shore of departure. The area covered from the EU operation is only close to the EU shores, thus many migrants are destined to die at the sea,

470 Regulation EC No. 2007/2004 of 26 October 2004, O.J.L. 349, 25 November 2004, p.1-11.

471 Directive 2008/115/EC, 16 December 2008, O.J.L. 348, 24 December 2008, p. 98-107. Website www.eurlex.europa.eu.

472 European Ombudsman, Press release no. 20/2014, 22 October 2014.

473 Mos Maiorum, a shortsighted and inhuman policy clashing with the humanitarian issue at the foundation of Europe (2014), ASGI (Association for Juridical Studies on Immigration).

far away from the EU shores because their vessels will not be detected in most cases (also whether it continues to be applied the international law of the sea and SAR[474], which provides to rescue persons into the sea who risk their life). That could mean transforming the Mediterranean sea into a cemetery[475].

Moreover, operations such as MARE NOSTRUM have been useful in fighting against trafficking in human beings[476], but an operation such as TRITON did not seem have the suitable equipment and funds to achieve this aim.

Furthermore, the level of participation by Member States in Triton was not clear: it was not clarified whether the countries whose vessels will rescue smuggled migrants will disembark the latter on their territory or on the closest shore and therefore, it is not known which country should have taken the responsibility for possible asylum claims[477].

A new tool was launched on October 2016: the European Border and Coast Guard Agency, already briefly mentioned before, building on the basis of FRONTEX[478].

---

474 Website www.imo.org.

475 P. FARGUE, S. BONFANTI, *When the best option is a leaky boat: why migrants risk their lifes crossing the Mediterranean and what Europe is doing about it*, Migration Policy Center, EUI, 2014, Italy.

476 P. DE BRUYCKER, A. DI BARTOLOMEO, *Migrants smuggled by sea to the EU: facts, laws and policy options*, MPC Research Report 2013/09.

477 On 27 October 2014 the new Foreign Office Minister Lady Joyce Anelay announced that Britain will not support future search and rescue operations carried out in the Mediterranean to prevent the death of migrants at Europe's borders. The British Foreign Office has argued that they will not participate in TRITON because they claim that search and rescue operations in the Mediterranean have become a 'pull factor' which encourages people to migrate to Europe. Human rights organisations such as the British Refugee Council, Statewatch and Amnesty International have denounced the British government's decision as they consider that such operations are crucial in order to avoid further mass drowning of migrants. They state that by refusing to rescue people fleeing from war and persecution,
Britain is not living up to its international commitments. This is just one example of highly divergent views on the issue inside the European Union.

478 Regulation (EU) 2016/1624 of the European Parliament and of the Council of 14 September 2016 on the European Border and Coast Guard and amending Regulation (EU) 2016/399 of the European Parliament and of the Council and repealing Regulation (EC) No 863/2007 of the European Parliament and of the Council, Council Regulation (EC) No 2007/2004 and Council Decision 2005/267/EC, OJ L 251, 16.9.2016, p. 1–76.

The new Agency will have a stronger role in supporting, monitoring and, when necessary, reinforcing national border guards, focusing primarily on early detection and prevention of weaknesses in the management of the EU external borders.

The Agency's permanent staff will be more than doubled and the Agency will be able to purchase its own equipment. A rapid reserve pool of at least 1,500 border guards and a technical equipment pool will be put at the disposal of the Agency[479]. The European Border and Coast Guard will now ensure the implementation of Union standards of border management through periodic risk analysis and mandatory vulnerability assessments. In addition, the Agency will have a mandate to assist neighbouring non-EU countries in handling high migratory pressure[480].

NATO effectively contributes to the EU's efforts to stem illegal trafficking and irregular migration through intelligence, surveillance and reconnaissance in the Aegean Sea[481]. NATO maritime forces are deployed in the Aegean Sea to contribute with critical, real-time information to fight smuggling and break the business model of criminal networks. The mission, which was launched in February, includes early warning and surveillance activities and the sharing of operational information with FRONTEX and with the Greek and Turkish Coast Guards. In March 2016, Frontex and NATO reached a common understanding on the practicalities of their cooperation in the Aegean Sea.

NATO is considering possible additional support to international efforts in the Mediterranean, complementing and in cooperation with the European Union[482].

---

479 Regulation (EU) 2016/1624 of the European Parliament and of the Council of 14 September 2016 on the European Border and Coast Guard and amending Regulation (EU) 2016/399 of the European Parliament and of the Council and repealing Regulation (EC) No 863/2007 of the European Parliament and of the Council, Council Regulation (EC) No 2007/2004 and Council Decision 2005/267/EC, OJ L 251, 16.9.2016, p. 1–76.

480 Regulation (EU) 2016/1624 of the European Parliament and of the Council of 14 September 2016 on the European Border and Coast Guard and amending Regulation (EU) 2016/399 of the European Parliament and of the Council and repealing Regulation (EC) No 863/2007 of the European Parliament and of the Council, Council Regulation (EC) No 2007/2004 and Council Decision 2005/267/EC, OJ L 251, 16.9.2016, p. 1–76.

481 European Commission Report EU operations in the Mediterranean Sea, 4 October 2016.

482 European Commission Report EU operations in the Mediterranean Sea, 4 October 2016.

To take urgent action against traffickers and human smugglers in the Central Mediterranean, EU Naval Force Mediterranean Operation Sophia[483] was launched on 22 June 2015 following a decision by the European Council.

Its objective is to contribute to the wider EU efforts to disrupt the business model of criminal networks in the Central Mediterranean and thus prevent further loss of life at sea.

The operation's core mandate is to identify, capture and dispose of vessels and enabling assets used or suspected of being used by migrant smugglers or traffickers. The operation is designed around 4 phases. The first phase, which has been concluded, saw the deployment of forces to build a comprehensive understanding of smuggling activity and methods. The second phase includes the search, boarding, seizure and diversion of smugglers' vessels on the high seas under conditions provided for by applicable international law. Future phases, subject to the necessary legal framework established by UN Security Council Resolutions, will include taking operational measures against vessels and related assets suspected of being used by human smugglers or traffickers inside coastal states' territory[484]. All activities undertaken by the operation adhere to and are conducted under full respect of international law, including human rights, humanitarian and refugee law and the principle of non-refoulement[485].

5. Application of human rights law at sea

In relation to interceptions, rescues, or other encounters with migrant-smuggling vessels within a State's internal waters or territorial sea, there is no substantial difference in the application of the law: human rights and refugee law to which that State is bound will apply in exactly the same way as it would if the event were enterily contained within a State's land borders. It remains only to consider whether an obligation has in fact been

483 Operation Sophia has been named after a baby born on 24 August 2015 on board the German frigate Schleswig-Holstein, operating in the Central Mediterranean as part of the EUNAVFOR MED Task Force.

484 UN Security Council Resolution No 2240 (2015).

485 Political and Security Committee Decision (CFSP) 2018/1219 of 23 August 2018 on the appointment of the EU Force Commander for the European Union military operation in the Southern Central Mediterranean (EUNAVFOR MED operation SOPHIA) and repealing Decision (CFSP) 2017/2432 (EUNAVFOR MED/1/2018) ST/11334/2018/INIT, Official Journal L 226, 7.9.2018, p. 5–6.

breached and whether that breach can be attributed to the State in question. Once these two tests are satisfied then an internationally wrongful act, incurring that State's legal responsibility, will be established.

A much more difficult set of issues arise when the response occurs outside the territory of the State (on the high seas or in the territorial waters of another State). Territorial waters refers to that part of the ocean immediately adjacent to the shores of a state and subject to its territorial jurisdiction. The state possesses both the jurisdictional right to regulate, police, and adjudicate the territorial waters and the proprietary right to control and exploit natural resources in those waters and exclude others from them[486]. Territorial waters differ from the high seas, which are common to all nations and are governed by the principle of freedom of the seas.

The high seas are not subject to appropriation by persons or states but are available to everyone for navigation, exploitation of resources, and other lawful uses. The legal status of territorial waters also extends to the seabed and subsoil under them and to the airspace above them[487].

Whether and under what circumstances a state that is party to a particular human rights treaty (or under a customary law obligation) owes legal obligations under that treaty (or customary rule) to a person who is not within the territory of that State is a difficult question and in many respects the critical issue for the international law on migrant smuggling.

Commentators have identified the growing shift toward extraterritorial immigration control as motivated largely by a desire to avoid the substantive and procedural guarantees to which migrants, including those who have been smuggled, are entitled[488]. Even if this does not hold true for all smuggling-related interventions at sea, it is clearly essential to examine whether States are indeed able to shift or minimize their obligations in this way and, if so, under what circumstances. International human rights treaties generally specify their scope of application as extending to every person within their territory and/or under their jurisdiction[489].

---

486 Convention on the Territorial Sea and the Contiguous Zone, Geneva on 29 April 1958.

487 Art. 2, Section I, General Provisions, UNCLOS.

488 See generally B. RYAN, *Extraterritorial Immigration Control: What Role for Legal Guarantees?*, in B. RYAN and V. MITSLEAGAS eds., *Extraterritorial Immigration Control: Legal Challenges* 1, 2010.

489 For instance International Covenant on Civil and Political Rights, 999 UNTs 171, done Dec. 16, 1996, entered into force Mar. 23, 1976 (ICCPR), at Art. 2(1); Convention against Torture and Other Cruel, Inhuman or Degrading Treat-

The notion of being under the jurisdiction of a State has been interpreted by the Human Rights Committee in connection with the International Covenant on Civil and Political Rights (ICCPR) as meaning that a state Party must respect and ensure the rights laid down in the Covenant to anyone within its *de facto* jurisdiction, that is, persons who are *"within the power or effective control of that State Party, even if not situated within the territory of the State Party"*[490]. It futher confirmed that enjoyment of Covenant rights is not limited to citizens of States Parties but must also be available to all individuals, regardlessness of nationality or statelessness, such as asylum seekers, refugees, migrant workers and other persons, who may find themselves in the territory or subject to the jurisdiction of the State Party. This therefore applies to irregular migrants.

Althought not explicitly adopting the "power and control" test[491], the International Court of Justice has generally affirmed that provisions of human rights treaties will apply to actions of a State outside its territory even where the terms of the treaty do not envisage such extraterritorial application[492].

At regional level, the most substantial jurisprudence has emerged from consideration of the scope of application of the European Convention on Human Rights. The starting point is an acceptance of the essentially territorial nature of this instrument and a corresponding reluctance to interpret the Convention as being applicable to all State Party conduct everywhere. The focus has accordingly been on establishing the parameters of exeptions. Althought earlier cases of the European Court of Human Rights emphasized effective control over territory[493], judgments have moved toward recognition of the exercise of power and authority over individuals as sufficient to establish jurisdiction[494].

---

ment or Punishment, 1465 UNTS 85, done Dec. 10, 1984, entered into force June 26, 1987, at Art. 2.

490 UN Human Rights.

491 A. T. GALLAGHER, F. DAVID, *The international law of migrant smuggling*, Cambridge University Press,2014.

492 *Legal Consequences of the Construction of a Wall in the Occupied Palestinian Territory (Advisory Opinion)*, 2004, ICJ Rep 136 (*Israeli Wall Advisory Opinion*), at para. 111. See also *Armed Activities on the Territory of the Congo (Democratic Republic of the Congo v. Uganda)*, (2005) ICJ Rep 168, at para. 216.

493 Most famously *Bankovic and Others v. Belgium and Others*, (2007) 44 EHRR SE5 (ECHR, Dec. 12, 2001). For further analysis of this case references to the extensive and largely critical literature.

494 Most recently by the European Court of Human Rights in *Al-Skeini and Others v. United Kingdom*, 2011, 53 EHRR 18 ECHR, July 7, 2011; *Al-Jedda v. United*

A case, involving scenarios of relevance to the issue of smuggling by sea, deserves to be briefly mentioned: in the 2012 case of *Hirsi Jamaa v. Italy* (high seas interception and push-back to Libya of smuggled Somalia and Eritrean nationals by the Italian coast guard), the Court found that Italy had exercised both *de jure* and *de facto* jurisdiction over the applicant, specifically stating its view that *"The removal of aliens carried out in the context of interceptions on the high seas by the authorities of a State in the exercise of their sovereign authority, the effect of which is to prevent migrants from reaching the borders of the State or even to push them back to another State, constitutes an exercise of jurisdiction..."*[495].

The Court held that Italy's actions violated fundamental rights, including the prohibition on torture and inhuman or degrading treatment or punishment and the prohibition of collective expulsion of non-nationals, despite the relevant actions occurring outside Italy's territory. Critically, the fact that this was billed as a search and rescue operation, that the Italian authorities had not boarded the vessels, and that they had not used weapons, did not affect the Court's judgment on the point of jurisdiction and extraterritorial application of the European Convention on Human Rights. The ruling does appear to be, in the words of one commentator *"a resounding endorsement of the responsibility of States for their migration control activities at sea"*[496].

It is reasonable to argue that extraterritorial human rights obligations will arise *"when a State exercises control, power or authority over people or situations located outside its sovereign territory in a way that could have an impact on the enjoyment of human rights by those people or in such situation"*[497]. There can be little doubt that interception or rescue of a migrant smuggling vessel on the high seas or in the territory of another State, which involves con-

---

Kingdom, 2011, 53 EHRR 23, ECHR, July 7, 2011. For earlier examples of the same approach see *Ilascu and Others v. Moldova and Russia*, 2005, 40 EHRR 46, ECHR, July 8, 2004, at paras. 312, 314; and *Issa and Others v. Turkey*, 41 EHRR 27, ECHR, Mar. 30 2005, at para. 71.

495 *Hirsi Jamaa v. Italy*, ECtHR – Hirsi Jamaa and Others v Italy [GC], Application No. 27765/09, at para. 180.

496 C. COSTELLO, *Courting Access to Asylum in Europe: Recent Supranational Jurisprudence Explored*, 2012, in 12 *Human Rights Law Review* 287, at 300.

497 O. DE SCHUTTER, A. EIDE, A. KHALFAN, M. ORELLANA, M. SALOMON, and I. SEIDERMAN, *Commentary to the Maastricht Principles on Extraterritorial Obligations of States in the Area of Economic, Social and Cultural Rights*, 2013, 34 *Human Rights Quarterly* 1084, at 1090.

duct such as boarding the vessel, altering its course, or detaining persons on board fall within this "power, control or authority" test[498].

This leaves unanswered the question of whether States owe extraterritorial human rights obligations to smuggled migrants at sea who are not intercepted or rescued.

6. Further specific human rights issues

A relevant distinction between operations that are exclusively about search and rescue and those that are concerned with responding to irregular migration must also be considered, as there may well be a difference in the nature and substance of the applicable human rights obligations[499].

6.1. Use of force, inhuman treatment and violations of the right to life

Regarding the use of the force according to the Law of the sea, although certain provisions of the law of the sea support coercive action, the United Nations Convention on the Law of the sea (UNCLOS) itself does not provide specific rules on the use of force. It is widely accepted, however, that rules governing the use of force in other areas are generally applicable to actions of States at sea. This means that use of force must be avoided as far as possible. When force is used it must be proportionate[500]. Proportionality implies elements of both reasonableness and necessity. Critically, as the Law of the Sea Tribunal has affirmed, *"considerations of humanity must ap-*

498 A. T. GALLAGHER, F. DAVID, *The international law of migrant smuggling*, Cambridge University Press, 2014.

499 Tondini takes this position, arguing that it is not reasonable to expect that an official vessel engaged in a salvage operation be burdened in this way: "Human rights provisions such as the prohibition of collective deportation cannot be applied to a genuine SAR intervention, otherwise any rescue of people in distress at sea, even when not migrants, would turn into a possibly involuntary and virtual access of such people to the flag state´s territory, with all the consequences of the case, including the necessity to take them back inland for identification, possibly to a national port located thousands of miles away and irrespective of the survivors´ will to be disembarked to the closest´ safe third country." Tondini, "The Legality of Intercepting Boat People" at 73.

500 M. TONDINI, *The use of force in the course of maritime law enforcement operations*, in Journal on the Use of Force and International Law, 4:2, 2017, 253-272.

ply in the law of the sea as they do in other areas of international law"[501]. The search and rescue regime does not appear to envisage use of force, and it has been argued that such a regime could not reasonably be applied to irregular migrants against whom force is required to be used to effect the "rescue"[502].

That means that the States have a duty, when intercepting or otherwise dealing with a migrant smuggling vessel, its passengers, and crew, to avoid using force that causes any unnecessary harm. For instance, use of force under this standard may include towing a boat load of disstred migrants in an overcrowded vessel back to the point of embarkation, or using weapons to move unwilling migrants from one vessel to another. Human rights law provides an important additional constraint on the use of force in responding to smuggling by sea. The International Court of Justice has affirmed that the prohibition on inhuman and degrading treatment is "*among the rules of general international law which are binding on States in all circumstances, even apart from any treaty commitments*"[503].

That prohibition is likely to extend to the actions outlined previously as well as to other responses that lead or contribute to suffering or hardship of smuggled migrants and their crew, such as the withholding of medical treatment. The prohibition on inhuman and degrading treatment would also be violated through the failure of a State that is in a position to do so to come to the aid of migrants at sea who are at risk of physical harm whether from the circumstances of their journey or at the hands of their smugglers.

The right to life, recognized in all major human rights instruments, extends to all persons, including those who are smuggled by sea and their smugglers, irrespective of legal status, nationality, conduct, or any other consideration[504]. The Migrant Smuggling Protocol makes explicit reference to the international legal obligation on States to preserve and protect

---

501 M/V "Saiga", No.2. Case St. Vincent and the Grenadines v. Guinea, judgment of International Tribunal for the Law of the Sea, at para. 155.

502 M. TODINO, *The Legality of Intercepting Boat People Under Search and Rescue and Border Control Operations with Reference to Recent Italian Interventions in the Mediterranean Sea and the Ecthr Decision in the Hirsi Case*, in Journal of International Maritime Law, April 2012, Vol. 18, No. 1, pp. 59-74. at 62: "*In the case of active resistance, the interception cannot fall within the SAR legal regime*".

503 *Ahmadou Sadio Diallo (Republic of Guinea v. Democratic Republic of the Congo)*, 2010, ICJ, Rep 639, at para. 87.

504 See, as example, ICCPR, at Art. 6(1): "Every human being has the inherent right to life".

the right to life of smuggled migrants[505]. Coercive actions that threaten or result in loss of life whether deliberate (such as the pushback of an unseaworthy vessel) or accidental (such as occurred in the situation that was the subject of the Xhavara case[506]) would appear to be in violation of the positive obligations attached to the right to life[507]. Failure of State to come to the rescue of smuggled migrants or migrant smuggling vessels that are in distress, would also constitute a clear violation of this core human rights obligation.

6.2. Arbitrary detention

Smuggled migrants intercepted or rescued at sea (and their crew) may be detained on the vessel of interception/rescue. They may also be returned to the place of disembarkation and subsequently placed under detention. In brief, provided States are in a position to lawfully exercise enforcement jurisdiction, the detention of persons intercepted or rescued at sea, including smuggled migrants and persons seeking asylum is not, per se, arbitrary[508]. However, the prohibition on arbitrary detention[509] has been interpreted as requiring legally authorized detention to be reasonable and necessary in all of the circumstances of the case, and to be a proportionate means to achieve a legitimate aim[510]. Deprivation of liberty provided by law must not be "manifestly disproportional, unjust or unpredictable"[511]. The man-

505 Migrant Smuggling Protocol, Art. 16(1): "*In implementing this Protool, each States Party shall take, consistent with its obligations under international law, all appropriate measures, including legislation if necessary, to preserve and protect the rights of persons who have been the object of conduct set forth in article 6 of this Protocol as accorded under applicable international law, in particular the right to life and the right not to be subjected to torture or other cruel, inhuman or degrading treatment or punishment* ".

506 Xhavara case, 2017/C 424/01, Court of Justice of European Union.

507 For a consideration of State obligations to take positive measures to ensure the right to life, see M. NOWAK, *U.N. Covenant on Civil and Political Rights – CCPR Commentary*, 2nd revised ed. 2005, *Novak, CCPR Commentary*, at 122-124.

508 See A. v. Australia, UNHCR Comm. No. 560/1993, UN Doc. CCPR/C/59/D/560/1993, Apr. 30, 1997, decided Apr. 3, 1997, at para. 9.3:"There is no basis for the claim that it is per se arbitrary to detain individuals requesting asylum.".

509 Article 9 (1) ICCPR.

510 See Hugo van Alphen v. The Netherlands, UNHRC Comm. No. 305/1988, UN Doc. CCPR/C/39/D/305/1988, Aug. 15, 1990, decided July 23, 1990, at para. 5.8.

511 Nowak, CCPR Commentary, at 225.

ner in which a decision is taken to deprive someone of his or her liberty must be capable of being deemed appropriate and proportionate in view of the circumstances of the case. A detention situation that was originally not arbitrary might become arbitrary if it continues over time without proper justification. Irrespective of the lawfulness of the detention, smuggled migrants detained at sea or following a rescue or interception at sea must be treated with humanity and with respect for the inherent dignity of their person[512].

6.3. Collective expulsion

The term "collective expulsion" refers to any measures compelling non-nationals, as a group, to leave a country or the territory of a country, except where such a measure is taken on the basis of a reasonable and objective examination of the particular case of each individual member of the group. International law prohibits States from engaging in collective expulsion[513], irrespective of the legal status of the individuals concerned, and even when those expulsions do not violate the prohibition on *non refoulement*. The requirement of a reasonable, objective, and individualized assessment is unlikely to be met through a process carried out on board a migrant smuggling vessel or a vessel of interception or rescue.

The obligation of individual determination was highlighted in the judgment of the European Court of Human Rights in *Hirsi Jamaa v. Italy*, mentioned above, which included considerations of whether a high seas inter-

512 ICCPR, at Art. 10(1).

513 The prohibition set out in Article 4 of Protocol 4 to the ECHR is also recognized in other international and regional conventions. It is noted that Article 19(1) of the Charter of Fundamental Rights of the European Union also provides that 'Collective expulsions are prohibited.' Similarly, Article 22(1) ICMW stipulates as follows: 'Migrant workers and members of their families shall not be subject to measures of collective expulsion. Each case of expulsion shall be examined and decided individually.' Notable also is Article 7(1) of the Draft Articles on Expulsion of Aliens, provisionally adopted by the Drafting Committee of the International Law Commission (ILC) in its ongoing work on the subject. It may therefore be observed that the prohibition of collective expulsion has evolved as a principle of general international law. Report of the International Law Commission, Fifty-ninth session (7 May-5 June and 9 July-10 August 2007), U.N. Doc. A/62/10, para. 239; United Nations Committee on the Elimination of Racial Discrimination, General Comment 30 on the Rights of Non-Citizens, U.N. Doc. CERD/C/64/Misc.11/rev.3 (2005), para. 26.

ception and removal of smuggled migrants to a third country (deemed to be an exercise of jurisdiction by Italy) violated the European Convention on Human Rights prohibition on collective expulsion. In that case the Court found that Italy had indeed violated the prohibition of collective expulsion in its interception and transfer of smuggled migrants back to Libya because *"the transfer of the applicants to Libya was carried out without any form of examination of each applicant´s individual situation"*[514]. The Court rejected a territorial limitation on the prohibition on collective expulsion. The Court further noted that this would create discrepancy between the protections available to migrants traveling by sea as compared to those using land routes[515].

6.4. An obligation of non-refoulment at sea

International human rights law prevents States from returning smuggled migrants who are rescue or intercepted at sea back to their point of embarkation or to another place where there is a credible risk that such return will result in serious violations of human rights, including torture and arbitrary deprivation of the right to life[516].

International refugee law imposes the same obligation with respect to asylum-seekers who are at risk of persecution on one of the established grounds. The obligation of non-refoulment applies, not just to persons who are formally recognized as refugees or beneficiaries of complementary protection under human rights law, but also to asylum-seekers pending a final determination of their claim[517]. Interception of smuggled migrants

514 *Hirsi Jamaa v. Italy*, at para. 185, and futher: *"It has not been disputed that the applicants were not subjected to any identification procedure by the Italian authorities, which restricted themselves to embarking all the intercepted migrants onto military ships and disembarking them on Libyan soil. Moreover, the Court notes that the personnel aboard the military ships were not trained to conduct individual interviews and were not assisted by interpreters or legal advisers"*.

515 ECtHR, Hirsi Jamaa and Others v Italy [GC], Application No. 27765/09.

516 Convention against Torture and Other Cruel Inhuman or Degrading Treatment or Punishment, 1465 UNTS, 10 December 1984, entered into force 25 June 1987 (Convention against Torture) as well as major regional human rights instruments.

517 UNHCR Advisory Opinion on the Extraterritorial Appliation of Non-refoulment Obligations, at para. 6.

on the high seas does not, of itself, violate the prohibition on refoulement[518].

However, the risk is certainly present. UNHCR has made clear its view that *"interception measures should not result in asylum-seekers and refugees being denied access to international protection, or result in those in need of international protection being returned, directly or indirectly, to the frontiers of territories where their life or freedom would be threatened on account of a Convention ground, or where the person has other grounds for protection based on international law."*[519].

The obligation of non-refoulment relates to the actual risk of a person being subjected to a serious human rights violation or persecution as a result of his or her expulsion or return. As a result, States are prevented from returning smuggled migrants to a country that will, in turn, return them to a place where their life or liberty is in danger[520]. This prohibition was a key basis for the European Court of Human Rights′ finding in *Hirsi Jamaa v. Italy* that Italy′s return of intercepted migrants to Libya was unlawful[521].

II. Hot Spot

As part of a package of immediate actions to counter the unfolding migration crisis, the Commission announced a series of measures in May 2015,

518 G. GOODWIN-GILL, J. MCADAMAT, *The Refugee in International Law,* Oxford University Press, 2007.

519 UN High Commissioner for refugees Executive Committee, *Conclusion on protection Safeguards in Interception Measures*, Doc. No. 97 (LIV) – 2003, Oct. 10, 2003, at para. (a)(iv).

520 This situation, generally referred to as "chain *refoulement*", has been described by UNHCR as follows: *"the risk that the person would be sent by the Third State to another State in which he or she would not receive effective protection or would be at risk of being sent from there on to any other State where such protection would not be available"*: UN High Commissioner for Refugees, *Summary Conclusions on the Concept of "Effective Protection" in the context of Secondary Movements of Refugees and Asylum-Seekers (Lisbon Expert Roundtable, 9-10 December 2002), Feb. 2003 (UNHCR, Summary conclusions on the Concept of "Effective Protection" in the Context of Secondary Movements of Refugees and Asylum-Seekers),* at para. 15(c).

521 *Hirsi Jamaa v. Italy*, at paras. 146-148, 209, and at 80 (concurring opinion of Judge Pinto de Albuquerque). For a similar finding by the Australian High Court in Plaintiff M70 and Plaintiff M106 v. Minister for Immigration and Citizenship (Plaintiff M70/2011 and Plaintiff M106/2011 v. Minister for Immigration and citizenship (2011) 244 CLR 144 (Aus. HC, Aug 31, 2011), at para. 249.).

including the "hotspot approach" and "relocation measures"[522]. Both were endorsed by the European Council with the hope of better containing the growing flows of irregular migration *inter alia* through the "*reinforcement of the management of the Union's external border*"[523].

In the European Agenda on Migration, hotspots were presented as an initiative to assist frontline states to swiftly identify, register and fingerprint incoming migrants – or as comprehensive and targeted support by the EU Agencies to frontline Member States. As the official definition of the Commission, a "Hotspot" is a section of external borders characterized by specific and disproportionate migratory pressure, consisting of mixed migratory flows. The "hotspot approach" means that EU Agencies intervene in a coordinated manner through "Migration Management Support Teams", relying essentially on personnel and equipment to be made available by other Member States.

Italy and Greece are the first two Members States where this Hotspot approach is currently being implemented. Other Member States can also benefit from the Hotspot approach upon request. Indeed, the EU, in the Conclusions of 25-26 June 2015[524] of the European Council charged the Commission in collaboration with the Member States to draw up a roadmap by July 2015 on the legal, financial and operational aspects of the "Hotspots". This explanatory note[525] elaborates on the concept of the "Hotspot" approach.

The European Asylum Support Office (EASO), the EU Border Agency (FRONTEX), the EU Police Cooperation Agency (Europol) and the EU Judicial Cooperation Agency (Eurojust) work on the ground with the authorities of the frontline Member State to help to fulfil their obligations under EU law and swiftly identify, register and fingerprint incoming migrants. The work of the agencies will be complementary to one another[526].

522 COM/2015/0240 final, European Agenda on Migration.

523 COM/2015/0240 final, European Agenda on Migration.

524 EUCO 22/15, 26 June 2015.

525 The annexes to this explanatory note consist of two roadmaps setting out the way in which that approach is implemented in practice in Italy and in Greece, and an annex consisting of a flowchart setting out the workflow under the "Hotspot" approach. The explanatory note and the roadmaps have been prepared in close collaboration with the EU Agencies and with the host Member States, in this case, Italy and Greece.

526 M. SAVINO, *La crisi migratoria tra Italia e Unione Europea: diagnosi e prospettive*, Editoriale Scientifica, 2017.

The Hotspot approach will also contribute to the implementation of the temporary relocation schemes proposed by the European Commission[527]: people in clear need of international protection will be identified in frontline Member States for relocation to other EU Member States where their asylum application will be processed.

Not included in this "comprehensive and targeted support" are the reception of claimants and the processing of claims. Returns also remain essentially in the hands (and on the budget) of the host state despite some funding and assistance being available from the EU. The host state must finally submit a "roadmap" setting out "complementary measures" to be adopted to manage the situation (e.g. building reception facilities). Below a more detailed analysis of the Hotspot approach will be conducted.

1. The hotspot approach

The aim of the Hotspot approach is to provide a platform for the agencies to intervene, rapidly and in an integrated manner, in frontline Member States when there is a crisis due to specific and disproportionate migratory pressure at their external borders, consisting of mixed migratory flows and the Member State concerned might request support and assistance to better cope with that pressure. The support offered and the duration of assistance to the Member State concerned would depend on its needs and the development of the situation[528]. This is intended to be a flexible tool that can be applied in a tailored manner.

In the European Agenda on Migration, the Commission committed itself to setting up a new "Hotspot" approach[529]. The Agenda does not provide a definition of a "Hotspot" but rather describes how the "Hotspot" approach is to be applied. Accordingly, in such a "Hotspot" approach, the European Asylum Support Office, Frontex and Europol will work on the ground with frontline Member States to swiftly identify, register and fingerprint incoming migrants. The work of the agencies will be complementary to one another. Those claiming asylum will be immediately channelled into an asylum procedure where EASO support teams will help to process asylum cases as quickly as possible. For those not in need of protec-

527 COM/2015/0240 final, European Agenda on Migration. Briefing, March 2016, Hotspots about emergency relocation, State of Play, European Parliament.

528 COM/2015/0240 final, European Agenda on Migration, on 13 May 2015.

529 COM/2015/0240 final, European Agenda on Migration, on 13 May 2015.

tion, FRONTEX will help Member States by coordinating the return of irregular migrants. Europol and Eurojust will assist the host Member State with investigations to dismantle the smuggling and trafficking networks.

A "Hotspot" is characterized by specific and disproportionate migratory pressure, consisting of mixed migratory flows, which are largely linked to the smuggling of migrants, and where the Member State concerned might request support and assistance to better cope with the migratory pressure. The triggering of the "Hotspot" approach is based on both the assessment of the Member State concerned and the risk analysis provided by the relevant EU Agencies, in particular FRONTEX and EASO. In principle, an external border section should be considered to be a "Hotspot" for the limited period of time during which the emergency or crisis situation subsists and during which the support of the "Hotspot" approach is necessary.

The "Hotspot" approach is to be triggered upon the request of a Member State. The requesting Member State would need to submit its request and proposal outlining its needs to the Commission and the relevant Agencies. Under the overall coordination of the Commission, the Agencies will assess the request and the accompaning proposal with the aim of defining a comprehensive support package that would meet the needs of the Member State concerned without delay. This approach would avoid overlap or duplication of efforts on the ground[530].

In those instances where despite facing high migratory pressures, a frontline Member State does not request support from all of the Agencies or only requests emergency funding, the Commission will consider suggesting to that Member State that it requests the triggering of the "Hotspot" approach[531].

On the ground, operational coordination is necessary. For practical reasons an EU Regional Task Force (EURTF) would take responsibility for the overall coordination of the work of the different teams of experts involved in the "Hotspot" approach and the information exchange among these teams[532]. The EURTF is the organisational entity to implement the "Hotspot" approach in administrative and operational terms. The "Hotspot" approach consists of a headquarters hosting the EURTF and operational expert teams that support the work of the host Member State on

530 COM/2015/0240 final, European Agenda on Migration, on 13 May 2015.

531 COM/2015/0240 final, European Agenda on Migration, on 13 May 2015.

532 COM/2015/0510 final, Managing the refugee crisis: State of Play of the Implementation of the Priority Actions under the European Agenda on Migration.

the ground (e.g. registration and screening of irregular migrants at the ports of disembarkation, pre-return assistance in pre-removal centres).

It is essential that officers from all Agencies directly concerned, namely Frontex, EASO and Europol, as well as national authorities are present in this EURTF[533]. Eurojust and other EU Agencies may also consider deploying staff to this EURTF, depending on the situation. Representatives from relevant Member States' authorities could be temporarily deployed to the EURTF upon previous agreement with the host Member State, and only for purposes related to a relocation scheme.

Close links must be built with the competent national authorities and the coordination structures, in particular the International Coordination Centre for FRONTEX Joint Operations. The operational support and assistance to be provided by closer interaction among national and EU actors can be further enhanced by liaising with international actors such as Interpol, IOM, UNHCR and relevant NGOs[534].

The EURTF, in close cooperation with the competent national authorities, will facilitate the overall coordination of the teams of experts from the different Agencies deployed on the ground, and ensure information exchange. The EURTF will coordinate its efforts with competent national authorities.

Depending on whether the major challenge is pressure at the external borders, or processing asylum applications or investigating criminal networks, the relevant Agency would need to take up the role of coordinator in the EURTF in cooperation with the competent authority of the host Member State. The coordinating EU Agency will take care of the administrative and logistical arrangements in cooperation with the competent authority of the host Member State. The EURTF shall carry out its tasks without prejudice of the competences and responsibilities of the relevant national authorities, and in close collaboration with them.

It could be that more than one external border section in the same Member State would be considered a "Hotspot" at the same moment in time. Therefore, the EURTF could be coordinating efforts with regard to more than one "Hotspot".

The operational support to be provided using the "Hotspot" approach will be tailored to the specific situation at the external sea or land borders

533 Managing the refugee crisis: State of Play of the Implementation of the Priority Actions under the European Agenda on Migration.

534 COM/2015/0240 final, European Agenda on Migration, on 13 May 2015.

of the frontline Member State. The following operational support could be included[535]:

1. registration and screening of irregular migrants by FRONTEX to determine their identity and nationality, and provision of information, where appropriate, concerning the asylum process. Fingerprinting and registration in EURODAC will be carried out by Member State authorities, and if requested with the support of the relevant EU Agencies and specialized expert teams from the Member States. At this stage, each individual undergoes a first screening interview. Following the screening it should be possible to distinguish between the following categories of persons:
   a) persons who wish to apply for asylum;
   b) persons who can be returned immediately: procedures for immediate return (actors: national competent authority with the support of FRONTEX);
   c) persons with regard to whom the situation may remain doubtful: the normal procedure applies. Special attention will be paid to vulnerable groups, including children particularly unaccompanied children who need specific protection.
2. Debriefing of migrants supported by FRONTEX at the frontline to understand routes, *modus operandi* and to gather information, including on secondary movements, with a view to contributing towards investigations into smuggling networks and for criminal analysis. Europol is provided with relevant information and intelligence from all debriefing interviews to support and initiate investigation with the concerned Member State[536].
3. Stepping up investigations (including forensic/operational support), information and intelligence exchange on facilitation of irregular transit and stay within the EU. This enhanced cooperation should deal with criminal networks facilitating migration to the EU as well as secondary movements from the Member State of disembarkation to the final destination (actors: host Member State, in particular national prosecutors and judicial authorities, Europol, Eurojust as needed).
4. Asylum support by channelling asylum seekers into the appropriate asylum procedure (normal, accelerated/border procedure, prioritized/ Article 78(3) procedure, according to the relevant national legal system)

535 COM/2017/0201 final, on the operationalisation of the European Border and Coast Guard, on 2 March 2017.

536 COM/2015/0240 final, European Agenda on Migration, on 13 May 2015.

and assisting with registration of asylum seekers and subsequent preparation of case files. In this framework EASO teams, alongside with UNHCR, should focus on persons in clear need of international protection in order to ensure swift processing possibly linked to relocation (Article 78(3) decision).

5. Coordination of the return of migrants that do not have the right to stay in the EU legally, in particular with regard to pre-return assistance and the coordination of return flights. Support for the acquisition of travel documents from countries of origin, including by setting up teams from identified countries of return to carry out interviews and speed-up the issuance of travel documents (Actors: host Member State and other Member States which can assist in the contacts with the relevant countries of origin or transit with the support of FRONTEX).
6. Interpretive language to facilitate the work of the experts provided by the Agencies for the above tasks will be provided by the Agencies and/or Member States. The "Hotspot" approach does not provide reception facilities to its host Member States but builds on their existence and functioning. The expert teams deployed under the "Hotspot" approach support the work of the host Member State in its national reception facilities and pre-removal centres (for those not in need of protection). The existence and functioning of national reception facilities and pre-removal centres is therefore necessary for the successful implementation of the "Hotspot" approach[537].

2. The European agencies are involved in the hotspot approach

As specified above, the European Agencies which cooperate in the implementation of this Hotspot approach are: FRONTEX, EASO, Eurojust, Europol[538].

FRONTEX: provides operational cooperation through joint operations and rapid interventions, upon request from the Member States[539]. Since 2006 the Agency has been coordinating and financing many joint opera-

537 COM/2015/0240 final, European Agenda on Migration, on May 2015.

538 EASO, www.easo.europa.eu, EUROPOL, www.europol.europa.eu, EUROJUST, www.eurojust.europa.eu, FRONTEX https://frontex.europa.eu.

539 F. CASOLARI, *The EU's Hotspot Approach to Managing the Migration Crisis: A Blind Spot for International Responsibility?*, in *The Italian Yearbook of International Law*, 2015, Vol. 25.

tions hosted by the Member States affected by exceptional irregular migration across their external maritime and land borders (e.g. Spain, Italy, Malta, Greece, Bulgaria, Hungary and Poland), based on risk analysis, including an assessment of Member States' capacity to face pressures at their external borders, as already explained earlier in the Chapter. This Agency supports Member States in the identification procedures through screening. Moreover, it provides tailored products and services within the context of EUROSUR (for instance, vessel traffic monitoring, vessel detection or vessel of interest tracking and analysis layer deliverables)[540]. Furthermore, the European Agency collects information for its own analysis and supports Member States' competent authorities in investigations by carrying out debriefing interviews to gather information concerning routes, *modus operandi* and facilitators. FRONTEX also organises and coordinates return operations of Member States.

EASO: provides or coordinates the provision of operational support, *inter alia* through the deployment of asylum support teams to support Member States in particular with expert know how in the different steps of the asylum process and to facilitate the analysis of asylum applications under examination by the competent national authorities, for example, through joint processing[541]. Currently a number of Member States receive assistance coordinated by EASO through Operational Support Plans (Italy, Greece, Bulgaria and Cyprus)[542].

EUROPOL: supports Member States by providing secure information-sharing opportunities, expertise, strategic and operational analysis relating to cross-border serious and organised crime and terrorism[543]. Europol offers support on the spot including forensic assistance to the authorities of the affected Member States and cooperation with other services involved (e.g. EUNAVFOR MED). Europol staff may participate in a supporting capacity in joint investigation teams. Joint Operational Team (JOT) Mare was launched in March 2015 as the EU information hub for criminal (in-

---

540 F. CASOLARI, *The EU's Hotspot Approach to Managing the Migration Crisis: A Blind Spot for International Responsibility?*, *The Italian Yearbook of International Law*, 2015, Vol 25.

541 EASO: provides or coordinates the provision of operational support, inter alia through the deployment of asylum support teams to support Member States in particular with expert know how in the different steps of the asylum process and to facilitate the analysis of asylum applications under examination by the competent national authorities, for example, through joint processing.

542 EASO, www.easo.europa.eu.

543 EUROPOL, www.europol.europa.eu.

cluding personal) data on smuggling of persons by sea and specifically intended to tackle related organised criminality.

EUROJUST: supports and strengthens coordination and cooperation between national investigating and prosecuting authorities in relation to serious crimes affecting two or more Member States, in order to render their investigations and prosecutions more effective[544]. Eurojust can ask the competent authorities of the Member States, also in cases involving third countries, to undertake an investigation or prosecution. Eurojust can assist in the execution of European Arrest Warrants and requests for mutual legal assistance, advise on jurisdiction and support in the setting up and running of Joint Investigation Teams, including financial support. Eurojust contributes to facilitating swift prosecution of criminal networks of smugglers.

3. The added value of the hotspot approach

The benefit of this "Hotspot" approach is that comprehensive and targeted support is provided to the frontline Member State by the relevant EU Agencies with regard to all challenges that arise due to specific and disproportionate migratory pressures at the external borders. The "Hotspot" approach is envisaged to contribute to facilitating the implementation of the relocation scheme established on the basis of Article 78(3) TFEU. This approach also allows for parallel efforts in respect of tackling smuggling based on real-time law enforcement analysis of the situation on the ground. At the same time, this approach contributes to enhancing the return policy. The support offered by the Agencies can already be provided by them within their respective mandates. The "Hotspot" approach would help avoid duplication and better pooling of efforts.

It is an opportunity for the Agencies to make best use of information, capabilities and systems which they already have available for the benefit of the frontline Member States. The result of combining information, operational support and capacity building activities from all relevant EU Agencies should amplify the impact of this assistance, which would be greater and more visible than when provided by EU Agencies separately.

This should enable the frontline Member State to address the migratory pressure in a swifter and more effective manner in full compliance with

544 EUROJUST, www.eurojust.europa.eu.

fundamental rights and also strengthen its capacities for facing migration and asylum as well as internal security challenges in the future.

4. Considerations on the hotspot approach

On the whole, notwithstanding the "assistance" rhetoric, hotspots are clearly designed to shift back all the responsibilities States (theoretically) shoulder under current EU legislation onto the frontline states: to identify migrants, to provide first reception, to identify and return those who do not claim protection, and to channel those who do so towards asylum procedures in the responsible state – in most cases, none other than the frontline state itself.

This is where temporary relocation schemes become relevant. Established by the two Decisions of 14 and 22 September 2015 as temporary emergency measures under Art. 78(3) TFEU[545], the relocation schemes constitute a derogation from Dublin: by September 2017, the responsibility for a number of applications (66,400 from Greece and 39,500 from Italy) has to be transferred to other Member States. In conformity with the goal of the scheme – re-establishing EURODAC/Dublin "normality" in frontline states – applicants may only be relocated after applying for protection there, being properly fingerprinted, and after the responsibility of Italy and Greece under Dublin has been established (Art. 3(1) and 5(5) relocation Decisions). Furthermore, only applicants "in clear need of international protection" are eligible, i.e. those who possess a nationality for which the EU-wide recognition rate at first instance is 75% or higher (Art. 3(2) relocation Decisions).

The policy link with the "Hotspot approach" is made explicit in Articles 7 and 8 of the relocation Decisions: relocation is to be accompanied by "increased operational support", and may be suspended should the beneficiary state fail to comply with its "Hotspot approach". It is clear that hotspots and relocation have so far failed to produce any tangible results. The setting-up of hotspots is behind schedule in both frontline states and, in the words of the Commissioner in charge, relocation schemes are "not working".

---

545 Council Decision (EU) 2015/1601 of 22 September 2015 establishing provisional measures in the area of international protection for the benefit of Italy and Greece No longer in force, Date of end of validity: 26/09/2017 OJ L 248, 24.9.2015, p. 80–94.

The causes of such delays appear to be manifold. Italy and Greece have been more or less openly accused of feet-dragging on hotspots, even by UNHCR. It is of course an open question whether – willing or not – it would be possible at all for Greece or any other EU State of comparable size and wealth to organize screening and reception for arrivals similar to those recorded in 2015.

Be that as it may, a rather less discussed aspect of the situation is that the other Member States are themselves failing to provide the assistance required to make the whole scheme work: the calls by EU Agencies for personnel to be deployed in hotspots (about 775 officers for FRONTEX by the end of January 2016 and about 370 for EASO by the third quarter of 2017) have not been successful so far, and relocation places have been made available in insufficient numbers and subject to many conditions.

It is quite a range of different causes, and each one would deserve analysis before the next moves are decided. Finger-pointing, however, is proving to be irresistibly attractive. It is a matter of "homework" not done properly, and a percetption that once Europe flings Greece out, all will be well in the Schengen area. The states are indeed "assisted" both operationally and financially. However, as noted above, the hotspot approach leaves most or all of the main costs to the host state (reception, processing, detention and expulsion costs) subject to modest financial support from the EU. More importantly, frontline states are in fact "assisted" to better shoulder the full extent of their responsibilities under the existing Schengen and Dublin arrangements.

Insisting that every arriving migrant should be registered and identified at the point of entry is entirely acceptable. For this to be done, however, identification should be decoupled from the responsibility to organize the reception, protection or return of every arriving migrant[546]. Coupling identification with further responsibilities is a sure-fire way to induce border states to look the other way, as experience shows, and amounts to assigning overwhelming responsibilities on the basis of geographical location – arguably the allocation principle farthest from "the principle of solidarity and fair sharing of responsibility" (Article 80 TFEU).

546 F. MAIANI, Professor at University of Lausanne, Hotspots and Relocation schemes: the right therapy for the Common European Asylum System, in http://eumigrationlawblog.eu/.

III. The detention and return of irregular immigrants

In the European Union legal framework on irregular migration, one of the tools used to deal with this phenomenon is the return provision which is hotly debated especially concerning human rights.

The main tool at the EU` s disposal is the Return Directive of 2008[547], which establishes a new approach to return which is now extended to the country of transit. Its implementation also covers undocumented non-EU citizens who have not yet reached the age of 18. It envisages the possibility of keeping irregular immigrants in detention in special or prison facilities, formalizing this as one of the most important aspects of European Union policy in this area[548].

The EU Return Directive, mentioned earlier, which entered into force in 2010, sets common standards and clear, transparent and fair common rules for the return of irregularly staying migrants, in full respect of fundamental and human rights. However, its inconsistent transposition into national legislation has had a negative impact on the effectiveness of EU return policy. Many Member States did not implement the Directive correctly as shown by several judgments of the European Court of Human Rights[549]. In the next Chapter this issue will be explored in depth withparticular reference to Italy.

The European Council in its Conclusions of 20-21 October 2016[550] called for the reinforcing of national administrative processes for returns and the Malta Declaration of Heads and State of Government of 3 February 2017[551] highlighted the need for a critical review of European return policy with an analysis of how the tools available at national and at Union level are applied.

547 Directive 2008/115/EC of th,e European Parliament and of the Council of 16 December 2008 on common standards and procedures in Member States for returning illegally staying third-country nationals, OJ L 348, 24.12.2008, p. 98–107.

548 COM(2015) 240 final, European Agenda on Migration, on 13 May 2015.

549 Some example: ECtHR, *N.D. and N.T. v. Spain*, Application No 8675/15 and 8697/15, 3 October 2017; ECtHR – Hirsi Jamaa and Others v Italy [GC], Application No. 27765/09; ECtHR – Sharifi and Others v Italy and Greece, Application No. 16643/09; ECtHR – De Souza Ribeiro v France [GC], Application No. 22689/07.

550 European Council, EUCO 31/16, 21 October 2016.

551 COM/2017/0350 final, Fourth Progress Report on the Partnership Framework with third countries under the European Agenda on Migration, on 3 February 2017.

The return procedure, which also provides for the detention of irregular migrants before their return, is a case in which issues regarding the protection of human rights and their violation frequently arise. Because of the complexity of this phase a more detailed analysis of this tool and its impact on human rights will be provided.

1. The return procedure

The migrants who are subject to the return procedure are: third-country nationals who do not have the legal right to stay on the territory of a Member State, thus irregular migrants. This includes persons whose claim for asylum has been rejected, persons who have stayed longer than the period allowed by their visa and who no longer fulfil the conditions for stay in the EU and those who are subject to return as a criminal law sanction.

Directive 2008/115 is one of the first acts through which it was decided to regulate one of the aspects of migratory flows, irregular migration, by adopting common standards and procedures for returning irregular third-country nationals. One of the most important innovations is the possibility of arranging the return of undocumented people not only to their country of origin, but also to a country of transit[552]. A part of the Directive is also dedicated to possible detention in specific facilities.

Before starting the full analysis, it is useful to make a comparison between the different language versions of the Directive, and observe differences that inevitably affect the interpretation of the Directive in the Member States. Taking into consideration the Italian, French and English versions, a first difference arises in the title: while in the Italian, and French versions refers to the Third Country National (TCN) as "soggiorno regolare" and "en sejour irregulier" (underlining the irregularity of the position), the English version, refers to "illegally staying" TCNs.

The difference is important because while the concept of irregularity refers to a position of an administrative nature, the idea of illegality refers to a more rigorous concept, to violation of the law, certainly assuming more severe consequences. In the legal system of the European Union the sources of law are all authentic, whatever the language version. This can create problems relating to their interpretation.

Concerning the Directive's application *ratione loci*, the Act has been adopted in the Area of Freedom, Security and Justice (AJFS). Hence, not

552 Article 3.3 of the Return Directive.

all Member States are bound by it[553]. At the same time the Act is binding for countries outside the EU (Norway, Iceland, Liechtenstein and Switzerland, members of the Schengen Agreement[554]) because it constitutes a development of the Schengen acquis.

As to application *ratione personae*, the Directive will apply to TCNs who are staying illegally in a Member State´s territory when the conditions laid down by the Schengen Borders Code, or by other conditions of entry, stay or residence fixed by the national laws, are not respected or are no longer fulfilled (e.g. when a stay permit expires) (Article 2 of the Return Directive).

The Directive provides for different exeptions in which Member States can refuse to apply it: first of all, according to Article 2.3, when the persons involved (and their families) are non-EU citizens following EU citizens exercising their right of free movement. Member States, however, have the option not to apply the Directive in two other circumstances: first, in a situation of refusal of entry, or when immigrants are apprehended or intercepted in connection with irregular crossing of the border and they have not subsequently obtained an authorization or right to stay in that Member State. The result of this provision is that the Directive can be applied to situations where the citizen is still in the country, but not all cases where irregular citizens are in the states´s territory. Thus, the EU has missed the opportunity to set a common procedure for regulating one of the most delicate situations in the phenomenon of migration.

The second circumstance may occur if the TNCs are subject to return as a criminal law sanction, or as a consequence thereof according to national law, or if they are subject to extradition procedures. The purpose of Article 2.2 (a)-(b) does not seem to interfere with judicial activities, but it is true that its broad interpretation could also involve exercising an exeption in cases where the penalty arises directly as a consequence of the crime of committing illegal entry to the state in question. On this point the court should clarify the meaning of this provision but, considering the general principles of EU law (general duty of cooperation and effectivness), it seems to exclude the possibility of denying the effectiveness of the Directive.

Although the term "return" normally involves citizens going back to their country of origin, either voluntary or forcibly, according to Article

553 Denmark, the UK and Ireland did not take part in its adoption, nor are these three member states subject to its application).

554 OJ C 340, 10.11.1997, p. 93.

3.3 of the Directive "return" also covers situations where the individual goes back to a country of transit (before arrival in Europe) or, to a third country; in this last case only with the immigrant's consent[555].

The two scenarios need an agreement: between the EU (or a member state) and the country of transit in the former case; or between the EU (or a member state) and the third country in the latter case. In this case, "return" to that country should be accepted by the immigrant.

Return to country of transit raises some concerns, because that type of decision is possible with the agreement of the country involved, but without the acceptance of the immigrant. It is likely that the European Parliament and the Council chose this solution to overcome obstacles that authorities might meet when having to identify undocumented citizens. Some problems can be traced to a lack of enforcement by the state, others are attributable to a lack of cooperation from the authorities of the potential country of origin including the possibility of denial that the immigrant concerned is even a citizen of that state. This possibility is not so far from reality, especially taking into account the administrative burdens and difficulties present in the countries of origin of the vast majority of irregular migrants.

It is clear that, in such a situation, persons irregularly staying in the EU often suffer the consequences of the structural deficiencies in their countries of origin. In most cases they are solely responsible for having crossed the border without the right to stay in the EU, and are not carrying the pertinent documentation.

According to the EU Charter of Fundamental Rights, the same Directive, the treaties, and the European Convention on Human Rights, which apply to all EU member states, this rule's application must respect fundamental rights in the country of transit. Moreover, once forced to return to their country of origin, migrants might be victims of human traffickers and, in general of international criminal organizations for a second time.

In its recent comprehensive evaluation of EU readmission policy, the Commission concluded that the EU readmission agreements are useful for repatriating irregular migrants, but that "*it is equally clear that readmission negotiations with several countries, including with the most important countries of origin and transit of irregular migration, are difficult*" [556].

---

555 M. CECCORULLI, N. LABANCA, *The EU, Migration and Politics of Administrative Detention*, Routledge London, 2014.

556 COM11(76)final, Communication of the Commission on the evaluation of EU Readmission Agreement, on 23 February 2011.

Some elements can confirm doubts and concerns. In fact, the Commission reports that immigrants who have been readmitted to a transit country may find themselves in a particularly precarious situation in countries with a weak system of human rights and international protection.

For instance:*"there is…a risk of disproportionate administrative measures that are not allowed under general human rights standards (e.g. prolonged or indefinite detention period pending onward expulsion to their country of origin) or of further readmission to their country of origin, despite legitimate fears of persecution in the latter"*[557].

Even being free in the transit countries is a risk because people who are not detained may face difficulties with regard to their means of subsistence during their stay in the country of readmission.

In that situation, the Communication recommends that any readmission agreement " *should contain a clause whereby the parties explicitly confirm that they will treat TCNs in compliance with the key international human rights conventions to which they are a party. If the readmitting country has not ratified the key international human rights conventions, the EURA should explicitly oblige that country to comply with the standards set out in those international conventions"*[558].

In addition, it underlines the need for a mechanism to monitor what happens to persons after their readmission, especially to find out if the third country has respected the human rights of persons after return has taken place. This fact confirms how difficult it is for the rule to take effect and to use the instrument of readmission agreements in full respect of human rights.

In general, return to the country of origin follows a return decision that declares that the stay is illegal, which may be followed by a removal action, namely "the physical transportation out of the Member State", except in the event of "voluntary departure"[559].

The latter possibility seems to be encouraged. However, it should be recalled that the ban cannot exceed five years and it is normally connected to forced return. So, the entry ban will certainly be present in a situation of forced return or non-compliance with the obligation to return, but it may

557 COM11(76)final, Communication of the Commission on the evaluation of EU Readmission Agreement, on 23 February 2011.

558 COM11(76)final, Communication of the Commission on the evaluation of EU Readmission Agreement, on 23 February 2011.

559 Article 7-11 of the Return Directive 2008/115/EC, OJ L 348, 24.12.2008, p. 98–107.

also be present if the immigrant is granted a period within which to voluntary leave the member state´s territory. On the other hand, a "reward" is suggested when the person demonstrates full compliance with the return decision. Indeed, in such cases the state may provide for entry ban to be suspended or revoked.

There are situations in which it is possible to waive a return decision. As established by Article 6, if the TCN holds a valid residence permit or other authorization issued by another Member State, they must immediately go to that state. In this event the return decision process is only activated if the subject does not comply with the requirement. The same situation arises when there are reasons of public policy or national security that require immediate departure[560]. Member States may refrain from issuing a return decision if the immigrant is taken back by another Member State under bilateral agreements or arrangements already existing on the Directive´s date of entry into force.

In such a case, the Member State which has taken the migrant back will decide on their return by adopting a return decision. Some doubts may arise about this return decision, in particular regarding whether the second Member State has to adopt this Act or not.

In those state legislations implementing the Directive, it might be envisaged that the national authorities grant the right to stay for "compassionate, humanitarian or other reasons". An already-issued return decision can be withdrawn or suspended for the duration of the validity of the residence permit or other authorization offering the right to stay.

During the renewal of residence permits a Member State may refrain from issuing a return decision until the pending procedure is finished. In principle, the return decision has to provide for an appropriate period for voluntary departure (7-30 days)[561], during which the undocumented persons must leave the country. If national legislation sets out that this period is only granted following a specific request, the authorities must inform the TNC of the possibility of submitting such request.

Whatever time limit the national legislator has chosen to impose, the competent authorities have the obligation to take into account the specifi-

560 Article 6.2 of the Return Directive 2008/115/EC, OJ L 348, 24.12.2008, p. 98–107.

561 Article 7 of the Return Directive 2008/115/EC, OJL 348, 24.12.2008, p. 98-107.

ties of the case at hand, the existence of other family and social links[562], so as to be able to make an extention to meet specific needs.

The removal will be postponed if the TNC has appealed against the return decision before a court, or if the return would violate the principle of non-refoulment. In the latter case, a more appropriate period of time can be allowed, taking into account the specific circumstances of the case, such as physical state or mental capacity; technical reasons, such as lack of transport capacity; or failure of the removal due to lack of identification.

It is very likely, therefore, that the rules intend to assert the possibility of postponing removal due to lack of identification also prevents verification of the existence of special status rights. To proceed with a removal would be in conflict not only with international law, but with the same Return Directive that mentions the protection of fundamental human rights and human rights law as being the higest principles of EU law[563].

If necessary, and even if a period for voluntary departure has been granted, the return decision must provide for all necessary enforcement measures and measures to prevent the individual from escaping justice. In that case the period for voluntary departure may be suppressed or granted for less than seven days, but only for reasons strictly connected to the fact that the application for legal stay has been dismissed as manifestly unfounded or fraudulent, or if the person concerned poses a risk to public policy, public security or national security[564].

The Directive also provides procedural safeguards[565]: the formal requirements of the decision are identified, the remedies provided, as well as the additional minimum safeguards that must be taken into account before departure to the country of origin or the country of transit, whether it be voluntary or forced. This way, migrants are more capable of protecting themselves by understanding and using the legal process; hence, it is essential to establish the way to inform them of their rights. Every return decision, entry ban and removal decision must be issued in writing, motivated in fact and in law, and offer information about the legal remedies available. The national law may limit reasons of fact in order to safeguard national securi-

562 Article 7 and 8 of Return Directive 2008/115/EC, OJL 348, 24.12.2008, p. 98-107.

563 Introductory part point 24 of the Return Directive 2008/115/EC, OJl 348, 24.12.2008, p.98-107.

564 Article 7. 4 of the Return Directive 2008/115/EC, OJ L 348, 24.12.2008, p. 98–107.

565 Article 12, Chapter III of the Return Directive 2008/115/EC, OJ L 348, 24.12.2008, p. 98–107.

ty, defence, public security and to protect the carrying out of investigative activities.

Upon request, the competent authorities are required to offer a written or oral translation of the main elements of the Act related to the removal. This possibility triggers more than one perplexity, particularly as far as the effectiveness of the right to a defence is concerned, especially insofar as the Directive allows authorities to translate the Act orally[566].

The Directive extends the possibility of issuing a return decision against unaccompanied minors, including the option of them being taken back to a country of transit, albeit on condition that they are returned *"to a member of his or her family, a nominated guardian or adequate reception facilities in the state of return"* (Article 10 of the Return Directive). The rule seems capable of ensuring the protection of minors, even if its inherent weakness appears to result from a failure to consider the existence of family models other than the (stereotypical) European one[567].

Part of the Directive, in particular Article 11, refers to those who, as victims of human trafficking, were granted a residence permit under directive 2004/81, which provides for a residence permit of limited duration to those who cooperate in the fight against such trafficking or against actions to facilitate irregular immigration. The exception will not be applied if the

566 Article 12, 2 of Return Directive 2008/115/EC, OJ L 348, 24.12.2008, p. 98–107.

567 Removal may be initiated in one of the following three alternative situations, which must be present before the decision is adopted. First, unaccompanied minors will be removed only once public authorities are sure that they will be returned to a member of their family, though there are problems of interpretations here. It is therefore important to understand which family members it referes to. The same goes for verifying the successful return of unaccompanied minors to an appointed guardian. In this case the characteristics of that figure must be identified, making reference to the definition in the European legal order and, potentially, the existence of similar figures in the legal system of the state of return. Finally, although for different reasons, reference to adequate reception facilities is not immune from criticism. What constitutes "adequate" is very vague and can be interpreted in broad terms. For instance, the control and presence in such facilities of associations or organizations whose aim is to protect the rights of minors does not appear sufficient in itself to pass the adequancy test. In all probability checks and guarantees need to be established to ensure that these rights are effectively respected; only by interpreting these provisions in a restrictive sense would full protection of the rights of minors be guaranteed.

person concerned represents a threat to public policy, or public or national security[568].

2. Detention and its limits

One of the critical issues related to the fight against irregular migration is the checking and identification of those citizens who have reached the territory of a Member State without respecting the law. In this case, it is important to balance respect for people´s freedom with the right afforded to every state to authorize entry into its territory and to carry out verification activities. If a person´s identity is to be verified, it appears necessary to allow the competent authorities to keep the person in detention for a certain period of time, which should be both reasonable and no longer than strictly necessary to identify them[569].

According to the Directive, a citizen without the legal stay requirements will be detained for the purpose of removal, but only: [570]*(a) "to prepare the return and/or carry out the removal process; (b) unless other sufficient but less coercive measures, still capable of achieving the aim, can be applied effectively in a specific case* "[571].

Detention should be as short as possible, that is, only *"as long as removal arrangements are in progress and executed with due diligence"*[572] which will necessarily depend on the national authorities involved and the workload that they are subject to. While the Directive makes reference to the briefest possible detention period, it turns out that, in most cases, this does not happen. It is the same Directive that fixes the maximum time limit at six months. Something that clashes with what is underlined in the preamble

568 It can be assumed that non-EU nationals staying illegally in a member state´s territory, who have previously been granted a residence permit as victims of human trafficking, can never be the addresses of an entry ban, except in the hypothesis of objective danger. In situations outside the scope of directive 2004/81/EC, the member states "may withdraw or suspend an entry ban in individual cases or certain categories of cases for other reasons".

569 Articles 15 and 16, Chapter IV Return Directive 2008/115/EC, OJ L 348, 24.12.2008, p. 98–107.

570 Court of Justice C-61/11 PPU, EL Dridi, EC Rep. 28, April 2011, p. I-0000; Court of Justice C-329/11, Achghbabian, EC Rep, 6 December 2011, p. I-0000.

571 Court of Justice C-61/11 PPU, EL Dridi, EC Rep. 28, April 2011, p. I-0000; Court of Justice C-329/11, Achghbabian, EC Rep, 6 December 2011, p. I-0000.

572 Article 15 paragraph 1 of the Return Directive 2008/115/EC, OJ L 348, 24.12.2008, p. 98–107.

of the Directive is the possibility to extend it for a period *"not exceeding a further twelve months"*[573]. This means that the period may reach a total of 18 months if the removal operation from the country is likely to last longer owing to *(a) a lack of cooperation on the part of the immigrant, or (b) delays in obtaing the necessary documentation from the third countries involved*[574]. In any case, in counting the maximum duration of detention, the period of detention completed before the rules in the Directive become applicable must also be considered[575].

The extention of the period of detention may depends as much on the conduct (or negligence) of the TCN, as on reasons related to administrative inefficiency in the third country. First, the extention of detention may be authorized due to lack of cooperation by the national in question. In this case, this will only be possible if the immigrant's behaviour serves to avoid or impede the removal process. It follows that detention is conditioned by the active approach of the individual concerned, but it deciding on the extension of the envisaged six-month term (with maximum of three renewals, i.e. from six to 18 months), with the risk of not adhering to the reasonableness and brevity required by the general rule the competent authorities may take into account passive behaviour as well. Second, detention can be extended for so long as required to obtain documentation from third countries.

Thus, the extention of the detention period will not depend on the liability or conduct of the TCN, who will instead bear the consequences of the national administration's efficiencies and ineffectiveness. The detention may be ordered by administrative or judicial authorities, but in the latter case, a speedy judicial review should be made as to its lawfulness, which should take place as quickly as possible. The terms for challenging the decision are determined by national procedural law, but the verification will be activated *ex officio*. This can also be deduced from the Directive, which, as an alternative to the methods of control described above, grants the immigrant the right to appeal, and to submit the lawfulness of the detention measure to a speedy judicial review a decision which has to be ruled on as soon as possible.

---

573 Court of Justice (2009) C-357/09PPU, Kadzoev, EC Rep. 30 November 2009, p. I-11189.

574 Article 15 paragraph 6 of the Return Directive 2008/115/EC, OJ L 348, 24.12.2008, p. 98-107.

575 Court of Justicce C-357/09PPU, Kadzoev, EC Rep., 30 November 2009, p. I-111199.

The detention will cease, with the immigrant consequent release, when it is deemed to be unlawful, it is no longer justified and there is no risk of escape, when the immigrant´s behaviour hampering the removal and/or the expulsion ceases, or when it appears that there no longer exists a reasonable prospect of removal owing to legal or other considerations that are not further identified by the rule. A linguistic observation must be made when speaking about the procedure and the procedure and the places where the citizens in an irregular position can be detained for the purposes of their identification and/or removal. In this case, the French and Italian versions use "trattenimento" and "retention", while the English version uses the term "detention".

It is a difference that can be explained by the nature of the two legal systems and, probably therefore, different legal cultures: in the Italian and French system, detention ("detenzione", "detention") can only be a consequence of a court decision, following a judgment of convintion or as a preventive measure in particularly serious cases; on the other hand, detention in the meaning of "retention" and "trattenimento" can even be enforced by the police for a short, and specific, length of time, for purposes identified by the law, not necessarily for "criminal" reasons but also, for example, in order to identify someone[576]. In the other systems, it seems that this linguistic distinction does not exist.

Another difference concerns the places where people in an irregular position are held. They are "centri di permanenza temporanea", i.e. temporary stay facilities, in the Italian version, but "centres de retention specialises" in the French version; in this case they have a meaning that is closer to that of the English version, that is "specialized detention facilities".

However, in this case too the concept transmitted goes beyond the simple linguistic distinction. Both the French and the English versions characterize the structures by their "specialized" nature, while the Italian version seems to stress the temporary nature of the position of those concerned, who may then be allowed onto the state territory or be repatriated. Therefore, it can be seen that the same purpose of the rule could be interpreted in a different way, depending on the language version of the Directive that is taken into account.

Once the TCNs have been notified of the detention decision, they will be kept in a detention facility. Under the Directive, the detention may

576 E. MITZMAN, *Il rimpatrio dei migranti irregolari*, in M. SAVINO, La crisi migratoria tra Italia e Unione Europea: diagnosi e prospettive, Editoriale Scientifica, Napoli, 2017.

even take place in a prison, although only in cases where the state cannot provide accommodation in a specialized detention facility[577]. In the absence of a specific rule in this regard, the evaluation is carried out on a case-by-case basis. However, it is not desirable for this rule to be used as a remedy against overcrowding in these facilities.

Although the directive distinguishes between immigrants and ordinary detainees, the provision is characterized by a negative connotation; on the one hand, it favours the connection between crime and irregular immigration (all undocumented immigrants are criminal), while on the other hand it does not consider that the needs of those people in detention for removal purposes, especially those falling into the category of vulnerable people, are completely different from those of criminal detainees, requiring specialized staff whose training is clearly different from that normally received by prison staff.

Once detained the possibility to contact legal representatives, family members and competent consular authorities is only granted "in due time". This extremely vague expression can only be interpreted with regard to the need to protect rights and in particular the right to a defence, requiring the person to get in contact with a legal representative as soon as possible[578]. The balance between the state's action and the interests of the detainee may also be achieved through one of the Directive's earlier provisions, providing that Member States immediately inform detainees about their right of appeal against the detention decision. It would not be acceptable to stretch the interpretation of the concept of "due time" to render it more difficult to judicially protect the rights of TNCs[579]. As for the conditions of detention, they must respect human dignity, not only with reference to the physical aspect afforded, but also the obligation to ensure emergency healthcare and the essential treatment of diseases[580].

A different ruling concerns unaccompanied minors or families with minors, whose detention is only to be applied *"as a measure of last resort"* and

577 Article 16 paragraph 1 of the Return Directive 2008/115/EC, OJ L 348, 24.12.2008, p. 98–107.

578 M. CECCORULLI, N. LABANCA, *The EU, Migration and Politics of Administrative Detention*, Routledge London, 2014.

579 E. MITZMAN, *Il rimpatrio dei migranti irregolari*, in M. SAVINO, La crisi migratoria tra Italia e Unione Europea: diagnosi e prospettive, Editoriale Scientifica, Napoli, 2017.

580 E. MITZMAN, *Il rimpatrio dei migranti irregolari*, in M. SAVINO, La crisi migratoria tra Italia e Unione Europea: diagnosi e prospettive, Editoriale Scientifica, Napoli, 2017.

"for the shortest appropriate period of time"[581]. In particular, it is ruled that families detained pending removal be provided with separate accommodation guaranteeing adequate privacy; at the same time, minors in detention will be given the opportunity to engage in leisure activities and have access to education. The best interests of the child are a primary consideration in the context of the detention of minors pending removal, as well as respect for their fundamental rights[582]. Different Member States have decided to set out the detention of minors in different ways[583].

Finally, in emergency situations, that is when an exceptionally large number of immigrants to be returned place an "unforeseen heavy burden" on the capacity of the detention facilities or the Member State's administrative or judicial staff, periods may be allowed for *"judicial review longer than those provided for under the third subparagraph of Article 15(2)"*, at the discretion of the Member States themselves; in addition, urgent measures may be taken concerning the conditions of detention, *"derogating from those set out in Article 16.1 and 17.2"* [584], including for minors and families. In this way, however, the Directive allows for facilities other than detention facilities to be used, thus enabling non-observance of the special guarantees attributed to families.

International and non-governmental organizations and bodies whose activities and expertise are universally recognized may organize visits to verify the condition of the detention facilities. The rule, in particular Article 16 paragraph 4, although acceptable for the purpose can however be criticized due to the fact that it gives Member States the choice to allow this procedure under authorization. The option of having a more effective checking instrument, that is, the unannounced visit, could be weakened,

---

581 Article 17 of the Return Directive 2008/115/EC, OJ L 348, 24.12.2008, p. 98–107.

582 M. CECCORULI, N. LABANCA, *The EU, Migration and Politics of Administrative Detention*, Routledge London, 2014.

583 For instance, in Lithuania unaccompanied minors are given accommodation at the Refugee Reception Centre run by the Ministry of Social Security and Labour, with personnel and facilities that take into account the needs of persons of their age. In Malta, unaccompanied minors are not placed in detention, except for a very short period while medical tests are carried out. It has to be said that, if difficulties are encountered in determining their age, the immigrants are housed in a detention centre with others, according to gender. In that situation the minors risk stayiong in a centre for a long time, without special assistance.

584 Article 18 paragraph 1 of the Return Directive 2008/115/EC, OJ L 348, 24.12.2008, p. 98–107.

allowing the national authorities to cover up the real conditions of the facilities where irregular immigrants are normally detained.

A final observation must cover the role of detention when it is a result of a criminal sanction and hence is imposed in accordance with a judgment. In this case, as pointed out by the EU Court of Justice, detention, including so called hose arrest is allowed, provided that it does not slow down the process of removal of those immigrants whose presence on the national territory is irregular[585].

3. Human rights protection during return procedures

FRONTEX, as mentioned above, has a clear mandate, under its current legal basis, to provide the necessary assistance to Member States for organising joint return operations of irregular migrants. In addition, it shall identify best practices on the acquisition of travel documents and on the removal of irregularly present third country nationals, including via cooperation with the authorities of third countries.

Within its current mandate, FRONTEX will provide, under the hotspot approach, as we saw, substantial and increased operational support to the frontline Member States Italy and Greece. This should enable these Member States' authorities to make a distinction early on between those that have a right to stay in the EU and those that need to be returned, and to carry out their swift return. The work of FRONTEX would focus on the nationals of those third countries that are a priority to return from the frontline Member States and would support those Member States in a number of stages (pre-return[586], return operations[587] and capacity building[588]).

585 Court of Justice C-430/11 Md Sagor, EC Rep., 6 December 2012, p. I-0000.

586 Frontex experts will help frontline Member States register apprehended and arriving migrants, both documented and undocumented, whether they apply for asylum or not. They will screen newly arrived migrants, thus helping establish their presumed nationality and reducing the risk of nationality swapping. This would help quickly assess migrants, to identify those that are returnable and the ones that need assistance and protection. Frontex will provide support in the identification of migrants, which is one of the biggest challenges for return. This is because migrants frequently have no travel or identity documents and often do not cooperate in establishing their countries of origin, to hinder return. Frontex will coordinate the deployment of experts offered by Member States to help with the screening of migrants in the frontline States. These should have expertise on the presumed countries of origin of migrants present in the front-

As anticipated previously, the return Directive is establishing minimum standards for the return systems of EU Member States. However, the margins of discretion contained in the Directive have led to an inconsistent ap-

---

line Member States. To support identification and confirmation of the presumed nationality of migrants by the frontline Member State, Frontex will facilitate cooperation with the embassies or consular services of countries of origin of the migrants, to help obtain emergency travel documents. For this, it will, in particular, assist Member States in inviting task forces gathering immigration/consular officers from countries of return to carry out interviews for identification and to speed up the issuing of travel documents for return. Frontex will draw on the work of existing networks of experts working on return, as appropriate. It will, for instance, make use of the Best Practices developed by the European Integrated Approach on Return Towards Third Countries (EURINT). To help increase the rates of voluntary return of irregular migrants from frontline Member States, the Member States' experts deployed should provide to migrants information about the assisted voluntary return options as well as about the prospects of forced return. The Commission supports assisted voluntary return programmes through AMIF, in cooperation with governmental and non-governmental actors, in particular the International Organization for Migration (IOM).

587 After the identification of migrants and the issuing of travel documents for their return, Frontex will assist to organise, will coordinate and finance the joint return operations to swiftly bring the migrants to their countries of origin or transit. The joint return operations include migrants subject to forced returns and – if this is a feasible alternative – also voluntary returns. Frontex coordinated joint return operations may involve irregular migrants from just one frontline Member State, or from several Member States. In view of the needs of the frontline States, Frontex should prioritise returns to the main countries of origin of irregular migrants present and check the needs of other Member States for returns to these third countries. While Frontex does not have yet the capability and the capacity to charter the aircraft for the return operations or to assist the Member State with the chartering, it can support them by reimbursing the costs for joint return charters. In addition, Frontex will explore the possibility to render financial support to return operations carried out by frontline Member States to return migrants that have been refused entry in line with the Schengen Border Code, or who are present in an area near the EU/Schengen external border. This includes, for instance, those persons arriving irregularly by boat who are apprehended upon or shortly after arrival. According to Article 2(2)a of the EU Return Directive, Member States may choose not to apply this Directive to such migrants, and to apply national rules instead. The Frontex Code of Conduct applied during all joint return operations coordinated by Frontex shall ensure that return is carried out in a humane manner and in full respect of fundamental rights. Forced return monitors, from the pool established under the project Forced Return Monitoring (FReM) may be made available, to provide unbiased and neutral reporting of return operations. Frontex can finance the costs of providing monitors for return operations.

plication in Member States with a negative impact on the overall effectiveness of the EU's return policy.

The Commission has found, based *inter alia* on the results of the Schengen Evaluation Mechanism, that the legal framework provided for by the Directive has so far not been fully used by all Member States. A more rigorous and realistic interpretation of the Directive in full compliance with fundamental and human rights is even more necessary as the migratory challenges have made an effective and efficient EU return policy more important than ever.

After the Malta Summit of 3 February 2017 highlighted the need for a review of EU return policy, the Commission proposed a renewed EU Action Plan on Return[589] and a set of recommendations to Member States on how to make return procedures more effective. The renewed Action Plan on Return and the Recommendation on making returns more effective when implementing the Return Directive focus on a better implementation of existing EU legislation. They show how faster procedures, stronger measures against absconding and better information exchange and coordination can lead to a higher return rate within the existing legal framework. That way, an immediate impact on the return rates can be achieved without compromising the fundamental and human rights of those being returned. The measures proposed by the Commission focus on a better implementation of the EU Return Directive and guidance on how to make

588 Frontex will continue providing training for escort leaders and escorts of Member States, helping for instance frontline States to establish pools of escorts close to the hotspots, to enable their swift deployment on return flights. Training includes theoretical as well as practical sessions, for instance focusing on the safety procedures on board of the aircraft during critical situations. It will serve as a hub for exchanging operational experience and knowledge in return matters among Member States, through the network of national operational return experts, the Direct Contact Points on Return. Frontex is central to the system of return management in the EU, by helping coordinate the networks and projects funded at the EU level focusing on the readmission of irregular migrants and on their reintegration in their home countries – EURINT, the European Reintegration Instrument Network (ERIN) and the European Return Liaison Officers network (EURLO). Frontex should seek to increase synergies between these networks and enable them to work in a mutually reinforcing way. It should provide these networks with support, as appropriate – the making available of the web-based platform Frontex One-Stop-Shop (FOSS) to EURINT for the information exchange and sharing of best practices on the acquisition of travel documents between the project members is a good example of such support.

589 COM (2017) 200 final on a more effective return policy in the European Union, on 2 March 2017.

better use of its provisions, no legal changes are being introduced and instead it is recommened that Member States:

- improve the coordination among all the services and authorities involved in the return process in each Member State to ensure that all skills and expertise required are available for effective returns while respecting the rights of the returnees;
- remove inefficiencies by shortening deadlines for appeals, systematically issuing return decisions that do not have an expiry date and combining decisions on the ending of a legal stay with the issuance of a return decision to avoid duplicate work;
- tackle abuses of the system by making use of the possibility to assess asylum claims in accelerated or, where considered appropriate, border procedures when it is suspected asylum claims are made merely to delay the enforcement of a return decision;
- prevent absconding by detaining people who have received a return decision and who show signs they will not comply such as refusal to cooperate in the identification process or opposing a return operation violently or fraudulently;
- increase the effectiveness of return procedures and decisions by only granting voluntary departure if necessary and if a request is made and giving the shortest possible periods for voluntary departure, taking into account individual circumstances;
- set up operational assisted voluntary return programmes by 1 June 2017 and ensure proper dissemination of information on voluntary return and assisted voluntary return and reintegration programmes[590].

The EU's policy on return and readmission is fully in compliance with international human rights standards, in particular the EU Charter of Fundamental Rights, the European Convention for the Protection of Human Rights and Fundamental Freedoms, the 1951 UN Refugee Convention and its 1967 Protocol, and the principle of non-refoulement.

590 Monitoring the effects of disparities between national voluntary return schemes (short term); funding through Asylum Migration and Integration Found of assisted voluntary return programmes in cooperation with governmental and nongovernmental partners such as IOM; promoting best practices on voluntary return and reintegration programmes through the EMN to encourage Member States to develop an effective framework enabling irregular migrants to have easy access to voluntary return programmes; support for joint reintegration programmes to improve both the quality of the support provided to migrants and its cost-efficiency.

Considering the renewed Action Plan on Return in more detail: it sets out steps at each stage of the return process to tackle key challenges for return both at EU level and in the cooperation with countries of origin and transit.

The action proposed at EU level include:

- increased financial support to Member States with € 200 million in 2017 for national return efforts as well as for specific joint European return and reintegration activities;
- improving information exchange to enforce return by collecting real time information at national level and sharing it using the existing Integrated Return Management Application, as well as speeding up work on adopting the proposals to reform the Schengen Information System and Eurodac and to establish an EU Entry-Exit System (EES) and a European Travel Information System (ETIAS);
- exchanging best practices to ensure reintegration packages are consistent and coherent among all Member States to avoid countries of origin favouring returns from countries offering higher reintegration packages or assisted-voluntary return-shopping by irregular migrants;
- offering full support to Member States by the European Border and Coast Guard Agency with the Agency called on to step up pre-return assistance, increase its return support unit staff and set up a commercial flight mechanism for financing returns by June, as well as step up the training of third country authorities on return by October;
- overcoming the challenges of readmission by working to swiftly conclude the negotiation of Readmission Agreements with Nigeria, Tunisia and Jordan and striving to engage with Morocco and Algeria.

Within the Partnership Framework collective leverage in a coordinated and effective manner is employed through tailor-made approaches with third countries to jointly manage migration and further improve cooperation on return and readmission[591].

The EU Return Directive requires Member States to take all necessary measures to ensure the effective return of irregular migrants while setting out specific safeguards to guarantee the protection of returnees' rights during the whole return process. It notably contains a robust set of norms, including the possibility of effective remedies to challenge a return decision, respect for family unity and the best interests of the child and the special needs of vulnerable persons. The standards and procedures set out by the

591 See also report on the implementation of the Partnership Framework: IP/17/402.

Return Directive respect fundamental rights and international law, in particular refugee protection and human rights obligations. The Return Directive sets minimum rules and common procedures for ensuring the respect of these rights, as shown above.

Detention is a delicate issue in relation to human rights, but can be necessary for the successful preparation and organisation of return operations by ensuring that illegally staying third-country nationals do not abscond[592]. The detention period, with respect of human rights, should always be as short as possible and with a view to completing the return procedure successfully. However, the maximum period of detention used by several Member States is currently significantly shorter than the time needed to complete the return procedure. This has hindered the effective return of irregular migrants. The Commission therefore recommends that all Member States implement the possibility to make use of, in cases where it is necessary, the maximum detention period allowed for by EU law, in light of the individual circumstances of the case: a maximum initial period of detention of six months and the possibility to prolong detention up to a maximum of 18 months when necessary. The Commission also recommends that Member States bring detention capacity for return in line with actual needs.

The Commission is recommending that Member States provide for the legal possibility, under national legislation, to make use of the detention periods allowed for by EU legislation in specific cases where it is necessary to allow for the completion of the return procedure. Detention should only be used if no other sufficient but less coercive measure can be applied effectively and when there is a risk of absconding. Detention periods should be adapted by judicial authorities in the light of the individual circumstances of the case.

---

592 The Commission also sets out a number of criteria to assist Member States in assessing whether a risk of absconding exists. Objective circumstances for a risk of absconding include for example the refusal to cooperate in the identification process (e.g. by using false or forged documents), violent or fraudulent opposition to a return operation, failure to comply with measures aimed at preventing absconding such as reporting to the competent authorities or staying at a certain place when required to do so and unauthorised secondary movements to another Member State. Indicative criteria to be taken into account by the relevant authorities should be an explicit expression to not comply with a return decision, non-compliance with a period for voluntary departure and an existing conviction for a serious criminal offence in an EU Member State.

Supporting Member States in the return of irregular migrants is one of the priority tasks of the European Border and Coast Guard. This role has been further strengthened since the Agency became operational under its new mandate on 6 October 2016. The European Border and Coast Guard is composed of the European Border and Coast Guard Agency and the national authorities and coastguards responsible for border management.

A European Return Office within the Agency allows the deployment of European Return Intervention Teams composed of escorts, monitors and return specialists who will work to effectively return illegally staying third country nationals. A uniform European travel document for return will ensure a wider acceptance by third countries.

The limitations of the current EU border agency, FRONTEX, have hindered its ability to effectively address and remedy the situation created by the refugee crisis: it is not able to purchase its own resources, it does not have its own operational staff and relies on Member State contributions, it is unable to carry out its own return or border management operations without the prior request of a Member State and it does not have an explicit mandate to conduct search and rescue operations. The new Agency, European Board and Coast guard, mentioned,above, is strengthened and reinforced to address all these issues.

The Agency continues to coordinate forced return operations from Member States, but it now also has the possibility to propose the organisation of returns on its own initiative and to provide support to voluntary departures of migrants. Since January 2017, three return pools composed of escort, monitor and return specialists have been set up, and are available for deployment in the Member States, notably those facing particular pressure. When deficiencis are identified, the Agency will be empowered to require Member States take timely corrective action. In urgent situations that put the functioning of the Schengen area at risk and when deficiencies have not been remedied, the Agency will be able to step in to ensure that action is taken on the ground even where there is no request for assistance from the Member State concerned or where that Member State considers that there is no need for additional intervention. The new Agency will ensure Union standards for border management are implemented at all external borders. The external borders will be constantly monitored with periodic risk analyses and mandatory vulnerability assessments to identify and address weak spots. Liaison officers will be seconded to Member States where the borders are at risk. They will be fully integrated into the national information systems and able to relay the information back to the Agency. The Agency[593] will have a new mandate to send liaison officers and launch joint operations with neighbouring third countries, including operating on their territory.

4. Some considerations on detention and return procedures

It seems that a security approach to the problem prevails, with the idea that TNCs staying illegally necessarily represent a public order issue. The idea of removing them from the country, regardless of the consequences that this may entail, and accepting that these people may be moved to other countries less interested in respecting their human rights is of concern. In particular, it is important to consider modifying the rule that provides for removal of unaccompanied minors, a real weakness of this text, along with the possibility of "returning" the TCNs to a country of transit with weak control over the respect of human rights. It is clear that, when used properly, the EU readmission agreements do provide added value with regard to the readmission of nationals, especially to the countries neighbouring the European Union. As such they are an important tool in tackling irregular migration from third countries[594].

From this point of view we must take into consideration the Commission communication on the effect of the agreements recommending a coherent mobility package which should be offered to the negotiating third countries that, following the agreements with EU, are establishing specialized detention facilities in their territories.

In that case, it would not be acceptable, and not only for legal reasons originating from international conventions or agreements, to reduce the guarantees of these people´s fundamental rights just because they are held

593 The Agency's permanent staff will be more than doubled and for the first time, the Agency will be able to purchase its own equipment and deploy them in border operations at a moment's notice. A rapid reserve pool of border guards and a technical equipment pool will be put at the disposal of the Agency – meaning there will no longer be shortages of staff of equipment for Agency operations. Moreover, the Agency will include cross-border crime and terrorism in its risk analysis, process personal data of persons suspected to be involved in acts of terrorism and cooperate with other Union agencies and international organisations on the prevention of terrorism.

594 M. BORRACCETTI, *The EU, Migration and the Politcs of Administrative Detention*, 2014, Routledge.

in territories outside the Union following agreements between the EU and third countries[595].

Moreover, if Member States simplified administrative procedures and reviewed the restrictions on the possibilities for TCN migrants' mobility within the EU and between the EU and third countries, without losing acquired rights of residence and employment, this would help make labour markets function better. It is also desirable to eliminate the possibility for keeping these citizens in detention for up to 18 months for reasons of establishing identification, an excessive time limit which goes beyond the reasonable, and which could be reduce by at least a third through better identification services and better cooperation between Member States following the principle of solidarity underlined by Article 80 of the Treaty on the Functioning of the European Union.

---

595 M. BORRACCETTI, *The EU, Migration and the Politcs of Administrative Detention*, 2014, Routledge.

Chapter III: The implementation of human rights for irregular migrants in the Member States

Introduction

After the analysis of the European Union legal framework on the protection of the human rights of irregular migrants in the entry phase into Member States, the specific Italian and German cases will be addressed. Specifically, the kind of guarantee of human rights provided in the context of high sea, hot spots and during the detention and return procedures in these two Member States will be explored. How the European Union legislation is implemented by Member States and the provisions from the domestic jurisdiction which complement that will further be discussed.

Italy and Germany are two states which differ in many aspects such as the cultural and legal traditions. However, they have several similarities: both are members of European Union and consequently are subjected to the same supranational legal system. However, these two countries are representative of different realities in terms of the management of irregular migration in the EU and how the legislators of these states reconcile the requirements of public security and migration flow control with the protection of fundamental rights at the core of protection.

For geographical reasons the Italian shores on the Mediterranean sea are one of the first points where irregular migrants land when they arrive from the sea, in particular via the central Mediterranean route, which is the main path many currently use, when they leave from Third Countries, especially from the African continent. This is the reason why Italy has to face a large number of irregular arrivals especially from the African shores and these arrivals are often concentrated in particular periods of the year (spring, summer and early autumn). Germany, because of its geographical position can better control and stop the irregular entry of migrants even if Germany is one of the favourite countries of destination in the EU for migrants because of the opportunities for family reunification and the relatively open labour market.

How, in these different contexts, the European Union legislation has been implemented, is an interesting point of comparison. It could be interesting to see how these two countries have implemented the same EU legislation and if a comparison between the different implementing laws could be useful and serve as inspiration to improve the overarching legal framework.

To understand if a combination of the positive aspects of the two legal systems could bring benefits to both national systems, and whether it could be considered to be an inspiration to the European Union to better deal with the irregular migration phenomenon, provides a useful point of reflection.

A. *Italy: the protection of human rights of irregular migrants in the entry phase within the Italian legal system*

I. The phenomenon of irregular migration within Italian legislation

1. Categories of migrants under the Italian regulation

Italy was transformed from an emigrant country to a country of destination as many studies underline[596]. In recent years, especially with the increase of the democratic instability of the Mediterranean region, as shown by the "Arab Spring"[597] and the tragic wars which are characterizing the Middle East[598], the number of persons who flee from their countries to reach the European shores has been growing.

Before analysing the protection of human rights of irregular migrants in Italy and in order to have a clear framework of the complex Italian context in mind, a description of the categories of migrants in Italy's legal system will follow. Before the single text on immigration, so called TUIM[599], there was no systematic and complete approach to the matter of immigration. Even under TUIM, however, no appropriate measure to regularize ir-

---

596 For a detailed reconstruction under an historical point of view of the Italian immigration policy, see L. EINAUDI, "*Le Politiche dell' Immigrazione in Italia dall 'Unita' ad oggi* ", Laterza, 2007.

597 Wave of pro-democracy protests and uprisings that took place in the Middle East and North Africa beginning in 2010 and 2011, challenging some of the region's entrenched authoritarian regimes (Jasmine Revolution in Tunisia 2010, Egypt Uprising of 2011, Yemen Uprising of 2011–12, Libya Revolt of 2011, and Syria Uprising of 2011–12.).

598 For instance: Egyptian Revolution 2011; Lybian war 2011; Syrian Civil war 2011-2018; Turk-Syrian Kurd Conflict 2018.

599 Legislative Decree, coordinated text, 25/07/1998 No 286, Official Journal No 191, 18 August 1998.

regular migrants has been provided. The consideration of the particular categories of foreigners from other EU Member States has not altered this structure. It is important to emphasize that the overall set of categorizations tends to divide into two blocks, namely the so-called economic migration and that of so-called humanitarian migration.

The first category remains subject to the previous (or ordinary) framework under the TUIM and its periodic modifications. The latter, is characterized by special legislation that also implemented supranational and international norms.

1.1. Titles of regular entry in Italy

The entry into the territory of the state, as a rule, is allowed for migrants who have a visa issued by the consular authorities or Italian diplomats present in the State from which the alien comes[600].

The visa can be issued for several reasons and depends on the condition of stay of the alien on Italian territory. In particular, leaving aside the situation of refugees and those who have obtained some form of protection, a first distinction concerns the length of stay[601].

A further distinction is made on the reason for which the residence permit has been issued: some types of residence permits may identify and be linked to the working activity of the requesting party (for seasonal work, self-employed, etc.) or for others special residence permits linked to specific situations of the alien or his/her family (for family reunification, for family reasons, for medical care or for reasons of justice)[602].

As for the duration, it is the TUIM which establishes the maximum limits of time extension and spells of residence. Residence permits for work reasons in accordance with the provisions must be requested from the

600 Legislative Decree 25 July 1998, n. 286 Official Journal number 191 of 18 August 1998, Ordinary Supplement number 139.

601 The duration may be short, up to 90 days, in the case of a tourist visa, or may last for several months or until indefinite, subject to certain conditions. Legislative Decree, coordinated text, 25/07/1998 No 286, Official Journal No 191, 18 August 1998. See F., CORTESE, *La difficile classificazione dei migranti* in M. SAVINO, *La crisi migratoria tra Italia e Unione Europea: diagnosi e prospettive*, Editoriale Scientifica, 2017.

602 Legislative Decree, coordinated text, 25/07/1998 n. 286 Official Journal No 191, 18 August 1998. Changes made by Law 11 January 2018, n. 3, of the Law of 14 July 2017, n. 110 and by Law 7 April 2017, n. 47.

Questor of the province in which the foreigner is located, within eight days of his/her entry into the state territory[603].

The granting of a residence permit is only in the framework dictated by the so-called "Decree Flows": that is a decree adopted periodically by the Interior Minister, in implementation of the provisions of TUIM, aimed at regulating the flows of entry of foreigners in our country[604].

The coordinated immigration text also includes some types of residence permits to ensure specific protection for the alien or /her his family, in the presence of special conditions. The first and perhaps the most significant of these, is the residence permit for family reunification, governed by Article 29 TUIM and aimed at guaranteeing the fundamental right to the alien's family unit. A foreigner who holds a valid residence permit may apply for reunification with his / her spouse, minor children (with the consent of the other parent), any dependent children (if they cannot objectively provide for their sojourn), dependent parents or parents over sixty-five.

In order to qualify for family reunification, the foreigner who requests such reunification must demonstrate possession of suitable accommodation and the availability of an annual income not less than the amount of social security and health insurance.

In the light of the fundamental rights of the foreigner Article 36 TUIM makes provision for a residence permit for health reasons. In this case, and in addition to the provisions of Articles 34 and 35 of the TUIM guaranteeing access to health services to foreigners who are regularly or irregularly present in the territory of the state, provision is made for the possibility of requesting a specific residence permit to enjoy certain medical benefits within Italy.

For the protection of the right of defence of the alien, a residence permit for reason of justice was introduced, governed by Article 17 TUIM which can be issued to a foreigner who has been charged or offended in criminal proceedings and who has been authorized to return to Italy from the judicial authority.

Furthermore, in order to protect particular conditions of vulnerability, TUIM provides for the possibility of issuing a residence permit for social protection purposes[605] and for the protection of victims of domestic vio-

---

603 Legislative Decree, coordinated text, 25/07/1998 n. 286, Title III – Discipline of work (Articles 21-27-sexies). Official Journal, No 191, 18 August 1998.

604 Art. 21 TUIM.

605 The discipline of which has been recently amended as a result of Article 8, paragraph 1, Legislative Decree 4 March 2014, No 24.

lence[606] may issue a residence permit to allow a foreigner to avoid the violence and the criminality of the criminal organization and participate in a program of social assistance and integration. In the first case, the commissioner can issue a residence permit to allow the foreigner to escape the violence and the conditions of the criminal organization and to participate in a program of assistance and social integration, when in the course of investigations or criminal proceedings are ascertained situations of violence or exploitation against a foreigner and there is a real danger to his safety.

Finally, Article 9 of the TUIM regulates the requirements for applying for a long-term EU residence permit that marks the transition from the temporary state of residence of a foreigner to the permanent state. The rule, as amended by Legislative Decree no. 12, constitutes the result of a procedure for the adoption of the law of the European Union[607].

1.2. The status of irregularity in Italy

An irregular migrant is a migrant who illegally entered the territory of a state by avoiding frontier controls or who, already present in the territory of the state, is no longer in possession of a valid residence permit because of, for example, its expiration or failure to comply with the conditions that legitimize its release or renewal[608].

In the first case, the migrant has never been in possession of a residence permit entitling his or her presence in Italy and therefore has never entered into a direct or legitimate relationship with the institutions of the host country. In the latter case, however, the alien transits from a condition of regularity and perfect legitimacy of his or her stay to one of irregularity, which results in the loss of many benefits stemming from the validity of the residence permit.

One of the most significant changes made by the so-called 2009 Security Package to the TUIM concerns the so-called illegal immigration offence,

606 Ex Article 18 bis TUIM, introduced by Article 4, paragraph 1, Decree Law of 14 August 2013, No. 93, converted, with amendments, by law October 15, 2013, number 119.

607 F. CORTESE, *La difficile classificazione dei migranti*, in M. SAVINO, La crisi migratoria tra Italia ed Unione Europea: diagnosi e prospettive, Editoriale Scientifica, Napoli, 2017, p. 153, 154.

608 Consider the reasons for the renewal of the residence permit: art. 4, paragraphs 3 and 6 TUIM.

governed by Article 10 bis of the same Legislative Decree no. 286/1998[609], which will be analysed in more detail below.

Under this rule the foreigner was punished for his/her status with a sanction of 5,000 to 10,000 euro. Since its inception, the law has been subject to a heated debate that has divided jurists in favor of criminalizing the phenomenon of so-called "illegal immigration" and scholars who, instead, declared themselves against the creation of a crime considered difficult to prosecute[610].

On the constitutionality of the offence, the Italian Constitutional Court then intervened with the judgment 250/2010[611] that the issues of constitutional legitimacy of the contested provision were partly without foundation and in part manifestly inadmissible. According to the judges, the identification of punishable conduct and the configuration of its sanctioning treatment fall within the discretion of the legislator and are subject to the constitutional court only in the limits of their non-arbitrariness and unreasonableness[612].

It is possible to identify a level of protection of the subjective legal situations of irregular migrants that public authorities have to take on. In particular, it is TUIM itself to provide conditions and modalities for the protection of the right to health even for the irregular, to which the urgent or otherwise essential, even continuative, sickness and accident benefits cannot be denied and are extended preventive medicine programs to safeguard individual and collective health[613]. Among these modality are mentioned the social protection of pregnancy and maternity, the protection of

609 Legislative Decree 25 July 1998 No 286, Official Journal No 191 of 18 August 1998, Ordinary Supplement No. 139.

610 M.SAVINO, *La crisi migratoria tra Italia e Unione Europea: diagnosi e prospettive*, Editoriale Scientifica, Napoli, 2017.

611 Judgment No 250, 5 July 2010, Official Journal No 28, 14/07/2010. See also the judgments number 249/2010 (on aggravating illegal immigration) and 359/2010 (on non-compliance with the removal order). With the law number 67/2014, the Parliament had delegated the Government to adopt a legislative decree aimed, inter alia, to decriminalize the crime of illegal stay on the territory of the state, making it an administrative offense. But this delegation has expired without a positive follow-up on this point. In spite of this, the need to put a hand on the discipline has been recognized by the Government several times.

612 C. MAZZUCATO, *Il reato di ingresso e soggiorno illegale nel territorio dello stato. La posizione della Corte Costituzionale e i persistenti dubbi di legittimita´ riguardo ad una norma lucidamente incoerente*, in *Gli Stranieri*, review of studies and four-monthly jurisprudence, No 2, 2010.

613 Art. 35 TUIM.

the health of the child, as well as vaccinations, prophylaxis, diagnosis and treatment of infectious diseases[614].

Another important point in the protection of fundamental rights of irregular aliens concerns the right to education of the child based also the implementation of international human rights standards. Article 6 TUIM explicitly excludes access to compulsory school attendance. It follows that a minor without a residence permit has the right to be enrolled in the compulsory schools and to obtain the certificates awarded at the end of the school year.

Among the changes introduced by the 2009 security package, there was also an amendment to Article 116 of the Italian Civil Code, according to which the matrimonial publications were subordinate to the submission of residence documents. By judgment no. 245/2011, the Constitutional Court declared this provision unlawful, stating that, despite the fact that the rule can be attributed to a general aim of controlling migratory flows and of counteracting so-called marriages of convenience[615], the sacrifice imposed by that provision for freedom of marriage is considered disproportionate and unreasonable.

2. The protection of the human rights of irregular migrants in Italy: an overview

Prior to the examination of the protection of fundamental rights of irregular migrants, this section briefly analyse the case of the other categories of migrants who are grant the international protection. These categories of migrants are related to the status of irregularity because, very often, at the moment of their arrival into the Italian territory, these migrants do not have any regular status in the Italian territory.

In Italy, in the last twenty years, several laws have been implemented to regulate the matter of asylum law. The first attempt took place in 1990 with the Martelli Law [616], which defined and expanded refugee status through the regulation of its procedure for recognition. Later, in 1998, this

614 Art. 35 TUIM.

615 Marriages contract for the purpose of obtaining a residence permit. See F. CORTESE, *La difficile classificazione dei migranti* in M. SAVINO, *La crisi migratoria tra Italia e Unione Europea: diagnosi e prospettive*, Editoriale Scientifica, 2017.

616 Martelli Law 28 February 1990, No. 40, Official Journal No 49 of 28 February 1990.

legislation was amended by Turco-Napolitano Law[617] on Immigration, and then merged into the Consolidated Immigration Act[618] still in force, TUIM.

In 2002, the matter was governed by the Bossi-Fini Law[619], but it did not receive full implementation until April 2005. Some of the rules in these laws are now in the TUIM mentioned above which regulates the matter of immigration generally. It is important to underline that the TUIM has been criticized in particular on refugee legislation because it is not effective. Scholars and civil associations who work in this field, highlight the need of an Asylum Law which should be effective, homogeneous and systematic[620].

Firstly, at the domestic level, there are two forms of asylum protection: constitutional asylum and the granting of the refugee status, as follows:

a) the individual who can obtain constitutional asylum, according to Art. 10, paragraph 3 of the Italian Constitution[621], is "….a foreigner[622] who, in his home country, is denied the actual exercise of the democratic freedoms guaranteed by the Italian constitution shall be entitled to the right of asylum under the conditions established by law"[623].

---

617 Turco–Napolitano Law no. 40, 6 March 1998, Official Journal No 59 of 12 March 1998, Ordinary Supplement 40.

618 Legislative Decree of 25 July 1998, n. 286, Official Journal No 191, 18 August 1998.

619 Bossi-Fini Law 30 July 2002, no. 189, Official Journal No 199, 26 August 2002.

620 M.SAVINO, *La crisi migratoria tra Italia e Unione Europea: diagnosi e prospettive*, Editoriale Scientifica, Napoli, 2017.

621 Italian Constitution. Received from http://www.quirinale.it/qrnw/statico/costituzione/pdf/Costituzione.pdf on 5.6.2016.

622 The foreigners are the strangers, evidently, who are not Italian citizens. However, different rules apply to foreigners "Community", i.e. citizens of countries belonging to the European Union, from the ordinary citizen "non-EU". But also between the latter is necessary to further distinguish between those who are in possession of a residence permit for work reasons (so called "legally residing"), and other (so called "legally or not legally residents"). Therefore, it is important to distinguish the typologies of foreigner to identify the rules that the Italian law applies. Different classification: communitary citizens; citizens who not belong to the European Union (non-EU); resident aliens; non-EU foreigners "not legally residing"; foreign non-EU spouse of an Italian citizen (or European Union citizen); foreign children; foreigner with multiple citizenship; apolidi; asylum seekers.

623 Italian translation of the Art. 10, paragraph 3 of the Italian Constitution: "*…. Lo straniero, al quale sia impedito nel suo paese l'effettivo esercizio delle libertà democratiche garantite dalla Costituzione italiana, ha diritto d'asilo nel territorio della Repubblica, secondo le condizioni stabilite dalla legge..*".

Thus, the absence of effective exercise of democratic freedoms guaranteed by the Italian Constitution in the country of origin of allows foreigners to get the constitutional asylum protection. Despite the provision in the Constitution, legislation to that effect on asylum does not exist yet.

Nevertheless, several rulings of the Corte di Cassazione (Italian Supreme Court) have established that the right to asylum enshrined in the Constitution is set up as an individual right[624] and not merely as a legitimate interest and is to be afforded to a foreign citizen[625], even in the absence of ordinary laws that give effect to the constitutional principle[626]. However, this absence of law does not allow clarification of what are the consequences in terms of protection of rights, social benefits, obligations and so on, for a person granted constitutional asylum.

b) In order to obtain, on the other hand, the refugee status, the situation in which the foreigner finds themselves must be in accordance with the Art. 1 of 1951 Geneva Convention[627], "*...owing to well-founded fear of persecution for reasons of race, religion, nationality, membership of a particular social group or political opinion, is outside the country of his nationality and is unable or, owing to such fear, is unwilling to avail himself of the protection of that country; or who, not having a nationality and being outside the country of his former habitual residence as a result of such events, is unable or, owing to such fear, is unwilling to return to it...*". The Convention and its Protocol has been ratified by Italy through Law no. 722 of 1954[628].

Moreover, in recent years, Italy has implemented relevant EU directives aimed at harmonizing the material among Member States. Among these the most important are the Qualification Directive 2011/95/EC[629] "on stan-

---

624 Art. 10, paragraph 3, Italian Constitution, Official Journal No.298 of 27 December 1947.

625 M.SAVINO, (2017), La crisi migratoria tra Italia e Unione Europea: diagnosi e prospettive, Editoriale Scientifica, Napoli.

626 The competent organ to judge on the request of constitutional asylum is the Civil Court.

627 Geneva Convention on Refugee Status of 1951.

628 Italian Law 24 July 1954, no. 722 which ratified the Geneva Convention, Official Journal No 196 of 27 August 1954. Moreover, the request to get the refugee status has been forwarded to the competent Territorial Commission.

629 "Qualification Directive": Council Directive 2004/83/EC of 29 April 2004,repealed by Directive 2011/95/EU of the European Parliament and of the Council of 13 December 2011 on standards for the qualification of third-country nationals or stateless persons as beneficiaries of international protection, for a uniform status for refugees or for persons eligible for subsidiary protection, and for the content of the protection granted, OJ L 337, 20.12.2011, p. 9–26.

dards for third-country nationals or stateless persons to beneficiary of international protection, for a uniform status for refugees or for persons which qualify for subsidiary protection and the content of the protection recognized" and Procedure Directive 2005/85/EC[630] "on minimum standards on procedures in Member States for granting and withdrawing refugee status“.

The Italian State, based on the Qualification Directive, which was implemented in Italy by Legislative Decree of 21 February 2014, no. 18[631], which came into force on 22 March 2014, has introduced the status of subsidiary protection, which represents a form of international protection with secondary and supplementary nature to political asylum. The beneficiary of the subsidiary protection, according to Art. 2, is "*...person eligible for subsidiary protection' means a third- country national or a stateless person who does not qualify as a refugee but in respect of whom substantial grounds have been shown for believing that the person concerned, if returned to his or her country of origin, or in the case of a stateless person, to his or her country of former habitual residence, would face a real risk of suffering serious harm as defined in Article 15, and to whom Article 17(1) and (2) does not apply, and is unable, or, owing to such risk, unwilling to avail himself or herself of the protection of that country...*".

The competent authority[632] has to evaluate the request to grant one or the other status on examination of the basic presuppositions of the request.

630 "Procedure Directive": Council Directive 2005/85/EC of 1 December 2005, Official Journal L326/13 of 13 December 2005.

631 Legislative Decree of 21 February 2014, no. 18 which came into force on 22 March 2014, Official Journal No 55 of 7 March 2014.

632 The bodies in which the procedure for granting the refugee status or the beneficiary of subsidiary protection is sought are the territorial commissions for the recognition of international protection. The current organization, which is part of a National Asylum Commission that directs and coordinates the work of the territorial commissions, is essentially the result of the changes made to the original discipline of the so-called Martelli law of 1989 and Bossi Fini. The latter in particular, has given a new and still common name to the Central Commission, called the "National Commission on Asylum Law", and established the Territorial Commissions, decentralized bodies with the task of conducting a comprehensive examination of asylum applications. Territorial Commissions, originally established in number ten, were brought to twenty by virtue of the Decree Law 119/2014, converted by law no. 146/2014, in order to cope with the unremitting increase in the number of international protection applicants. Some of them have been set up, some detached sections formed by the substitute members of the Commissions themselves. There are 47 offices in which the Commissions perform their activities concretely.

The denial of international protection can be challenged before the special sections on immigration[633] in the civil court.

Indeed, despite the fact that the territorial commission has the nature of an administrative body, its decisions can be challenged before the ordinary court as they deal with subjective rights which are within the competence of ordinary judges. The appeal must be filed within 30 days of notification of the decision.

In the case of a successful application, the authority issues a measure granting the alien to a residence permit of five years which is renewable and issued by the policy headquarters[634]. The residence permit for subsidiary protection can be converted into a residence permit for work reasons. The holders may, after having met the necessary requirements, submit the application for the issuance of a residence permit for long-term residents[635].

With regard to their composition, the committees are appointed by decree of the chairman of the council of ministers, who are superseded by the Minister of the Interior and are made up of four members, that is, a prefectural career official with the function of chairman, a police officer State, by a representative of a territorial entity designated by the State Conference, city and local autonomy and an UNHCR representative.

The National Commission has the task of directing and coordinating the work of the Territorial Commissions, also training and updating components, as well as collecting data and information useful for completing the database on the socio-economic situation of the countries or origin.

It is nominated by a decree of the President of the Council of Ministers, but on a joint proposal by the Ministers of Interior and Foreign Affairs. It consists of a Director of the Presidency of the Council, a diplomatic career officer and a prefectural career by a head of the Department of Public Safety of the Ministry of the Interior. Also in this case the duration of the nominee is three years and renewable. UNHCR delegates may attend meetings but without voting rights.

633 Established at the courts of Bari, Bologna, Brescia, Catania, Catanzaro, Florence, Lecce, Milan, Palermo, Rome, Naples, Turin and Turin.

634 Art. 23 legislative decree 19 November 2007 No 251, Implementation of Directive 2004/83 / EC laying down minimum rules on the assignment, to third-country nationals or stateless persons, of the status of refugees or persons otherwise in need of international protection, as well as minimum standards on the content of recognized protection, Official Journal No 3 of 04-01-2008.

635 Art. 23 legislative decree 19 November 2007 No 251, Implementation of Directive 2004/83 / EC laying down minimum rules on the assignment, to third-country nationals or stateless persons, of the status of refugees or persons otherwise in need of international protection, as well as minimum standards on the content of recognized protection, Official Journal No 3 of 04-01-2008.

If, however, in the case of a refusal, the Commission considers that there are serious humanitarian grounds, it shall forward to the Questor the documentation of the procedure for the issue of a residence permit for humanitarian reasons, governed by Article 5, paragraph 6 of the TUIM.

The Qualification Directive mentioned above, also introduced the case of refugee "sur place", namely a refugee who is such because of present conditions in the country of origin during his/her absence in that country. The Directive has codified the concept of a refugee sur place in art. 5, implemented by the Italian legislature in Article. 4 of Legislative Decree No. 251/2007[636], which provides that the risk of suffering persecution or serious harm may arise from:

a) "events occurring after the departure of the applicant" or

b) "activities carried out by the applicant since he/she left his country of origin".

Another case of protection of European derivation introduced in Italy is the temporary protection, introduced by Legislative Decree No. 85/2003[637]. This is a procedure of exceptional character which provides immediate and temporary protection to the people, in case of massive and imminent influx of displaced persons from non-EU countries and who cannot return to their country of origin. This security measure is intended to prevent the collapse of the asylum system in the event of particular emergency situations[638].

The procedures mentioned so far are defined "Procedure for Recognition of International Protection" and thus comprise the several categories of protection. In Italy a foreigner who flees because of persecution, torture or war, although he/she crossed the borders irregularly and is undocumented, can apply for the procedure of International Protection[639].

---

636 Legislative Decree 19 November 2007, no. 251.

637 Legislative Decree No. 85, 7 April 2003, Official Journal, No 93, 22 April 2003.

638 In order to apply this protection is necessary a decision at the European Union level. Until now, this Directive has been never used. In 2011, Italy has requested the European Commission the application of the Directive due the emergency situation consequently the "Arab Spring" but to the demand nothing is followed. The European Union does not show a real will to implement this protection because the consequence would mean the entrance of a high number of foreigners. But at this point, the questions it could be: if European Union does not use this protection now, to handle the current critical situation, then when?

639 Art. 23 legislative decree 19 November 2007 No 251, Implementation of Directive 2004/83 / EC laying down minimum rules on the assignment, to third-country nationals or stateless persons, of the status of refugees or persons other-

Finally, there is a further form of protection of national nature. During the procedure for recognition of International Protection, where the Italian Territorial Commission finds that the elements giving rise to International Protection of the migrant are not present but "*...considers that there may be serious humanitarian reasons..*," it has the possibility to ask the police station to release a Residence Permit for Humanitarian Reasons[640]. Humanitarian reasons can be for instance: health assistance or natural disasters. This permit is valid for two years and it is important to underline that does not guarantee all the right of the refugee status: for example, it is not possible to invoke the right to family reunification. This limitation is due to the subsidiary and specific aim: protecting the concrete situations that are not provided for by the Consolidated Immigration Act. Thus the legislator considered it useful to insert this safeguard clause, usable if situations deserving protection for serious humanitarian reasons occur, or which impose the need to adapt the ordinary constitutional or international processes with particular regard to those relevant to human rights.

Coming back to the TUIM, which underwent some major amendments in 2002[641], when Law No. 189, the so called Bossi-Fini modified the rules on immigration in a significant manner. Although the general structure of the TUIM was kept intact, the changes resulted in a noteworthy turning-point in Italian migration policies[642]. The main intent of the legislator was that of making the regulation of migration more restrictive to combat irregular immigration. As pointed out by the Italian Supreme Court, security has become the central topic with Law 189/2002. As the Supreme Court pointed out "some aspects of security and public order had already as-

---

wise in need of international protection, as well as minimum standards on the content of recognized protection, Official Journal No 3 of 4/01/2008.

640 Art. 5, co. 6 and 19, co. 1, Legislative Decree No. 286/98, Consolidated text of the provisions concerning the regulation of immigration and rules on the condition of the foreigner, Official Journal No 191 of 18-08-1998 – Ordinary Supplement No. 139.

641 Law No. 189 of 30 July 2002, amending previous legislation on immigration and Asylum. After 2002 and before the security packages, the Single Text was modified as a result of adaptation to the EU directives, especially in matters of expulsion, and of certain rulings of the Constitutional Court and the adoption of some measures to combat terrorism.

642 B. NASCIMBENE, *Nuove norme in materia di immigrazione. La legge Bossi-Fini: perplessita´ e critiche*, Corriere Giuridico, 2003, 532; K. TOUZENIS, "*Migration and Human Rights in Italy: Prospects for the ICRMW*" in R. CHOLEWINSKY, P. DE GUCHTENEIRE, and A. PECOUD (eds), *Migration and Human Rights: The United Nations Convention on Migrant Workers´ Rights*, 2009, 343.

sumed a greater role in Law 40 of 1998, but they became the central theme with Law 189 of 2002[643].

Despite the aspiration of the 1998 Single Text on Immigration to regulate migration effectively in all its phases for the first time, the strong presence of irregular migrants in Italian territory has however remained an issue that is both difficult to resolve and fraught with controversy. Concerns about the struggle against irregular immigration have started to occupy an increasingly central role in political debate, due also to the public outcry resulting from some grave news items involving irregular immigrants[644]. Insecurity attributable to irregular migration was one of the key topics of the 2008 electoral campaign. It was no coincidence therefore that immediately after being appointed, the government set the adoption of new stricter measures as a priority, with the aim of discouraging and reducing irregular flows. Although official statistics show that crime has fallen since the 1990s, the need to adopt a "security package" was supported by the widespread perception – fuelled by politicians and the media – that Italy was facing a national security emergency, largely caused by irregular migrants[645].

As a result, criminal law provisions were strengthened. The 2008 security package included a draft law (which was then adopted in its final form in the 2009 security package), a law decree and two legislative decrees. The 2009 Security Law concerns five areas: immigration, organized crime, widespread crime, road safety, urban décor. The bill on security according to Interior Minister Roberto Maroni[646] was a very important step towards ensuring the safety of Italian citizens. On the matter of immigration, certain standards against the phenomenon of irregular immigration are set which will increase the results obtained with the rules of the security package already in force, as the decree converted into Law 125/08[647] (Press release, 2 July 2009). The 2008 security package also included a draft legislative decree aimed at introducing and integrating the provisions of Legis-

643 Judgment of the Cassazione Penale Court, Third section, of 23 January 2003, No. 3162, Official Journal No 298 of 22 December 2003.

644 M. SAVINO, *La crisi migratoria tra Italia e Unione Europea: diagnosi e prospettive*, Editoriale Scientifica, Napoli, 2017.

645 M. BARBAGLI (ed.), *Rapporto sulla criminalita´ in Italia*, 2007.

646 Roberto Maroni was Minister of Interior on 10 May 1994 until 17 January 1995 and on 8 May 2008 until 16 November 2011.

647 Law No 125 of 6 August 2008, Official Journal No. 188 of 14 August 2015, Ordinary Supplement 49.

lative Decree No. 30 of 2007[648], (which transposed EU Directive 2004/38[649]).The existing rules were also made more restrictive in relation to various aspects including the expulsion of foreigners, and EU citizens, detention in view of their removal, family reunification, citizenship acquisition through marriage, and the procedure for granting and withdrawing refugee status. In many respects, and especially those concerning rules applicable to EU citizens, these changes have raised doubts not only as regards fundamental rights, but also their compatibility with EU law[650].

3. The crime of irregular migration and aggravating circumstance

One of the main and most controversial changes introduced by the 2008 security package was the aggravating circumstance applicable to aliens with irregular status[651]. In 2009 the criminal legal system was further strengthened through the introduction of the so-called "crime of illegal entry and stay"[652]. The first revision implemented an aggravation of the penalty imposed for the commission of a crime by up to one-third, solely by virtue of being a foreigner not complying with immigration law requirements, whereas in the second case illegal entry and stay became an offence punishable with a fine of a criminal character from euro 5000 to euro 10.000[653].

---

648 As mentioned by A. Lang "Le modifiche al decreto legislative n.30 del 2007 sui cittadini comunitari", 10 Diritto, Immigrazione e Cittadinanza (2008) 120.

649 Directive 2004/38, Official Journal L 158, 30 April 2004, p. 77–123.

650 M. SAVINO, *La crisi migratoria tra Italia e Unione Europea: diagnosi e prospettive*, Editoriale Scientifica, Napoli, 2017.

651 Art. 61, para. 11-bis of the Criminal Code as amended by Law No. 125 of 2008. In its original wording, the rule seemed to nay foreign national, including EU citizens, thus raising the profile of non-compliance with EU law. With the 2009 security package, it was made clear that this aggravating circumstance did not concern EU citizens.

652 Art. 10-bis of the Singe Text on immigration as amended by Law No. 94 of 2009. The initial draft was limited to illegal entry, but in the end the typical conduct of the incriminating rule was extended to also encompass the case of illegal stay, characterized in that the presence of foreigners in the territory, which was originally supported by a legitimate title, has become irregular at a later date.

653 Detention initially envisage in the draft proposal was them replaced with a fine, which is nonetheless a criminal sanction.

These amendments have met criticism and been discussed for several reasons. One critique has been in relation to the principles of subsidiarity and proportionality of criminal punishment, both of which are enshrined in the Italian legal system and which certainly represent an orientation criterion for the legislature in the field of criminal law[654]. The restriction of rights, which is implied in criminal sanctions, should be subject to ascertaining the absence or ineffectiveness of other less coercive and afflicting sanctions. A second criticism has been made is that these provisions are also questionable in view of the principle of non-discrimination, as the level of punishment seems mainly to rely on the status of the offender. Many Italian commentators considered this to be a crime which is inherent in people – that is, in irregular migrants – and therefore the cornerstone of a new criminal law based on geopolitical (or citizenship) discrimination[655]. Discussion also focused on whether criminal prosecution of undocumented migrants may be considered an effective measure to discourage and prevent irregular migration, and the limits of the legislature´s discretion in this respect[656].

Not surprisingly, then, the Constitutional Court was very quickly called upon to assess the constitutionality of the two major innovations introduced by the 2008 and 2009 security packages. The Court declared the aggravating circumstance unconstitutional[657], whereas it dismissed the objections raised against the so-called crime of illegal immigration[658].

More generally it can also be asked on what grounds the state applies a sanction of a criminal character to a foreigner with irregular status. Breaches of immigration laws have been defined as victimless crimes, since "*to the extent that harm is done at all, it is to the integrity of the states´s border and immigration control laws*"[659]. As noted by the Special Rapporteur on the human rights of migrants, irregular entry or stay are not per se crimes against persons, property, or national security[660].

---

654 A. DI PASCALE, *Italy and Unauthorized Migration: Between State Sovereignty and Human Rights Obligations*, Oxford Scholarship Online, 2014.

655 Constitutional Court, Judgment No. 250 of 8 July 2010.

656 F. VIGANO´, Diritto penale e immigrazione: qualche riflessione sui limiti alla discrezionalita´ del legislatore (Criminal law and immigration: some reflection on the limits of discretion of the lawmaker), 12 *Diritto, Immigrazione e Cittadinanza* (2010) 65.

657 Constitutional Court, Judgment No. 249 of 8 July 2010.

658 Constitutional Court, Judgment No. 250 of 8 July 2010.

659 Commissioner for Human Rights (n.39) at 8.

660 UN Doc A/HCR/20/24, para. 13.

The discriminatory nature of the aggravating circumstance was promptly denounced by commentators, who considered that it required a difference of treatment and punishment among citizens and regular and irregular immigrants, without the slightest justification. In the aftermath of its introduction, the President Emeritus of the Constitutional Court pointed out that it effectively discriminated between persons on grounds of national origin and personal circumstances, in violation of Articles 2 and 7 of the Universal Declaration of Human Rights, Article 14 ECHR and Article 26 ICCPR, as well as Article 3 of the Italian Constitution[661]. Similar doubts about the discriminatory character of the new provisions were expressed by supranational bodies such as the European Commission and the European Parliament, and the Commissioner for Human Rights at the Council of Europe[662].

As the Constitutional Court emphasised in its ruling on the aggravating circumstance, the challenged provision is effectively based on a general and absolute presumption that third-country irregular migrants are more dangerous, which is reflected in the sanction being applicable to any violation of criminal law that they may have committed. The fact that EU citizens were subsequently expressly excluded from its scope of application was deemed to confirm this logic[663].

The Court confirmed that the relevant provision was contrary to the principle of equality, since it established an unreasonable aggravation of a penalty based on the unlawful presumption of undocumented migrants being more dangerous. Moreover, it was also deemed unacceptable that

661 V. ONIDA, *Efficacia non scontata per il ricorso al penale*, Il Sole 24 Ore, 22 May 2008.

662 The Commissioner took note of the EU Commission´s declaration of 23 September 2008 according to which the above-mentioned law decree poses problems of compatibility with Community Law, in particular concerning the rules on the automatic expulsion of EU citizens. Reported by Thomas Hammarberg, Commissioner for Human Rights of the Council of Europe, following his visit to Italy on 13-15 January 2009, CommDH (2009) 16, 16 April 2009, at para. 63. On 15 September 2008, the legal service of the European Parliament delivered an opinion which stated that an aggravation of the penalty imposed for the commission of a crime based exclusively on the quality of being a non-national European citizen not complying with immigration law requirements, would be discriminatory and contrary to the principles behind Directive 2004/38 and the case law of the Court of Justice on the matter.

663 A. DI PASCALE, Italy and Unauthorized Migration: Between State Sovereignty and Human Rights Obligations, Oxford Scholarship Online, 2014.

migrants were not punished more severely for their conduct, but for being irregular, according to the logic of personal criminal law[664].

The Court asserts "..*Assuming that illegal migrants are inherently more dangerous than citizens or foreign nationals with a legal status means to attach to them a stigma, which grounds different criminal treatment…the qualities of the individual to be judged are reconducted to the general quality established by law, based on an absolute assumption that identifies a type of author, who is subject, always to a more severe treatment…*"[665].

The Court´s assessment appears to conform to certain positions taken by international bodies on the prohibition of discrimination in national legislation and the administration of justice. In particular, the Committee on the Elimination of Racial Discrimination stipulated that under the Convention, differential treatment based on citizenship or immigration status will constitute discrimination if the criteria for such differentiation, judged in the light of the object and purpose of the Convention, are not applied pursuant to legitimate aim, and are not proportionate to the achievement of this aim[666].

Possible stigmatization of the condition of undocumented migrants was, however, assessed with a different approach in relation to the new crime of irregular immigration. The Court considered firstly that the new offence did not object to "a way of being" of the person, but a specific type of behaviour[667].The Court held that the incriminating rule was not intended to penalize the conduct of life and the intentions of the irregular migrant, but rather the lack of compliance with the rules on entry and stay of foreigners in the state. The condition of irregularity is not a pre-existing and unrelated circumstance, but is instead the consequence of the same criminal conduct which is made illegal[668].

The Court identified the interest of the state to control and manage migratory flows, in accordance with a regulatory framework. In this respect,

664 A. DI PASCALE, *Italy and Unauthorized Migration: Between State Sovereignty and Human Rights Obligations*, Oxford Scholarship Online, 2014.

665 Constitutional Court, Judgment No. 249 of 8 July 2010, para. 9.

666 *General Recommendation No.30: Discrimination Against Non Citizens*, 1 October 2004, para.4. See also *General recommendation 31 on the prevention of racial discrimination in the administration and functioning of the criminal justice system*, para. 5(a).

667 A. DI PASCALE, *Italy and Unauthorized Migration: Between State Sovereignty and Human Rights Obligations*, Oxford Scholarship Online, 2014.

668 A. DI PASCALE, (2014), Italy and Unauthorized Migration: Between State Sovereignty and Human Rights Obligations, Oxford Scholarship Online.

resorting to criminal sanctions cannot be considered arbitrary, since such interest can actually be infringed by illegal entry and stay of aliens[669].

In particular, the control of migration necessarily involves that conduct in violation of these rules is construed as a crime[670].

The analysis carried out by the Court raises the issue of balance between border control and the protection of fundamental rights. In this respect, the Court makes reference to its case law that "*the reasons for human solidarity cannot be established outside of the proper balancing of the values at stake*"[671]. However, according to the Court, the reasons for human solidarity are not in themselves contrary to the rules on immigration aimed at guaranteeing orderly migration flows and appropriate reception and integration of foreigners. The Court also reiterated that Italian legal framework "*provides a different regulation – even in the Constitution (Article 10(3)) for entry and stay of foreigners in the country, according to whether they are applicants for asylum or refugees or economic migrants*"[672].

These statements are all the more significant as a trend is emerging in many countries that provides for greater resort to criminal sanctions against undocumented migrants. The remark made by Constitutional Court, and placed among the reasons of the decision, that the choice made by the Italian legislator is far from being isolated in the international scene. In fact, the Court has emphasized that standards of a similar nature, sometimes accompanied by penalties even significantly more stringent than those imposed by the provision in question, are present in the legislation of several European Union countries[673]. Criminal law sanctions in relation to entry and stay have been adopted in Germany, where irregular

---

669 The orderly management of migration flows is qualified by the Court as instrumental to the implementation of an advanced form of protection of complex final public goods, having constitutional significance, which may be compromised by uncontrolled immigration. Constitutional Court, Judgment No. 250 of 8 July 2010, para. 6.3.

670 Determining the most appropriate penalty for a violation, and whether it should have a criminal sanction rather a purely administrative one (as was the case before the entry into force of Law No. 94 of 2009), are judged to be under the discretion of the legislature. The quality and level of repressive intervention resulting from this can vary significantly over time in relation to the changing characteristics and dimensions of migration and the significance of the different needs associated with it.

671 Constitutional Court, Decision No. 353/1997, Official Journal, first series, 1997.

672 Constitutional Court, Judgment No. 249 of 8 July 2010, para. 9.

673 Constitutional Court, Judgment No. 250 of 8 July 2010, para 6.5. regarding French legislation, see the remarks in the ECJ decision in Achughbabian (n.42).

entry (and residence) is an offence under criminal law. The sanction for the least severe form is imprisonment for up to one year or a fine and in addition expulsion[674].

According to the Italian Court, the legislature enjoys broad discretion in limiting the access of foreign nationals to the state. This is in fact the outcome of a balancing of values that are relevant and a discretionary exercise which are questionable only if the choices made are manifestly unreasonable, which in any event, also applies to the selection of the repressive instruments (whether of a criminal or administrative nature). Far from being universally shared, these considerations are at the heart of an issue that is of growing importance, as is the treatment of irregular migrants and tools that can be legitimately used to discourage the phenomenon.

Different international bodies have different positions on the subject, which clearly show the contrast between statements that express concerns more oriented to the development of absolute values and the need to protect fundamental rights, as the statements of the Special Rapporteur on the human rights of migrants or the Commissioner for Human Rights, and other underlying concerns related more towards the protection of state prerogatives. At the European level, the ECJ has undoubtedly had an influence, and thus contributed to redefining the national laws on the matter. The Court ruled specifically in relation to Article 10-bis of the Italian Consolidated Text at the end of 2012. The ruling does not consider the norm providing for a criminal prosecution incompatible with the principles stated in the Return Directive itself, which can lead to a fine for which an expulsion order may be substituted, since it has markedly different effects from those of legislation providing for a criminal prosecution which may lead to a term of imprisonment in the course of the return procedure. However, the Court has further specified the limits of its lawful application[675].

674 Similar sanctions were provided for irregular entry in Greek immigration law. In France, under the direct influence of the earlier mentioned ECJ case law (El Didri, Achughbabian), and referring to the norm that provides up to one year imprisonment and a fine of up to euro 3750 in case of entry and stay of the foreigner in breach of immigration rules, the Supreme Court affirmed that a third-country national who is only accused in relation to the crime provider for in Article L. 621-1 CESEDA cannot be placed in custody on that account alone.

675 Case C-430/11, *Md Sagor,* judgment of 6 December 2012, not yet published. See also Case C-522/11, *Mbaye,* order of 21 March 2013, not yet published, where the Court has confirmed its position stating that the third-country nationals accused or convicted of the offence of illegal stay provided for by the legislation of

4. Irregular migrants and the restriction of their human rights in Italy

In the 2009 the provision of a large area of activities corresponding to fundamental rights which has been made subject to presentation of the residence permit, was introduced by the security package. These restrictions concerned the application for licences and public authorizations and the capacity to marry, while access to medical care remained excluded.

In Italy, access to essential health care in case of disease and injury is guaranteed to any foreigner, irrespective of their legal status. In 2008, the government proposed to amend the system by introducing a provision that would have required health professionals to report a suspected crime.

Further to the introduction of the so-called crime of irregular migration, and in the absence of a specific exemption, health professionals would have in fact been obliged to inform the public authorities if they had treated a foreigner in a position of irregularity. In the final text of Law 94/2009[676], this provision was abandoned, partly because of the tough stance of doctors, who strongly disagreed with the obligation to report, claiming breach of their ethical obligations[677]. The mere rumour about the introduction of that rule had, however, caused a series of episodes that illustrate the practical consequences of an approach that deprives migrants of the enjoyment of fundamental rights. The right to health is in fact guaranteed under several human rights instruments, introducing a duty on health professionals to report undocumented migrants and thus using health care and services as an instrument of immigration control policy, was condemned by UN Commissioner for Human Rights, who affirmed that it had the effect of preventing migrants from gaining effective access to health care even if there was no express prohibition[678].

The request for licences, permits, registrations, and the like from a public authority was instead made subject to the possession of a residence permit. An exception to this rule in addition to access to health care and

---

a member state may not, on the sole crime of illegal stay, be exempted from the scope of Directive 2008/115/EC.

676 Law No 94 of 15 July 2009, Official Journal No 170 of 24 July 2009, Ordinary Supplement 128.

677 A. DI PASCALE, *Italy and Unauthorized Migration: Between State Sovereignty and Human Rights Obligations,* Oxford Scholarship Online, 2014.

678 Report of the United Nations High Commissioner for Human Rights, UN Doc E/201/89, 1 June 2010. See also V. CHETAIL and G. GIACCA, *Who care? The right to Health of migrants*, in A.CLAPHAM and M. ROBINSON (eds), Realizing the Right to Health (2009) 244.

mandatory schooling-applies only to measures relating to sports and recreational activities of a temporary nature[679]. Compared to the existing provision, the new wording removed two references to acts of civil status and access to public services, for which in the past a residence permit was not required. A strict reading of the rule would have appeared contrary not only to the Constitution but also to Article 7 and 8 of the United Nations Convention on the Rights of the Child of 1989, which requires state parties to ensure the immediate registration of the birth of a child, and to preserve their identity and family life. Birth registration was then later specifically excluded from the scope of the new provision[680].

Particular attention must be turned to the norm which linked the possibility of marriage to the demonstration of the alien´s regular position, as similar rules, which set conditions and requirements to avoid situations of fraud, were also introduced elsewhere and were deemed inconsistent with fundamental rights by national and supranational courts as will be analysed below. The amendment brought in 2009 to Article 116 of the Civil Code required any foreigner who wished to get married in Italy to present the registrar with documents certifying the legality of their stay in Italian territory, in order to prevent sham or simulated marriages. The right to marry and found a family is in fact specifically enshrined in Article 16 of the Universal Declaration of Human Rights, in Article 12 of the ECHR and in Article 9 of the European Charter of Fundamental Rights.

The new condition introduced in Italy was added to the already existing requirements which burdened the alien with the submission of a statement issued by the competent authority of his or her country, providing clearance for the marriage according to the laws to which he/she is subject. A subsequent ministerial circular made it clear that the regularity condition only applies to non-EU foreign nationals, thus excluding EU citizens[681].

The rule, which makes the capacity to marry of non-EU citizens in Italy subject to the requirement of regularity of their stay, was challenged on the grounds of its compatibility with the constitutional principles relating

679 Art 6 of TUIM.

680 See Circular of the Ministry of the Interior of 7 August 2009, No. 19, see website Ministry of the Interior www.interno.gov.it.

681 See Circular of the Ministry of the Interior of 7 August 2009, No. 19 see website Ministry of the interior www.interno.gov.it.

to freedom of marriage as a fundamental human right, and international obligations[682].

Similar issues had been examined in the case of *O′ Donoghue and Others v. the United Kingdom*[683] which concerned UK legislation requiring that, in order to marry, persons subject to immigration control had to have either entry clearance expressly granted for the purpose of enabling them to marry in the United Kingdom or a Certificate of Approval. The ECtHR ruled that the UK legislation on immigration related to the marriage capacity of foreign nationals violated Articles 12 and 14 of the ECHR[684]. The arguments of the Court appear particularly relevant to Italian law. The Strasbourg Court first stated that the fundamental right to marry and start a family, provided by Article 12 of the ECHR, may be subject to limitations and restrictions by states, when these respond to legitimate purposes including the orderly regulation of migration flows[685]. This may also include preventing sham marriages; that is, those designed to circumvent the regulations on entry and residence of foreigners. However, such limitations and restrictions must meet the criterion of proportionality[686] and must not impair the essence of the right to marry. According to the Strasbourg Court therefore, the presumption of bad faith of the marriage of an alien in an irregular position or holding a short-term residence permit, resulting in automatic and indiscriminate restriction on the right to marry, is contrary to the European Convention in that it goes beyond the margin of appreciation granted to states[687].

This decision was followed by the Italian Constitutional Court in July 2011 in a case concerning the legality of the amendments to Article 116 of the Civil Code. The Court said that while the legislature is allowed to regulate the entry and stay of foreigners in Italy, this must be reasonable and proportionate (particularly when the enjoyment of a fundamental right is

682 Constitutional Court, Judgment of 25 July 2011 No 245, Official Journal No 32 27/07/2011.

683 O′ Donoghue and Others v. the United Kingdom, ECHR (2010) Appl. No. 34848/07, judgment of 14 December 2010.

684 O′ Donoghue and Others v. the United Kingdom, ECHR (2010) Appl. No. 34848/07, judgment of 14 December 2010.

685 O′ Donoghue and Others v. the United Kingdom, ECHR (2010) Appl. No. 34848/07, judgment of 14 December 2010.

686 O′ Donoghue and Others v. the United Kingdom, ECHR (2010) Appl. No. 34848/07, judgment of 14 December 2010.

687 O′ Donoghue and Others v. the United Kingdom, ECHR (2010) Appl. No. 34848/07, judgment of 14 December 2010.

at issue) and not in contravention of international obligations[688]. Thus, while a foreigner may be treated differently on certain grounds subject to balance of various public interests, such as those concerning safety and public health, public order, the international and national obligations on immigration, their legal status cannot be used in order to allow discriminatory treatment[689].

Although the aim of the protection of borders and controlling migration flows is legitimate, imposing a general impediment to marriage was not proportionate to that aim, especially since the immigration law in force already contained provisions to tackle sham marriages[690].

In the situations described above, it is not disputed that the national legislature, which has the power to mediate between constitutional values, can legitimately set conditions aimed at limiting cases of fraud, or more generally at regulating the entry and treatment of non-EU citizens. However, such requirements cannot have the effect of making the exercise of a fundamental right impossible. As the Italian Court affirmed, the legislature- far from making it easier to ascertain any element of convenience of the marriage-has instead created a general impediment to marriage by unauthorized third-country nationals presence in the state[691].

According to the ECtHR judgment in *O′Donoghue and Others v. the United Kingdom*, the margin of appreciation granted to the states cannot extend so far as to introduce a general, automatic and indiscriminate restriction on a vitally important right[692].

From what has been analysed so far, it is possible to deduce that the Italian legislative system regarding irregular immigration is experiencing a strong tension between two opposite needs: guaranteeing the security of the territory and the control of irregular flows and, on the other hand, protecting the fundamental rights of migrants, although irregular and therefore without a residence permit. The balancing of these two reasons seems to be a difficult objective to achieve with an imbalance in favor of the secu-

688 Constitutional Court, Judgment of 25 July 2011 No 245, Official Journal No 32 27/07/2011.
689 Constitutional Court, Judgment of 25 July 2011, No 245, Official Journal No 32 27 July 2011, recalling Decision No 249 of 2010, para 4.1.
690 Constitutional Court, Judgment of 25 July 2011, No 245, Official Journal No 32 27 July 2011.
691 Constitutional Court, Judgment of 25 July 2011, No 245, Official Journal No 32 27 July 2011.
692 O′ Donoghue and Others v. the United Kingdom, ECHR (2010) Appl. No. 34848/07, judgment of 14 December 2010.

rity needs that have led to an intensification of the policy towards the phenomenon of irregular immigration leading to a significant legislative stigmatization for example with the introduction of the crime of irregular immigration. In addition to the introduction of new measures, the legislator has chosen to reduce the protection of the fundamental rights of this category of migrants, so as to hinder or even prevent their inclusion in the social fabric of the state and in the hope of discouraging arrivals in the country by force of this treatment. An example of what has been said are the restrictions on obtaining licenses and public authorizations and on the subject of marriages: in both areas the attempt, curbed by the national and international courts in charge of safeguarding fundamental rights, has been to reduce the protection of rights which are by their nature undeniable to any person regardless of their status.

II. The sea: irregular migrants by sea and the protection of human rights

1. Arrivals of migrants by sea in the Euro-Mediterranean area: the situation on the Italian shores

The control of the migration flow by sea is particularly difficult in terms of finding a balance between the human rights protection and the aim of the State controlling their borders: the issue is very complicated considering the complex framework and the high number of actors who are involved in this control of maritime borders[693].

The European borders are managed with forms of police cooperation, including the bilateral relations between countries which overlook the same sea. Moreover, it is necessary to add to that a complex juridical framework of international legislation on sea law, refugee law, European Union law and the Convention on Human Rights which are crucial for the control activity[694].

---

693 G. CAMPESI, *L´Italia e il controllo delle frontiere marittime*, in M. SAVINO, *La crisi migratoria tra Italia e Unione Europea: diagnosi e prospettive*, Editoriale Scientifica, Napoli, 2017.

694 For instance Conventions 1982 United Nations Convention on the Law of the Sea (UNCLOS); 1974 International Convention on the Safety of Life at Sea (SOLAS); 1979 International Maritime Search and Rescue Convention (SAR); European Convention of Human Rights;1951 Geneva Convention on Refugee Status; EU Directive 2011/95.

Border surveillance is regulated by rules of a regional nature, such as the Schengen Border Code, which governs surveillance activities aimed at preventing unauthorized crossings and imposes on member states the provision of appropriate and adequate staff and resources, as well as permanent cooperation between the competent national services and those belonging to several member states, possibly coordinated by Frontex[695].

The Mediterranean area can be divided into three strategic areas[696] with respect to maritime border control:

1) the first area is that of the Atlantic and the western Mediterranean, which pivots on Spain and its relations with neighbouring countries (Morocco, Mauritania, Senegal);

2) the second area is that one of the Central Mediterranean, in this case irregular migration control activities point to the role of Italian police forces and have been influenced by the difficult relations with Libya in recent years;

3) the third is that one of the eastern Mediterranean in which Greece has a central role.

These strategic areas are different for geo-morphological characteristics, relations between neighbouring countries and institutional capacities of the main member countries of the region.

In 2015, Italy had welcomed 153,000 migrants and international protection applicants, fewer than in 2014 but representing an increase of 565% compared to the average of the arrivals of the decade 2003-2013[697]. The migratory routes have profoundly changed changed during the first nearly 20 years of this millennium. The migratory pressure has started to concentrate on the Sicilian coast, particularly on the island of Lampedusa, gradually reducing the number of migrants who land in Apulia[698]. The main starting points are Libya and, to a lesser extent, Tunisia, while the route of the low

---

695 Art. 16, comma 2, regulation (EC) 562/2006. For the origin and functions of FRONTEX: G. Campesi, *Polizia della Frontiera e la Produzione dello Spazio Europeo*, Deriveapprodi, Roma, 2015.

696 G. CAMPESI, *L´Italia e il controllo delle frontiere marittime*, in M., SAVINO, *La crisi migratoria tra Italia e Unione Europea: diagnosi e prospettive*, Editoriale Scientifica, Napoli, 2017.

697 Source: Annual Risk Analysis.

698 Apulia 1998 28.458 and 2015 11190 landings; Sicilia 1998 8.828 and 2015 104.709 landings. Source: processing of data contained in government reports on police activity and the state of security.

Adriatic and the route from the eastern Mediterranean (Turkey or Egypt) to the Ionic sea are almost irrelevant[699].

In Italy the incidence of people from areas plagued by serious political and / or civil crises has progressively increased, while the number of foreigners coming from neighbouring Balkan or North African countries has drastically decreased.

The reasons are probably[700]: on one hand the facilitations in obtaining visas granted to these countries as a counterpart to their cooperation with the so-called external dimension of EU[701] migration policies or the reserved visas for visas granted by Italy in exchange for bilateral cooperation on irregular immigration[702]; on the other hand to the growth of geopolitical instability and the driving factors that trigger forced migratory movements towards Europe from the immediate regions of the Mediterranean[703].

Crossing by sea is now a mobility strategy largely reserved for refugees and migrants from Sub-Saharan Africa, the Horn of Africa and the Middle East crisis areas, while the citizens of the Western Balkans and North Africa, which in the 1990s and 2000s represented the main nationalities that landed in Italy, now have different migration channels that allow the possibility of traveling to Europe freely without a visa requirement.

---

699 P. MONZINI, *Il traffico di Migranti per via marittima: il caso dell'Italia*, in P.MONZINI, F.PASTORE, G.SCIORTINO, *L'Italia Promessa. Geopolitiche e dinamiche organizzative del traffico di migranti verso l'Italia*. Studies Centre of International Policy, Roma 2004, p.48.

700 G. CAMPESI, *L'Italia e il controllo delle frontiere marittime*, in M., SAVINO, *La crisi migratoria tra Italia e Unione Europea: diagnosi e prospettive*, Editoriale Scientifica, Napoli, 2017.

701 F. TRAUNER, I. KRUSE, "*EC visa facilitation and readmission agreements: A new standard EU foreign policy* tool?", in *European Journal of Migration and Law*, 10(4), 2008, pp. 411-438.

702 P. CUTTITTA, *Readmission in the Relations between Italy and North African Mediterranean Countries*, in J.P. CASSARINO(ed), *Unbalanced Reprocities: Cooperation on Readmission in the Euro-Mediterranean Area.*, Middle East Institute, 2011, p. 40.

703 A. NOURAN, P. MONZINI, F. PASTORE, *The Changing Dynamics of Cross-border Human Smuggling and Trafficking in the Mediterranean*, Istituto Affari Internazionali, Roma, 2015, p. 20.

2. The structure of the Italian maritime border system

Over time, Italy has developed a complex legal, political and diplomatic instrument for controlling irregular migrations by sea, redefining it with the adoption of Law 189/2002 (Bossi / Fini) which has supplemented Legislative Decree 286/1998, as already mentioned previously.

2.1. Normative aspect

The Italian rules governing maritime patrols are similar to international ones, especially the 1982 *United Nations Convention on the Law of the Sea* (UNCLOS). It is possible to distinguish between: territorial, contiguous and international waters.

Territorial waters are an extension of state sovereignty within which the passage of vessels flying a foreign flag must be guaranteed, unless it endangers peace, good order and the security of the coastal state[704]. Threats to good order include violations of customs and tax laws, regulations, drug trafficking or immigration[705].

The adjacent band extends for 24 miles beyond the territorial waters. Within this band the state has no full sovereignty but has significant prerogatives. In fact it can exercise the necessary controls in order to prevent and / or punish violations of its customs, tax, health and immigration laws and regulations[706].

Within this area of operation, police service ships therefore enjoy extensive power of inspection and stopping. According to Italian law, if there is proof that the boat carries irregular migrants, it can be escorted to the nearest port and placed under judicial seizure[707].

Outside the territorial waters and the adjacent area, the principle of the freedom of the seas applies and the boats are subject only to the jurisdiction of the flag state. International waters are not subject to any exclusive jurisdiction and, on the basis of Article 87 (1) Unclos, are to be considered as an open space.

704 Principle of innocent passage of the Law of the Sea. N. Klein, *Maritime Security and the Law of the Sea*, Oxford University Press, Oxford 2011, p. 75; Y.TANAKA, *The International Law of the Sea*, Cambridge University Press, Cambridge 2012, p. 85.

705 Art. 19 (2), UNCLOS.

706 Art. 33(2), UNCLOS.

707 Art. 12. Comma *9-bis*, D.lgs 286/1998.

An exception is the "right of access" to ships suspected of being involved in piracy, slave trafficking, abusive broadcasts, or in any case without flag, or in cases where there are bilateral or multilateral agreements between the states concerned[708].

Another exception to the principle of freedom of navigation in international waters is provided in the 2001 Protocol against the Smuggling of migrants by Land, Sea and air (Smuggling Protocol), attached to the 2000 United Nations Convention against Transnational Organized Crime, which is the only multilateral agreement to give States the "right of visit" with the aim of countering irregular immigration[709].

In line with international law, Italian law reflects the design drawn up by the international law of the sea, stating that the powers of inspection and stopping exercised in territorial waters can also be exercised offshore, within the limits of international law and multilateral /existing bilateral, when the ship flies a flag of another state, or is flag-free[710].The current rules offer wide margins to exercise the powers of controlling irregular migration by sea, as most of the vessels carrying migrants are flag-free[711].

The "right of visit" undoubtedly implies the exercise of a power of interdiction, that is, the adoption of measures aimed at halting the movement of the vessel to be subjected to checks. Such measures may involve the use of force, although the applicable international standards do not specify in detail the extent to which the use of force is legitimate. Evidently the use of force can only be carried out within the limits of the principle of proportionality and strict necessity[712].

These principles have been further clarified in the Italian order with the "rules of return" contained in the Decree of the Minister of the Interior of

---

708 Art. 110, UNCLOS.

709 E. PAPASTAVRIDIS, *The Interception of Vessels on the High Seas: Contemporary Challenges to the Legal Order of the Oceans*, Hart Publishing, Oxford and Portland 2013, p. 278.

710 Art. 12, comma 9-quater, D.lgs 286/1998.

711 G. CAMPESI, *L'Italia e il controllo delle frontiere marittime*, in M., SAVINO, *La crisi migratoria tra Italia e Unione Europea: diagnosi e prospettive*, Editoriale Scientifica, Napoli, 2017.

712 N. KLEIN, *Maritime Security and the Law of the Sea*, cit., p. 117. Even if there is space for arguing in favor of marginalization of legitimacy even more limited, especially in view of the fact that many of these operations are conducted in an exceptional situation with respect to the general principle of the freedom of the seas and to limit the mobilization of humans who are formally exercising their right to emigrate or seek shelter in another country (E. PAPASTAVRIDIS, *The Interception of Vessels on the High Seas*, cit., p. 309).

14 July 2003 containing Provisions on the matter of irregular immigration. It stipulates that the action is "always focused on safeguarding of the human condition and respect for the dignity of the person"[713].

The right of access must be "made in the best possible way to safeguard the security of the inspection team and the migrants themselves"[714], while in the case of recourse to coercive means, the intensity, length and length of the response must be proportionate to the intensity of the offence, to the actuality and the actuality of the threat[715].

The exercise of sovereign powers in border control encounters a limitation in international law on refugees and in particular the prohibition of *refoulment* provided for by Art. 33 of the Geneva Convention[716]. The Italian rules on the control of maritime borders do not explicitly mention this principle, although Article 2 (1) of Legislative Decree 286/1998 states that "*the fundamental rights are recognized in the foreign state at the frontier or in the territory of the state of the human person envisaged by the rules of national law, the international conventions in force and the generally recognized principles of international law*".

The prohibition of *refoulment* was instead placed at the top of the legal order of the European Union, to the point that Article 78 (1) of the Treaty on the Functioning of the European Union requires the development of a common asylum policy aimed at "any third-country national who needs international protection", as well as "ensuring that international protection is respected "as well as" direct to ensure compliance with the principle of non-*refoulment*".

In relation to the control activities of the common borders of the Schengen area, Regulation (EC) No 562/2006[717] also requires that its provisions be applied without prejudice "to the rights of refugees and those seeking international protection, in particular as regards non-*refoulment*"[718]. It is le-

713 Art. 7, comma 1, D. M. 14 July 2003.

714 Art. 7, comma 4, D.M. 14 July 2003.

715 Art. 7, comma 5, D.M. 14 July 2003.

716 E. LAUTERPACHT, D. BETHLEHEM, *The scope and content of the principle of non refoulment, in* E. FELLER, V. TÜRK, F. NICHOLSON (eds), *Refugee Protection in International Law: UNHCR's global consultations on international protection,* Cambridge University Press, Cambridge 2003, p. 89-177.

717 Regulation (EU) No 265/2010 of the European Parliament and of the Council of 25 March 2010 amending the Convention Implementing the Schengen Agreement and Regulation (EC) No 562/2006 as regards movement of persons with a long-stay visa, Official Journal L 85, 31.3.2010, p. 1–4.

718 Art. 3, regulation (EC) 562/2006.

gitimate to intervene in international waters if committed to enforcing rescue obligations and therefore to carrying out humanitarian interventions.

The obligation to provide relief to ships in difficulty is an ancient principle of customary law which has also been adopted in international treaties. Unclos states that states may require flag vessels to intervene and rescue boats in difficulty, to the extent that it is possible, reasonable and does not endanger their safety, while at the same time obliging coastal states to prepare search and rescue services in agreement with neighbouring countries[719].

Other conventional instruments regulate relief activities at sea, the most important of which are undoubtedly the 1974 International Convention on the Safety of Life at Sea (Solas), which provides for Art. 10 (a) an obligation to assist ships in difficulty, or to alert the competent authorities, and the 1979 International Maritime Search and Rescue Convention (Sar), which divided the sea into search and rescue regions for which one or more coordinated states are obliged to take responsibility for any search and rescue operations. Italy joined the Sar in 1979[720].

Italy has adhered to Sar with law number 147/1989[721] and with a subsequent implementing regulation[722] created an organisational structure dedicated to maritime relief, whose summit is constituted by the General Command of the Corps of the Harbor Capitals (*Guardia Costiera*) at the Ministry of Infrastructure and Transport. The Decree of the Minister of Interior of 2003 stipulates that relief and police operations may be concurrent[723], although in the case of aspects related to irregular immigration, the adoption of rescue measures must obviously take priority[724].

2.2. Political and institutional aspects

Maritime border control was explicitly conceived as an interforces activity whose strategic direction was directed at the Ministry of the Interior. The latter has the task of promoting appropriate coordination measures be-

719 Art. 98, UNCLOS.

720 Italy has joined the Convention with the Law No 147/1989 and with a subsequent implementing regulation D.P.R. No 662/1994.

721 Law No 147 of 3 April 1989, Official Journal No. 97 of 27 April 1989, Ordinary Supplement 31.

722 D.P.R. n. 662/1994.

723 Art. 2, comma 4, D.M. 14 July 2003.

724 Art. 2, comma 3, D.M. 14 July 2003.

tween competent Italian authorities, European agencies, as well as promoting agreements with countries of origin or transitory irregular flows aimed, in general, on "*cooperation in the fight against illegal immigration*"[725].

At the Ministry of the Interior, the Central Directorate for Immigration and Border Police was set up in 2002, it is entrusted with the tasks of coordinating border control activities and combating irregular immigration, functions that are at the local level coordinated by the Prefects of the land border provinces and the prefectures of the capitals of the regions concerned at the maritime border[726]

The modes of coordination between the various security agencies involved in maritime border control are specified in the aforementioned Decree of the Ministry of Interior of 2003, at Art. 2, paragraph 1, identifies three main areas of contrasting activities of irregular migration by sea:

1)the activities held in the third countries of origin and / or transit of the migrations, also thanks to diplomatic activity and to the agreements of cooperation;

2) the activities carried out in international waters, where the navy operates, although with the possibility of supporting police forces, whose intervention is extraneous "*in the exercise of the police powers of the high seas directed to monitoring, surveillance, identification, control of naval navigation objectives and the acceptance of illegal immigration flows*"[727];

3) the activities carried out in the territorial waters, where the Finance Guard police service operates, albeit on the occasion of the military navy or the means of other police forces, whose intervention is directed at the repression of crimes and the discovery of connections with transnational organizations that facilitate irregular migration[728].

Finally, port capitals have been attributed a "transversal" function, relating to the coordination of life-saving activities and the direction of the research and rescue activities. The competences of the Coast Guard in the matter were as mentioned above already governed by D.P.R. n. 662/1994[729] and remain unchanged even after the adoption of Law 189/2002[730].

---

725 Art. 11, comma 1-bis, D.lgs 286/1998.
726 Art. 11, comma 3, D.lgs. 286/1998.
727 Art. 3, comma 2, D.M. 14 July 2003.
728 Art. 3, comma, D. M. 14 July 2003.
729 D.P.R. No. 662 of 28 September 1994, Official journal No. 281 f 1 December 1994.
730 Art. 2, comma 2, D.M. 14 July 2003.

The Navy traditionally carries out police duties in the high seas and since the late nineties has been competing for the control of irregular migratory flows. Since 2002, its competences have been made more explicit and since then a constant surveillance activity on the high seas has been set up "*aimed at the localization, identification and tracing of suspected traffic smugglers, by means of employment of all available aircraft*"[731].

The co-ordination of sea-going activities was entrusted to the Navy Command, while the navy-controlled control device was based on coastal radars, maritime patrol vehicles, the seafront units and coastal naval units[732].

The body is equipped with an articulated para-military apparatus for border control, which today can leverage 3 aeronautical groups: 1 Aeronautical Exploration Group and 15 Aeronautical Departments[733].

This apparatus has been progressively strengthened and converted to control irregular migration by sea. Since 2006, furthermore, the action of the Guardian of Finance in the area of territorial waters and adjacent areas has been supported by the work of the Frontex agency[734].

The coordination of these operations, involving the participation of units belonging to several European countries, was entrusted to the Guardian of Finance through the Aeronautical Operation Command of Sea Practice, where the International Coordination Centre was established[735].

The action of the Italian and European security forces acting in the framework of the complicated operations launched by the Frontex Agency

731 Report on the Status of Military Disciplinary and Armed Forces Organization, 2003, Doc. nnnVI No 4, Presented by the Minister for Relations with Parliament, Senate of the Republic, Chamber of Deputies, XVI Legislature, Bill of Rights and Relationships, Rome, 2004, p. 112.

732 Since 2004 it has been operating on a permanent basis in the Sicily channel and intervenes on an occasional basis in the lower Adriatic and Ionian Sea, absorbing on average 15 % of the naval activity and 80 % of the units' activities Seaplane aerial.

733 Report on the activities of the police, on the state of order and on public security and organized crime (year 2014), Volume II, Doc. nnnVIII n.3, presented by the Minister of the Interior, Senate of the Republic, Chamber of Deputies, XIII Legislature, Bill of Rights and Relations, Rome 2015, p. 1308.

734 G. CAMPESI, *Polizia della frontiere*. Frontex e la produzione dello spazio europeo, Derive Approdi Editor, cit., pp. 176-185.

735 Reports on the activities of the police, on the state of order and on public security and on organized crime (year 2014), item I, Doc. nnnVIII n. 3, presented by the Minister of the Interior, Senate of the Republic, Chamber of Deputies, XIII Legislature, Bill of Rights and Relations, Rome 2015, p. 1301.

also leverages technical-operational cooperation with the forces of third countries of origin and / or transit, according to a migration management model that has been effectively defined as "external governance"[736] or "extra-territorial"[737] control of the frontier[738].

The objective of cooperation with third countries is to advance control activities by acting in foreign territorial waters, so as to intercept the movement of ships carrying migrants before they can leave the jurisdiction of the country of origin and / or transit.

Bilateral cooperation between the member countries and their closest neighbours remains a decisive factor in the organisation of the various local Euro-Mediterranean border control regimes. Italy is an emblematic example in that, it has entered into a long series of police and intensive technical cooperation agreements with the main countries of origin and / or transit of migratory flows[739].

Particularly intense was cooperation with Albania, Tunisia and Libya, which are the countries with the largest number of vessels loaded with migrants[740]. These countries have agreed to technical assistance programs for training of police personnel, exchange of liaison officers as well as strategic, operational and investigative information and on the return of irregular migrants and, above all, have initiated forms of patrolling the alliance of maritime borders.

---

736 S. LAVENEX, N. WICHMANN, *The External Governance of EU Internal Security*, in *Journal of European Integration*, 31, 2009, pp. 83-02.

737 J. RIJPMA, M. CREMONA, *The Extra-Territorialisation of EU Migration Policies and the Rule of Law*, EUI Working Papers, Law 2007/1, Fiesole 2007; V. MITSILEGAS, *Extra-territorial Immigration Control in the 21st Century: The Individual And The State Transformed*, in B. RYAN, V. MITSILEGAS (eds), *Extraterritorial Immigration Control*, cit., pp. 38-64.

738 G. CAMPESI, *L'Italia e il controllo delle frontiere marittime*, in M., SAVINO, *La crisi migratoria tra Italia e Unione Europea: diagnosi e prospettive*, Editoriale Scientifica, Napoli, 2017.

739 Cooperation agreement on the fight against terrorism, organized crime, drug trafficking and illegal immigration, signed in Algiers on 22.11.1999 and entered into force on 28 January 2008 and other cooperation agreements with Tunisia, Egypt and Libya.

740 P. MONZINI, *Il Traffico di Migranti per via marittima*, 2004-2008, Cespi working paper, cit, p. 45.

3. The different phases of the Italian policies for the control of maritime borders

In Italy it is possible to see a progressive evolution of security oriented actions, which, in addition to having to respond to the changed political geography of irregular migration by sea, see the political-institutional reference scenario changing. It is possible to detect three phases.

The first phase is represented by the five-year period from 1997 to 2002, at the end of which *Apulia* ceased to be the main destination for landings of migrants. This phase, besides being marked by the first genuine migratory crisis experienced by our country due to geopolitical instability in the Western Balkans region, sees Italy develop its maritime border control. The strategy of extra territorialisation of Italian control already highlighted many of the tensions between humanitarian needs and the securitization drive that would characterize the maritime border control policies for the years to come.

Cooperation with Albania evolved in years of serious humanitarian crises powered by the political instability that plagued the Western Balkans, culminating in the 1999 exodus of Kosovars. Italy was confronted with mixed migratory flows in which refugees fleeing from wars and persecutions mixed with Albanian citizens migrating for economic reasons[741].

The political response was contradictory: on the one hand, the government granted limited temporary protection measures to those who had reached Italian soil by escaping economic political instability in Albania in 1997 and the Kosovo crisis in 1999, and on the other hand the cooperation of police officers with the Albanian authorities aimed to halt the migratory flow before it reached Italian territory[742]. Such a strategy allowed to project the control capabilities of Italian security forces beyond domestic jurisdiction, without which also an extension of the burdens arising from the exercise of sovereign powers[743].

---

741 It is insufficient to recall that of the 46,000 migrants who landed in Puglia in 1999, over 22,000 were of Kosovar origin and 7.4000 Roma (P. MONZINI, *Il Traffico di Migranti per via marittima*, 2004-2008, Cespi working paper, cit., p.44).

742 M.C. PUGH, *Europe´s boat people: maritime cooperation in the Mediterranean, Institute for Security Studies*, Western European Union 2000, p. 36.

743 T. BASARAN, *Security, Law, Borders. Spaces of Exclusion, in International Political Sociology*, 2(1), 2008, pp. 339-354.

The second phase covers nearly a decade and is interrupted by the explosion of the so called "Arab Spring" in 2011[744], when the geopolitical scenario of the Mediterranean area changes dramatically. This period is characterized by the structure of the Strait of Sicily as the main transit space for irregular migration by sea and Libya as a the most common starting point not only for migrants from North Africa but also for migrants from sub-Saharan Africa, Asia, and from the Middle East[745].

In 2004, the Navy launched an international water patrol operation called Constant Vigilance, putting in place a naval control device that crossed into international waters in permanent service and could draw on the coastal radar network, patrol vehicles Sailboat of 41st fever in Sigonella, plus more united aeronautics rooms at Augusta base ready for rapid intervention in case of need[746].

In parallel, multinational action has also been intensified, with the launch of the first joint operations co-ordinated by the European front-facing agency[747]. The response to the increase of migratory flows in the Sicily channel did not diminish the simple enhancement of the control measures. Italy has also attempted to operate a genuine "policy transfer" by replicating the integrated control model of the maritime border experienced with Albania. The shifting of the main points of departure to Libya has led the Italian government to look for forms of co-operation similar to the Gaddafi regime with which the first arrangements of a technical nature were stipulated in 2003[748].

744 Arab Springs is the term referred to as Arab Revolutions: it was a revolutionary wave of demonstrations, protests, riots, coups and civil wars in north Africa and Middle East, started in Tunisia on December 2010. Other countries in revolution were: Libya, Egypt, Yemen, Syria, Bahrain. Demonstration took place in Morocco, Iraq, Algeria, Iranian, Lebanon, Jordan, Kuwait, Oman and Sudan. Minor protests: Djibouti, Mauritania, Palestinian territories, Saudi Arabia.

745 P.MONZINI, *Il traffico di Migranti per via Marittima*, 2004-2008, cespi working paper cit., p. 58-59.

746 Reports on the state of military discipline and on the state of the organization of the armed forces (year 2008), Doc. nnnVI No 2, presented by the minister for relations with Parliament, Senate of the Republic, Chamber of Deputies, XVI Legislature, Drawings of the law and reports, Rome 2010, p. 124.

747 The first operation was Nautilus only active for a few years for the contrasts between Italy and Malta on who would be charged with the burden of receiving migrants intercepted in the course of activities at sea. Then Hermes had hitherto acted to cover the route from Algeria to Sardinia, and Aenea, which had an operational scope moved more to the Ionian Sea.

748 S. HAMOOD, *Eu-Libya Cooperation on Migration: A Raw Deal For Refugees and Migrants?*, in *Journal of Refugee Studies*, 21, 2008, p. 33; S. KLEPP, *A contested asy-*

Cooperation with Libya improved with the conclusion of the Treaty of Friendship of 30 August 2008[749], which was executed by the police cooperation agreement of December 2007. Italy pledged to provide military means for the joint patrol of the Strait of Sicily and Libya agreed to repatriate migrants intercepted during sea operations[750].

Those agreements which led to the condemnation of Italy by the European Court of Human Rights in *Hirsi Jamaa and Others v. Italy* (2012)[751] were progressively incorporated into a European framework[752], so that in the absence of a definitive test of Frontex's cooperation in the back-up of operations in 2009, it can be argued that the action of Italian naval vehicles took place within the framework of Joint operation *Nautilus*, mentioned above, whose operational plan from 2008 provided for the possibility of landing migrants in Libyan territory [753].

For Italy, immediate results were achieved with a rapid decline in landings registered in Sicily in 2009 and 2010. The Italian government considered joint patrol operations as a major achievement of diplomacy, while the frontline indicated the availability of Libya for "*repatriation of illegal migrants as a factor that strengthened the deterrent effect of joint operations*"[754].

The European Court of Human Rights held a different opinion that in the case of *Hirsi* defined the refusal operations carried out by Italy in col-

lum system: The European Union between refugee protection and border control in the Mediterranean Sea, in *European Journal of Migration and Law*, 12, 2010, p. 4.

749 Law 6 February 2009, No 7 Ratification and implementation of the Treaty of friendship, partnership and cooperation between the Italian Republic and the great Arab Jamamatic People's Socialist Republic, made in Benghazi on 30 August 2008. Official Journal General Series n.40 of 18-02-2009.

750 L. BIALASIEWICZ, *Off-shoring and Out-sourcing the Borders of Europe: Libya and EU Border Work in the Mediterranean*, in *Geopolitics*, 17, 2012, p. 854.

751 ECtHR – *Hirsi Jamaa and Others v Italy* [GC], Application No. 27765/09.

752 D. LUTTERBECK, *Migrants weapons and oil: Europe and Libya after the sanctions*, in *The Journal of North Africa Studies*, 2009, No 14, p. 172; E. PAOLETTI, F. PASTORE, *Sharing the dirty job on the southern front?, International Migration Institute working paper, December 2010*, cit., p. 19.

753 Frontex, *Frontex go ahead for Nautilus*, Press release of 7 June 2008, http://frontex.europa.eu/news/go-ahead-for-nautilus-2008-M1QUcT (last access: 9 August 2016).

754 Frontex, *Annual Risk Analisis 2010*, Warsaw 2010, p. 18; Frontex, *Programme of Work 2010*, Warsaw 2010, p. 18.

laboration with the Libyan authorities as a genuine extraterritorial exercise of sovereignty, which involved a violation of the *refoulment* ban.[755]

Italy, on the other hand, argued that the migrants had not been rejected, but aided and landed in the most secure and nearest port. Such a topic used the lacuna of the international humanitarian law regime of the seas, which, while providing for rescue obligations[756], does not regulate the related landing burdens, enabling states to choose a safe harbour to land migrants.

As suggested by the literature on the subject and the most recent international standards, it is impossible to assess the safety of the chosen landing site, regardless of the rules of asylum law[757].

The European Court of Human Rights, in the *Hirsi* case, has reiterated that research and rescue operations should also take into account the risk of persecution and inhuman and degrading treatment which migrants may expereince at the landing site.

The controversy triggered by Italy's pushback operations was an opportunity to further clarify at European level the legal framework governing operations at sea. Although not all of the Member States were convinced of the need for a reform of the Schengen Border Code on labour, fearing in particular the weakening of the fight against irregular immigration, the Council came to adopt Decision 2010/252 / EU, *"no one can be landed or otherwise handed over to a country's authorities in violation of the principle of*

755 M. GIUFFRE´, Watered-Down Rights on the High Seas: Hirsi Jamaa and Others v. Italy, in *International and Comperative Law Quartely*, 2012, No 61, pp. 728-750.

756 The Art. 98, paragraph 1 (obligation to provide assistance) of UNCLOS (United Nations Convention on the Law of the Sea) and Chapter V, Regulation 33 (distress situation: obligation and procedures), paragraph 1 of the SOLAS (International Convention on the Safety of Life at Sea), state that every State shall require the master of a ship flying its flag the rescue of people in danger without any distinction of status or nationality and it must also guarantee assistance until disembarkation in the nearest place of safety.

757 A. FISCHER-LESCANO, L. TILLMANN, T. TOHIDIPUR, *Border Controls at Sea: Requirements under International Human Rights and Refugee Law*, in *International Journal of Refugee Law*, 2009, No 21, p. 290; V. MORENO-LAX, *Seeking Asylum in the Mediterranean: Against a Fragmentary Reading of EU Member States´ Obligation Accruing at Sea*, in *International Journal of Refugee Law*, 2011, 23, p. 199. Also *Maritime Safety Committee, Resolution* 167(78), 20 May 2004, *Guidelines on the Treatment of Persons Rescued at Sea*, MSC 78/26/Add.2, Annex 34, para 6.17.

non-refoulment or where there is a risk of being flushed or repatriated to another country in violation of that principle"[758].

The decision, which was annulled by the Court of Justice for procedural reasons, although it remained in force for a long time in the light of the approval of a replacement law, was finally adopted by Regulation (EU) No. 656/2014[759], however, was limited to the joint operations co-ordinated by Frontex. Because of this, Italy has been able to continue to provide migrants with help in neighbouring third countries in international waters, as evidenced by the most recent reports on police activities issued by the Ministry of the Interior[760].

The first arrangements for co-operation in the control of irregular immigration had been agreed with the Tunisian transition government on 5 April 2011 and subsequently consolidated in March 2012, with a memorandum of understanding signed between the Interior Ministers. The objectives of these agreements were the readmission of Tunisians irregularly in Italy and technical cooperation with the Tunisian National Guard, to which media and training activities were offered[761].

Much more complex was the management of relations with Libya post the Gaddafi regime. In April 2012, the interior ministers signed a verbal process involving the exchange of liaison officers, a readmission agreement, training activities for the Libyan police and the restoration of centres[762].

On 7 October 2013, a delegation of the Minister of the Interior led by the Directorate General for Immigration and Border Police then took on the commitment to support the Libyan border police with targeted train-

758 Council Decision 2010/252/EU, Attachment, Part I, Art. 1, comma 2.

759 Regulation (EU) No 656/2014 of the European Parliament and of the Council of 15 May 2014 establishing rules for the surveillance of the external sea borders in the context of operational cooperation coordinated by the European Agency for the Management of Operational Cooperation at the External Borders of the Member States of the European Union, Official Journal L 189, 27.6.2014, p. 93–107.

760 Decision of the Council 2010/252 / EU, annex, part I, art. 1, paragraph 2.

761 The agreement provides for simplified procedures for the recognition and repatriation of Tunisian nationals, which have repatriated a total of 3,290 people between 2012 and 2013.

762 Report on the activities of police forces, state of order and public security and organized crime (year 2012), cit. p. 27.

ing activities and assistance in maritime patrols by means of Guard of Finance[763].

At the same time, Italy had repeatedly called for European intervention, particularly in the wake of the launch of a joint defence and security policy operation in support of the Libyan security forces, especially in terms of maintaining order and border control[764].

The hopes of Italy were finally achieved with the adoption of Decision 2013/233/CFSP[765] which started the civilian mission for integrated border management assistance called EUBAM Lybia[766].

4. The North Africa crisis and the solution to manage the new migration flows

In 2011, the season opened with Libya plunging into a spiral of violence that led Italy and Europe to suspend any kind of collaboration pending stabilisation of the country. The consequence has been a progressive increase in the number of migrants sailing from the Libyan coasts since 2013.

In the Strait of Sicily, following these events, surveillance has been enhanced with the deployment of increasingly sophisticated and expensive media and technologies such as EUROSUR, the information platform created with the approval of EU Regulation no. 1052/2013[767] which integrates all national surveillance systems located along the southern frontier of Europe.

---

763 Report on the activities of police forces, state of order and public security and organized crime (year 2013), p. 1618.

764 Report on the activities of police forces, state of order and public security and organized crime (2012), p. 29.

765 Council Decision (CFSP) 2016/1339 of 4 August 2016 amending and extending Decision 2013/233/CFSP on the European Union Integrated Border Management Assistance Mission in Libya (EUBAM Libya), Official Journal L 212, 5.8.2016, p. 111–112.

766 European Union External Action, EU Integrated Border Assistance Mission in Libya (EUBAM Libya), January 2015, in http://eeas.europa.eu/csdp/missions-and-operations/eubam-libya/pdf/factsheet-eubam-libya-en.pdf (last access: 8 August 2016).

767 Regulation (EU) No 1052/2013 of the European Parliament and of the Council of 22 October 2013 establishing the European Border Surveillance System (Eurosur), Official Journal L 295, 6.11.2013, p. 11–26.

The system is designed to enhance maritime border control capabilities, providing the security agencies with a detailed information framework for tracking, locating and intercepting unauthorized crossings[768].

The first initiative was launched by the Italian government following the wreck near the Lampedusa Island on October 3, 2013, where more than 350 people died. The Italian response to such tragic events was the launch of a unilateral operation called *Mare Nostrum*[769] which in fact increased the patrol activity of the Sicily channel that the Navy had been staging since 2004 with Constant Vigilance.

Mare Nostrum used a quantity of men and means that had no precedent in the history of maritime control of Italian maritime borders and was presented as an operation whose main objective was to safeguard human life at sea and humanitarian assistance. For the first time the rhetoric was to speak of assisted migrants and not intercepted clandestines[770].

The humanitarian purpose of the operation gained consensus on the Italian government's action that has even been judged by many NGOs as a kind of humanitarian corridor *de facto* through the central Mediterranean. The operation was then ended with the aim to stimulate the EU take charge of the problem, but it raised a lot of protests[771]. And even after *Mare Nostrum*, the Navy's presence in the Strait of Sicily did not fall after November 2014. In fact, it operates a new Maritime Surveillance and Security Instrument (DSSM), although the latter operates on a small operational area using a number of lower tools[772].

768 J. RIJPMA, M. VERMEULEN, *EUROSUR: saving lives or building borders?, in European Security*, 2015, 24 (3), pp. 454-472.

769 The Mare Nostrum Operation was launched by the Italian Government on 18 October 2013, as a military and humanitarian operation aimed at tackling the humanitarian emergency in the Strait of Sicily, due to the dramatic increase in migration flows. The Operation ended on 31 October 2014, coinciding with the start of the new operation called Triton.

770 Relations with the State of Military Discipline and Status of Armed Forces (2014), Doc. nnnVI n.3, Presented by the Minister for Constitutional Reforms and Relations with Parliament, Senate of the Republic, Chamber of Deputies, XVII Legislature, Bill of Rights and Relations, Rome 2015, p. 89.

771 UN High Commissioner for Refugee, Profonda preoccupazione per la fine di Mare Nostrum, Comunicato stampa 16 ottobre 2014, in Http://www.unchr.it/news/unhcr-profonda-preoccupazione-per-la-fine-delloperazinoe-mare-nostrum (last access: 5 September 2015); Amnesty International, Lives Adrift. Refugees and Migrants in Peril in the Central Mediterranean, Peter Benenson House, London 2014, p. 25.

772 Report on the activities of police forces, on the state of order and public security and on organized crime (2014), cit., p.7; Reports on the state of military disci-

The attitude of the European institutions to Italian action has been ambivalent. *Mare Nostrum* has raised some perplexity in European partners, worried that the rules of engagement adopted were revealing a powerful attraction for irregular migrants[773]. Italy invoked more European intervention and stimulated a broad debate on the type of commitment Frontex could have been able to guarantee[774].

It was clear that Frontex would not be able to replicate a similar operation *Mare Nostrum* but it was not just a matter of the means to be put in place. All the Commission's concerns were expressed by Frontex in the document outlining the strategic lines for the future *Triton* operation, which would replace the previous operations in the region[775]. The document suggested that the presence of Italian ships near the Libyan coasts encouraged potential migrants to embark on a sea voyage with boats that were poorly equipped and unsuitable for crossing[776].

The governments of the other member countries, for their part, expressed some reluctance to participate in the new operation that the agency was about to launch, fearing that this also would work to act as an attraction factor for irregular migrants[777]. *Triton* was finally approved only on condition that its operational area was strictly circumscribed at the margins of Italian territorial waters and its objectives strictly limited to the surveillance of the European frontier[778].

It was only after another tragedy at sea, when in April 2015 the lives of more than 800 migrants were lost, that the mandate of the *Triton* operation was extended and its budget tripled in order to equip it with means

---

pline and on the state of the organization of the Armed Forces (2014), cit., P. 91.

773 S. CARRERA, L. den HERTOG, *Whose Mare?*, CESP paper in *Liberty and Security in Europe*, January 2015, No 79 cit. p. 4.

774 G. CAMPESI, *L'Italia e il controllo delle frontiere marittime*, in M., SAVINO, *La crisi migratoria tra Italia e Unione Europea: diagnosi e prospettive*, 2017, Editoriale Scientifica, Napoli.

775 Frontex, Concept of reinforced joint operation tackling the migratory flows towards Italy: JO EPN-Triton, Warsaw 2014, p. 4.

776 Frontex, *Concept of reinforced joint operation tackling the migratory flows towards Italy: JO EPN-Triton*, Warsaw 2014, p. 4.

777 G. CAMPESI, L'Italia e il controllo delle frontiere marittime, in M., SAVINO, La crisi migratoria tra Italia e Unione Europea: diagnosi e prospettive, 2017, Editoriale Scientifica, Napoli.

778 S. CARRERA, L. DEN HERTOG, *Whose Mare?*, CESP paper in Liberty and Security in Europe, January 2015, No 79 cit. p. 4.

capable of conducting similarly large rescue operations to those carried out under the *Mare Nostrum* operation[779].

The *Triton* operation took place in a political context in which humanitarian inspiration continued to dominate the debate, but the document which the board sent to the commission to increase the presence at sea of Frontex pointed out that strengthening the search and rescue capabilities of the joint operations coordinated by the agency should have always been carried out within its mandate, that is, control and surveillance of its borders. Therefore there was an intensification of the securitization and the humanitarian speech has ended up being incorporated into the talk of combating migrant traffic and smuggling[780].

The new framing of the humanitarian issue called for rethinking the response by abandoning the search and rescue approach and developing a maritime border management model inspired by military action against piracy. For these reasons, the European Council of 23 April 2015 imagined the launch of a military security operation and common defence policy with radically different ends from the predominantly humanitarian and border surveillance. The operation would have dismantled the traffickers' networks, assuring the perpetrators of justice and seizing their property, taking systematic measures to detect, stop, and destroy the boats before they were used by traffickers[781]. This provided for military action, such as the preventive destruction of potentially usable boats for smuggling, which needed a legal base capable of legitimizing raids on the territory of the third countries concerned.

The operation *Eunavfor Med*, subsequently renamed *Sophia*, was finally approved by Council Decision PESC 2015/778[782] and started its operations on 22 June 2015 and was organized in three successive phases:

---

779 Frontex, *Frontex expands its Joint Operation Triton*, press release, 26 May 2015, in http://frontex.europa.eu/news/frontex-expands-its-jointoperation-triton-udpbHP (last access: 8 August 2016).

780 G. CAMPESI, *L´Italia e il controllo delle frontiere marittime*, in M. SAVINO, *La crisi migratoria tra Italia e Unione Europea: diagnosi e prospettive*, Editoriale Scientifica, Napoli, 2017. European Commission, Questions and answers on the European Agenda on Migration, Fact sheet, 13 May 2015, http://europa.eu/rapid/press-release_MEMO-15-4957_en.htm (last access: 8 August 2016).

781 European Council, Special meeting of the 23 April 2015 – Statement, cit.

782 Council Decision (CFSP) 2015/972 of 22 June 2015 launching the European Union military operation in the southern Central Mediterranean (EUNAVFOR MED), Official Journal L 157, 23.6.2015, p. 51.

1) a first direct patrolling in international waters and intelligence gathering on traffickers' modalities;

2) a second in which military unions will be able to board, search, and hijack suspected ships to be used to promote irregular immigration. Such activities will be carried out at international waters, and subsequently also in territorial and domestic waters of third countries, "*in accordance with the applicable United Nations Security Council Resolutions or the consensus of the coastal State concerned.*"[783];

3) a third stage in which the mission, "*in accordance with the United Nations Security Council resolutions or with the consent of the coastal State concerned, shall stop, carry out inspections, seizures and hijackings on the high seas or in the territorial and internal waters of that State, of ships suspected of being used for trafficking and trafficking in human beings, under the conditions laid down in that resolution or consent*"[784].

Eunavfor Med Sophia is officially started on 22 June 2015 with the involvement of 22 countries.

In the early stages it covered a first zone that from the southern operating margin of *Triton* pushed down to the Libyan and Tunisian territorial waters. The transition to the second phase took place in October 2015, with the United Nations Security Council resolution no. 2240 of October 9, 2015[785]. In addition to reiterating the powers of action on the high seas already provided for by international law, it also grants *Eunavfor Med Sophia* the power of dispatching ships intercepted, destroying them in international waters without having to file it with judicial seizure[786]. The resolution represents a political investment of European action by the international community, but offers a fairly weak legal cover for the operation of *Eunavfor Med Sophia.*

In fact, the resolution does not grant the mandate to act in Libyan territorial waters without the consent of the state concerned, indispensable for the transition to the next steps of the operation. This has forced *Eunavfor Med Sophia's* means of limiting itself to international actions, effectively re-

---

783 Art. 2(2)(b)(ii), Decision (PESC) 2015/778 of the Council.

784 Art. 2(2)(c), Decision (PESC) 2015/778 of the Council.

785 Political and Security Committee Decision (CFSP) 2016/118 of 20 January 2016 concerning the implementation by EUNAVFOR MED operation SOPHIA of United Nations Security Council Resolution 2240 (2015) (EUNAVFOR MED operation SOPHIA/1/2016), Official Journal L 23, 29.1.2016, p. 63–64.

786 G. CAMPESI,, *L´Italia e il controllo delle frontiere marittime*, in M., SAVINO, *La crisi migratoria tra Italia e Unione Europea: diagnosi e prospettive*, Editoriale Scientifica, Napoli, 2017.

ducing research and rescue operations in all respects to those carried out by *Mare Nostrum.*

The scenario seems to have changed in March 2016, when the Fayez Al-Serraj-led government was set up in Libya. The European Union has begun negotiations to gain consensus on Libyan territory's extension of *Eunavfor Med Sophia's* action, as well as the resumption of technical assistance operations interrupted in 2013[787]. The Italian diplomatic initiatives have the obvious objective of reaching a Libya-like cooperation agreement similar to that between the European Union and Turkey[788].

In this context, the EU began to work to create conditions necessary to operate in Libyan territory with the cooperation of the security forces of the new government to reconstruct the security device in Libya, also assigning to this operation also technical assistance tasks originally unplanned[789].

On 20 June 2016 the operation was extended for a year, with a significant extension of its mandate. It now also has the task of providing technical assistance to the Coast Guard and the Libyan navy, as well as to ensure the implementation of the embargo on the sale of weapons in Libya on the basis of United Nations Security Council resolution no. 2292 of 14 June 2016[790].

Taking up the reflection expressed in conclusion in Part I, the tension between the need for security and the protection of fundamental rights is well highlighted in the phase of entry by sea, a context in which the regulatory framework appears to be very complex given the need to respect simultaneously international conventions on maritime law such as SAR, international refugee legislation such as the Geneva Convention and the Human Rights Conventions, such as the European Convention on Human Rights, whose application is crucial during the control activities. Italy appears to adopt a contradictory behaviour. On the one hand, on several occasions Italy has violated the principle of non-refoulment, as for example

---

787 G. CAMPESI, *L´Italia e il controllo delle frontiere marittime*, in M. SAVINO, *La crisi migratoria tra Italia e Unione Europea: diagnosi e prospettive*, Editoriale Scientifica, Napoli, 2017.

788 Agreement between the European Union and the Republic of Turkey on the readmission of persons residing without authorisation OJ L 134, 7 May 2014, p. 3–27.

789 G. CAMPESI, *L´Italia e il controllo delle frontiere marittime*, in M., SAVINO, *La crisi migratoria tra Italia e Unione Europea: diagnosi e prospettive*, Editoriale Scientifica, Napoli, 2017.

790 Decision (PESC) 2016/993 of the Council.

in the case Hirsi Jamaa and Others v. Italy, to reject the entry of illegal immigrants, and has signed agreements with third countries of origin or transit in order to reduce irregular flows without, however, a sufficient guarantee of protection of the fundamental rights of these migrants stopped in the moment of departure towards Europe in those countries. Italy has thus become responsible for violations of international human rights treaties. On the other hand, it has been used in search and rescue operations with operations carried out even by itself at sea like Mare Nostrum. This contradiction found in these legislative measures alongside violations of important principles that regulate fundamental rights, is accentuated by European legislative measures that are not always effective enough, for example in the case of joint operations at sea that have come only after great tragedies of deaths at sea as Triton, therefore finding Italy in a European regulatory framework that does not always seem to effectively apply the principle of solidarity. Moreover, the geographical position of Italy forces it to be one of the countries most exposed to the phenomenon of irregular flows, making the solution to the mentioned tension more difficult.

III. Reception: irregular migrants, first and second reception and the protection of human rights

1. Hotspots and the protection of human rights

One of the most controversial issues on the management of migratory flows is the issue of the treatment reserved to irregular migrants immediately after their arrival in the Italian State[791].

The criticisms are related to the mode of management of the very first operations after the arrival. It is important to clarify on the basis of which procedures are to be distinguished from those who are in a position to be able to claim the recognition of some form of international or humanitarian protection and can therefore be included in the host system by those who are economic migrants. Indeed, they are not in one of the situations

791 L. MASERA, G. SAVIO, *La "prima" accoglienza, in M., Savino, La crisi migratoria tra Italia e Unione Europea: diagnosi e prospettive,* Editoriale Scientifica, Napoli, 2017.

of needing protection and are therefore quickly subjected to the administrative repatriation process[792].

Until 2015, there was no organic law of the first reception. This was regulated in various regulatory texts, all issued in the execution of Community-wide obligations. The very first phase of identification and assignment to the category of asylum seekers or economic migrants, in spite of its extreme delicacy in terms of respect for fundamental rights, was characterized by a lack of law that was solved by relying on the absolute discretion of the policy authority.

Italy tried to organize in a organic manner the subject by Legislative Decree 142[793] of 18 August 2015 implementing Directive 2013/33 / EU[794] laying down rules on the reception of applicants for international protection and also Directive 2013/32 / EU[795] laying down common procedures for the recognition of the withdrawal of International protection. Despite that, in this legislation there are still questions concerning serious violations of the fundamental rights of foreigners.

The following is a brief *excursus* on the normative situation before the 2015 reform and then the current situation post reform will be analysed.

2. Centres of first aid and reception and reception centres for asylum seekers ante reform

Before the reform in 2015 all irregular foreigners came into a First Aid Centre (CPSA) after landing, usually located near the places where landings occurred frequently. In these centres, the identification of all foreigners and the separation between asylum seekers and economic migrants should take place: the first category to be sent to a reception centre for asylum seekers (CARA), the second to immediate repatriation, wherever pos-

---

792 L. MASERA, G. SAVIO, *La "prima" accoglienza, in M., Savino, La crisi migratoria tra Italia e Unione Europea: diagnosi e prospettive*, Editoriale Scientifica, Napoli, 2017.

793 Legislative Decree No 142 of 18 August 2015, Official Journal No 214 of 15 September 2015.

794 Directive 2013/33/EU of the European Parliament and of the Council of 26 June 2013 laying down standards for the reception of applicants for international protection, Official Journal L 180, 29.6.2013, p. 96–116.

795 Directive 2013/32/EU of the European Parliament and of the Council of 26 June 2013 on common procedures for granting and withdrawing international protection, Official Journal L 180, 29.6.2013, p. 60–95.

sible. Alternatively they should be detained at a centre for identification and expulsion (CIE) to await repatriation, or if there were no CIE with available places, they were issued with a quick order to leave the state territory within seven days[796].

Completely deficient in terms of regulatory discipline was the phase of the very first reception of the CPSA. Such centres were mentioned in Article 23, paragraph 1, of the Decree implementing the Single Immigration Act (D.P.R. 394/1999)[797], where it was established that the activities of first reception, assistance and those carried out for the sanitary needs associated with the relief of the foreigner may also be carried out outside the centres referred to in Article 22 (CIE) for the time necessary for the establishment of such centres or for the adoption of the measures necessary for the provision of specific forms of state aid.

Regarding the modalities of these centres, the regulation was limited to referring to the content of Decree Law 451/95 and its law of conversion (Law 563/1995, known as "Law of Apulia")[798].

This decree had been issued to meet the demands that emerged in that period following the massive influx on the Apulia Coasts of irregular migrants from Albania, and contained emergency provisions authorizing prefects for the use of military personnel in coastal control. Article 2 then allocated the sum of three billion lire (old Italian coin before the introduction of the Euro) to the institution, by the Ministry of the Interior, after hearing the Apulia Region, of three centres located along the maritime border of the Apulian coasts for the needs of first aid to the aforementioned groups of foreigners. However, there were no references to the legal nature of

796 Some of these phases found their source of regulation in a different regulatory source. The procedure for the repatriation of non-asylum-seeking economic migrants was governed by the provisions of Legislative Decree 286/98 (Article 10 regulates the dismissal institute, Article 13 on administrative expulsion, Article 14 contains the rules governing the execution of expulsion and of CIE retention); the procedures for formalizing the application for protection and the first reception measures (reception in the CARA) were governed by Legislative Decree 25/2008 implementing Directive 2005/85 / EC laying down minimum standards for procedures in Member States for the purpose Recognition and revocation of refugee status and Legislative Decree 140/2005 implementing Directive 2003/9 / EC laying down minimum standards for the reception of asylum seekers.

797 Decree of the President of the Republic August 31st 1999, n. 394, Official Journal n.258 of 03-11-1999 – Ordinary Supplement No. 190.

798 Law of 29 December 1995, n. 563, Official Journal No 303 of 30-12-1995.

these centres, which were not even specified whether it was closed places or otherwise host facilities from which the alien could freely leave[799].

The only provisions devoted to them merely envisaged the possibility of establishing centres of first aid and reception without specifying anything about the modalities in which such assistance was to be provided and even without mentioning the identification and registration of the protection applications that were made there. As it was easy to foresee, such anomaly not only caused a situation of absolute uncertainty but also led to police practices that were severely detrimental to fundamental rights[800].

Moreover, it is important to underline that a fundamental and transversal role in all the operations related to the recognition of the status of migrants and the concrete management of all matters related to the assistance and reception of immigrants is conducted from the administration of the interior. The administration of interior is also responsible for the establishment of the hotspots of the CPSA, CPA and CIEs. Further details on these centres will be provided subsequently[801].

The administration of the interior is also responsible for the "second reception" system, managed through SPRAR, the Protection System for Asylum Seekers and Refugees, as will be explained later[802]. This network is made up of a Central Service, located at the Department of Civil Liberties and Immigration and managed in agreement with ANCI (National Association of Italian Municipalities)[803].

The actual linkage of the network, however, is driven by all the municipalities that voluntarily adhere based on specific territorial projects (funded by the National Fund for Asylum Policies and Services), which are designed to guarantee and manage, also in collaboration with third sector

799 L. MASERA, G. SAVIO, *La "prima" accoglienza, in M., Savino, La crisi migratoria tra Italia e Unione Europea: diagnosi e prospettive*, Editoriale Scientifica, Napoli, 2017.

800 ECtHR, sez. II, *Khaifia and others v Italy*, 16483/12, 1 September 2015. See M. SAVINO, (2015), L'amministrativizzazione della liberta' personale e del due process dei migrant: il caso Khaifia, in Dir. imm. citt., 2015, No 3-4, p.50.

801 See p. 157 and following, Reception, Part III, Chapter III.

802 See p. 144 and following, Reception, Part III, Chapter III.

803 L. MASERA, G. SAVIO, *La "prima" accoglienza*, in M., SAVINO, *La crisi migratoria tra Italia e Unione Europea: diagnosi e prospettive,* Editoriale Scientifica, Napoli, 2017.

subjects, integrated reception activities for all asylum seekers who request it[804].

Local administrations do not play their role in participating in the SPRAR network, because they are in charge of important functions related to the guarantee of many of the social rights enjoined by refugees, and because they are in fact also affected by first reception. Asylum seekers are deployed in the territory of the Municipalities on the basis of a regional distribution plan, which in turn provides for the establishment of the Regional Centres/ Hubs, where they can carry out all the activities they can be carried out in the CARA and, where appropriate, assist in the formulation of international protection instances and the compilation of the relevant module formulated by the internal administration.

The Prefects still have the prerogative to promote, in agreement with the Municipalities, any useful initiative for the implementation of the use of international protection applicants on a voluntary basis, in the field of social utility in favour of local communities, within the framework of the current normative provisions.

The most well-known among the CPSA was one on Lampedusa: in the years that this centre was operational, until its provisional closure at the end of 2013, all the tens of thousands of irregular foreigners who landed on the island crossed, for more or less long periods, to the interior of the centre in question, where the identification and separation of economic migrants from asylum seekers was carried out. Since it was not at the regulatory level of a CIE, but a place of reception and there was no contingency procedure for detention, which was indispensable under Article 13 Const., if it had been a structure in which foreigners were deprived of their personal freedom, it would have been obvious that the centre on Lampedusa, like other active CPSA in Sicily or in other southern Italian regions, it was not a closed structure, but a place of assistance from which foreigners were free to move away. In fact, over the years there has been a *de facto* transformation of the CPSA into places of detention similar to CIE[805].

---

804 L. MASERA, G. SAVIO, *La "prima" accoglienza*, in M. SAVINO, *La crisi migratoria tra Italia e Unione Europea: diagnosi e prospettive*, Editoriale Scientifica, Napoli, 2017.

805 On the circumstance that the centre of Lampedusa, like other Sicilian centres, was a closed structure, from which strangers could not escape because they were massively guarded by the forces of order, testimonies are so numerous and unique that there is no reason to doubt it. For an analysis of landing management in Sicily during 2011 and 2012, see Vassallo Paleologo, Diritti sotto seque-

The use of the centre on Lampedusa as a CIE had been denounced not only by innumerable Italian and foreign NGOs, but also by two authoritative Commissions (the first instituted by the Senate of the Italian Republic and the second by the Parliamentary Assembly of the Council of Europe)[806] which in 2011 noted that they were a detention facility, in which foreigners were also detained for several weeks outside the court's jurisdiction and without any explanation being given about the grounds for detention[807]. The criminal judiciary was on more occasions urged to investigate the criminal relevance of such a serious violation of the right to the personal liberty of migrants.

However, they were all filed with a few lines of action and without the completion of any investigation activity, on the basis of the fact that the Lampedusa Centre was a reception centre and migrants were not detained, and the police authorities responsible for the centre were located there in order to deal with any serious emergency and threat to public security.

The issue was then brought to the attention of the European Court of Human Rights in an appeal filed by three Tunisian citizens who, in September 2011, had been detained for a few days in the Lampedusa Centre[808]. The applicants complained of the violation of Article 3 of the European Convention for the Protection of Human Rights, inhumane and degrading detention during which they had been placed in the centre and on ships; of Article 5 by virtue of the factual detention by the police without any legal basis (Article 5, comma 1), without judicial review (Article 5, comma 4) and without any provision of information on the reasons for de-

---

stro-Dall′ emergenza umanitaria allo stato di eccezione(Rights under seizure-from humanitarian emergency to state of exception), Aracne, 2012.

806 The judgment of the Commission for the right and protection of human rights, established by the Italian Senate and which ended its work on March 6, 2012, in the "Report on the state of human rights in prisons and in reception and detention centers for migrants in Italy ", available on the Italian Senate website.

807 See report on the visit to Lampedusa on 23-24 May 2011 by members of the *Ad Hoc Sub-Committee on large scale arrivals of irregular migrants, asylum seekers and refugees on Europe's southern shores*, established at *the Committee on Migration, Refugees and Population of the Parliamentary Assembly of the Council of Europe* concluding their reconnaissance stating that *"the conditions to which they were subjected were similar to the detention and deprivation of liberty... In practice, they are imprisoned there without access to a judge"*, and inviting the Italian authorities *"to clarify the legal basis for the de facto detention in the reception centre of Lampedusa* "(the report text is available on the Council of Europe website).

808 ECtHR, sez. II, *Khlaifia and others v Italy*, 16483/12, 1 September 2015.

tention (Article 5, paragraph 2); of Article 4 Prot. 4[809], by reason of the collective nature of the repatriation to which they were subjected under their nationality; and Article 13, because of the lack of the possibility of effective recourse against detention and repatriation[810].

The Court in Strasbourg, with a first judgment of September 2015, accepted all the main complaints of the applicants, landing in December 2016 for a more cautious decision only in reference to the violation of recalled art. 4 Prot. 4[811]. The condemnation of Italy by the Court is equivalent to the statement that the whole system of first reception, as structured in 2011, is in conflict with the fundamental rights of migrants.

The Court states, first of all, that any form of deprivation of liberty, even of an irregular alien, must take place in the strictest respect of the requirements laid down in Art. 5 of the European Convention. As regards the elements justifying the qualification of an expulsion as collective, and therefore contrary to Art. 4 of the Protocol, the Court has clarified that the mere identification is not enough to exclude the existence of a collective expulsion, since it is necessary for the expulsion of those who have been expelled to have the opportunity to express their specific situation of the repatriation[812].

3. 2015 Reform

The need to implement the European legislation and Europe's pressures, so that Italy would set up a more effective migration flow control system, led the legislator to re-write the system of the first reception. Legislative Decree 18.8.2015, n. 142[813], in force since 30.9.2015, is the implementation of Directive 2013/33 / EU laying down rules for the reception of applicants for international protection (recast of Directive 2003/9/EC[814]), as well as of Directive 2013/32 / EU, laying down common procedures for the recogni-

---

809 Art. 4 of Protocol 4 of 1951 Geneva Convention on refugee status.

810 ECtHR, Grand Chamber, Khlaifia, spec. § § 238 and 248.

811 European Court of Human Rights, Grand Chamber, *Khlaifia and others v Italy*, appeal n. 16483/12, 15 December 2016, 237-254.

812 European Court of Human Rights, Grand Chamber, *Khlaifia*, 238 and 248.

813 Legislative Decree 18 August 2015, n. 142, Official Journal No. 214 of 15 September 2015.

814 Council Directive 2003/9 / EC of 27 January 2003 laying down minimum standards for the reception of asylum seekers in the Member States, Official Journal L 31, 6 February 2003, p. 18–25.

tion and withdrawal of the international protection status: the abrogation of Legislative Decree No 140/2005[815] (implementation of Directive 2003/9/EC laying down minimum standards for the reception of applicants Asylum in the Member States), and introduces amendments to Legislative Decree 25/2008[816](implementation of Directive 2005/85/EC on minimum standards for procedures applied in the state of refugee for the recognition and withdrawal of refugee status).

The scope, as indicated in Article 1, includes measures for the reception of third-country nationals or stateless persons seeking international protection in the Italian territory and those subject to the so-called Dublin procedure for determining the State responsible for examining the application for asylum[817].

Such measures must have applied from the time of manifestation of the will to ask for international protection. In fact, the new Article 2 bis of Article 26, Legislative Decree 25/2008, stipulates that the statement containing the applicant's declarations must be drawn up within three working days of the request for protection, within six working days if the information has been given to border police offices or these terms may be extended by ten working days in the event of a high number of applications due to arrivals of a high numbers of applicants close together[818].

The relevance of the time when the applicant is willing to apply for protection is evident, since from that moment it is obligatory to prepare the reception measures provided for in the decree in question. Exactly at this moment there is a first criticism of the concrete ways of information about the right to seek asylum and the timeliness of the voluntary declaration.

According to Article 3 of the decree, the information booklet on the reception conditions (referred to in Article 10 of Legislative Decree 25/2008) is delivered and explained, with the help of cultural interpreters and mediators, after the submission of the application, when the choice to ask for

---

815 Legislative Decree 30 May 2005, n. 140, Official Journal No.168 of 21 July 2005.

816 Legislative Decree January 28, 2008, No. 25, Official Journal No. 40 of 16 February 2008.

817 Regulation (EU) No 604/2013 of the European Parliament and of the Council of 26 June 2013 establishing the criteria and mechanisms for determining the Member State responsible for examining an application for international protection lodged in one of the Member States by a third-country national or a stateless person, OJ L 180, 29.6.2013, p. 31–59.

818 G. CAMPESI, *L´Italia e il controllo delle frontiere marittime*, in M. SAVINO, *La crisi migratoria tra Italia e Unione Europea: diagnosi e prospettive*, Editoriale Scientifica, Napoli, 2017.

protection is already formalized: but nothing in the decree says anything about the information that must be provided to the alien regarding the possibility of asking for protection before such a will has already been in manifested in any form.

After the formalization of the request for protection, a residence permit for a six-months asylum application is issued to the applicant in Italy, renewable until the decision and, in the event of a judicial remedy, until the applicant has been authorized to remain in Italy (Article 4, paragraph 1). This permits allows the exercise of an employment activity after two months from the submission of the application.

The overall reception system is structured, as in the past, on three levels:

1)a first phase of rescue, first reception and identification, contained in the CPSA (Article 8);

2) a first reception phase in appropriate government centres (CPA) where the applicant formalizes the application for international protection (Article 9);

3) a second phase of reception concerning the applicant who has formalized the application and who has no means of subsistence; he/she will be sent to the centres of the protection system for asylum seekers and refugees, SPRAR, Art. 14 and following.

3.1. First aid and reception centers

Article 8, paragraph 2 provides that the rescue and first reception and identification functions continue to be carried out in facilities set up pursuant to Decree Law 451/95, converted into Law 563/95[819]. The decree adds nothing to the very first reception phase. The legislature limited itself to a reference to the above-mentioned Apulia Law, which provides for the possibility of establishing such centres without any specificity regarding their functioning.

The Decree Law of 17 February 2017, no. 13[820], paragraph 1 of Article 17, provides that *"the alien was admitted for the needs of rescue and first aid at special points of crisis set up within the facilities referred to in Law Decree 451/1955 converted into Law 563/95"*. Therefore is not provided any discipline of the centres called "crisis points" (hotspots according to the termi-

819 Law December 29, 1995, No. 563, Official Journal No. 303 of 30 December 1995.

820 Decree Law converted in Law by the Convertion Law 13 April 2017, n. 46.

nology of the European Commission), for which the reference is to regulatory texts that do not specify the nature of these sites and their functions[821].

The specific purpose of this organizational strategy is to facilitate Member States quickly identifying the people who are entitled to seek international protection as opposed to migrants who have been induced to enter Europe for various reasons and to detect irregular migrants who can be repatriated.

Within each structure, as mentioned in the previous chapter, there are officials of EUROPOL, EUROJUST, FRONTEX, EASO, UNHCR and OIM. There are also spaces dedicated to the national police offices and the territorial commission for the recognition of international protection.

In Italy, these structures have been identified in Lampedusa, Pozzallo, Porto Empedocle, Trapani, Taranto and Augusta. Their activity has been the object of a vast critical debate, since in these centres, several operations are carried out simultaneously and often indistinctly, some of which are subject to statutory and jurisdictional reservations, as restrictive of personal liberty guaranteed by Article 13 Const.

Beyond the inability of authorities to force foreigners to undergo fingerprinting and biometric identification, EU and international legislation stipulates that some basic essential rights will always be guaranteed at hotpots: the right to understandable information, the right to manifest at any time the will to seek asylum, the right not to be expelled before a full assessment of the individual personal situation, the right to be guaranteed the presence, in all operations of UNHCR and of other humanitarian organizations[822].

In 2017, however, the Interior Ministry published the Standard Operating Procedures that should be followed at each hotspot. These procedures were strongly criticized by the observers in order to be able to replicate

821 Regional Law (Legge Puglia) 24 March 1995, No 8, Official Journal 3 Special Serie, No 51, 23 December 1995.

822 The protection of these rights does not appear to be guaranteed in a widespread manner, for example, cases of deferred dismissal, prolonged retention of unaccompanied minors under conditions of serious promiscuity with adults, information and collective care, indefinite limitation of personal freedom, of a substantial grouping of migrants for predominantly homogeneous groups depending on their origin.

and settle the police practices mentioned above[823]that constitutes a violation of the law on foreigners (Article 10, paragraph 2, of the law).[824]

The rule also acknowledges that the CPSA does not only perform first aid but also identification functions, and that in order to render the activity identifiable effectively, a government programming document provides that the places where the first identification occurs are closed structures, from which the foreigner has not been allowed to leave.

Despite the fact, there is no legal basis for detention in these centres in open violation of Article 13 of Const. and Art. 5 of the European Convention on Human Rights this gap remains the most critical in the first reception system in Italy.

3.2. First reception centres (CPA)

Article 9, para. 1 provides that *"for the needs of first reception and for the completion of the operations necessary for the identification of the legal position, the foreigner has been admitted to the special government offices established by the Ministry of Interior Decree"*.

The management is entrusted to local authorities, public or private bodies working in the field of assistance to immigrants and asylum seekers, in accordance with the procedures for relying on public contracts. In the CPA, First Reception Centres, the international protection applicant was initiated by the prefect and was accepted for the time needed to complete the identification procedures (which began in the CPSA), the statement of the application for protection (compilation of the already mentioned model C3) and the initiation of the procedure of examination of the application itself.

At the same time, the applicant's health condition is assessed, in order to verify the existence of vulnerable applicants such as those with special needs as unaccompanied minor, pregnant women, old persons, etc. Once the formalities have been completed, the applicant who has no resources and requests it, is moved to the second reception facilities, that is the SPRAR system.

---

823 Reflections of Fulvio Vassallo Paleologo, available at: http://www.meltingpot.org/Hotspot-Le-Procedure-Operative-Standard-SOP.html. V4POwfmLTIV.

824 G. CAMPESI, *L'Italia e il controllo delle frontiere marittime*, in M., SAVINO, *La crisi migratoria tra Italia e Unione Europea: diagnosi e prospettive*, Editoriale Scientifica, Napoli, 2017.

Article 10 governs reception arrangements in CPA: "*respect for the private sphere is ensured, including gender differences, age-related needs, the protection of the physical and mental health of applicants, the unity of family nuclei consisting of spouses and relatives within the first degree, preparing the necessary measures for people with special needs*".

It is suggested that it is allowed to leave the centre in the daytime hours, with the obligation to return at night, and that the foreigner may ask the prefect for a temporary leave of absence for longer periods, with the obligation to justify any denial. Finally, it the possibility to communicate with representatives of UNHCR, guardianship institutions, ministers of worship, lawyers and family members was guaranteed.

Article 11 on reception arrangements provides that "*in the event of temporary availability of facilities within the structures referred to in Articles 9 (CPA) and 14 (SPRAR), due to the substantial and close involvement of applicants, reception can be arranged by the prefect... in temporary facilities, specially set up* " (CAS, extraordinary reception centres); pursuant to paragraph 3 previously mentioned in this Chapter, the stay in such centres is limited to the time strictly necessary for the transfer to the above structures[825].

CPA are also open structures in which foreigners seeking protection are not deprived of personal liberty, but are limited in freedom of movement. If they meet the requirements for the retention of the applicant in the expectation that his application will be assessed, it will be within the CIE, where possible in separate areas from non-applicants.

3.3. Hotspot approach

A few weeks after the issuance of Legislative Decree 142/2015[826], the Italian Roadmap was announced. This is a non-legislative instrument that

825 Article 12 provides that the Minister of the Interior shall issue by decree the tender specifications for the supply of goods and services in all the different categories of centres "in order to ensure uniform levels of hospitality in the national territory, in relation to the peculiarities of each type of centre". Then it is foreseen "the identification of forms of participation and involvement of the applicants in the conduct of their lives in the structures". Finally, under Article 13, the unjustified removal from the centre involves the withdrawal of the reception conditions.

826 Legislative Decree 18 August 2015, No. 142, Official Journal 214 of 15 September 2015.

does not regulate but clarifies the future Italian will with respect to the response to the current migration crisis[827].

It was announced on 28 September 2015 giving a framework of the current situation and the prospects for reception and management of asylum seekers and it has been followed by a circular of 6 October 2015 of the Department for Civil Liberties and Immigration of the Ministry of the Interior.

The text clarifies how the administration intends to implement the system outlined in Legislative Decree 142/2015 in execution of "further commitment by Italy for the Common European Asylum System (CEAS)"[828].

In line with the European Migration Agenda, Italy has adopted a new hotspot approach, namely a plan to channel the arrivals by sea into a number of selected landing ports where all prescribed procedures such as health screening, pre-identification, recording, finger printing and the taking of biometrics are conducted.

In September 2015, four ports were identified as hotspots: Pozzallo, Porto Empedocle, Trapani and Lampedusa, CPSA with a capacity of 1,500 each[829]. By the end of 2015, two other areas were opened, Augusta and Taranto.

The government with the terms Hubs and hotspot seems to refer to the government reception centres, CPA, which together with the CAS constitute the first welcome facilities at the regulatory level.

The ministerial document clearly indicates what hotspots are and what they are used for. First of all, this is similar to closed centres without any further specification. The government expects the alien to be deprived of personal liberty, at least for the time needed for the execution of the indictment (the 24-48 hour arch is only indicative especially in periods of increased inflow). However without there being any rule of law which gives

827 G. CAMPESI, *L'Italia e il controllo delle frontiere marittime, in M., Savino, La crisi migratoria tra Italia e Unione Europea: diagnosi e prospettive*, Editoriale Scientifica, Napoli, 2017.

828 According to the data reported in the ministerial roadmap, updated September 28, 2015, the Italian reception system has a total capacity of 96,945 seats, while the first reception capacity has gone from about 5,516 seats in 2012 to about 12,000 in half 2015. The first reception system is made up of structures belonging to former government centres that are being configured as "Regional Hubs" and which provide for an increase of up to 15,550 by December 2016. The extraordinary reception system consisting of CAS (in which It can be done both first and second reception) has a capacity of 68.093 seats.

829 Source Minister of Interior, Piano Accoglienza 2016.

legal basis for such deprivation of liberty it is to be determined whether and to what judicial authority it should be communicated, for the purpose of validating it. Again, this represents a breach of the guarantees referred to in Article 13 Const. and 5 of the Convention on Human Rights.

The procedures implemented in these hotspots are as follows:

a) subjected to medical screening, in order to ascertain immediate health problems; b) submission to the pre-identification procedure, consisting of interviews by officials of the immigration offices, for the compilation of the so-called "newsletter" containing the identification elements of the person, his/her photograph, basic information, and indication of whether or not to seek international protection and finally the identification of persons who might be part of the relocation[830] procedure.

The Roadmap states that "there will be a first differentiation between asylum seekers / potentially relocated and unregulated persons; c) submission to investigative or intelligence interviews with investigative police officers, of Frontex and Europol towards those who, on the basis of the first findings, are presumed to be able to provide useful information; d) separation, after pre-identification, of persons who are reported as CAT 1 (asylum seekers, even relocated, who will be sent for formalization of applications in the regional hubs, CPA) or CAT 2 (persons in position which do not require protection, destined to be transferred to CIE in view of the most recent repatriation)[831].

The government therefore expects that at this stage of the first reception, the fundamental selection of applicants for asylum, to be sent to the circuit of the reception, and irregular or economic migrants to be started in the return procedures. An aspect to be considered critically is the prediction that in the hotspots areas the interview and preselection activities are exclusively carried out by law enforcement agencies (immigration offices, scientific and investigative police) assisted by officials of Frontex, Europol and EASO agencies without presence of UNHCR or NGOs members, in closed centres where family or lawyer access was denied.

There are therefore no external controls over the correct and timely information of the right to seek international protection, not to mention

830 The so-called "relocation" allows the transfer from Italy to other member states of persons with obvious international protection needs belonging to nationals who have received a 75 % or more 75 % protection rate according to Eurostat data (To date only Syrians, Eritres and Iraqis).

831 G. CAMPESI, *L´Italia e il controllo delle frontiere marittime*, in M., SAVINO, *La crisi migratoria tra Italia e Unione Europea: diagnosi e prospettive*, Editoriale Scientifica, Napoli, 2017.

that the pre-identification phase takes place in the immediacy of landings, in relation to highly traumatized persons and certainly under conditions of stress, using a standard "news sheet"[832] in which the entries appear in different languages (Italian, French, English and Arabic) to indicate the reasons for their arrival in Italy.

To think that the whole fate of the migrant rests on the basis of this scarce information, does not suggest a respect for fundamental rights (the right to information about the possibility of protection and the problem of collective repatriation). Furthermore, the roadmap devotes considerable scope to the implementation of voluntary repatriation procedures, forced return, and foresees an increase in posts in CIE.

4. Criticism of the reform

The analysis in this paragraph and the subsequent subparagraphs, will be dedicated to the problems of the reception phase immediately after the arrival of the rescue services in Italy, both for asylum seekers and for economic migrants under the new reform. This is a very delicate phase because the fundamental rights of migrants are involved.

4.1. Personal freedom in the first aid and reception centres (CPSA)

The *Khlaifia* ruling ruled that the detention of irregular foreigners in closed facilities such as the one that was practiced for years on Lampedusa constitutes a detention in fact, without a legal basis, in violation of Article 5 of the Convention on Human Rights. The court has affirmed: “in the case of deprivation of liberty, it is particularly important to satisfy the general principle of legal certainty. Therefore, it is essential that the conditions of deprivation of liberty under domestic law are clearly defined and that the law itself is predictable in its application, so as to meet the legality requirement set by the law”[833]

832 Came to Italy for: 1) work, 2) reaching family members, 3) fleeing from poverty, 4) escaping for other reasons, 5) seeking political asylum.

833 *“lorsqu'il s´agit d´ une privation de liberte´, il est particulerment important de satisfaire au principe general de la securite´ juridique. Par consequent, il est essentiel que le conditions de la privation de liberte´ en vertu du droit interne soient clairement definies et que la loi elle-meme soit previsible dans son application, de facon a´ rem-*

As already mentioned, the CPSA which are not regulated at regulatory level are often administered by the police authority as closed structures, from which the alien cannot leave until he/she has been identified and categorised as an applicant for protection.

The police practices that the European Court of Human Rights have criticised in relation to the management of the Lampedusa Centre in 2011 are still being practiced today in the same manner as before, and the Government itself admits, in an official document that hotspots are closed structures, although they have no legal basis. There is a need for regulatory action to clarify whether and to what extent the deprivation of liberty is permitted for the purpose of first identification, otherwise a serious violation of Article 13 Const. will continue to go on.

4.2. The violation of the right to a correct information and ban on collective expulsion

The right of migrants to be informed about the possibility of requesting immediate international protection is of fundamental importance in a correct first aid system compliant with fundamental rights, it is also expressly recognized by a set of European and national norms[834]. As already described, the first and the second reception are different from the moment when the migrant expressed on his/her request for protection. So the right to be properly and timely informed of this possibility is a crucial moment for the fate of the migrant, from the arrival of the hotspot-CPSA. Indeed, as already mentioned, this is where a first selection is made between protection applicants and economic migrants. The first ones will be sent to the reception facilities, the second will be initiated for repatriation procedures and possibly temporarily destined for CIE. Even the detention in one of these CIE will then be able to formulate a request for asylum but in a condition of restriction of its freedom and with different procedures, as regulated by art. 6 and 7 of Legislative Decree 142/2015.

However, these clear provisions run the risk of being left out, considering in particular that the legislation does not provide for the presence of

---

plir le critere de legalite´ fixe´ par la Convention", ECtHR, sez. II, Khlaifia, 2015, § 69. It conforms to the point the judgment of the Grand Chamber (2016).

834 L.MASERO, G. SAVIO, *La prima accoglienza*, in M. SAVINO, *La crisi migratoria tra Italia e Unione Europea: diagnosi e prospettive*, 2017, Editoriale Scientifica Napoli, p. 56.

independent NGOs, lawyers and bodies in the very first post-landing stages, which could play a vital role in assisting the administrative authority in providing information to migrants, how to monitor the ways in which this information is actually guaranteed[835].

Connected to the subject of adequate information there is the ban on collective expulsion, as interpreted in the above quoted *Khlaifia*. The foreigner who is expelled or rejected who wants to complain to the omission of information that has led him to not apply for protection and consequently to suffer measures restricting his liberty, may claim his reasons in front of the ordinary judge when validating the retention or appeal against expulsion or rejection. However, it should be pointed out that if a migrant is categorized as an economic migrant from certain countries (e.g. among other, the so-called safe countries, Tunisia and Egypt), citizens of these countries are subject to expedited repatriation procedures, which concretely prevent them from having access to the defence in court.

Therefore, when the European Court of Human Rights imposes on the state, an order not to violate the prohibition of collective expulsion, to provide a foreigner the right to oppose repatriation, it imposes a guarantee that the foreigner is really put in the condition of advancing his demands, instead of being repatriated on the sole basis of his own nationality. Therefore it is reiterated that foreigners should be provided with correct information about their right to be informed and that they are guaranteed the opportunity to exercise their right in an individual interview.

4.3. The use of physical coercion

Article 9 of the EU Regulation 603/2013[836] establishing the EURODAC for fingerprinting compels each Member State to fingerprint any international protection applicant older than 14 years and to transmit that data to the central system as soon as possible and in any case within 72 hours of the

---

835 L.MASERO, G. SAVIO, *La prima accoglienza*, in M. SAVINO *La crisi migratoria tra Italia e Unione Europea: diagnosi e prospettive*, Editoriale Scientifica Napoli, 2017.

836 Regulation (EU) n. 603/2013 of the European Parliament and of the Council, of 26 June 2013, establishing "Eurodac" for the comparison of fingerprints for the effective application of Regulation (EU) no. 604/2013 which establishes the criteria and mechanisms for determining the Member State responsible for examining an application for international protection, Official Journal L 180, 29 June 2013, p. 1-30.

submission of the application for protection. Such an obligation has been proscribed by article 14 towards the foreigner in relation to the irregular crossing of an external frontier.

Fingerprinting takes place mainly in CSPA and the question should be asked: to what extent police forces can resort to physical coercion for fingerprinting against people who oppose and or offer passive resistance?

To answer the question it is necessary to consider the Code of Criminal Procedure, Article 349, allows the police to identify the persons under investigation to perform dactyloscopic, photographic and biometric identification. Paragraph 2 also stipulates that, if such investigations involve hair prediction or saliva and there is not the consent of the person, the compulsory sample shall be taken in accordance with the dignity of the person and with the prior approval of the public prosecutor. This is the only rule that authorizes the use of force in identification procedures, limited to hair removal or saliva, and as a rule it affects the fundamental rights of the subject, it does not seem possible to have an analogous extension.

The legislator in the case of goods protected by Article 13 Const. has the burden of clearly establishing the limits of coercive action, while respecting the legal and jurisdictional guarantees provided by the constitutional norm. In the absence of a specific authorizing rule, any coercive action which, as in the case of fingerprints, shifts into a restriction of personal freedom, must be considered in breach of Article 13 Const.

4.4. First reception centres and the protection of human rights

When the alien is initiated to the CPA, his/her asylum seeker status has already been recognized, though provisionally, and the centres where he/she is hosted are open structures, for which there are no problems with respect to Article 13 Const.[837] The problem at this stage is not of a regulatory nature but on the real capacity of the public administration to manage asylum seekers′ flows according to the dictates of the law.

In the absence of a sufficient number of places in the centres of reception, the hotspots have to take extraneous functions, often being the only structures where, at times of increased inflow, foreigners can be located even after rescue operations and first identification after which should end

---

837 Article of Italian Constitution on personal freedom. G. CAMPESI, *L′Italia e il controllo delle frontiere marittime,* in M., Savino, La crisi migratoria tra Italia e Unione Europea: diagnosi e prospettive, Editoriale Scientifica, Napoli, 2017.

their function. Foreigners so often remain in hotspots several days despite being identified and possibly already even having formulated a request for protection[838].

Therefore the problem of the lack of legal a basis of the deprivation of freedom, analysed above becomes of the utmost importance, when for reasons of inefficiency of the reception system, such retention continues for longer periods and without reasons related to the difficulty of identification. The legislator also did not intend to remedy the provisions of Article 17, paragraph 1, Decree Law 13/2017, which merely invokes the Apulia Law without adding anything else[839].

5. The jurisdiction: ordinary, administrative and the supranational court

Regarding the concrete definition of the different categories of migrants and the rights that are afforded to them, the role of judges is very significant. The role of judges is particularly intense in the places where individual interested parties are concerned, to react to volunteer manifestations with which the state defines the terms of the restrictive procedures to which they may be subject, or their right to remain in the national territory, or enjoy a certain stay regime, or access certain benefits.

This articulated and differentiated set has two characteristics: remedial pluralism linked to the progressive overlap of the different normative regimes, so that every specific intervention of the legislator has always followed the assignment of a specific jurisdiction for all the relevant issues.

On the other hand, the frequent allocation of jurisdiction to the ordinary court, despite the privileged approach of the law, has always focused on the central value of the provisional recognition of the status that it actually is. The choice of the ordinary judge can be justified not only by reference to the nature of the legal situation of the alien, who is the holder of subjective rights but also for practical reasons, of greater coverage of the territory because there are more court of ordinary jurisdiction on the territory.

838 G. CAMPESI, *L'Italia e il controllo delle frontiere marittime*, in M. SAVINO, *La crisi migratoria tra Italia e Unione Europea: diagnosi e prospettive*, Editoriale Scientifica, Napoli, 2017.

839 G. CAMPESI, *L'Italia e il controllo delle frontiere marittime*, in M. SAVINO, La crisi migratoria tra Italia e Unione Europea: diagnosi e prospettive, Editoriale Scientifica, Napoli, 2017.

On this point, the intervention of supranational courts (European Court of Justice) is also relevant, which may come into play in accordance with the usual mechanisms outlined in the Treaties (TFEU and ECHR), and which are largely of the concrete definition of the extent of the rights of migrants who come into contact with national procedures for the recognition of their status or the guarantee of specific prerogatives that are related to them.

From what has been analysed so far, the Italian system of first acceptance (relating to the phase immediately following the entry of irregular migrants) is the subject of various criticisms regarding the protection of fundamental rights within this system. An attempt to reform the subject in a more organic way has been done with the reform of 2015 but in spite of this there are still critics with respect to situations of violation of fundamental rights, as for example with respect to personal liberty sanctioned as inviolable by Art. 13 of the Constitution. In fact, the legal basis on which the definition of the CPSAs as closed centers, where thus detention is possible, is not clear, with consequent violation of art. 13 of the Constitution. Moreover, this violation also derives from the bad management of the CPAs (considered open centers where thus detention is not possible), and to the limited number of available places within these structures, which leads to the use of hotspots, closed centers, in their replacement: a relevant example is the case of Lampedusa treated in this Part.

IV. Return: the return of irregular migrants and the protection of human rights

1. Irregulars and the expulsion trend

There are numerous treaties and international conventions, especially with regard to human rights, which set out some common standards of protection for expulsion[840]. Among the treaties, certainly one of the most important is the European Convention on Human Rights: in fact the role of control carried out by Strasbourg has contributed to shaping national policies by implementing fundamental principles such as the right to life, the right not to be subjected to torture, etc.

840 IOM, International standards on immigration detention and non-custodial measures, November 2011. http://www.ohchr.org/Documents/Issues/Detention/DraftBasicPrinciples/IOM3.pdf.

The role played by European Union law is becoming more and more important, especially after the entry into force of the Treaty of Lisbon and, in particular, with the delivery of the Directive 2008/115/EC[841] mentioned and analysed in the previous Chapter.

On the merits, the right of the European Union clearly indicates the tension between the objective of expulsion effectiveness and the objective associated with the protection of rights. On the one hand, the Charter of Fundamental Rights of the European Union, and in particular the prohibition of torture and inhuman and degrading treatment (Article 4), the right to liberty and security (Article 6), the right to an effective remedy and a fair trial (Article 47), as well as specific limits on expulsion (art 19) and asylum law (Article 18), and also the text of the return directive, provide for different guarantees for the protection of the foreigner, on the other hand, the effectiveness of repatriation measures is one of the fundamental objectives of the European legislator, also conforming to several judgments of the European Court of Justice.

One of the main problems is that of the effectiveness of the administrative instruments to combat irregular immigration, namely the difficulty observed not only at the national level but also at the European level, to bring concrete implementation of particular and complex administrative measures such as repatriation measures of foreigners who receive the order to leave the EU, between 40,000 and 50,000 each year, only about 40% of them are actually repatriated.

The problem of the effectiveness of repatriations, however, manifests itself to a different extent in the various European states: there are evident quantitative differences between countries such as Great Britain and Germany, which show return rates significantly higher than the European average, and countries such as Italy, which are well below this average[842]. Dating back to 2015, confirm this gap, in fact the Europe of the 28 of 533,395 repatriation measures issued saw 226,800 (42 %) performed while

841 Directive 2008/115/EC of the European Parliament and of the Council of 16 December 2008 on common rules and procedures in Member States for returning illegally staying third-country nationals, Official Journal L 348, 24 December 2008, p. 98–107.

842 In 2015: Germany 102,3% and Italy 17,1%. Eurostat source: all data are referred to all return provisions, judicial and administrative, towards Third Countries and Member States.

in Italy, 27,305 repatriation measures were issued 4.670 (17 %) performed[843].

Returns data have an oscillatory trend, for example, between 2009 and 2011 the incidence of expulsion and rejection of irregular presence in Italian territory increased in relation to the so-called North Africa emergency. While the number of repatriations issued seems to be more regular, with decreasing tendency[844]. The system of expulsions is not compared to the phenomenon of irregularity, widely disseminated in Italy and in Europe.

Concerning Italy, the numbers of irregulars declined between 2010 and 2012,according to some observers[845] because the country was seen as less attractive. But since 2013 the numbers are again on the rise probably due to the considerable increase in international protection and in mixed flows, which have contributed to increase the number of repatriation measures that however are often not implemented.

2. The expulsion procedure

From a procedural point of view, the decree of expulsion must always be justify with a motivation, signed and communicated, respecting specific translation requirements in a language known to the recipient[846] and decided on a case by case basis (Article 13, paragraph 2). However, it is not possible to hear the alien before the adoption of the provision and no early communication is envisaged[847].

The most delicate phase of this process is certainly the practical execution particularly in relation to the possible use of coercive powers. The re-

---

843 Source Eurostat. Elaboration of Eurostat data referring to all repatriation, judicial and administrative accounts, to EU third countries. As for the clarifications about the differences between the series, the traceability of data and the breakdowns of the statistical series, please refer to the explanatory notes on the Eurostat website, http://ec.europa.eu/eurostat.

844 The positive trend seems to be confirmed by the most recent figures made available by the government, according to which up to September 15, 2015 3,731 return decisions were made on 15,686, or 23.7 % of the total. See Roadmap Italy, September 2015.

845 E. MITZMAN, *Il rimpatrio dei migranti irregolari*, in M. SAVINO, *La crisi migratoria tra Italia e Unione Europea: diagnosi e prospettive*, Editoriale Scientifica, Napoli, 2017.

846 Supreme Court, civil section VI, judgment 8 March 2012, n. 3678/12 on the rights of translation to penalty of nullity.

847 Supreme Court, civil section VI, 28 February 2013.

turn directive on this point expresses a principle of gradualness in the ways of executing expulsion and a preference for voluntary departure[848], supported by economic incentives in the state, preferable as it is less expensive for administration and more dignified for the person concerned. Indeed, the person decides to voluntarily repatriate without a forced procedure[849].

However, the number of voluntary assisted repatriations is still relatively low in Italy and reveals the absence of government initiatives in this regard. Indeed, the Italian legislature seems to rely principally on the coercive instruments, regulating in broad terms the accompanying measures at the frontier, listed in art. 13 of TUIM, whose execution was subject to the Court's validation of the Judge of Peace by sacrificing instead the voluntary departure process, which only applies upon request by the foreigner.

In the last few years, there has been an attempt to enhance the voluntary departure. However, to be effective, these efforts would require more continuity, the introduction of incentives, as well as a more precise knowledge of the voluntary return institution, both in terms of its potential and its limits[850]. The availability of the countries of origin to receive the citizens expelled from other countries is very important for a good return policy. For this reason, the readmission agreements signed by Italy with third countries have a strategic role. The nationalities which see the most successful return are those of the countries with which one of these agreements has been concluded: the main agreements signed by Italy are with Tunisia[851], Nigeria[852], Egypt[853] and Morocco[854]. Finally, there is also the Memorandum of Understanding between the Department of Public Security of the Italian Ministry of the Interior and the National Police of the Ministry of Interior of Sudan, August 2016.

---

848 See Frontex, Risk Analysis, p. 32; EMN, Programmes and Strategies in the EU Member States fostering Assisted Return to and Reintegration in Third Countries, 2011; European Migration Network (EMN), Country factsheet: Italy 2014.

849 E. MITZMAN, *Il rimpatrio dei migranti irregolari*, in M. SAVINO, *La crisi migratoria tra Italia e Unione Europea: diagnosi e prospettive*, Editoriale Scientifica, Napoli, 2017.

850 E. MITZMAN, *Il rimpatrio dei migranti irregolari*, in M. SAVINO, *La crisi migratoria tra Italia e Unione Europea: diagnosi e prospettive*, Editoriale Scientifica, Napoli, 2017.

851 09/02/2017 Framework agreement. Source Italian Ministry of Interior.

852 12/06/2011 Memorandum of understanding. Source Italian Ministry of Interior.

853 Police agreement signed on 06/18/2000 and entered into force 09/01/2007. Source Italian Ministry of Interior.

854 Agreement 27/07/1998. Source ministry of Interior.

In recent years the European Union has also been helping cooperation with third countries in the readmission of migrants, concluding specific readmission agreements and including this strategy among the priorities for the coming years[855].

However, the agreements are problematic due to the lack of transparency in the content and the related trading procedures, the lack of specific provisions for the respect of human rights in the texts of the treaties themselves, as well as the tendency to suggest quick and accelerated expulsion procedures, based only on the mere identification of specific foreigners[856].

There are other tools that can be used to find agreements, such as the Memorandum of Understanding, operational protocols, etc., as envisaged in the Roadmap 2015 mentioned previously. However, this approach can speed up the use of unclear negotiation procedures and exclude parliamentary intervention, it involves the shift of the legal reserve that the Constitution provides for the legal status of a foreigner (Article 10, second paragraph).

Finally, another problematic aspect in this matter is given by coordination between European national authorities[857].

A strategic role was also played by the Frontex agency, as well as in border surveillance[858], in joint repatriation operations[859]. However, this involvement is not particularly cumbersome, given that statistically most of the repatriations are still carried out by the Member States' authorities without Frontex or other organizations[860]. In this context there is the strengthening of the functions of the agency, with the establishment of a

---

855 See http://www.europarl.europa.eu/atyourservice/it/displayFtu.html?ftuld=FTU_5.12.3html.

856 See FRAU, Fundamental rights at Europe´s southern sea boarders, March 2013; FRA, Fundamental Rights Conference 2014 "Fundamental rights and migration to the EU: Conference conclusions", November, 2014.

857 The European Union intervenes with specific funding, faces the creation of networks between operators, and maintains common databases (with visas information systems, VIS, and the Schengen information system, SIS).

858 See Regulation 656/2014 regulating maritime surveillance at sea borders, also in the light of the principle of *non-refoulment.*

859 Article 9, paragraph 1, FRONTEX Regulation and Code of Conduct of 7 October 2013 on joint repatriation operations.

860 Joint operations represent only 2.8 % of forced returns to third countries, while IOM repatriations represent 18 % of voluntary repatriations. See Frontex Annual Risk Analysis, p. 65.

genuine European coast and border guard, endowed with personal and autonomous means and operationally independent of the states[861].

These developments, which certainly represent improvements, make the solutions of some of the criticisms already present with Frontex more urgent, especially as regards the transparency of operations and the liability regime for possible violations of human rights during the course of its activities. As evidenced by the recommendations made by the European Ombudsman, at the end of an investigation conducted in 2014 (OI / 9 / 2014MHZ, 4 May 2015)[862], highlighting the need to improve training activities for Frontex officials, to regulate some JRO profiles in more detail, as well as instituting a remedy against the acts of the agency.

3. Administrative detention

Administrative detention is a measure which prevents the alien from escaping from the authorities.

However, this measure, as will be explained, is ineffective in relation to the management costs that are very significant. At a supranational level, this hypothesis is expressly governed by Art. 5 lett. f) of the European Convention on Human Rights: if a different interpretation was initially established, for which administrative detention was not warranted by particular circumstances, some more recent pronouncements have established more stringent parameters (e.g. in cases where reasonable expulsion perspectives[863] are no longer present or in relation to particular circumstances such as the detention of minors or vulnerable foreigners[864] have come to an end), and consider this tool as an *extrema ratio* to any other less restrictive measures[865].

---

861 EU 2016/1624 Regulation of the European Parliament and of the Council of 14 September 2016 on the European Border and Coast Guard amending Regulation 2016/399 of the European Parliament and of the Council.

862 Own-initiative inquiry OI/9/2014/MHZ concerning the means through which Frontex ensures respect for fundamental rights in joint return operations (JRO). Decision of 4 May 2015.

863 See for instance European Court of Human Rights, *Mikolenko v. Estonia*, 8 September 2009, n. 10664/05.

864 See for instance European Court of Human Rights, *Yoh-Ekale Mwanje v. Belgium* 20 Dicember 2011, n. 10486/10; European Court of Human Rights, *Popov v. France* 19 January 2012, nn. 39472/07 and 39474/07.

865 *"A privation de liberte´ est une mesure si grave qu´ elle ne se justifie que lorsque d´ autre mesures, moins severes, onte ete´ considererees et jugees insuffisantes pour sauve-*

It is important to point out that the Return Directive is relatively ambiguous on the ground because, on the one hand, it stipulates that retention may be made in limited cases and for definite purposes[866], but on the other hand it provides for rather generous extensions, up to a maximum of 18 months (even in the event of delays in obtaining the necessary documentation from third countries, which is in fact one of the most common obstacles in practice) that seems contradictory to the initial intent.

Within the Italian system, the institute has been progressively expanding over the years, assuming an almost punitive value as a sanction for the irregularity of the stay. Even in the constitutional view, this institution is criticized: in fact it is a limitation measure of personal freedom, which is devoid of the character of exceptionality, thus contrary to art. 13 of the Constitution.

In 2014, however, a reduction in the maximum length of retention was introduced (only 30 days, which can be extended to a further 60 only under precise conditions, which can be disputed during validation)[867], thus restoring a clearer instrumentality compared to repatriation[868] and favouring a decrease in average retention times.

In the first half of 2014, the average time spent in the various CIE was shorter than in 2010 and 2011: 55 days in Bari, 24 days in Caltanissetta, 32 days in Rome and Turin, and 50 days in Trapani[869].

The retention of asylum seekers remains a delicate problem. The institute has recently been amended by Legislative Decree 142/2015, extending its terms to 12 months. This seems to be worrying with regard to administrative detention, especially in the light of frequent complaints about the poor living conditions of foreigners in detention centres that expose peo-

garder l′ interet personnel ou public exigeant la detention"(par. 73). English translation: "deprivation of liberty is a measure so serious that it is only justified when other, less severe, measures are considered and considered insufficient to safeguard the personal or public interest in detention" (paragraph 73).

866 Such hypotheses are the risk of escape or if the foreigner hinders the procedure. It may also be prepared where other sufficient but less coercive measures can not be effectively applied (Article 15).

867 Law 161/2014 (European Law 2013-bis).

868 The detention in the CIE must be interrupted if there is no reasonable prospect of the concrete circumstances that the removal can be carried out and that the alien can be retaken from the State of origin or where he/she comes from, in accordance with the principles expressed in *Kadzoev* Causa C-357/09 *PPU*.

869 Senate of the Republic, Extraordinary Commission for the Protection of Human Rights, Report on CIE in Italy, July 2014.

ple to treatments potentially contrary to supranational protection standards.

The increase in the financial resources invested in this field[870], the codification of the treatment standards within CIE, and the intervention of the National Guard for the rights of persons detained or private in personal freedom[871] are positive signs.

However, it is evident how both the national and European systems continue to play a central role in the administrative detention of the alien, especially in the light of the emerging logic of the last year in relation to the hotspots strategy, which is based on new forms of limitation of the personal liberty on a large scale, reducing the improvement signals at the regulatory level[872]. The Italian government has pledged to increase the number of places available in CIE, in line with European priorities and to meet the needs created by the hotspot approach. In September 2015, the overall capacity of CIE actually increased[873].

In this context, however, a problem is the poor adoption of alternative measures to administrative detention, namely the delivery of documents, the obligation to reside and the obligation to submit to the public office. Analyses, on the one hand, acknowledge the limits of alternative measures to the risk of the alien fleeing and, on the other hand, show greater economic sustainability and greater compatibility with the principles of human rights protection[874].

---

870 The per capita amount has been increased from € 30 to € 40. Ministry of Internal Source.

871 Decree of March 11, 2015, n. 36, *Regulation laying down the structure and composition of the Office of the National Guarantor of the rights of detained or private persons of personal liberty.*

872 E. MITZMAN, *Il rimpatrio dei migranti irregolari*, in M. SAVINO, *La crisi migratoria tra Italia e Unione Europea: diagnosi e prospettive*, Editoriale Scientifica, Napoli, 2017.

873 In September 2015 the total capacity was 872 seats, disaggregated in 716 places for men and 156 for women (the latter available only in the CIE of Rome). See Roadmap Italia 2015. At the beginning of 2016, however, it appears that there are six CIEs operating (Bari, Brindisi, Caltanissetta, Crotone, Rome, Turin), with 720 seats available. See Senate of the Republic, Extraordinary Commission for the Protection of Human Rights, Report on CIE, February 2016. E. MITZMAN, *Il rimpatrio dei migranti irregolari*, in M. SAVINO, *La crisi migratoria tra Italia e Unione Europea: diagnosi e prospettive*, Editoriale Scientifica, Napoli, 2017.

874 See FRA, *Alternatives to detention for asylum seekers and people in return procedures*; and in EMN, *The use of detention and alternatives to detention in the context of immigration policies*, Synthesis Report fort he EMN Focussed Study 2014.

It would seem to be useful for the legislator and administrations to make more effort to focus on alternative means of detention, which would favour a differentiated approach in relation to the needs of each concrete case[875].

4. The rejection system

The rejection procedure is a special measure because it is characterized by faster expulsion procedures and intervenes at a time when the foreigner is more vulnerable when he has just come to the frontier. The return directive allows members to exclude from their scope such measures which are governed by a few provisions of the Schengen Code. The EC Regulation No 562/2006 of the European Parliament and of the Council of 15 March 2006 provides for an obligation to state reasons and to notify the refusal, as well as to the right to appeal, but does not regulate other issues such as the modalities of execution (Article 13 and Annexes Part B). Furthermore, it is expressly set down that the initiation of the appeal procedure has no suspensive effect on the dismissal measure (Article 13, 3).

At the national level, however, dismissal has long been considered a mere public administration behavior, without the guarantees of the actual measure. This is true, especially for the so-called immediate rejection by the border police, which is the classic rejection case (Article 10, paragraph 1 TUIM).

The abovementioned rejection distinguishes from the deferred rejection, provided by the Questor when the foreigner was temporarily admitted to the territory for reasons of public relief, or was removed from the frontier controls, being stopped at the entrance or immediately afterwards (Article 10, 2, TUIM). Execution is carried out by means of coercive accompanying at the border and, if necessary, detained within CIE but judicial validation is not required by the legislator. Again, there is a problem of compatibility with Article 13 Constitution: in fact no jurisdictional validation is envisaged and the requirement of the exceptionality and residuality of these forms of coercion is not respected.

The provisions of the measure are defined in relatively vague terms, in particular as regards the failure to indicate a maximum time interval be-

875 E. MITZMAN, *Il rimpatrio dei migranti irregolari*, in M. SAVINO, *La crisi migratoria tra Italia e Unione Europea: diagnosi e prospettive*, Editoriale Scientifica, Napoli, 2017.

tween the entry of the alien into the territory and its rejection, thus giving rise to the risk of abuse, as well as of actual violations of constitutional and supranational rules.

There are cases of limitation of personal freedom, sometimes justified by demanded rescue needs, extended for several days or weeks, prior to the formal adoption of the dismissal order and the communication of detention to the court of peace, violating the article 13 of the Constitution[876].

The question of the possible overlap between the cases of deferred rejection and the expulsion of the irregular alien who is actually remitted by the discretion of the administration that chooses the type of measure to be taken is particularly delicate. In fact, if the alien is found in an irregular state, it is enough for the administration to say that he has crossed the border recently to adopt a deferred dismissal rather than expulsion.

The criticisms of the Italian case came to light in the judgment of the European Court of Human Rights, the *Khlaifia* case, which also introduced significant details of the procedural safeguards implicit in the ban on collective expulsions (Article 4, Protocol 4 of the European Convention on Human Rights) as already seen.

The judgment points out the need for more precise legislative provisions in the matter of refusals, including the need to provide each migrant with an effective opportunity to put the reasons for expulsion before the administration prior to the adoption of the measure[877].

Another particular case is that of dismissal in the high seas, considered in the *Hirsi Jamaa*[878] judgment, in which the European Court of Human Rights found against Italy for breach of the principles of *non-refoulment*, individuality of dismissal and right to an effective remedy. In order to arrive at the review of the measure by an independent authority before its execution, rather than at a later date.

876 Constitution of the Italian Republic. Official Journal General Series n.298 of 27-12-1947.

877 E. MITZMAN, *Il rimpatrio dei migranti irregolari*, in M. SAVINO, *La crisi migratoria tra Italia e Unione Europea: diagnosi e prospettive*, Editoriale Scientifica, Napoli, 2017.

878 ECtHR, Hirsi Jamaa and Others v Italy (GC), Application No. 27765/09.

5. Judicial protection

There is a division of competences between the administrative judge, the ordinary judge and the justice of peace in respect of legal protection against expulsion and dismissal.

On the merits the legislature provides for elements of *favour* to the appellant in the conduct of the judgments, such as the exemption of certain acts of the proceeding from any tax and duty[879], or access to free legal aid regardless of income for certain proceedings. Despite this, the procedure provided presents several problematic aspects.

a) The first problems stems from the presence of legislative gaps: as far as refusals are concerned, there is a complete lack of legislative indication of the modalities of appeal, and only recently case law has come to a solution by establishing the jurisdiction of the ordinary court[880]. The choice is based on the finding that the rejection measure affects fundamental rights, in particular as regards the international protection of Article 3 of the European Convention on Human Rights. However, there are various uncertainties about the rite to be applied and the definition of the powers of the judge with respect to the contested measures which are incompatible with various constitutional and supranational principles of the process and the right to defence.

In fact, in the absence of any legislative indication, the ordinary court did not have the power to cancel or suspend the administrative measures. There is therefore a need for clarification from a constitutional point of view in the light of the provisions of Article 113, paragraph 3 of the Constitution, as well as in the light of the right to an effective remedy (Article 13 of the European Convention on Human Rights) in virtue of the requirements of certainty of the right underlying them[881].

As regards the administrative detention in CIE, the right to compensation for unjust injury, as protected by the Article 5 of the European Convention on Human Rights is not yet governed by the legislature[882].

---

879 Art. 18, Legislative Decree of 1 September 2011 No. 150, Official Journal No. 220 of 21 September 2011.

880 See Supreme Court United Sections, judgment 17 June 2013, No. 15115 for the deferred rejections and state Council, section III, 13 September 2013, n. 4543, for the border rejections.

881 See judgments: ECtHR *Čonka v Belgium*, Application No. 51564/99, 5 February 2002, ECtHR *Gebremedhin (Gaberamadhien) v France*, Application No. 25389/05 and ECtHR *Hirsi Jamaa and Others v Italy* (GC), Application No. 27765/09.

882 European Court of Human Rights, *Seferovic c. Italia*, 8 February 2011, 12921/04.

b) Another big problem is the appealing to different jurisdictions

An explanatory example is that the judgment on the denial of residence permit is held in front of the Regional Administrative Court and the judgment on the expulsion order that comes to that denial, takes place in front of the judge of peace[883].

The Supreme Court tends to deny both the possibility for the court of peace to suspend its judgment pending the conclusion of that before the Regional Administrative Court and the possibility of incidental knowledge of the illegality of the decision on the stay[884].

The judge of peace is thus emptied of his powers and the utilization of the possible admissibility of the appeal by the Regional Administrative Court is compromised in the case the expulsion order has already been executed.

Finally, a third problem is given by the choice of the Italian legislator to attribute to the judge of peace, a judge without toga, who has more conciliatory functions, the guarantor of the legitimacy of restrictive measures such as expulsions and administrative detention and the appeals are allowed only to the Supreme Court[885].

To attribute this matter to a court of law would seem more appropriate, even on the basis of national and supranational jurisprudence, which reaffirms that the judicial review of administrative detention must be carried out in an in-depth, also in order to ensure compliance with important international principles.

The Supreme Court clarifies that the court of peace was not only obliged to consider the existence of reasonable prospects for foreign repatriation (on the basis of the return directive) but also to assess the manifestations of manifest illegitimacy of the decree of expulsion, as a preventive measure[886].

The European Court of Justice has ruled that judicial review of the prolonged retention of custody entails the exercise of a merit of unity, in

883 See Supreme Court, United Civil Sections, 16 October 2006, n. 22217, which denies the cross-border syndicate of the court of peace on the legitimacy of the denial of residence permit.

884 E. MITZMAN, Il rimpatrio dei migranti irregolari, in M. SAVINO, La crisi migratoria tra Italia e Unione Europea: diagnosi e prospettive, Editoriale Scientifica, Napoli, 2017.

885 As well as providing that the premises and the support needed to conduct validation hearings are offered by the police and not by the Ministry of Justice.

886 Supreme Court, Civil Section VI, 5 June 2014, n. 12069, and 11 July 2014, n. 17407.

which the pertinent authority must be able to not only know all the relevant facts and law but also replace decision with that of the administration[887].

Recently, there has been an establishment at the ordinary courts of specialized sections on immigration, international protection and free movement of citizens of the European Union (Decree Law No 13 of 17 February 2017[888]) which constitutes an improvement because judges are the most specialized. However, the competences in this matter are still in the hands of the judge of peace and the specification of the ordinary court's powers is still unclear with respect to the contested decisions.

6. Returns

The phenomenon of irregular migration is tackled by the Italian legislator as well as by the European one with increasing penal measures. In Italy, both in order to suppress conduct related to irregular immigration and to incriminate the illegality of the alien, in particular through the offence of clandestine offences (Article 10-bis TUIM), through the offensc of inadmissibility to the order of expulsion (Article 14, paragraph 5-ter TUIM), the crime of re-entering the territory (Article 13, paragraph 13 TUIM), as well as through the aggravating of clandestinity (Article 61 n.11-bis Penal Code, subsequently declared Unconstitutional in 2010 Constitutional Court, No. 249/2010[889]). The European Court of Justice and its case law partially stopped this tendency.

If it is true that criminal law and criminal procedure rules are, in principle, within the competence of the Member States, the European Union law must be affected by this legal field, in order to ensure that the application of criminal law does not compromise the useful effect of the return directive (*El Dridi*, points 53 and 54).

The law of the Union does not prohibit a Member State from applying a law that categorises the irregular stay of a foreigner as a criminal offence, including penalties and imprisonment in order to prevent and repress such offences. However, they are incompatible with Union law and criminal

---

887 C-146/14, Bashir Mohamed Ali Mahdi.

888 Decree Law 17 February 2017, No. 13, Official Journal No.40 del 17 February 2017.

889 Judjment of Constitutional Court No 249 of 8 July 2010, Official journal 14/07/2010 n. 28.

law whose application may be an obstacle to the pursuit of the return directive objectives[890].

In response to the judgment *El Dridi*, the Italian lawmaker replaced the sentence for a crime with a pecuniary fine for the offence of inadmissibility to the order of expulsion from the territory. While, in response to another case, *Sagor*[891], a special prevalence mechanism for expulsion proceedings has been envisaged on the performance of measures such as home stay and work of public utility.

The adoption of penalty detention measures can take place in the pre-repatriation stage or at the next stage. In the first case, the margins of criminalization for the national legislature are particularly subtle, limiting the adoption of instrumental measures to repatriation itself (e.g. arrest or detention aimed at identifying the alien and verifying his/her status), so as not to delay the adoption of the repatriation or commencement of the proceedings[892].

In the second case, however, the detention may be made only against a foreign national whose repatriation procedure has already been applied, where all the instruments, including the coercive measures provided for by the directive for the purposes of enforcing the return order have been concluded, even if unsuccessfully.

An analogous reading of the case law of the Court led to believe that the crime of re-entering the territory of the state, which is the only case of irregular residence still punished by the Italian ordinance with the custodial sentence, should be considered contrary to the useful effect of the Directive, constituting the seizure of a potential obstacle of a new expulsion procedure[893].

However, in the *Celaj* case[894] the court adopted a different interpretative line, stating that the return directive does not preclude the criminalization of such conduct or the repression of prison sentences. In fact, irregular entry in breach of a prohibition imposed under Article 11 of the return direc-

---

890 C-61/11 PPU – El Dridi point 59; *Achughbabian*, C:2011:807 points 37-39 and 45; C-430/11 *Sagor* point 33.

891 Case C-430/11, Md Sagor, judjment of 6 December 2012.

892 CJEU: Judgment C-47/15 Affum point 88.

893 E. MITZMAN, *Il rimpatrio dei migranti irregolari*, in M. SAVINO, *La crisi migratoria tra Italia e Unione Europea: diagnosi e prospettive,* Editoriale Scientifica, Napoli, 2017.

894 Case C-290/14 Skerdhan Celaj, Fourth Chamber of the Court of Justice of the European Union, 01-10-2015.

tive would complement a different case from the mere irregular entry into the territory[895].

This reading seems to be confirmed by a more recent case, *Affum*[896], cited above, in which the Court reiterated, as a case of mere irregular entry, the overriding objective of the removal from the punitive demands of the State, also underlining the differences compared to *Celaj* case[897].

The sentence of imprisonment for the crime of reinstatement in the territory of the state may therefore be compatible with the return directive, provided that the limits expressly invoked by the court are respected, including compliance with art. 11 of the Directive, the fundamental rights of the person, and where applicable, the provisions of the Geneva Convention, and in particular Article 31 (1) thereof, which prohibits the punishment of refugees with criminal penalties because of their illegal entry or residence.

In the Italian system, criminal immigration policies are not only criticized in relation to the protection of human rights, but also in terms of effectiveness. The most significant case was represented by the illegal entry and stay case introduced by Law 94/2009[898] in a framework of a total hardening of the instruments of repression of irregular immigration[899].

After seven years from its introduction, the view is that this is useless and damaging, both in relation to the apparent impossibility of enforcing financial penalties for indigent foreigners and the substantial ineffectiveness in the contrast to irregular immigration[900]. The Italian Government has expressly preferred not to exercise such a case, according to the delega-

895 L. MASERA, *La Corte di giustizia Ue dichiara il delitto di illecito reingresso dello straniero espulso (art. 13 comma 13 TUIMM) conforme alla direttiva rimpatri (2008/115/CE)* in *Contemporary Criminal Law*, October 5, 2015.

896 CJEU: Judgment C-47/15 Affum.

897 Case C-290/14 Skerdhan Celaj, Fourth Chamber of the Court of Justice of the European Union, 01-10-2015.

898 Law of 15 July 2009, No 94 Provisions on public security. Official Journal General Series No 170 of 24 July 2009 – Suppl. Ordinary No 128.

899 E. MITZMAN, *Il rimpatrio dei migranti irregolari*, in M. SAVINO, *La crisi migratoria tra Italia e Unione Europea: diagnosi e prospettive*, Editoriale Scientifica, Napoli, 2017.

900 IOM, IOM's proposals for managing irregular immigration effectively and respecting the rights of migrants (http://www.italy.iom.int/images/pdf/PROPOSTE_OIM.pdf).

tion under Law 67/2014[901], therefore, it is hoped that new legislative initiatives will be initiated[902].

As analysed so far, the measure of repatriation at European level is diversified and as regards Italy the number of repatriation seems not to be high. It is possible to identify various violations of the human rights of irregular migrants in relation to repatriation. The reason seems to be twofold: partly there is the responsibility of European legislation that is often ambiguous and contradictory (for example, by stating the exceptional nature of administrative detention but allowing a duration of up to 18 months) thus leaving Member States more easily with an application sometimes more restrictive of the fundamental rights of migrants, as stated in the *Khlaifia*[903] ruling, highlighting the need for migration with an effective opportunity to put before the administration for the expulsion of the priority. On the other hand, there are criticisms in the field of judicial protection that hinders the protection of fundamental rights, such as for example due to regulatory holes in appeal procedures or the fact that judging the legitimacy of restrictive measures such as expulsions and detention administrative, it is the judge of peace, which is not a professional judge, and considering the relevance of the rights at stake this appears not very guaranteed. Although on this latter point has been established the competence of the ordinary courts of specialized sections on immigration, international protection and free movement of citizens of the European Union, the competences in this matter are still in the hands of the judge of peace.

At the end of this review, it is possible observe that the system of entrance and first reception is particularly fragmented. Significant problems arise on the normative and organisational level, which consequently affect the human rights protection of the irregular migrants. In this framework, as already underlined, it is evident the tension between the need of security and reduction of the irregular flows and the need of protection of fundamental rights of this category of migrants. Indeed, the situation at the sea, into Mediterranean area, paths used by migrants to reach the EU shores, sees the particular difficulty on reaching the solution for this tension. The juridical frame is very complex with several international and European

901 Law 28 April 2014, No. 67, Official Journal No 100 del 02 May 2014.

902 Even in line with the abrogation choices already adopted by other European regimes, such as France (After the *Achghbabian* ruling, the French legislature abolished the offense of irregular residence; Which could in future be extended to the offense of illicit entry, which is the subject of the *Affum* judgment).

903 ECtHR, sez. II, Khaifia and others v ITaly, 16483/12, 1 September 2015.

legislations that have to be implemented simultaneously: SAR, UNCLOS, ECHR, Geneva Convention on Refugee Status, ect. Several violations occurred by Italy respect with some of these legislations as some judgment from ECtHR affirmed in Hirsi Jaamal v Italy with the violation of the principle of non-refoulment and ECHR concerning collective expulsions, thus with the violation of fundamental rights, in particular to the right to life. At the same time, Italy took the responsibility to conduct also alone some operations of search and rescue into the sea to save life, not always with the adequate support of EU.

Another important restriction of the fundamental rights of irregular migrants, in particular related to personal freedom, occurred in the subsequent phase of the entrance immediately after the detection at the sea: the first reception phase. The criticisms in this phase and system are several and are at both normative and organizational as mentioned above. Notwithstanding the attempt to realize a reform that guarantees more flexibility to the matter, there remain several relevant violation to the fundamental rights and freedom of these migrants: important to underline is in particular the Art. 13 Cost on personal freedom which is violated because of the vagueness of the legal framework. Indeed it is not clear the juridical base to consider the restriction of this freedom within the CPSA, and for the scares and not efficient organization of CPAs, that not provide the restriction of Art. 13 Cost., but are not enough in the territory and are for these reasons used CPSA at their place with consequent restriction of the Article.

Violation of human rights are also presented in the judicial system in which the level of protection is not always efficiently guaranteed, such as for example due to regulatory holes in appeal procedures or the fact that judging the legitimacy of restrictive measures such as expulsions and detention administrative, it is the judge of peace. The recent reform that introduced some good measure as at the ordinary courts of specialized sections on immigration, international protection and free movement of citizens of the European Union, however the competences in this matter are still in the hands of the judge of peace and the specification of the ordinary court's powers is still unclear with respect to the contested decisions, as already mentioned.

In conclusion the balance between the two different needs, security and protection of human rights, has been not found yet. The legislative measures seem oriented to a security approach which prevail on a full enjoyment of the human rights, some example are the restriction obtaining licenses and public authorizations and on the subject of marriages, as analysed at the beginning of this Part. This seems possible also for the ambiguity and not always clarity of the EU legislation that somehow allows Member States to implement the law incorrectly with the scope of the same legislation. Therefore, in the opinion of the author a stronger will from the EU to guarantee the protection of this specific category of migrants who are particularly vulnerable given their status is necessary, and on the other side Italy should improve their measures to find a balance ensuring the human rights.

Conclusion

At the end of this review, taking into account what has been considered with respect to the classification of migrants, on regulatory and administrative regimes, it possible observe that the system is particularly fragmented. Fragmentation that has also led to frequent simplification between an economic migrant and a recipient of international protection or humanitarian protection, without considering that even these categories within them are inhomogeneous as shown by mixed flows.

Significant problems also exist on the organizational level, which consequently affect human rights. In fact, some facilities, as well as hotspots, as described above, have the primary and preliminary purpose of selecting migrants and identifying those who may, even temporarily, hold a right to remain in Italy or in the European Union. These structures are particularly concentrated where the phenomenon of irregular arrivals occurs more massively.

Other facilities, as seen, have the purpose of offering to the already selected subjects useful and sustainable areas of assistance and possible and subsequent integration, spread throughout the national territory. These structures are set to rise in all regions and make use of the necessary support from local authorities.

However, this organization, which is partly rational and functional, generates also great ambiguity, as the delays or inefficiencies of the first structures oblige the legislator to place on the second structures also part of the tasks of identifying and accepting responsibility for first.

In addition to that, when the Municipalities participate in the integrated reception system, the possible coordination between the activities carried out by the local authority in that specific is normally left unmanaged. To handle these situations, the Italian legislature resorts to a special discipline and not to the ordinary one, generating new coordination issues.

The hope is that there will be a high of an absorption action of the special system in the ordinary one, making some changes to the assumptions governing the ordinary one, so that the holders of international or humanitarian protection can access more easily the ordinary regime[904]. The government must set up an appropriate first reception system to ensure the first reception for who come every year in Italy because otherwise any legislative reform would be unsuccessful in achieving significant results both from the point of view of the efficiency of the identification procedures and the effective respect of the fundamental rights of migrants.

In the current context described in this part of this last Chapter dedicated to Italian system, the strong increase in the flow of migrants to Italy and Europe in general, has heightened the already existing criticisms of the national and European return system, overlapping and interweaving with the problems of the reception. At both levels, therefore, return policy is a key part of the strategy for addressing migratory crisis.

It is important to point out that, in the current migration crisis, a new season of strengthening of control instruments is likely to be present and, by adding new problems to those already existing, presents the risk of a regression in the area of the protection of rights. Specifically, it is necessary to ensure adequate judicial safeguards on the forms of administrative detention that are carried out in the early stages of reception and identification of migrants, leading to the adoption of any ablative measures. It is necessary to deepen the instructing profiles and the procedural guarantees that precede the adoption of the rejection order, even in the light of the ban on collective expulsion.

As regards the system of expulsions, the concern is still the central role played by the coactive execution of the measure enforcement rather than voluntary execution, as well as the regular use of coercion instruments, which should constitute an *ultima ratio*. It might be necessary to make greater efforts in the area of voluntary repatriation and in the application of alternative measures to detention to return to make the deprivation of liberty of the person a case of exception as the Constitution itself requires.

As far as cooperation with third countries is concerned, greater transparency should be required with regard to content and forms of implementation of readmission agreements, in order to ensure, both textually

904 F. CORTESE, *La difficile classificazione dei migranti* in M. SAVINO, *La crisi migratoria tra Italia e Unione Europea: diagnosi e prospettive*, Editoriale Scientifica, 2017.

and practically, full respect for the standards of protection of rights under national law and supranational law.

Finally, it must be remembered that the objective of the protection of the right to protection cannot be secondary to that of the effectiveness of expulsion. Recent expulsion data, which seem to indicate recovery in the rate of return of refugees, can be welcomed as a positive signal provided that the rights of migrants are ensured, that is, the increase in the number of expulsions is not realized at the expense of the quality of the tutelage.

Another piece to deal with the growing migration crisis is also to try to better face the migratory phenomenon by sea. As outlined in the Chapter, Italy has developed an articulated legal, political and diplomatic instrument for controlling sea migration over the last few years, especially with a view to combating clandestine migration.

The Arab spring has produced a significant change in the political-diplomatic scenario in which the control activities have been carried out, prompting the government and European institutions to find a way out of the crisis. The actions condemned between 2013 and 2015 have been inspired by radically different and not necessarily compatible political goals, reflecting the political controversy over the management of the migratory crisis that crosses Europe.

Italy seems to be oriented towards extra territorialisation of maritime border control, also through the active presence of European and Italian security forces in foreign territory.

The current Italian critical area is above all the territory of the Sicilian Channel, given the difficulty of treading a vast stretch of sea, the flows have never been totally arrested. The policy of increased patrols has resulted in increasing the risk of crossing and also modifying the practices of smugglers.

For this reason patrolling has also become the focus of search and rescue, and in the absence of viable other alternatives, it forces the military and police authorities to allow landing on the Italian soil of those who are intercepted at sea.

The search for practicable alternatives seems to find obstacles of a political and legal nature difficult to solve. In fact, it is necessary to obtain the availability of a third country of origin to allow the landing of migrants intercepted at sea, but this acceptance depends on the political-diplomatic relations between the countries of origin and the destination of migratory flows concerned.

In the case of Libya, the country of origin or transit from which many migrants arrived, seems to be difficult to establish good relations of this kind for several reasons. Libya has always been a transit country and not a source of migratory flows, that has a significant impact on the local economy. Therefore, it has never been interested in the offer of migration quotas or visa facilitations, but it used irregular migration as a diplomatic surge. On the other hand, the extra territorialisation of border control meets rigid legal constraints.

Today, given the political situation in Libya, characterized by the lack of a single interlocutor, it is very difficult to enter into agreements to redeploy the Libyan government for migrants intercepted and assisted in the Sicilian channel.

A possible solution to reduce the number of landings and then deaths at sea could be to open up humanitarian channels to allow safe access to European territory to those who have legitimate international protection claims[905].

Therefore, it could affirm the need for the Italian lawmakers to work on several aspect in order to improve the system of entrance from the protection of human rights point of view and develop a better management system of entrance, balancing of these fundamental aspects.

B. *Germany: the protection of human rights of irregular migrants in the entry phase within the German legal system*

I. Irregular migration law

1. Categories of regular and irregular migrants in the German legal system

The Immigration Act[906] (Law on Stay, Work and Integration of Foreigners into Federal Territory), of 30 July 2004, which came into force on 1 January 2005, is made up of the Residence Act, the Act on the General Free-

905 Similar experiences have been experienced by international bodies such as UNHCR, see http://www.unhcr.it/cosa-facciamo/soluzioni-durevoli/reinsediamento. But also from non-governmental organizations such as the Federation of the Evangelical Churches in Italy, the Tavola Valdese and the Community of Santo Egidio, which have launched a cooperation with the Ministries of Interior and Foreign Affairs for a pilot project for the recoilization of about 1000 Refugees from Lebanon, Morocco and Ethiopia, see http://www.santegidio.org/pageID/1165/langID/it/itemID756/Scheda-Cosa-sono-i-corridoi-umanitari.html.

906 Gesetz über Den Aufenthalt, Die Erwerbstätigkeit und die Integration von Ausländern im Bundesgebiet – Aufenthaltsgesetz, AufenthG.

dom of Movement for EU Citizens and amendments to additional legislation[907]. The Immigration Act for the first time provides a legislative framework for controlling and restricting immigration as a whole. The new law also contains measures to promote the integration of legal immigrants in Germany.

The Immigration Act contains provisions on the entry of foreigners into Germany, their residence in the country, various residence purposes, the termination of residence and asylum procedures. It will hereinafter be referred to as the Residence Act (*Aufenthaltsgesetz*).

Amendments to the Act took effect on 28 August 2007[908]. These amendments include provisions to implement eleven European Union directives on residence and asylum rules, to prevent sham or forced marriages, to enhance internal security, to implement decisions of the German Conference of Interior Ministers on nationality law, to facilitate the immigration of company founders and, above all, provisions to foster the integration of legal immigrants[909].

The Residence Act stipulates for the first time ever that a visa is of itself a kind of residence permit. This provision is of significance for short stays. A visa now expressly permits the holder to reside in Germany for its duration; under the old legislation[910] only residence permits acquired after entry into Germany entitled the holder to stay in the country[911].

In the case of longer stays, the only distinction that is still made is between (temporary) residence permits and (permanent) settlement permits. First-time entry into the country still requires a visa for Germany (national visa), which is then converted into a residence or settlement permit once the holder has arrived in the country. Residence permits are issued for the purposes specified in the Act (education or training, gainful employment, international-law, humanitarian, political or family reasons). Settlement permits are issued if a foreigner has possessed a residence permit for five years and meets the additional requirements (secure income, no criminal record, adequate command of the German language, etc.). These can be issued more quickly to highly qualified foreigners and holders of an EU Blue Card. The amended Immigration Act also introduced the "long-term

---

907 Residence Act as amended on 25 February 2008, (BGBl) Federal Law Gazette I p. 162, which was last amended by Article 1 of the Law of 8 March 2018 (BGBl) Federal Law Gazette I p. 342.

908 Federal Law Gazette (BGBI) I, 19 August 2007 p. 1970.

909 Federal Office for Migration and Refugees, www.bamf.de.

910 Foreigners Act, Federal Law Gazette I, p. 1950.

911 Federal Office for Migration and Refugees, www.bamf.de.

residence permit" as a separate residence permit which is very similar to the settlement permit.

Implementation of the EU Council Directive on the conditions of entry and residence of third-country nationals for the purposes of highly qualified employment (the so-called Blue Card Directive)[912], meant introducing a new residence category with effect from 1 August 2012: the EU Blue Card which is very similar to a temporary residence permit[913] but makes it easier to get a settlement permit.

The provisions concerning the entry and stay of aliens who are not nationals of the countries of the European Union or the European Economic Area are contained in the Immigration Act which Constitutes, as mentioned above, the main legal basis for entry, removal and residence of for-

912 Council Directive 2009/50/EC of 25 May 2009 on the conditions of entry and residence of third-country nationals for the purposes of highly qualified employment, OJ L 155, 18.6.2009, p. 17–29.

913 Foreigners may be issued with a renewable residence permit for the purpose of applying to and studying at a state or state-recognized higher education institution or comparable training establishment. After graduating, they may have their residence permit extended for up to one year (from 1 August 2012 for up to 18 months) for the purpose of seeking employment relevant to their field of study.
A residence permit can also be issued to those wishing to participate in a language course without thereafter going on to university. Residence permits to enable a child to attend school can only be issued in exceptional cases.
If the Federal Employment Agency gives its approval, residence permits may also be issued for the purpose of completing in-company initial and continuing training. Graduates of German schools abroad who wish to complete a qualified in-company training course for a state-recognized or similarly accredited training occupation may be granted a residence permit without the approval of the Federal Employment Agency.
A new kind of residence permit that also grants access to the labour market was introduced on 1 January 2005, replacing the previous system of separate residence and work permits. Foreigners will thus now only have to deal with one authority. Abroad this will be the German missions (embassy and consulate visa sections), in Germany the foreigners authorities. The labour authorities will be contacted as required by the missions or foreigners authorities themselves.
The Act provides for highly qualified persons to be granted permanent residence from the outset. They may obtain a settlement permit immediately upon arrival. Their family members who come to Germany with them or join them at a later date are entitled to take up gainful employment.
Self-employed persons can be issued with a residence permit if there is particular economic or specific regional interest in the planned business project. To this end, each case is examined also taking due account of the impact on the economy and the securing of financing.

eign nationals in Germany. It is also applicable to refugees and asylum seekers in the measure that the legislation on asylum procedure does not include special rules. § 60 *AufenthG* also establishes the ban on expulsion or removal of asylum seekers and refugees who have been granted the right to stay.

According to the provisions of § 14 *AufenthG* migration is considered irregular if the foreigner does not have a passport or other passport replacement document valid for entry into the territory of the Federal Republic, or any kind of residence permit, and is not otherwise authorized to enter German territory or has been recipient of a removal order. Therefore, if the foreigner does not meet the requirements of the law for entry, then his or her stay a in German territory is not allowed.

Likewise, a foreigner is obliged to leave the federal territory (cf. *Ausreisepflicht*) in cases where the conditions necessary for his or her stay (§ 50 *AufenthG*) are no longer met or he or she no longer holds a valid residence permit.

§ 51 *AufenthG*, paragraph 1, lists the cases in which a residence permit is no longer valid: the expiry of the validity period; having a cancellation status; withdrawal and revocation of the residence permit; expulsion of the alien; notification of an expulsion order; failure to return to Germany for a foreigner within six months or a longer period determined by the competent authorities; submission of an asylum application.

In order to obtain the release of any type of residence permit, the foreigner must prove that he or she is in compliance with the passport or other entry document and has adequate means of subsistence; their identification information have to also be known. Finally, nationality and the presence on the territory must not be a threat to the interests of the Federal Republic (§ 5 *AufenthG*).

1.1. The German legislation on the irregular entrance or staying of migrants

In Germany, the irregular immigrant's sanctioning treatment is governed by *Gesetz zur Zuwanderung und zur Regelung des Aufenthalts und der Integration von Unionsbürgern und Ausländer* (the Law on the Management and the Limitation of Immigration and the Discipline for the Stay and the Integration of Citizens of the European Union and of Foreigners), the so-called

"*Zuwanderungsgesetz*" of 30 July 2004, which entered into force on 1 January 2005, and is subject to amendments[914].

This is a unique text in which the first article includes the law on living, working and integration in the Federal territory with reference to non-EU citizens "*AufenthG*". In the second article, however, the rules on the free movement of Community nationals or members of the EEA (the so-called EU Free Movement Act) are laid down. Subsequent articles govern, by amending the existing legislation, further cases concerning the phenomenon of immigration, including asylum, citizenship, legal status of expatriates[915] and stateless persons in German territory, as well as social rights.

Alongside the provisions that deal with the irregular alien, complex legislation deals with sactions to be applied to the conduct of those who makes it possible or favour irregular immigration of aliens[916]. It is emphasized that generally the German legislature differentiates the sanctioning treatment of the immigrant or irregular resident depending on whether the irregularity concerns citizens of European Union countries or non-EU nationals.

Irregular immigration by non-EU foreigners is configured according to their conduct, and in particular depending on the degree of guilt, as a crime or an administrative transgression. The entry and stay of all non-EU foreign[917] nationals are governed by the law *Aufenthaltsgesetz* issued on 30 July 2004 in the context of the above-mentioned *Zuwanderungsgesetz*. The *Aufenthaltsgesetz* contains the main legal bases regarding the entry, removal and residence of aliens in Germany.

---

914 Statue of 30 July 2004, Federal Law Gazette (BGBI) 2004 I, p. 1950 ff. E. Guild, P. Minderhoud, (2006), Immigration and criminal law in the European Union: the legal measures and social consequences of criminal law in Member States on trafficking and smuggling in human beings, Martinus Nijhoff Publishers.

915 German ethnicity from the republics of the former Soviet Union, Estonia, Lithuania, Latvia, arrived in Germany after 31 December 1992.

916 Moreover, a number of criminal cases have specifically targeted the violation of certain provisions of the laws contained in *Zuwanderungsgesetz* made by German nationals or foreigners, both regular and irregular.

917 The foreign term identifies all persons who are not German citizens within the meaning of Article 116, paragraph 1, Basic Law: "*Save the law, a German citizen is considered to be a German citizen for the purposes of this Basic Law anyone who possesses German citizenship or has received a reception, As a refugee or expelled from ethnic affiliation to the German people, or as a spouse or descendant, in the territory of the German Reich within the boundaries in force on 31 December 1937*".

The *AufenthG* applies also to recognised refugees and to applicants for asylum insofar as the law on asylum procedure does not provide for special rules. In addition, § 60 of *AufenthG* provides for the prohibition of expulsion or removal of asylum seekers or refugees who have been granted the right to stay[918].

In Germany, criminal conduct and criminal offences inherent in immigration are listed and governed by § 95 *AufenthG*. Under the terms of this provision, irregular immigration of non-EU nationals has been configured, in the presence of certain conduct and / or depending on the degree of guilt of the offender, as a criminal offence: § 95 regulates sanctions, including both imprisonment (*Freiheitstrafe*), from one to three years, and a financial penalty (*Geldstrafe*). In addition, § 98 *AufenthG* provides for certain sanctions of an administrative nature to determine the conduct of non-EU citizens constituting an administrative offense. Illegal stay without *dolo* but negligent, is considered to be an administrative and unlawful transgression.

The criminal offences related to irregular foreigners are: the stay (voluntary) in German territory without a passport or other valid identity document; the stay (voluntary) in German territory without the necessary residence permit (also with reference to the work activity) or on the slope of an enforceable removal order or a ban on entry; illegal entry as provided for in Article 14, and also fraud or false or incomplete disclosure of personal data within the meaning of Article 49, paragraph 2 of *AufenthG*.

Other provisions may be related to irregular immigration: membership of an association or group whose existence, whose purpose or activity is deliberately kept secret from the authorities, is a violation of the provisions of the protection of internal security (Article 46, 47 and 49), failure to comply with the obligation of complaint and registration (Article 54a). The stay with a formally valid leave but issued as a result of fraud or other crim-

918 Moreover, with regard to Turkish nationals, a special discipline applies to the Agreement signed in Ankara on 12 September 1963, which created an association between the European Economic Community and Turkey (*BGBl.* 1963 II, p. 509) Of the Additional Protocol of 23 November 1970 (*BGBl.* 1972 II, p. 385) and of the subsequent resolutions of the Association Council (ARB) Nos. 1/80 and 2/76, which provide related to the *AufenthG* for some privileges to Turkish citizens. With reference to Switzerland, the Agreement of 21 June 1999 between the Swiss Confederation, on the one hand, and the European Community and its Member States on the other, on the free movement of persons (*BGBl.* 2001, II, p 810), which states that Swiss nationals enjoy the same rights as Community citizens.

inal activity is punishable under the law following a recent amendment of the law[919].

Pursuant to §§ 96 and 97, any citizen (foreign and German) may be punished by imprisonment up to 10 years, depending on the conduct, or a pecuniary penalty if he/she facilitates entry or residence of irregular persons in the German territory in order to gain an economic advantage (the penalty is increased if the irregular alien dies or if the activity is carried out professionally or in the context of a criminal offence).

With regard to the sanctions, the sentence of one year of imprisonment is foreseen for the first illegal entry and stay, a period of up to three years for repeat offenders, or immigrants who have already been expelled, enter or reside in German territory despite a prohibition and use or provide false information in order to obtain a residence permit for themselves or for others. Germany makes use of conditional deferral of the sentence, when the judge believes that the conditions for a favorable prognosis for social reintegration exist. Pursuant to § 95, a judge may, as an alternative to imprisonment, impose a financial penalty.

The sanction regime contemplated under § § 95 and 98 *AufenthG* is only one of the consequences of illegal entry and residence. The law provides, in fact, in § § 15 and 50-62 detailed legislation on the removal and forced expulsion of foreigners on an administrative basis, not only irregular but also of regular foreigners, in response to certain conduct and conditions.

These are police and security measures, or measures aimed at stop and preventing dangers, falling within the competence of the administrative authorities and not in the jurisdiction of the judges. Under § 71 of *AufenthG*, the Länder may determine which authorities within the Land are competent for various measures envisaged in the *AufenthG*. This issue will be analysed further in the Part III of this Chapter.

Expulsion represents an alternative to criminal sanction. The Prosecuting Attorney has a discretionary power to waive the charge or the execution of the sentence in the presence of a measure involving expulsion or the removal of a foreigner, including refusal. However, waiving of criminal prosecution is not allowed in the case of crimes of some gravity, partic-

919 This provision should reconsider the orientation expressed in the Federal Supreme Court's (BGH) ruling of 27 April 2005 (2 StR 457/04), which excluded from the current regime the punishment in the presence of a formally valid permit, irrespective of its material validity. The *BGH* opted for the formal point of view, especially in view of the lack of a specific law provision in the contrary (now contained in § 95, paragraph 6) and in the light of the principle of legal certainty.

ularly in the case of offences for which the imprisonment is foreseen without conditional suspension or in the case of offensces whose prosectution is in the public interest. It is also required, for the purpose of a possible waiver, that the expulsion or removal order be enforceable and may be enforced immediately upon conviction[920].

1.2. The German legislation on the entry and stay of irregular European citizens

The Law on the Free Movement of Community Citizens (*Freizügigkeitsgesetz/EU*), inserted in Article 2 of the new Law on Immigration, regulating entry, movement and residence of Community nationals in the German territory. For these, the law on the stay of non-EU nationals does not apply, except where this last law contains more favourable provisions than *Freizügigkeitsgesetz/EU* (§ 11, paragraph 1, last term). Criminal sanctions with respect to such citizens is governed by Articles 9 (Penal Code) and 10 (Administrative Offense) of the aforesaid law. The law provides for a criminal sanction, in the form of imprisonment up to one year, or a fine for immigrant citizens or residents who have lost their right to freedom of movement. The determination of the loss of that right and the consequent withdrawal of the relevant certificates attesting that right of residence are subject to very strict conditions and the existence of reasons of public policy, public security and / or public health protection.

There must be a present and particularly serious danger to public order and security, which is of fundamental importance to society. This danger must be based on a citizen's personal conduct (Article 6 (2) of the Law on Free Movement). Only convictions that have not yet been removed from the federal register, which reveal a personal conduct of the citizen that represents an imminent threat to public order, can be taken into consideration[921].

The evaluation of the assessment of the loss of the right must also take account of the principle of proportionality and hence the duration of the

920 With respect to the execution of the sentence under § 456a Code of Criminal Procedure (*StPO*), the waiver is normally only exercised once the half of the prison term is taken. The anticipation of resumption of the execution of the sentence in case of return of the defendant expelled has to be underlined.

921 For instance, convictions for harassment and imprisonment for a minimum of five years.

stay of the European citizen[922], his age, his state of health, his economic and family situation, his social and cultural integration in Germany and his bond with his state of affiliation.

§ 11 of the EU Free Movement Act provides for the application by Union nationals of certain provisions of the law on the stay of non-EU citizens by analogy, including some criminal provisions. In particular, Article 95, paragraph 1, 4 and 8, paragraph 2, subparagraph 4, and §§ 96 and 97 are applied.

Therefore, a Union citizen who opposes an executive measure referred to in § 46, Paragraph 2, periods 1 and 2 (prohibition of leaving the country), 47, paragraph 1, number 2 and paragraph 2 (prohibition or restriction of certain political activities contrary to the interests of the Federal Republic of Germany), or Part of an association or a group of foreigners kept secret in order to avoid the prohibition by the competent authorities may be punished by imprisonment up to one year or with a financial penalty.

According to §§ 96 and 97 (analogously), a European citizen may be punished by imprisonment of up to 10 years or by a financial penalty if he or she facilitates entry or residence of foreigners on German territory in order to obtain an economic advantage (punishment is increased if the alien dies or if the offence takes place professionally or in the context of a criminal offence).

In addition to criminal sanctions, the EU Free Movement Act provides for some administrative sanctions. The administrative offence referred to in Article 10 of the Law, for which a fine of up to two hundred and fifty thousand euros is envisaged, refers solely to the violation of the obligation to possess and / or display upon request a passport or a valid replacement document.

In addition, § 11 of the EU Free Movement Act provides for the application of Article 98, paragraph 2, number 2, paragraph 2a, paragraph 3, number 3, and paragraphs 4 and 5 of the Law on the Stay of Non-EU Citizens and therefore the application of some provisions on analogous administrative malpractice.

The definitive determination of the loss of the right of residence to which it may be linked in certain circumstances also implies the obligation

922 After five years of regular residence in the German territory, Community citizens and their family members acquire permanent status, which is recognized irrespective of the existence of the requisite conditions for the freedom of movement and residence; in the presence of status, the assessment of the loss of the right is justified only for very serious reasons.

of the Community citizen to leave German territory (Article 7 of the Freedom of Movement Act). In the relevant communication of the competent authority, the time within which the territory is to be left must be indicated, and the eventual expulsion must be acknowledged. If the Community citizen fails to comply with that precept, he may be forcibly expelled.

According to § 11, paragraph 2 of the Act, *AufenthG* applies in the event that the administrative authority has ascertained the non-existence or loss of the right to freedom of movement, subject to special provisions contained in the EU Free Movement Act. The provisions on expulsion and the forced removal of non-EU nationals are therefore generally applicable[923]. The assessment of the loss of the right to freedom of movement as a precondition for the expulsion of a Community citizen requires a very strict examination.

As described, irregular immigration can be categorised as a crime, as well as as an administrative transgression. This circumstance necessarily implies a differentiation even with regard to the treatment of an irregular immigrant who commits other offences.

The punishment of the offence of clandestine crime is *a priori* excluded with reference to foreigners who enjoy special protection for special situations such as those who are granted a residence permit for situations of particular discomfort, for political reasons, international public or for humanitarian reasons, as well as irregular foreigners with a status as "tolerated" or those who would still have the right to obtain such status.

The categorisation of irregular immigration as a criminal offence generally implies that the commission of an offence by another unlawful alien to another criminal act is a competition of crimes. The competition of crimes may be, depending on the criminal activities committed, qualified both as an ideal or a formal one (rarely seen, for example, with regard to criminal offences of falsifying documents or in the presence of criminal conduct that accompanies permanent offence of illegal stay) or as real or material. As it is evident, the offence of illegal entry and residence may by nature be committed only by a foreigner, which, in the presence of other offences, may have different sanctions than those affecting German citizens who commit the same conduct, but in absence of this competition. While a German citizen who commits a crime is punished for that offence, the irregular immigrant who committed the same type of crime is regular-

923 The assessment of the loss of the right to freedom of movement as a precondition for the expulsion of a Community citizen requires a very strict examination.

ly exposed to a greater punishment because of the commission of crimes that it comes to categorise. That is why it is possible to identify a peculiar nature of aggravating circumstances that is attached to irregular immigration.

In any case, a double punishment must be avoided and, with reference to the material contest, they must not affect the determination of the cumulative penalty for imposing the same criteria or mitigating or aggravating considerations already taken into account in committing the punishment for the individual offenses.

Foreign status in itself does not constitute an aggravating or mitigating factor for the German legislation. But it can affect the discretionary sentence in an aggravating way if the foreigner enters federal territory precisely with the intention of committing crimes[924].

On the other hand, the punishment cannot be increased by the fact that in the country of origin of the alien there are expected to be more severe penalties for the conduct committed, while they may, to a certain extent, affect attenuating the education and the different culture of the alien if they lead to a different assessment of the meaning of justice that has influenced the criminal conduct that has been put in place (the sense of justice must, however, be in accordance with the order of the country of origin)[925]. However, an evaluation is always required on the basis of the individual case and a detailed analysis of the personal motives of the alien. In a mitigating way, language and communication problems, different habits and difficulties that relate to family and social relationships and contacts can also be considered, in the presence of special and motivated circumstances[926].

2. Asylum procedure

Since 2012, Germany has received the highest annual numbers of asylum applications in the European Union (EU). The increase in the number of

924 E. GUILD, P. MINDERHOUD, *Immigration and criminal law in the European Union: the legal measures and social consequences of criminal law in Member States on trafficking and smuggling in human beings*, Martinus Nijhoff Publishers, 2006.

925 E. GUILD, P. MINDERHOUD, *Immigration and criminal law in the European Union: the legal measures and social consequences of criminal law in Member States on trafficking and smuggling in human beings*, Martinus Nijhoff Publishers, 2006.

926 These circumstances may, in each case, also affect the judge's assessment of the effect that punishment and execution might have on the offender.

people searching for international protection in the EU since 2015 led to a significant rise in asylum applications in Germany. In 2016, Germany received 745,155 asylum applications, which accounted for almost 60 percent of all the asylum applications in the EU and almost six times more than Italy, which ranked second (with almost 123,000 applications)[927]; however, the *ratio* becomes different if the number of asylum applicants is compared with the total population. Despite rising numbers of asylum seekers, Germany offered them a generous welcome. In September 2015, Germany's government under Chancellor Angela Merkel agreed to open German borders to more than 10,000 asylum seekers stranded in Hungary[928].

Thousands of volunteers have been active in providing accommodation, language training, legal support, and other services to asylum seekers. However, more recently, the administration has moved toward more stringent policies, including increased rate of deportations to Afghanistan, limitation of family reunion rights[929], plans to set up shelters for returned children in Morocco[930].

---

927 Eurostat, "Asylum and Dublin statistics," accessed 17 July 2017, http://ec.europa.eu/eurostat/web/asylum-and-managed-migration/data/database.

928 Allan Hall and John Lichfield, "Germany opens its gates: Berlin says all Syrian asylum-seekers are welcome to remain, as Britain is urged to make a 'similar statement'," Independent, 24 August 2015, http://www.independent.co.uk/news/world/europe/germany-opens-its-gates-berlin-says-all-syrianasylum-seekers-are-welcome-to-remain-as-britain-is-10470062.html; Kate Connolly, "Angela Merkel defends Germany's refugee policy after attacks," The Guardian, 28 July 2016, https://www.theguardian.com/world/2016/jul/28/merkel-rejects-calls-to-change-germanys-refugee-policyafter-attacks.

929 AITIMA, "*Serious Problem Regarding Family Reunification For Asylum Seekers In Germany Under*
Dublin III Regulation" 14 July 2017, http://aitima.gr/index.php/en/news/421-14-07-2017-seriousproblem-regarding-family-reunification-for-asylum-seekers-in-germany-under-dublin-iii-regulation.
6 L. GAZZOTTI, German plans to send migrant children to reception centres in Morocco ignore
lessons from history, The Conversation, 29 June 2017, http://theconversation.com/german-plans-tosend-migrant-children-to-reception-centres-in-morocco-ignore-lessons-from-history 78012?utm_source=twitter&utm_medium=twitterbutton.

930 L. GAZZOTTI, German plans to send migrant children to reception centres in Morocco ignore lessons from history, The Conversation, 29 June 2017, http://theconversation.com/german-plans-tosend-migrant-children-to-reception-centres-in-morocco-ignore-lessons-from-history.

Article 16a of the Fundamental Law (*Grundgesetz – GG*) guarantees all refugees a fundamental individual right to asylum. The procedure for the recognition of this right is governed by a special law, the *Asylverfahrensgesetz* (Law on Asylum Procedure), which grants a federal authority the Federal Office for Immigration and Refugees (*Bundesamt für Migration und Flüchtlinge – BAMF*), the competence to examine asylum applications. As of 1 December 2013, with the entry into force of the Law of 28 August 2013 implementing Directive 2011/95 / EU "laying down rules on the qualification of third-country nationals or stateless persons" beneficiary of international protection, uniform status for refugees or persons entitled to subsidiary protection, as well as on the content of the recognized protection ", each asylum application shall include both verification of the conditions of entitlement to asylum pursuant to art. 16a, paragraph 1, GG, and the assessment of needs of international protection (§ 1, paragraph 1, No 2 AsylVfG). In the case of international protection, refugee protection is covered by the Geneva Convention of 28 July 1951 (§ 3, paragraph 1 AsylVfG) and c.d. subsidiary protection (§ 4, paragraph 1 AsylVfG).

It is not possible to appeal for the foreigner entering the territory of the right of asylum of the Federal Republic coming from a Member State of the Union European or other safe third State, which guarantees the application of the Geneva Convention on the Status of Refugees and the European Convention for the Protection of Human Rights and Fundamental Freedoms. By means of the chamber federal law, which requires the consent of the Bundesrat, those States can be identified outside the European Union[931], in which, due to the legal situation, the application of law and general political relations, it appears guaranteed that no political persecution, no degrading punishment or degrading treatment, or contrary to the sense of humanity, occurs. It is therefore presumed, as it states in § 16a, paragraph 3 of the GG, that a foreigner should not be persecuted in one of these States until he/she presents any factual situation which gives rise to the doubt that he/she, contrary to this presumption, is persecuted politically.

According to § 3, paragraph 1 *AsylVfG* the refugee status is afforded to a foreigner (*Flüchtlingseigenschaft*) if, for the well-founded fear of being persecuted because of race, religion and nationality, for his/her political beliefs or his/her membership of a particular social group lies outside the country

931 These States are Norway and Sweden (Annex I to the Asylum Procedure Act), Ghana, Senegal, Bosnia and Herzegovina, Macedonia and Serbia (Annex II, last Amended by the law of October 31, 2014).

of origin, which protection he/she can not claim or because of this fear does not want to claim. The aforementioned § 60, paragraph 3 of the *Aufenthaltsgesetz* explicitly states that persecution for belonging to a particular social group may occur even if the threat is based solely on sex (persecution Gender specifics).

Although the scope for recognition of the refugee status is wider than that of political persecution, the legal consequences of both decisions are the same: both asylum seekers and foreigners who have been afforded refugee status at first receive one permanent residence permit (*befristete Aufenthaltserlaubnis*) authorizing them to pursue paid employment. After three years they are granted an unlimited residence permit (*Unbegrenzte Niederlassungserlaubnis*), provided that there are no grounds for withdrawal or withdrawal of recognition (§ 26, paragraph 3 *AufenthG*).

A foreigner looking for protection, who does not meet the requirements for the subsidiary protection (*Subsidiärer Schutz*), when there are well-founded grounds for believing that he or she is seriously injured in his/her country of origin (§ 4, paragraph 1, *AsylVfG*). Severe harm means the imposition or execution of the death penalty, torture or inhuman or degrading treatment, punishment or individual threat of life or of the person's innocence due to indiscriminate violence within an internal or international armed conflict[932].

A foreigner who is granted subsidiary protection is granted a one-year residence permit entitling him/her to work in paid employment. After seven years he can obtain an indefinite stay permit without the need for verification by the Federal Office for Immigration and Refugees of the persistence of the reasons for the protection. It is also possible, after five years of residence in the Federal territory, to grant a EU residence permit for long-term residents: this residence permit is issued by Germany as a Member State of the EU pursuant to § 9a 2 *AufenthG* with reference to Directive 2003/109 / EC.

In case of refusal of the application for asylum and of the request of international protection, the Federal Office for Immigration and Refugees checks whether there are prohibitions on expulsion (*Abschiebungsverbote*) under paragraphs 5 or 7 of § 60 *AufenthG*. This national protection from expulsion – as it is not regulated in the aforementioned European Qualifications Directive (2011/95 / EU) – applies only in the event of dangers that undermine the applicant's foreign country in the country where he/she is to be expelled to. A further ban on expulsion, pursuant to § 60, paragraph

932 § 4, paragraph 1, *AsylVfG*.

7 *AufenthG*, may occur when an ongoing illness is likely to be worsened considerably with the return to the country of origin. The competent authority must also take into account the dangers associated with the abandonment of the Federal territory, such as the inability to travel due to illness.

With a prohibition of expulsion, a residence permit must be issued for at least one year (§ 26, paragraph 1 *AufenthG*). This permit, pursuant to § 25, paragraph 3 *AufenthG*, is not allowed if it is possible and reasonable to expatriate in another state if the alien repeatedly or seriously violates the corresponding co-operation obligations or if there are reasons to suppose: he/she has committed a crime against peace, war crimes or a crime against humanity; has committed a crime of great importance; that he/she has been guilty of actions contrary to the objectives and principles of the United Nations; or ultimately posing a danger to the community or a security risk for the Federal Republic[933].

It is possible to state that the Immigration Act which entered into force on 2015 has clarified who is an irregular migrant and the options of visa, resident permit, settlement permit and EC long-term residence permit which guarantee a regular status. Irregular status, in Germany, is treated severely[934]: Irregular immigration by non-EU foreigners is caegorised according to their conduct, and in particular depending on the degree of guilt, as a crime or an administrative transgression. The sanctions include both imprisonment and financial penalties and in the absence of *dolo* but negligent, the conduct is considered an administrative and unlawful transgression and there are cases of exclusion of the sanctions as for *duldung*[935]. However, it is possible to affirm that based on the status of irregularity, the person receives a stronger punishment: a German citizen who commits a crime is punished for that offence, the irregular immigrant who commit-

---

933 E. GUILD, P. MINDERHOUD, *Immigration and criminal law in the European Union: the legal measures and social consequences of criminal law in Member States on trafficking and smuggling in human beings*, Martinus Nijhoff Publishers, 2006.

934 Sanctioned according to the Law on the Management and the Limitation of Immigration and the Legislation for the Stay and the Integration of Citizens of the European Union and Foreigners.

935 Gesetz über den Aufenthalt, die Erwerbstätigkeit und die Integration von Ausländern im Bundesgebiet (Aufenthaltsgesetz – AufenthG) Inhaltsübersicht) Resident Act, Geographical Restriction Art. 61, 1. Residence Act in the version promulgated on 25 February 2008 (Federal Law Gazette I p. 162), last amended Article 10 (4) of the Act of 30.10.2017 (Federal Law Gazette I p. 3618; Gesetz zur Verbesserung der Rechtsstellung von asylsuchenden und geduldeten Ausländern of 23 December 2014, BGBI 2014.

ted the same type of crime is regularly exposed to a greater punishment because of the commission of crimes. That is why it is possible to identify a peculiar nature of aggravating circumstances which attach to irregular immigration.

II. Return: the protection of human rights within the detention and return procedures

1. Return procedure

In Germany the phenomenon of irregular migration does not have the same dimension that it has in Italy especially because in the latter country illegal entrance is facilitated by the geographical conditions: the arrival, especially from the Mediterranean Sea makes control at the maritime borders more complicated.

In Germany the irregular entrance occurs mostly via land and that allows easier detections of irregular arrivals, certainly, as it will be explained later, the irregular status can be given also from the lost of the regular status and other various situations, when the migrant is already within the German territory. Despite that, the phenomenon of irregular migration is also present in Germany and, as will be analysed, in relation to human rights most of the violations occur during the return procedures. That is the reason why this part of the Chapter is focused on an analysis of the return measures and problems concerning the protection of human rights.

The entry of a foreigner into Germany may be prohibited in the following cases:

a) if there are no conditions for adopting a measure of expulsion;

b) if there are well-founded reasons to believe that the actual grounds of the stay is different from the ones stated;

c) if the input conditions are not specifically provided from the Schengen Convention.

The law provides, in fact, §§ 15 and 50-62 of the *AufenthG*, a detailed regulatory scheme on removal and administrative expulsion not only of irregular but also of regular foreigners, in the presence of certain conducts or conditions. It deals essentially with police and security measures to prevent dangers, falling within the administrative sphere and not of judicial authorities. § 71 *AufenthG*, Paragraph 1, gives the *Länder* the power to determine which or which authorities within the *Land* are competent for the measures envisaged in the *Aufenthaltsgesetz*.

2. Deportation measures for irregular and regular migrants

In 2011, the UN Committee against Torture (CAT) and in 2015 the UN Working Group on Arbitrary Detention (WGAD) urged Germany to limit the number of immigration detainees[936].

For a few years, the number of immigration detainees has been decreasing in Germany. According to the National Agency for the Prevention of Torture, in 2013, the country detained 4,812 non-citizens, compared to 5,748 in 2012, and 6,781 in 2011[937]. According to official sources, in 2014 the country detained 1,850 non-citizens slated for removal and in the first half of 2015, 563[938]. However, according to information from organisations working in detention centres, the numbers of detainees have been on the rise: for instance, as of early August 2017, about 80 persons were held in the recently opened Eichstätt detention facility (Bavaria) and approximately 74 persons in Ingelheim am Rhein (Rhineland-Palatinate)[939].

---

936 Committee Against Torture, Consideration of Reports Submitted by States Parties under article 19 of the Convention: Concluding Observations of the Committee Against Torture: Germany, CAT/C/DEU/CO/5, 12 December 2011, www.ohchr.org/EN/countries/ENACARegion/Pages/DEIndex.aspx (Committee Against Torture, 2011); Working Group on Arbitrary Detention, Report of the Working Group on Arbitrary Detention: Addendum: Follow-up mission to Germany, A/HRC/30/36/Add.1, 10 July 2015, http://www.ohchr.org/EN/Countries/ENACARegion/Pages/DEIndex.aspx (Working Group on Arbitrary Detention, 2015).

937 Response of the Federal Government to the major interpellation of the deputies Ulla Jelpke, Jan Korte, Agnes Alpers, other MPs and the DIE LINKE: printed matter 17/10597: implementation of the deportation policy of the European Union and the practice of detention, Ministry of Interior, 4 September 2012, dipbt.bundestag.de/dip21/btd/17/105/1710597.pdf (Federal Government, 2012); National Agency for the Prevention of Torture, Annual Report 2013 of the Federal Agency and the Commission countries, April 2014, www.nationale-stelle.de/26.html (National Agency for the Prevention of Torture, 2013).

938 Federal government, Antwort der Bundesregierung auf die Große Anfrage der Abgeordneten Ulla Jelpke, Jan Korte, Sevim Dağdelen, weiterer Abgeordneter und der Fraktion DIE LINKE: Drucksache 18/3769, Drucksache 18/7196, 6 January 2016, http://dipbt.bundestag.de/doc/btd/18/071/1807196.pdf (Federal Government, 2016).

939 A lawyer who is an expert in immigration detention law has reported in May 2017 that since 2002 he had represented 1,299 clients in detention cases; in 666 of these cases courts have ruled that the respective clients had been unlawfully held in detention (Peter Fahlbusch, email message to JRS Germany, 8 May 2017).

2.1. Specific deportation measures

The first instrument by which a stranger can be removed is the forced rejection (*Zurückweisung*) of those who are trying to illegally cross the frontier (§ 15, paragraph 1, *AufenthG*). A second instrument is the forced removal (*Zurückschiebung*) of a foreigner who has already entered illegally: according to § 57, paragraph 1, *AufenthG*, this measure is to be immediately executed and should be put into place without notice, except for exceptional circumstances that justify the stay of the alien, such as for example the recognition of the "tolerance"[940] state (*Duldung*) or the special provisions for asylum seekers who, as a rule, cannot be removed.

The third instrument is the forced expulsion (*Abschiebung*), provided by § 58 *AufenthG*, of foreigners subject to an obligation to leave the territory (*Ausreisepflicht*) under the aforementioned § 50 *AufenthG*, because of not possessing the required residence permit or no longer being in possession of one because it expired. Foreigners without residence permits must leave the German territory immediately or within the time limit set by the competent authority. If the obligation to leave the territory is enforceable[941] and where there is a real danger of non compliance with this obligation, or if surveillance appears necessary for security reasons or for public order (for example, because it is presumed that the alien commits a crime), then forced expulsion is applied through which the foreigner is delivered to the border police which performs the removal, except in cases where there are prohibitions or impediments to such measure[942].

In particular, before the expulsion of an unaccompanied foreign minor, the competent authority must ensure that, in the State of return, he or she is handed over to a member of his family, to a person authorized to his/her custody or to an appropriate reception institute (§ 58, paragraph 1a).

---

940 See p. 220 and p. 228, paragraph 4, Italy and Germany: two legal systems in comparison, Chapter III.

941 The obligation of expatriation can be enforced by law in the event of illegal entry or in cases where the alien has not applied for the issue or renewal of the residence permit or in the case of a return decision by another Member State of European Union pursuant to art. 3 of Directive 2001/40 / EC on the mutual recognition of decisions to remove third-country nationals. In other cases, this obligation becomes enforceable only when the residence permit has been refused or if another administrative measure (revocation, withdrawal of the permit, expulsion order) has become executable, therefore no longer enforceable and immediately enforceable.

942 Federal Office for Migration and Refugees, www.bamf.de.

A foreigner who holds a long-term European residence permit or a corresponding legal position in another Member State of the European Union and who has the right to international protection in another Member State may be expelled only if the Member State guarantees protection (§ 58, paragraph 1b).

The requirement of expatriation is provided by law at the time the residence permit expires or comes to an end[943]. However, in practice, the competent authorities issue an obligation by providing for a period within which the same must be fulfilled. If the foreigner does not voluntarily comply with the requirement of expatriation, the authorities may proceed with expulsion, which, however, as it is said, presupposes the enforceability of the obligation itself.

The expulsion order (*Ausweisung*) referred to in §§ 53-56 *AufenthG* applies to regular aliens whose conduct endangers security, public order or other relevant interests of the Federal Republic. Following the order of expulsion, these foreigners, originally regular, must be considered "irregular" and are therefore required to leave the German territory. The reasons justifying an order of expulsion can be of various nature.

The expulsion is mandatory (*zwingende Ausweisung*) in the case of definitive criminal convictions for at least three years of imprisonment (or two years for drug trafficking or acts of serious disturbance of public order during demonstrations and court proceedings) and convictions for illegal immigration of foreigners (§ 53 *AufenthG*). As a rule (*Ausweisung im Regelfall*) the expulsion is then scheduled in mandatory cases listed in § 54 *AufenthG*[944].

943 The residence permit may be terminated by law (if it is not renewed or if the foreigner has left the country) or following an administrative measure such as the order of expulsion, revocation or withdrawal of the permit, or the Notification of a deportation order.

944 Cases:
1) a final sentence of imprisonment (at least two years for minors) without conditional suspension; 2) proven participation in illegal immigration; production, import and sale of narcotic substances; 3) participation in acts of violence committed during unauthorized public events that have in any way jeopardized public security; 4) proven membership, present or past, as an active member, to flanking organizations of terrorism; 5) Carrying out activities aimed at endangering the foundations of democratic coexistence in the Federal Republic; 6) participation in violent acts or incitement or threat to resort to violence for political ends; 7) issuing false statements to public authorities about previous periods of stay in Germany or issuing false and incomplete information on relevant aspects of relationships with people involved in terrorist acts; 8) the command

§ 55 *AufenthG* is a general clause regulating the (numerous) cases in which the administrative authority may with discretion (*Ermessensausweisung*) impose an expulsion measure where the stay of a foreign national may affect the public policy or other relevant interests of the Federal Republic.

The fourth and final tool to remove an alien from the federal territory is the immediate removal order (*Abschiebungsanordnung*) provided by § 58a *AufenthG*: this is a competence assigned to the *Länder* for security and defence against particular dangers for the Federation and in the event of a terrorist threat. In such cases the law provides for the territorial jurisdiction of the Land authorities to order the expulsion of a foreigner with immediate effect, without any previous order of expulsion and without notice.

The Federal Minister of the Interior may assume direct responsibility for the expulsion order in case of a special interest of the Federation. The authorities of the *Land* are informed of this and the measure is carried out by the federal police. After the expulsion order, the foreigner still has the possibility to contact a trusted lawyer and he has right to be informed about the measure, its consequences and the possibilities of appeal.

Even in the case of an immediate removal order, an appeal may be filed within seven days in accordance with the applicable law on administrative proceedings. Therefore, the expulsion is not executed within seven days and, if the application is lodged, until the decision on the same[945].

The order of expulsion, forced removal and forced expulsion entails, pursuant to § 11 *AufenthG*, the ban on re-entry and stay in German territory (*Einreise- und Aufenthaltsverbot*). A foreigner who is expelled or removed is no longer granted a residence permit, even in the presence of other statutory requirements. On demand, such effects may be limited in time, except in cases where the alien has been expelled from the federal territory for offences relating to peace, war crimes or humanity, or on the basis of an order of deportation under § 58 *AufenthG*.

If the request is accepted, the time limit set for re-entry is fixed in the light of the circumstances of the case and may last for more than five years only if the alien has been expelled because of a criminal conviction or because it may be a serious threat to public security and public order. When determining the duration of the limit, account shall be taken of whether

---

of organizations declared illegal for purposes contrary to the criminal law, the constitutional order of the state or the international order.

945 Federal Office for Migration and Refugees, www.bamf.de.

the alien has left Germany in accordance with established times and voluntarily. The terms starts from moment of his/her departure from federal territory.

2.2. Detention

In order to ensure the execution of expulsion and forced expulsion, it can be arranged the c.d. *Abschiebungshaft*, which can be of two types: preparatory detention (*Vorbereitungshaft*) and prison precautionary detention (*Sicherungshaft*), both governed by § 62 *AufenthG*. The detention of the alien who has been notified the expulsion order is, as a general rule, a measure envisaged only when it is expected that the person concerned will not leave voluntarily.

Minors and families with minors may be taken into custody pending expulsion only in exceptional cases and for a reasonable time in consideration of the child's well-being (§ 62, paragraph 1).

Preparatory detention can last up to six weeks (maximum time allowed by law) and applies in cases where it is not possible to make an immediate decision regarding forced expulsion or deportation and, at the same time, execution of deportation may be compromised in the absence of restrictive measures of personal liberty (§ 62, paragraph 2).

Precautionary detention or arrest for security reasons shall be made if one of the following conditions applies:

1) that the alien is subject to the obligation to leave the federal territory as irregular;

2) that the maximum time for voluntary departure has elapsed without the person having obeyed the order;

3) that the alien has not been found in the place and day expected for expulsion;

4) that the foreigner has fulfilled the obligation in some way;

5) that there are reasonable grounds for suspecting that the alien will seek to circumvent the measure and intend to escape deportation (§ 62, paragraph 3).

Precautionary detention can be up to six months, but in cases where irregular foreigners hinder his/her expulsion, it may be extended for a further 12 months (§ 62, paragraph 3).

3. Detention Centre

Pursuant to § 62a *AufenthG*, introduced *ex novo* by the Law of 22 November 2011[946], which adopted a number of Union directives on the stay of foreigners, detention aimed at expulsion is normally carried out in specific detention centres for foreigners (*Hafteinrichtungen spezielle*).

If there are no such centres in the *Land* concerned, the execution of the detention measure takes place in normal prisons, but in places exclusively-for irregular foreigners in order to ensure an adequate level of privacy.

Those in custody awaiting expulsion are allowed to contact legal representatives, family members and competent consular authorities. A minor is guaranteed the application of Art. 17[947] of Directive 2008/115 / EC of 16 December 2008 laying down common rules and procedures in the Member States concerning the return of third-country nationals whose stay is unlawful. Upon request, employees of organizations involved in assistance and support for foreigners must be allowed to visit them in detention centres. Finally, the law provides that foreigners waiting for expulsion are informed about their rights and duties and the rules in force within the detention centre.

The largest foreign detention centre in Europe was the Büren Penitentiary Institute, near Paderborn (North Rhine-Westphalia), where approximately 530 migrants were detained pending expulsion. Subsequently closed, it was reopened from May 2015 as specific detention centre for foreigners awaiting expulsion (*Abschiebehaftanstalt*) with a capacity of 100[948].

---

946 BGBl. 2011 I, p. 2258.

947 This Article, concerning the treatment of minors and families, states that: 1) children are not accompanied and families with minors are detained only in the absence of other solutions and for a suitable period as short as possible; 2) families detained in the habit of leaving away are provided with separate accommodation that ensures their proper respect for private life; 3) the restrained minors are offered the opportunity to carry out recreational activities, according to their age and, depending on the length of their stay, access to education is provided; 4) unaccompanied minors are provided, as far as possible, in institutions with facilities and facilities to meet the needs of people of their age; 5) the child's best interest constitutes a fundamental criterion for the detention of minors awaiting removal.

948 Other detention centers in German territory are located in Berlin-Köpenick (160 seats), Eisenhüttenstadt (Brandenburg, 108 seats), Mühldorf am Inn (Bavaria, 68 Places for men, 14 places for women), Langenhagen (Lower Saxony, 15 to 30 seats), Ingelheim (Rhineland-Pfalz, 70 seats). Previously there were other deten-

The detention for the purpose of deportation has posed a number of problems of constitutionality, since, while not being configured as a penalty, it is practically implemented in the same manner as criminal detention. In some of its decisions, the Federal Constitutional Court (*Bundesverfassungsgericht*) has imposed the maximum acceleration of procedures and, by virtue of the principle of proportionality, the waiver of detention if the removal is not enforceable.

On 17 July 2014 a judgment of the Court of Justice of the European Union[949] found that Germany and the other EU Member States can ot rely on the lack of specific detention centres in a part of their territory, in order to accommodate irregular foreigners in common prisons. The Court has in fact, accepted the request of Attorney General Yves Bot, who strongly criticized the use of the prisons as a violation of the human dignity of immigrants[950].

The deprivation of liberty to them is not a punishment and therefore those people must be accommodated in special centres that also take into account the special needs of their families and children. The European Court has also ruled that foreigners awaiting expulsion cannot be accommodated in normal institutes of punishment even if there is the consent of the person to be detained.

In 2014, the daily detention costs per person ranged between approximately 43 euros in Bremen and 420 in Hannover Langenhagen[951]. The Residence Act (Section 66(1) and 67(1)) stipulates that costs relating to deportation, including the costs of detention, are to be borne by the non-citizen. Non-citizen should pay these costs to be permitted to re-enter Germany, even after the period of validity of re-entry ban[952]. Reportedly these costs are to be paid by non-citizen only in the event of deportation, thus

---

tion centers for immigrants in Rendsburg, Schleswig-Holstein, Mannheim (Baden-Württemberg) and Volkstedt (Saxony-Anhalt).

949 For instance: C-473/13, C-474/13, C-514/13.

950 Judgment of the Court (Grand Chamber), 17 July 2014, C-473/13 – Bero and Bouzalmate.

951 Federal government, 2016, op. cit.

952 C. GRAEBSCH, B. SELDERS, *Der Zugang zum Bundesgerichtshof ist das geringste Problem: Interview mit Christine Graebsch von Beate Selders*, In Haft ohne Straftat. Fakten und Argumente gegen Abschiebungshaft, Edited by Flüchtlingsrat Brandenburg, Flüchtlingsrat Schleswig-Holstein and Humanistische Union, Berlin, 2013, quoted in Federal Office for Migration and Refugees, 2014, op. cit.

the obligation to pay for deportation and detention functions acts as an incentive for migrants to leave voluntarily[953].

In cases of entry by air, non-citizens coming from a safe country of origin or those without identity documents who apply for asylum with the border authority may be kept in custody at airport premises during the asylum procedure for up to 19 days (Asylum Act, Section 18(a))[954]. In 1996, the German Federal Constitutional Court ruled that the placement of foreigners at airport transit zone premises does not constitute detention, as, according to the court, the people concerned have an option to leave by plane[955]. In contrast, the European Court of Human Rights ruled, in *Amuur v France*[956], that accommodation of asylum seekers in transit zones, even if they could freely leave the premises by leaving the country and irrespective of domestic classification of the practice, may amount to detention.

Under "custody to prepare deportation" (*Vorbereitungshaft*), a non-citizen may be detained to enable the preparation of deportation if a decision on deportation cannot be reached immediately and deportation would be much more difficult or impossible without such detention (Residence Act, Section 62(2)).

A person can be placed in "custody to secure deportation" (*Sicherungshaft*) for several reasons, including being required to leave the federal territory because of unlawful entry, having evaded or being presumed to intend evasion of deportation (Residence Act, Section 62(3)). This provision is used in most cases.

People subject to Dublin procedures may be detained if there is a risk of absconding and if a non-citizen has left another member state prior to the conclusion of Dublin or asylum proceedings. Under "custody to secure departure" (*Ausreisegewahrsam*), a foreigner may be detained in an airport transit area or in a special facility to ensure deportation once the period for voluntary departure has expired (Residence Act, Section 62b).

---

953 Federal Office for Migration and Refugees, 2014, op. cit.

954 Informationsverbund Asyl und Migration, "Country report: Germany," Asylum Information Database (AIDA), European Council on Refugees and Exiles (ECRE), December 2016, http://www.asylumineurope.org/reports/country/germany (Informationsverbund Asyl und Migration, 2016).

955 Bundesverfassungsgericht, judgment, 14 May 1996, 2 BvR 1516/93.

956 European Court of Human Rights, judgment, 25 June 1996, 17/1995/523/609.

4. Centre for refugees

As soon as they have arrived in Germany, asylum seekers are required to stay for six weeks, and for up to three months, in one of the first reception centres (*Erstaufnahmeeinrichtungen*). For the duration of his stay in the centres, the foreigner is obliged to be made available to the competent authorities and judicial bodies. Within 15 days from the submission of the asylum application, the centre of the first reception will inform them, possibly in writing and in a language understandable, to them about their rights and obligations under the law on the benefits for asylum seekers (*Asylbewerberleistungsgesetz*). They should also be given information about who can provide legal assistance and which associations can help with accommodation and medical care.

The Federal Office opens an electronic file containing the data of asylum seekers. Those who have reached the age of 14 are subject (*erkennungsdienstliche Behandlung*) photographs and fingerprint detection. These measures serve to ascertain whether the alien, possibly with a different name, has previously been in Germany or if another European state is in fact competent to carry out the asylum procedure.

An identification document, e.g. a residence permit (*Aufenthaltsgestattung*) is issued, which the alien must always carry with them and show in case of police checks. Subsequently (after a maximum of three months), asylum seekers are transferred to one of the second reception centres (*Anschlussunterbringungen*), spread across federal territory according to a system of allocation of hostels between *Länder* [957]. According to the provisions of § 44 AsylVfG, the Länder are obliged to provide the reception facilities necessary to accommodate and maintain asylum seekers and, in accordance with their reception quota, to make available the number of beds needed in relation to arrivals and requirements reported monthly by the Federal Ministry of the Interior.

Following the sharp increase in the number of foreigners seeking asylum in 2013 and even in 2014, some Länder have begun to expand and enhance the capacity of reception facilities. Alternatively, they have resorted to emergency accommodations such as barracks, hotels and hostels, containers and camps. In order to facilitate and speed up the projects by the

957 According to § 45 AsylVfG, the Länder may agree a coefficient for the reception of asylum seekers (Cd. reception fee, Aufnahmequote). In the absence or in the event of termination of the agreement, the shares shall be calculated taking into account the tax revenue and the size of the population of the various Länder.

Länder, a law was approved by the Bundesrat (specifically the Länder of Hamburg, Bremen and Baden-Württemberg) on measures in the building legislation to facilitate the accommodation of refugees ("Gesetz über Maßnahmen im Bauplanungsrecht zur Erleichterung der Unterbringung von Flüchtlingen"), in force since 26 November 2014.

The recent amendments to the Asylbewerberleistungsgesetz – AsylbLG Law and the Social Security Law (Sozialgerichtsgesetz), introduced by the Law of 10 December 2014, entered into force on 1 March 2015[958]. Purpose of the bill governmental act, approved without amendment by the Bundestag and the Bundesrat, is the implementation of the Federal Constitutional Court's judgment of 18 July 2012, by which the provisions relating to the basic contributions, in the form of cash grants, granted on the basis of the Asylbewerberleistungsgesetz, have been declared incompatible with the fundamental right to a decent level of subsistence[959].

Once again, the amounts of the subsidies were adjusted, adjusting them to the needs and establishing, for the future, their regular updating. In addition, foreigners entitled to aid provided for by the Asylbewerberleistungsgesetz can benefit from Social Assistance (Sozialhilfe) provided for in the Social Security Code (Sozialgesetzbuch – SGB), after an uninterrupted period of 15 months (previously 48 months) in federal territory.

With the law to improve the legal status of foreigners seeking asylum and tolerated (Gesetz zur Verbesserung der Rechtsstellung von asylsuchenden und geduldeten Ausländern) of 23 December 2014, in force since 1 January 2015[960], the primacy of the principle of performance in nature (so-called Sachleistungsprinzip) referred to in § 3 AsylbLG, was limited to the period of stay in the first reception centre. After this time, cash grants (Geldleistungen) are prioritised over the provision of and other necessities.

As shown previously by the statistical numbers, in Germany the phenomenon of irregular migration has a smaller dimension than in Italy and most of the violations of human rights of these immigrants occurred during the procedures of return. As analysed in this Part, there are several different measure of return: forced rejection, forced removal, forced expulsion and immediate removal order. To ensure the execution of expulsion

958 Federal Law Gazette I p. 2438.

959 Federal Office Migration and Refugees: Migration, Integration, Asylum Political Developments in Germany 2016 Annual Policy Report by the German National Contact Point for the European Migration Network (EMN).

960 BGBI 2014. Act on Improvement of the Legal Status of Asylum Seekers and (temporarily) tolerated Foreigners, 23 December 2014 (No. 64).

and forced expulsion, if it is expected that the person concerned will not leave voluntarily and will not be possible take more mitigated measures, then it provides a detention: preparatory detention and precautionary detention. This type of detention has posed several constitutional problem because as configured not as a penalty but however is implemented as a criminal detention. Indeed, it has been conducted very often in proper prison and not in specific and separate centres, as provided by the EU legislation, with the aim to accomplish this function, violating the human dignity of the migrants. As reported in this Part there were several judgment of conviction from the Court of Justice of European Union and European Court of Human Rights.

Conclusion: some reflections in particular on detention procedure

Since the expansion of the EU's eastern border in 2004, there have been fewer undocumented migrants entering Germany. Also, following the adoption of new detention legislation in 2009, domestic courts have reportedly rigorously scrutinized this practice[961].

As already analysed, unlike the vast majority of EU countries, Germany makes wide use of its prisons to hold non-citizens in administrative detention. Secondly, regional (*Länder*) governments, rather than the national government, are responsible for immigration detention.

The decentralized nature of immigration detention in Germany also presents important challenges in getting comprehensive information about detention practices and establishing accountability, particularly at the international level. Federal authorities typically claim that they do not have statistics on immigration detention because they are not in charge of this practice and regional authorities are sometimes not responsive to requests for information. Additionally, regional governments at times disagree with federal authorities on best practices, including over issues like whether prisons are adequate places to hold people for immigration-related reasons.

Germany's decentralised detention regime has been at the heart of two ground-breaking legal cases at the Court of Justice of the European Union (CJEU). In July 2014, the CJEU found that Germany's practice of using prisons for immigration reasons to be incompatible with the EU Returns

961 Pro Asyl and Diakonie Hessen 2013.

Directive. In its judgment in *Bero & Bouzalmate*[962] it ruled that Germany cannot rely on the fact that there are no dedicated detention facilities in a given *Land* to justify keeping non-citizens in prison pending their removal[963]. In *Pham*[964], the Court found that the same rule applies even if the detainee has consented to being confined in a penitentiary.

In particular, Germany's legal framework for immigration detention is provided in the 2008 Act on the Residence, Economic Activity and Integration of Foreigners in the Federal Territory (Residence Act) (*Gesetz über den Aufenthalt, die Erwerbstätigkeit und die Integration von Ausländern im Bundesgebiet or Aufenthaltsgesetz*) and 2008 Asylum Procedure Act (*Asylverfahrensgesetz*), as well as the 2009 General administrative regulation to the Residence Act (*Allgemeine Verwaltungsvorschrift zum Aufenthaltsgesetz*). Procedural rules are provided in the 2008 Act on Procedure in Family Matters and in Non-Contentious Matters (*Gesetz über das Verfahren in Familiensachen und in den Angelegenheiten der freiwilligen Gerichtsbarkeit*).

These legal provisions are intended to provide only a general framework for immigration detention. The Residence Act provides the grounds for detention, rules on the length of detention, and basic procedural safeguards. It contains few provisions dealing with conditions of detention. It is in the *Länder*'s capacity to adopt such laws, since they are in charge of immigration detention. Only three states (Berlin, Brandenburg, and Bremen) have adopted specific laws regulating enforcement of immigration detention. In the remaining thirteen states the Prison Act (*Strafvollzugsgesetz*), complemented by non-binding *Länder* standards, regulates conditions and overall detention regimes.

This situation has been criticized by the European Committee for the Prevention of Torture and Inhuman or Degrading Treatment or Punishment (CPT), which on numerous occasions has been frustrated in its ef-

962 CJEU – Joined Cases C-473/13 and C-514/13 *Adala Bero v Regierungspräsidium Kassel* and *Ettayebi Bouzalmate v Kreisverwaltung Kleve.*

963 At the time of the ruling, 17 prisons were in use. As of July 2017, German Länder operated five long-term dedicated centres: Pforzheim (Baden-Württemberg), Eichstätt (Bavaria), Hannover (Langenhagen) (Lower Saxony), Büren (North-Rhine-Westphalia), and Ingelheim am Rhein (Rhineland-Palatinate)[40]. In Bremen, a facility in the police headquarters compound is used to confine migrants. Another detention centre, Eisenhüttenstadt (Brandenburg) is temporarily closed for structural alteration works. In addition to these centres, Saxony (Dresden) and Hamburg operate detention facilities for the Ausreisegewahrsam. Also the Hannover (Langenhagen) centre is used for this purpose. Most of these centres were set up at the premises of former prisons.

964 CJEU – C-474/13, *Thi Ly Pham v Stadt Schweinfurt.*

forts to convince German authorities to reform immigration detention policies and practices, in part due to the decentralized nature of the country's immigration enforcement regime[965].

Because of Germany's widespread use of prisons for immigration detention, a critical question has been the extent to which administrative detainees are separated from criminal inmates. The National Agency for the Prevention of Torture told the Global Detention Project that immigration detainees are "*usually separated, even when an immigration detainee who is held in a prison receives medical attention in that prison's health clinic, it is against the law to put that person in the prison hospital. Prisoners and immigration detainees must not even mingle during sporting or leisure activities*"[966].

Many prisons that confine non-citizens appear to have specific areas for immigration detention (including those in Büren, Dresden, and Hamburg-Billwerder). On the other hand, several prisons do not have specific detention areas, including particularly in the case of facilities that confine female immigration detainees (such as in Chemnitz, Frankfurt III, Schwäbisch-Gmünd, and Rockenberg)[967].

While in practice non-citizens are not confined to the same cells as criminal detainees, they may have contact with them during meals or recreation time. Such a setting might be classified as not in line with the separation obligation[968]. In the *Pham* case, the CJEU ruled that immigration detainees shall be kept separated from ordinary prisoners. The Court noted that under the Return Directive, the obligation for migration detainees to

965 After its 2010 periodic visit to Germany, the CPT recommended that each state create special provisions for pre-removal detention. It expressed concern that in those Länder where immigration detainees are still being held in prisons, no specific regulations governing detention pending deportation exist. As a result, immigration detainees continue to be subjected to the same rules and restrictions as sentenced or even remand prisoners. Such a state of affairs is not acceptable, being a violation of human rights. In the CPT's view, conditions of detention of immigration detainees should reflect the nature of their deprivation of liberty, with limited restrictions in place. The CPT calls upon the German authorities to take immediate steps to ensure that, in all German Länder detention pending deportation is governed by specific rules reflecting the particular status of immigration detainees" (CPT 2012).

966 Dopp, Rainer (Head of the German Committee for the Prevention of Torture (National Agency for the Verhüting of torture). 2014. Interview with Michael Flynn (GDP). 11 April 2014.

967 Pro Asyl and Diakonie in Hesse and Nassau. 2013. Schutzlos behind bars detention in Germany. Pro Asyl and Diakonie in Hesse and Nassau. June 20 March 2014).

968 See Global Detention project, "Germany Immigration Detention" report 2014.

be kept separated from ordinary prisoners is not coupled with any exception. Moreover, they stressed that the separation requirement is more than just a specific procedural rule for carrying out detention in prisons and constitutes a substantive condition for that detention, without compliance of which such detention would, in principle, not be consistent with the Directive[969].

Germany is one of a very small number of European countries—Switzerland being another notable case—where prisons are used for the purposes of immigration-related detention. Because regional – rather than federal – authorities are in charge of carrying out immigration detention measures, detention practices can vary widely across the country.

The EU Returns Directive was expected to trigger changes in these German practices. Article 16(1) of the directive provides that "*detention shall take place as a rule in specialised detention facilities. Where a Member State cannot provide accommodation in a specialised detention facility and is obliged to resort to prison accommodation, the third-country nationals in detention shall be kept separated from ordinary prisoners*."

However, the federal nature of the German state and the country's decentralized immigration authority have continued to complicate reforms. Thus, while Article 62 of the Residence Act, which transposed article 16(1) of the directive, provides that "*[as] a general principle, custody awaiting deportation shall be enforced in specialised detention facilities*," the provision also states that if a Land "*has no specialised detention facilities, custody awaiting deportation may be enforced in other custodial institutions in that Land*" (Residence Act, Section 62a(1)). Thus, unlike the Returns Directive, which refers to the territory of the whole member state, the Residence Act allows using prisons in those *Länder* that do not have a dedicated immigration detention facility.

In 2011, the European Commission had to clarify the lack of consistency between the Residence Act and the Returns Directive. The commission responded stating that the directive's article 16(1) refers to the entire territory of a member state. Thus, *Länder* cannot legitimize detention of noncitizens in prisons if there are dedicated facilities available in other German federated states.

969 Majcher, Izabella, 2014, The EU Returns Directive and the Use of Prisons for Detaining Migrants in Europe, EU Law Analysis. July, Court of Justice of the European Union (CJEU), 2014B; *Pham* C-474/13, CJEU Curia.europa.eu/juris/document/document.jsf.

Following requests from German courts, in July 2014, the Court of Justice of the European Union (CJEU) rendered a long-awaited opinion on the use of prisons in Germany in two cases, mentioned above. The Court found this practice incompatible with article 16(1) of the EU Returns Directive, in the *Bero & Bouzalmate* case, it ruled that Germany cannot rely on the fact that there are no dedicated detention facilities some of its federated states to justify keeping non-citizens in prison pending their removal; in *Pham*, it found that the same rule applies even if a migration detainee consents to being confined in penitentiary[970].

The Court established that a federal country like Germany is not obliged to set up specialized centres in each of its states. However, it is obliged to establish procedures that enable *Länder* that do not have specialised facilities to place migrants in specialized facilities located in other states[971]. Similar mechanisms have already been set for certain cases. Thus, for instance, because not all *Länder* have facilities for confining women, they send female detainees to other *Länder*. Three states (Schleswig-Holstein, Hamburg, and Mecklenburg-Western Pomerania) have formal arrangements with the detention facility in Eisenhüttenstadt (Brandenburg) to hold female non-citizens. Also, in practice persons apprehended at the border in Saxony are sent to different places: men to Dresden and women to Eisenhüttenstadt. NGOs have documented several cases in which the deportations of family members detained in different facilities were scheduled at different times[972].

---

970 The court established that a federal country like Germany is not obliged to set up specialised centres in each of its states. However, it is obliged to establish procedures that enable federal states that do not have dedicated facilities to place migrants in specialised facilities located in other states. I. MAJCHER, The EU Returns Directive and the Use of Prisons for Detaining Migrants in Europe, EU Law Analysis, July 2014, eulawanalysis.blogspot.co.uk/2014/07/the-eu-returns-directive-and-use-of.html.

971 Majcher, Izabella. 2014. "The EU Returns Directive and the Use of Prisons for Detaining Migrants in Europe." EU Law Analysis. July. Court of Justice of the European Union (CJEU). 2014B. Pham. C-474/13.CJEU Curia.europa.eu/juris/document/document.jsf. Court of Justice of the European Union (CJEU). 2014a. Bero & Bouzalmate.C-473/13 & C-514/13. CJEU. 17 July 2014.curia.europa.eu/juris/document/document.jsf. Court of Justice of the European Union, 2014B, *Pham*, C-474/13, CJEU, Curia.europa.eu/juris/document/document.jsf.

972 Pro Asyl and Diakonie in Hesse and Nassau, 2013, Schutzlos behind bars detention in Germany, Pro Asyl and Diakonie in Hesse and Nassau, June 20 March 2014.

Another critical aspect concerning detention in Germany is that the quality of detention orders issued by district courts is sometimes very poor. A judge at the Federal Court has estimated that about 85 to 90 percent of detention orders issued by district courts had to be declared unlawful when reviewed by the Federal Court[973].For instance, judges frequently issue detention orders even when authorities have not sufficiently explained the reasons justifying this measure[974].

There is a possibility to apply for legal aid in the context of judicial review of detention[975]. However, free legal aid is dependent on how the court assesses the chances of success. Thus, in practice, free legal aid is rarely granted[976]. Migrants have the right to compensation for unlawful immigration detention but the rules are not explicitly laid down in the Residence Act. People concerned would need to rely on the Constitution and the Civil Code[977].

Related to alternative measures to detention, according to the Residence Act, pre-removal detention is not permissible if the purpose of the custody can be achieved by other, less severe means, which are also sufficient (Residence Act, Section 62(1)). However, unlike in most of the EU countries, the Residence Act does not clearly enumerate alternatives to detention. Consequently, it is very rare that alternatives to detention are checked in an individual case before a detention order is issued[978].

The WGAD addressed alternatives to detention during recent visits to Germany. Following its 2011 visit to Germany, the WGAD urged authorities to use alternatives to detention for non-citizens who do not have valid

---

973 J. Schmidt-Räntsch, Freiheitsentziehungssachen gem. §§ 415 FamFG. Neue Zeitschrift für Verwaltungsrecht (NVwZ), 2014, p. 110.

974 Peter Fahlbusch, Haft in Verfahren nach der Dublin II-Verordnung, Asylmagazin 9/2010, 289-295.

975 Federal Office for Migration and Refugees, 2014, op. cit.

976 Informationsverbund Asyl und Migration, 2016, op. cit.

977 K. HAILBRONNER and D. THYM, Completed Questionnaire for the project Contention: National Report – Germany, 2014, hhttp://contention.eu/country-reports/.

978 For the discussion on alternatives to detention see JRS Europe, From Deprivation to Liberty. Alternatives to detention in Belgium, Germany and the United Kingdom. Brussels, December 2011; JRS Deutschland, Abschiebungshaft vermeiden. Alternativen zur Abschiebungshaft in Belgien, Deutschland und dem Vereinigten Königreich. Berlin, April 2012.

visas[979]. Following its 2014 visit, the WGAD noted that the principles of necessity and proportionality under international law require the use of alternatives to detention[980].

In conclusion is possible to affirm there are some priorities[981] concerning immigration detention in Germany: to ensure that grounds justifying detention under the Residence Act and Asylum Act are clear and foreseeable in their application, in line with the requirement of lawfulness; to recognise that confinement of asylum seekers at the airport transit zones amounts to detention and consequently to ensure detention-related guarantees to these people; as recommended by the European Committee for the Prevention of Torture, to ensure that the Prison Act does not govern immigration detention in any federal states; also to ensure that detention is imposed only where it is necessary and proportionate given the person's individual circumstances. Relevant point, as recommended by the UN Committee against Torture and the UN Working Group on Arbitrary Detention, is to reduce the numbers of immigration detainees and to reduce the length of immigration detention. As recommended by the UN Committee on the Rights of the Child, also to apply detention to children as a last resort and for the shortest period of time. Moreover, to ensure that judges order detention only based on a case-by case examination of the individual circumstance, as required by the principle of necessity; to ensure that migrants are provided access to legal aid and to set up procedures facilitating access to compensation schemes for unlawful immigration detention. As recommended by the UN Working Group on Arbitrary Detention, to use alternatives to detention, in line with the principles of proportionality and necessity and to clearly enumerate alternatives to detention in the Residence Act.

Finally to ensure that private firms involved in operating detention centres are properly trained and accountable for their acts; to cease requiring immigration detainees to pay for their detention in order to ensure that detention is a non-punitive measure; to ensure adequate material conditions and regime of detention in all of the country's detention facilities and to

---

979 Working Group on Arbitrary Detention, Report of the Working Group on Arbitrary Detention: Addendum: Mission to Germany, A/HRC/19/57/Add.3, 23 February 2012, http://www.ohchr.org/EN/Countries/ENACARegion/Pages/DEIndex.aspx.

980 Working Group on Arbitrary Detention, 2015, op. cit.

981 GDP and Jesuit Refugee Service Germany, Submission to the Universal Periodic Review (UPR): Germany, 21 September 2017, Global Detention Project.

ensure that detention centres located in the former prisons provide a non-punitive environment[982].

In conclusion of this Chapter, it is possible to affirm that according to the German legislation, the irregular immigrant's sanctioning treatment governed by *Gesetz zur Zuwanderung und zur Regelung des Aufenthalts und der Integration von Unionsbürgern und Ausländer* (the Law on the Management and the Limitation of Immigration and the Discipline for the Stay and the Integration of Citizens of the European Union and of Foreigners), is severe. Indeed, under the terms of the provision § 95 *AufenthG*, irregular immigration of non-EU nationals has been formulated, in the presence of certain conduct and / or depending on the degree of guilt of the offender, as a criminal offense: § 95 regulates sanctions, including both imprisonment and financial penalty. Moreover, § 98 *AufenthG* provides for certain sanctions of an administrative nature to determine the conduct of non-EU citizens constituting an administrative offence. Illegal stay without dolo but negligent, is considered to be an administrative and unlawful illicit. Penalties are also foreseen for those who favor irregular immigration.

As it is clear, the provision related to the offence of illegal entry and residence may by nature be committed only by a foreigner thus the irregular immigrant who committed the same type of crime of a German citizen is regularly exposed to a greater punishment because of the commission of the crimes that it comes to configure. This makes evident as there is a peculiar nature of aggravating that connotes irregular immigration.

In Germany the phenomenon of irregular migration has a smaller dimension than in Italy. With respect to the subject of this analysis, namely the protection of fundamental rights of this category of migrants, most of the violations of their human rights are related to the procedure of return. There are four different kinds of deportation measures: the forced rejection (*Zurückweisung*) of those who are trying to illegally cross the frontier (§ 15, paragraph 1, *AufenthG*); forced removal (*Zurückschiebung*) of a foreigner who has already entered illegally; forced expulsion (*Abschiebung*), scheduled from § 58 *AufenthG*, against foreigners subject to the obligation of expatriate (*Ausreisepflicht*) under the aforementioned § 50 *AufenthG*, since not possessing the required residence permit or no longer in possession of as it expired and finally the immediate removal order (*Abschiebungsanordnung*)

982 Foreign Office for Migration and Refugeed. Izabella Majcher, "The EU Returns Directive and the Use of Prisons for Detaining Migrants in Europe," EU Law Analysis, July 2014, eulawanalysis.blogspot.co.uk/2014/07/the-eu-returns-directive-and-use-of.html.

provided by § 58a for security and defence against particular dangers for the Federation and in the event of a terrorist threat.

In order to ensure the execution of expulsion and forced expulsion, it possible to arrange the c.d. *Abschiebungshaft*, which can be of two types: preparatory detention (*Vorbereitungshaft*) and prison precautionary detention (*Sicherungshaft*), both governed by § 62 *AufenthG*. The detention aimed at expulsion is normally carried out in specific detention centres foreigners (*Hafteinrichtungen spezielle*) as provided by Art. 16 of the Return Directive in order to guarantee the fundamental rights of the migrants. If there are no such centres in the Land concerned, the execution of the detention measure takes place in normal prisons, but in destined places exclusively to irregular foreigners in order to ensure them an adequate level of privacy.

Specifically on this point several violations occur: as analysed, the detention for the purpose of deportation has posed a number of problems of constitutionality, since, while not being configured as a penalty, it is practically implemented in the same manner as a criminal detention. Indeed, as demonstrated in particular by two well known cases *Bero § Bouzalmate* and *Pham*, the detention of these migrants did not occurr in separate centres in violation of Art. 16 aforementioned, leaving the migrants in normal penitentiary structures justifying the decision with the lack of enough appropriate structures in the national territory.

However, the European Court of Justice did not consider this reason valid and affirmed the violation of the human rights of migrants forced to remain in criminal detention centres and therefore be treated as criminals, even if the detainees had consented to being confined in a penitentiary.

The violations of human rights underlined until here seem to be the result of a lack of good management and organization in the German territory of the structure mentioned above more than a policy aimed to restrict the fundamental rights of these category of migrants. This is a difference with the Italian policy that tries to restrict the human rights of these migrants using a more severe legislation. Although, also in German scenario a similar normative framework is into force towards the category of *duldung*, the foreigners who have a temporary suspension of deportation (these are often asylum seekers whose application is rejected and cannot be deported for humanitarian or other reasons). This will be explored further in the subsequent Chapter.

III. Italy and Germany: two legal systems in comparison

As already mentioned in the introduction to this III Chapter, there are some differences between the two countries which are quite evident and have determined the analysis on the protection of human rights of irregular migrants of these two legal systems following different lines and focusing on different points.

Irregular migration in Italy and Germany has different structures for several reasons. First of all a geographical one: Italy is one of the Member States at the border of European Union, with Greece and Spain to represent the main door to the Europe for third country nationals who want to enter the EU, so the arrival of the migrants, mostly irregular because they are without any legal status to enter, is very high. These migrants often arrive by boat reaching the Italian shores and this kind of entrance is very complicated to keep under control.

Moreover, these migrants consider Italy a transit country rather that a destination. They do not want to remain in the Italian territory in most cases, because often they already have part of their family or relatives in other Member States, because other countries guarantee a better labour market, and so on, and usually these countries are Germany, France and Sweden. For these reasons, they just try to cross Italy to reach other destinations.

However, they try to avoid identification in Italy because, based on EU Dublin III Regulation, already mentioned, they have to be processed for granting the status of asylum in the first state of identification, so very often Italy. This is why they try to avoid the identification in Italy and try to cross the country remaining irregularly.

Germany, instead, also for geographical reasons, it is surrounded by other Member States, does not have a high number of irregular entrances: identifying irregular migrants who arrive by bus or train often, allows controls to be conducted more easily. Moreover, Germany, as it has been said, is mostly a country of destination and that means the migrants who enter the territory usually submit an application for asylum. So, until the end of the procedure for the decision of international protection, as refugee status or subsidiary protection, guarantee the seekers the status of asylum seeker which is not an irregular status.

These are the main reasons why the phenomenon is different. In Germany, the irregular migrants are mostly falling into the category of *duldung* (tolerated) as it will be seen below and those who enter regularly and loses the resident permit which could be for a variety of reasons.

1. Reflections on the power of the Member States on the issue of irregular migration: the role of International Law

The subject of migration is a controversial one: indeed the policy makers often use the topic of migration, and in particular irregular migration, in order to gain more of the electorate stigmatising the phenomenon and consequently the migrants. This political approach prefers a security oriented policy with a consequent reduction in the protection of human rights of these migrants.

The role of the European Union policy and legislation in this field is very determinant: indeed, the sovereignty of the nations is understandable in relation to a phenomenon like irregular migration and given the differences of it in each country based on the geography, pull factors of the countries, and so on. However, the clarity and precision of the European framework is very important in order to avoid ambiguity where the States can take advantage of the application of rules which are not sufficiently respectful of human rights, as occurred in relation to the Return Directive as outlined in Chapter II[983], which let the States introduce rules not complying the international human rights standards. A correct balance between the coordination of the national and supranational level is important, as clear guidelines with precise points to be followed from the national law.

It possible to assert that the affirmation of human rights at international and supranational level, which have gradually extended their scope to a sector traditionally considered to reside within state sovereignty (such as the treatment of foreigners) has permeated this area to the extent that state power cannot be considered absolute[984].

The idea that state sovereignty should be exercised in accordance with international law, including international human rights law, backed up with increasing frequency by many international authorities, seems to have had an impact on national courts. Recent analysis of many different national and supranational rulings highlights the focus on common questions and the difficult search for a balanced position: how far does the margin of appreciation of states extend? How does the principle of proportion-

983 See p. 108, paragraph 1, Detention and return of irregular immigration, Special Part, Part IV, Chapter II.

984 A. PASCALE, *Italy and Unauthorized Migration: Between State and Sovereignity and Human Rights Obligations*, Oxford Scholarship Onlie, April 2014.

ality balance this?[985] The Member States in EU could have the possibility to increase the level of protection compare that one impose by international legal tools?

Thus, as already said, for a strong defence and application of human rights it is very relevant, a correct balance and complementarity between the two levels mentioned above.

Focusing on the last question the Member States in the matter of immigration could also make use of the more favourable provision clause in order to introduce stronger protection of human rights balanced with the security needs. Indeed, Member States are allowed to maintain or enact higher standards than those provided in EU law, as a consequence of the application of both their own legislation and international Treaties which they are bound to.

The implementation of this clause allows States to interact with EU fundamental rights, increasing the level of protection of these rights, accommodating EU legislation to national needs and contexts.

The difficulty in using such a clause could be detected at national policy level where often there is a lack of increase, or at least effective implementation, of the regulation of protection of fundamental rights in order to match the fears of the electorate especially in the last years with this wave of irregular migration flows.

Therefore, to have a strong and binding supranational regulation regarding the protection of human rights such as the ECHR and the Charter of Fundamental Rights of European Union is very important.

2. The concentration of the management of immigration phenomenon: to the overlap of the administrative and judicial system in Italy

One of the differences between the Italian system and the German one, concerning the issues in theme of immigration, that makes the latter more efficient, is the concentration of the powers which is attributed to the administrative apparatus. The powers are, indeed, distributed clearly between the jurisdictions, instead in the Italian case, based on the previous analysis of the legal classifications of migrants and their regulatory and administrative regimes, it can be seen that they have created a particularly fragmented system and this fragmentation also extends to the identification of compe-

985 A.PASCALE, *Italy and Unauthorized Migration: Between State and Sovereignity and Human Rights Obligations*, Oxford Scholarship Onlie, April 2014.

tent authorities or bodies case by case, to the legal definition of legal qualification, the provision of specific benefits or the resolution of potential disputes.

As can be seen, however, fragmentation is an attribute present both in the "ordinary" regime of immigration and in the "special" regime, and this must be recognized even in the face of the general unitarity of the administration responsible for all matter, which remains, basically, the government (i.e. the administration of the Interior).

However, this fragmentation[986] may be another element to challenge the frequent "simplification" of the dualism between a migrant and a migrant recipient of international or humanitarian protection. What is perhaps missing, for a complete overcoming of the distinction between an "ordinary" and a "special" regime, is the explicit link between one and the other. This goal could be better achieved where the law recognized the holders of protection international or humanitarian "specific" titles (so to speak) to access ordinary forms of permission or to achieve citizenship more quickly. The latter status, in truth, is the true "stone guest" of the whole theme discussed here, since the current legislation does not yet seem permeable to the recognition of systems capable of facilitating the positive outcome (with limitation, therefore, of the very wide administrative discretion) of an application for recognition presented by those who not only have accumulated heterogeneous residence permits, but, by virtue of those, have had experiences of qualified integration.

Even more specifically, organizationally, there is a peculiar "segmentation", especially in the "special" context, which is, as it has been said, the condition of those who may wish to have temporary residence permits in the territory reasons for international protection. In fact, there are a number of structures dealing with incoming identification, recognition of a subjective status, assistance and reception (first and second), and such organic heterogeneity is the result of institutional solutions that have happened over time (even at very short notice) and that, in spite of this, they still survive, living together.

986 Also quantitatively confirmed, given the different percentages of recognition of a residence permit depending on the different status of a foreigner.

2.1. The first reception centres and the German model

Some structures, in particular, among which there are also the "hotspots" and the territorial Commissions, have the main and preliminary purpose of selecting migrants and identifying those who may be holders of a right to remain, even temporarily, in the territory of Italy (or European Union): as such, similar structures are located in a "concentrated" way on single portions of the country, those most affected by significant phenomena of potentially illegal entry of foreigners. Other structures, on the other hand, also have the purpose of offering the same subjects that have already been selected useful and "sustainable" spaces for assistance and possible and subsequent integration, widespread throughout the national territory: as such, similar structures are destined to arise in all the Regions and to make use of the necessary support from local authorities.

However, this organization, which may seem rational, having proved in recent times to dispose of a particularly wide range of activities: is a source of great difficulty since, delays or inefficiencies of the first structures have forced the legislator to place on the second part also part of the identification and reception tasks of the former (and it is not often the case that individual migrants have difficulty accessing the sites of judicial protection, rooted in distant places of reception).

In addition, at the stage when the Municipalities participate in the "integrated reception system" (and thus become essential partners for the establishment of the second structures), the possible coordination of the activities carried out by the local authority in that specific term and other policies that the same entity (or even the internal administration) intends to pursue normally for the integration of aliens who are staying on the basis of administrative titles of the "ordinary" regime.

Therefore, as can be seen also based on the previous paragraph, the emergence and continuous evolution of the "special" matter has contributed to an intensification of the original fragmentation, generating also new coordination problems, both inter-organizational and intersubjective. Moreover, that can give rise, due to its peculiar fragmentation, to widespread phenomena of treatment disparity between holders, for expressive legislative recognition, of subjective situations that do not seem to admit, by definition, such differentiation.

The horizon of an action of total reordering of matter could be the absorption of the "special" into the "ordinary" system, with a mutation of the assumptions governing the second (so, that is, that at the second, the holders of international or humanitarian protection can access more easily)[987]. In conclusion, a more concentration in the administrative apparatus as in Germany, would simplify the Italian system.

3. Reflections on the measure of assisted repatriations: the efficiency of the German system

Another difference between the Italian and German system concerning the management of the irregular immigration, is related the return procedures: Germany adopts an efficient system of voluntary repatriation through the help of IOM which offers a program of assisted repatriation of migrants, reducing the use of forced return less compatible with the guarantee of human rights and more expensive. In Italy the return system is not efficient enough and it should be revised: Germany on this point could be a model of inspiration also to better implement the Return Directive provisions on this aspect which provide and allow the use of force in the return procedures as last option.

Indeed, Germany support through return programmes run by the federal government and the federal states who voluntary decide to leave the State. These programmes allow asylum applicants to permanently return to their home country or to migrate to a third country which has agreed to resettle them. The return programme includes not only logistic but also financial support. It consists of two connected elements which are commonly referred to as REAG/GARP ("Reintegration and Emigration Programme for Asylum-Seekers in Germany" / "Government Assisted Repatriation Programme"). REAG offers assistance with regard to transport and fuel costs (for car journeys) as well as travel benefits. GARP offers starter grants which help the asylum seeker to make a fresh start in another country. The International Organization for Migration (IOM) coordinates the exit journey through both funding programs. Since February 2017, an additional financial support named Starter Grant Plus or "*StarthilfePlus*" is also available in combination with REAG and GARP[988].

More in detail: the REAG/GARP-program is a humanitarian program assisting with financial and operational support the voluntary return and mi-

987 F. CORTESE, *La difficile classificazione dei migranti*, in M. SAVINO, *La crisi migratoria tra Italia ed Unione Europea: Diagnosi e Prospettive*, Editoriale Scientifica, Napoli, 2017. p. 171.

988 See German Federal Office for Migration and Refugees, www.bamf.de.

gration to third countries. It offers start-up assistance for defined nationalities and serves as a steering instrument for migration movements. The migrants eligible to benefit from the program are asylum-seekers, rejected asylum-seekers and recognized refugees as well as war and civil-war refugees, victims of forced prostitution or trafficking and other foreigners (eligible under § 1 *AsylblG*, the German asylum seekers' benefit Act), as well as migrants who have been granted residence due to humanitarian or political reasons.

The application of financial assistance within the programme REAG/GARP is organized in cooperation with German authorities, welfare organizations, specialized counselling centres, central information centres for voluntary return, and the United Nations High Commissioner for Refugees (UNHCR). To obtain REAG/GARP assistance, the appropriate applications can only be submitted through these authorities and organizations. Nationwide IOM works together with more than 1600 German authorities[989].

Within the framework of the program, the German Government grants the following types of assistance (defined in the Information booklet of REAG/GARP 2015): payment of travel costs (e.g. by plane or bus); additional travel assistance; initial start-up cash to people from countries that are particularly relevant in terms of migration[990].

3.1. The deficiencies of the Italian assisted repatriation measure and the German model

Regarding the situation of voluntary repatriation in Italy, the Central Directorate for Civilian Immigration and Asylum Services has been the Responsible Authority of the European Fund for Reimbursement (FR) 2008/2013, established at Union level under the SOLID Funds and aimed at supporting the efforts made by the Members States to improve repatriation management. In this context, the implementation of Voluntary Assisted Repatriation (RVA) programs has been supported, involving third-country nationals in integrated paths aimed at genuine re-accompaniment of the subjects involved in the country of origin at each stage related to repatriation, from pre-departure preparation, to return trip, expecting, in

989 See German Federal Office for Migration and Refugees, www.bamf.de.

990 See voluntary return program, German Federal Office for Migration and Refugees, www.bamf.de.

some cases, also a reintegration subsidy[991]. The total number of RVAs in the period 2009/2015 (30 June) was 3,947 and the first four repatriation nationals were Ecuador, Peru, Tunisia and Morocco.

Looking at the more recent situation, since the beginning of the five voluntary assisted return projects funded by the Interior Ministry in 2016, so far there has been a total average of 10-12% of departures from the planned target, which is about 3,000 voluntary repatriations. This has been denounced by the Italian Refugee Council (CIR), which one of the five entities that in May 2016 won the call for funding from the *Fondo, Migrazione e Integrazione Fami* 2014-2020 to carry out voluntary return projects assisted and reintegrated for migrants in Italy[992]. The head of the voluntary return project of CIR, said that this data is worrying. The projects last 18 months and they should end in March 2018 and ensure at least 6 months of monitoring in the original country, so repatriations should be completed before that deadline. The main problem of these low numbers depends on low information: since it is a measure that is activated by the manifestation of the will of the alien, the knowledge of the measure is fundamental[993]. Until now, very often the migrant that should have access to these program are not informed concerning that and consequently they cannot activate the measure.

The national information network, which should have accompanied the projects, has been assigned to the IOM, International Migration Organization, for the next three years only recently. That of assisted voluntary return is a measure often unknown by the operators as well. In addition, people who have received a postponed expulsion decree cannot access the measure, and irregular migrants who may access them often do not know the existence of the institution.

Another major issue is the duration of the projects, the fruits of work are often seen over a period longer than the period when the project is active. To work it should be always active so that everyone can realize a return

991 See voluntary return program, German Federal Office for Migration and the German model Refugees,
www.bamf.de.

992 See Italian Minister of Interior, www.interno.gov.it.

993 ANSA: the Associated Press Agency, commonly known as ANSA, is the first multimedia information agency in Italy and the fifth in the world after Reuters, AP, France Presse and EFE.
http://www6.ansa.it/ansamed/it/notizie/rubriche/politica/2017/04/19/migranti-rimpatri-volontari-finora-solo-10-dei-previsti_9794f319-7e3a-4e19-b48d-28325c483e80.html.

with their time. For the deficiencies illustrated, the German system could represent in this case a model of efficiency which allows the State to better guarantee the respect of fundamental rights during this measure and consequently also to better implement the Return Directive.

4. Reflections on the case of "duldung" in Germany and the violation of their human rights

The category of irregular migrants can cross with the category of asylum seekers: who enter a country without documents and then file an asylum application have an uncertain legal status until their application is processed; or who have exhausted all means for obtaining asylum, whose applications have not been accepted but who are, nonetheless, unable to leave the country and hence remain without residence status, yet with the knowledge and toleration of the authorities. This status may involve a formal suspension of enforcement action for a specific period of time, this is the case of *Duldung.*

This legal status is based on the Act on the Residence, Economic Activity and Integration of Foreigners in the Federal Territory (*Aufenthaltgesezt*) at Art. 60a, paragraph 2 on tolereted status – temporary suspension of deportation, affirms that asylum seekers whose application is rejected are granted the toleration status if they cannot be deported for humanitarian or other reasons. For instance, in the case of people whose origin cannot be determined, refused asylum seekers who cannot yet be returned, and witnesses in judicial processes, as mentioned above.

" ...*The deportation of a foreigner shall be suspended for as long as the deportation is impossible in fact or in law and no resident permit is granted...*".This suspension of deportation is granted for a short period of time and is repeatedly extended until return is possible.

Access to the labour market, to education and to social welfare benefits are severely restricted. For instance: under Section 18a of the Residence Act, qualified personnel whose residence has only been tolerated in Germany so far may receive a residence permit to engage in employment in keeping with their qualification after one of the following: a) completion of (two-year) qualified vocational training or a course of higher education in Germany; b) two years of employment in Germany in an occupation commensurate with a course of higher education abroad; c) three years of employment in Germany in an occupation requiring qualified (two-year) vocational training. The competent International Placement Services team approves residence permit issuance without a priority examination[994]. Another example is for medical insurance, the costs are only covered in cases of acute illness or pain; there is no right to family reunification (only in exceptional cases) and they are limited in access to university[995].

Analysing in detail the labour situation, which is fundamental for a dignified living in the state, they are subject to special conditions for access to the labour market. They can take up work, but they must obtain permission to engage in work from their immigration authority. The immigration authority decides in relation to the respective individual case whether permission to engage in work is granted. The authorisation of the local Employment Agency is also necessary as a matter of principle. The immigration authority will obtain the authorisation of the Employment Agency, and the individual does not need to obtain such authorisation themselves.

Persons who have a certificate of suspension of deportation may not engage in employment if they entered the country in order to obtain benefits under the Asylum-Seekers' Benefits Act (*Asylbewerberleistungsgesetz*) if they prevent residence-terminating measures by for instance providing misleading information with regard to their identity or nationality, or if they come from a safe country of origin and their asylum application was filed after 31 August 2015 and has been turned down. Moreover, persons with temporary suspension of deportation status who have good prospects to remain, have also had access to integration courses since November 2015.

Based on the points just mentioned, it is possible to detect some violation of fundamental rights of this particular category of migrants: they are forced to remain in the German territory, for some of the reasons seen above, but they see the exercise of one of the most important and essential right to live in the country, the right to work, limited and subject to a decision from the immigration authority as that one of the Employment Agency. This seems a violation of their human rights to limit them in the exer-

994 In the priority examination, the competent employment agency ascertains whether preferential applicants are available for a certain job. Precedence is accorded in Germany to Germans, Union citizens, citizens from EEA states and Switzerland and third-country nationals with unrestricted labour market access.

995 See (Gesetz über den Aufenthalt, die Erwerbstätigkeit und die Integration von Ausländern im Bundesgebiet (Aufenthaltsgesetz – AufenthG) Inhaltsübersicht) Resident Act, Geographical Restriction Art. 61, 1. Residence Act in the version promulgated on 25 February 2008 (Federal Law Gazette I p. 162), last amended Article 10 (4) of the Act of 30.10.2017 (Federal Law Gazette I p. 3618).

cise of the right to work which is the right that would allow them to live with dignity and with adequate sustenance although only temporarily.

Moreover, the legal provision based on which after four years of living in Germany it is nolonger necessary the authorization from the Employment Agency, it means the State considers as a concrete a duration of the permanence in the territory of this particular category of people for such a long time. However, the State does not provide the guarantee to fully exercise the right of work.

4.1. Italy and Germany closer in the restriction on human rights of irregular migrants

In the case mentioned above, which is not a case existing in Italy, the immigrants so called *Duldung* do not have a legal status to remain on the territory, however the German state, on the one hand accepts for practical reasons their irregularity without implementing any sanctions. On the other hand, these tolerated migrants do not have a full access to some fundamental rights purely because of their status which is also not the result of their free choice.

This particular form of status is not provided in the Italian legal system and this is one of the difference between the categories of irregular immigrants in the two Member States. However, this specific case falls into the bigger category of irregular migrants. That shows that, although it has been underlined that most violations of the fundamental rights of irregular migrants in Germany relate to the return measures for management reasons, there is a will from the State to restrict the exercise of significant human rights, such as the right to work, avoiding *de facto* the integration of these migrants who are forced to live in the German territory temporarily for a long time.

The toleration status brings the migrant into a legal and social limbo which forces the migrant to a situation of marginalization without protection. That appears not so different from the attempt of restriction of human rights conducted by the Italian state towards persons with an irregular status, as in the limitation analysed in the marriage and public authorisation cases.

5. Italy and Germany and the restriction of personal liberty based on the status

5.1. Crime of clandestinity in Italy

As it has been analysed in the Italian section of this Chapter, the provision of the crime of clandestinity has been criticised: indeed "*The idea of a criminal sanction envisaged and applied solely to condemn a subjective condition, without any offense being committed*"[996] is grossly wrong. This affirmed the Union of Criminal Chamber in Italy (UCPI), there is an evident violation of the dictation of the Italian Constitution and the Criminal Code, this provision does not reflect the main element and necessary which define a crime. That represents surely a violation of fundamental rights.

According to the UCPI, the debate on which are the most effective forms of control and repression of irregular immigration is undermined by ideological prejudices: criminalization did not have any deterrent effect, given that the offense is punishable by a fine ranging from € 5,000 to € 10,000.00, and no irregular immigrant is usually able to pay; moreover, any abolition would not eliminate the possibility of expelling irregular immigrants or undermining anyone's security.

In agreement with the National Magistrates Association, the UCPI Council believes that the only result of the rule was to tamper with the judicial offices, making it even harder to detect and repress the most serious conduct of those who organize and practice illegal trafficking.

It should be stigmatized the inspirational philosophy of the most recent lawmakers' interventions on justice: the tendency to solve problems "*solely on the tracks of usability / useless media or on the efficiency / inefficiency of the system*" rather than on the basis of constitutional principles, which "*require that a conduct for offense is actually offensive and does not simply reflect an abstract judgment of value, a rebuke for a mere subjective condition.*"[997]

The constitutional foundation can be deduced from the following normative references Art. 13 of the Italian Constitution, protecting personal freedom: so the imposition of a criminal sanction can only be issued as a reaction to a conduct that offends a rank of equal rank, based on the principle of offensiveness.

996 A. PASCALE, Italy and Unauthorized Migration: Between State and Sovereignity and Human Rights Obligations, Oxford Scholarship Online, April 2014.

997 A. PASCALE, Italy and Unauthorized Migration: Between State and Sovereignity and Human Rights Obligations, Oxford Scholarship Online, April 2014.

The principle of offensiveness for the law in force must be the parameter of constitutional legitimacy of the offenses envisaged meanwhile the irregular migrants are condemned to the payment of a financial penalty just for their subjective status.

5.2. Crime of clandestinity in Germany

The German regulation, as it has been seen, provides even a more strict and severe consideration of the status of irregularity: in Germany, criminal conduct and criminal offenses inherent in immigration are listed and governed by § 95 *AufenthG*. Under the terms of this provision, as already written, irregular immigration of non-EU nationals has been configured, in the presence of certain conduct and / or depending on the degree of guilt of the offender, as a criminal offense: § 95 *AufenthG* regulates sanctions, including both imprisonment (*Freiheitstrafe*), from one to three years, both the financial penalty (*Geldstrafe*)[998]. As already previously underlined, the offense of illegal entry and residence may by nature be committed only by a foreigner, which, in presence of other offenses, may have different sanctions than those affecting German citizens who commit the same conduct, but in absence of this competition. That demonstrates a peculiar nature of aggravating that connotes irregular immigration.

6. The violations of human rights during the return procedures: both Italy and Germany do not respect Art. 16 of Return Directive

From the analysis conducted until here, Germany and Italy, received several critics regarding the detention procedures in relation to the protection of human rights of the category of irregular migrants within the reception system.

Both States did not implement properly the European Union directive so called Return Directive, analysed in the previous Chapter. In particular the relevant problematics are connected the modality of detention of the migrants with an irregular status which have to be returned to their home

998 In addition, as already mentioned in the Chapter, § 98 AufenthG provides for certain sanctions of an administrative nature to determine the conduct of non-EU citizens constituting an administrative offense. Illegal stay without *dolo* but negligent, is considered to be an administrative and unlawful illicit.

country or transit country from which they come from. Both in Italy and Germany, the previsions of the Directive are not respected.

The Article 16(1) of the directive mentioned above provides that *"detention shall take place as a rule in specialised detention facilities. Where a Member State cannot provide accommodation in a specialised detention facility and is obliged to resort to prison accommodation, the third-country nationals in detention shall be kept separated from ordinary prisoners."*

In Germany, this provisions, is breached in several instances as outlined earlier: many prisons that confine non-citizens appear to have specific areas for immigration detention (including those in Büren, Dresden, and Hamburg-Billwerder). On the other hand, several prisons do not have specific detention areas, including particularly facilities that confine female immigration detainees (such as in Chemnitz, Frankfurt III, Schwäbisch-Gmünd, and Rockenberg). Although, in practice non-citizens are not confined to the same cells as criminal detainees, they may have contact with them during meals or recreation time. Such a setting might be classified as not in line with the separation obligation provided by the Directive. Where a Member State cannot provide accommodation in a specialised detention facility and is obliged to resort to prison accommodation, the third-country nationals in detention shall be kept separated from ordinary prisoners.

Therefore, a violation of the fundamental rights of migrants, as in the Italian case, can be affirmed: indeed in the Italian system the irregular migrants are often waiting for their return to their origin or transit country not in penitentiary institution but in different centres, as explained, with this function. However, very often these structures are more similar to jail than centres of identification and expulsion as they should be according to the European Directive.

The number of migrants who have to be returned and who are waiting in these centres does not match the capability of the structure, the number of the persons inside is higher ad consequently the conditions of life and the fundamental rights are not respected. Moreover, the return procedures very often last longer than what it is provided for by the European legislation and within the Italian system, the institute has been progressively expanding over the years, assuming an almost punitive value as a sanction for the irregularity of the stay. Even in the constitutional view, this institution is criticized: in fact it is a limitation measure of personal freedom, which is devoid of the character of exceptionality, thus contrary to art. 13 of the Constitution. Therefore, even if they are not detained as inmates, the migrants cannot enjoy their personal freedom so are no different to inmates.

The most difficult part for the Member States in the return phase is the management of the detention and during this phase several violations occure in both States. Although in the German case, the voluntary repatriation system is more efficient and reduce the case of forced return which is more expensive and less compliant with human rights. In this sense, Germany can represent a good model concerning the return phase for Italy.

Conclusion

A premise to this last conclusion: these final considerations are short because a specific conclusion has been written at the end of each Chapter. The aim of this last part of thesis is to focus on the main critical nodes highlighted during the research work. From these nodes, new paths of work can be identified for a research activity that aims to make the treatment of the human rights of irregular migrants, present in each territory of the member states, more uniform at European Union level.

The research project with respect to the initial aims illustrated in the introduction of the thesis, after detected and underlined precisely the category of irregular migrants and explained that one of the most critical aspects is the protection of their human rights within the European Union context, rebuilt a complete framework on the topic in reference to the European Union. The analysis conducted detailed a complete normative framework at European level reporting the main legislation by the institutions, as important directives and Agendas on Migration, and international and European Conventions such as the European Convention of Human Rights and the Charter of Fundamental Rights of the European Union, in order to understand the context in which the issue of protection of human rights of irregular migrants has been set in this dissertation.

The research project has outlined who are irregular migrants for the European Union legislation: a third-country national who does not fulfil, or no longer fulfils the conditions of entry as set out in Article 5 of the Schengen Borders Code or other conditions for entry, stay or residence in a Member State. This category includes not only undocumented people but also people who are in possession of forged papers or people who have assumed false identities with real papers.

The status of irregularity very often, as analysed in the first Chapter, defines the immigrant as "illegal". The concept of "illegal migration" is loaded with ideological meaning and it is highly politicised. It connotes criminal behaviour and should therefore be avoided. The term in question designates the act of entering a country in violation to national law and is confined to illegal border crossing, not to a stock of persons. This is the reason why the more neutral and correct term is irregular.

The strict and stigmatizing political approach to this category, just mentioned, reflects in particular in the weak protection of the human rights concretely guaranteed to these migrants. The protection of the fundamental rights of irregular migrants is provided by international legislation, suchs as the European Convention of Human Rights or the European Social Charter, by European legislation, such as the Charter of Fundamental Rights of the European Union, and by the national provisions, however the violations that occur against these legislation are many, as already mentioned.

For these reasons, given the innumerable violations of which Member States are guilty, it is also important to have clear international legislation to effectively impose the respect for the duty of protection of human rights of irregular migrants who are particularly vulnerable because of their status on the signatory States.

From the analysis conducted within this research project, the problematic aspects of the legal framework of European Union related to the protection of human rights of irregular migrants are several, and they come in particular from the difficulties in correctly balancing the strong tension there is between the need at the European level and at national level to guarantee the security of the borders and simultaneously the protection of the human rights of irregular migrants. To reach this balance is a challenge for the European Union that, notwithstanding several Conventions, Agenda on Migration, directives and so on to regulate the phenomenon and protect their rights, it seems to have had a security orientated policy approach. Given that European legislation is not always precise enough Member States have been allowed to implement it with too much discretion as seen, for instance, in the cases of the Return directive as analysed in the second Chapter.

In general, there is a tendency at European Union policy level to not create a legislation for the category of irregular migrants and the protection of their rights, but insted to recall the provisions in the international and European conventions which are applicable to everyone without any kind of distinction (as for instance enshrined in Art. 1 of ECHR) and leaving the Member States to correctly interpret those. Consequently, in this way, the issue is left to the domestic jurisdiction.

However, the Member States continue to have a strong tension between the need to guaranty security from illegal entrance and residence and the duty of protecting the human rights of the irregular migrants and the national legislation seems to be inclined towards an ineffective protection of human rights, as shows the comparative analysis between Italy and Germany. Thus, a correct balance and complementarity between the two levels mentioned above is very important for a strong defence and application of human rights.

Indeed, as it has been analysed, both States Italy and Germany, legally implement with different grade of intensity, a stigmatization of the irregular migrant who is consider, just for the fact of his status, a criminal who has to be subjected to a legal sanction. That seems to be not compliant with the human rights perspective: considering, for instance, the European Convention of Human Rights guarantees fundamental rights such as right to life, prohibition of slavery and forced labour, right to a fair trial, etc., and Article 1 enshrines the protection to all persons, regardless of their status, thus also to irregular immigrants. The same content is contained in the Charter of Fundamental Rights of the European Union. If the protection of fundamental rights has to be guaranteed without taking into consideration the status of the person, then it seems a paradox to condemn, from a legal point of view, a subject for his status, thus limiting his fundamental rights, including limiting their personal liberty, as provided in the German system, only because of the irregular status on the territory.

This limitation of the fundamental rights produced by a strict policy in two countries that experience a different phenomenon of irregular migration, as already said in terms of numbers being higher in Italy, are responsible for a strict and incorrect application of human rights in particular during the procedures for the return of these migrants to their countries of origin which is one of the most delicate phases. Indeed, in this phase the State has to act as guarantor of the protection of fundamental rights of these vulnerable persons. The most frequent violation is related to the limitation of the personal freedom: their presence in centre of first reception is too long and often conducted in centres that do not guarantee the facilities and conditions provided for in the Return Directive.

In Germany there have been many cases of irregular migrants being forced to stay in prison during their wait for return, having contact with prisoners that they should not have during the detention phase before return. In Italy because of poor management of the diverse centres where the migrants have to stay, irregular migrants waiting for return are also often treated as prisoners.

Notwithstanding that, the German case presents an efficient system of voluntary repatriation, as explained, through several programs that can be a good model not only for Italy but also improved and implemented at European Union level. This, indeed, would be progress on the issue of protection of human rights of irregular migrants by the European Union institution.

Another aspect that makes Germany more efficient, is the concentration of the powers related to the management of immigration, which is attributed to the administrative apparatus. The powers are, indeed, distributed clearly between the jurisdictions and there is not, as in Italy, the overlap of the administrative and judicial system, as mentioned in the Chapter on the Italian context. This also has an impact on the exercise of the fundamental rights by irregular migrants that see, in this unclear and sometimes unreasonable distribution of the power in Italy, judges that belong to different jurisdictions to decide their complaints.

The tendency in the Italian system is to create a "special" regime for migration issues creating a fragmented system. This fragmentation that generates inefficiency. For different reasons, this is also found at European level, in fact the European legislation is often applied unevenly by the Member States, which makes the supranational legislation inefficient including with reference to the protection of the human rights of migrants.

In general terms, the comparison showed as the recognition of important human rights, as the right of work, right of health, right to education is limited for irregular migrants during the time they have to stay in the European territory before to be returned. This limitation has been highlighted in the third Chapter both in Italy and in Germany, in the latter case in particular through the category of *duldung*, showing that these countries do not really protect the rights of these migrants and do not facilitate their integration when the migrants have to remain in the territory for a long period. Indeed the lack of the possibility to fully exercise their rights, as for example the right to work, would not give them the opportunity to integrate themselves in the society.

The main nodes emerging from this research project are: the poor protection of the rights of irregular migrants when they remain in the territory, albeit irregularly, and the issue of repatriations.

As it falls within the competence of the member states, the matter of immigration, is managed with too much diversity between the member states and the European legislation which regulates some aspect of the matter, allows too much discretion in its application by the member states, for the reasons illustrated previously, like the lack of clarity and ambiguity of some directives. There is a lack of specific legislation at European level, there are mainly references to international legislation, which in turn guarantees protection without providing strictly specific rules on this category of migrants. As long as the issue of immigration is not within the competence of the European Union, there will not be more precise and effective legislation or a common regulatory framework in all member states.

The system of voluntary repatriation should be further developed, which should be managed according to precise and binding procedures. Member states should be called to adequately promote this instrument. The European Union should have more initiative in signing agreements with the countries of origin in order to facilitate these voluntary repatriations.

Legislation (chronological order)

Agreements

Readmission Agreement EU-Hong Kong, OJ L 17, 24.1.2004, p. 25–39.

Readmission Agreement EU-Macao, OJ L 143, 30.4.2004, p. 99–115.

Readmission Agreement EU-Sri Lanka, OJ L 124, 17.5.2005, p. 43–60.

Readmission Agreement EU-Albania, OJ L 124, 17.5.2005, p. 22–40.

Readmission Agreement EU- Russia, OJ L 129, 17.5.2007, p. 40–60.

Readmission Agreement EU- Ukraine, OJ L 332, 18.12.2007, p. 48–65.

Readmission Agreement EU- Bosnia and Herzegovina, OJ L 334, 19.12.2007, p. 66–83.

Readmission Agreement EU- the Former Yugoslav Republic of Macedonia OJ L 334, 19.12.2007, p. 7–24.

Readmission Agreement EU-Montenegro OJ L 334, 19.12.2007, p. 26–44.

Readmission Agreement EU-Pakistan, OJ L 287, 4.11.2010, p. 52–67.

Readmission Agreement EU-Serbia, OJ L 334, 19.12.2007, p. 46–64.

Readmission Agreement EU- Moldova, OJ L 334, 19.12.2007, p. 149–167.

Readmission Agreement EU- Georgia, OJ L 52, 25.2.2011, p. 47–65.

Readmission Agreement EU- Armenia, OJ L 289, 31.10. 2013, p. 13–29.

Readmission Agreement EU-Azerbaijan, OJ L 128, 30.4.2014, p. 17–42.

Readmission Agreement EU-Cape Verde, OJ L 282, 24.10.2013, p. 15–34.

Agreement between the European Union and the Republic of Turkey on the readmission of persons residing without authorisation, OJ L 134, 7.5.2014, p. 3–27.

Conventions

Universal Declaration of Human Rights, UN General Assembly Resolution A/RES/217 (III) of 10 December 1948.

European Convention on Human Rights (ECHR), 1950.

International Convention on the Elimination of All Forms of Racial Discrimination (ICERD) 1965.

International Covenant on Civil and Political Rights (ICCPR) 1966.

International Covenant on Economic, Social and Cultural Rights (ICESCR) 1966.

Convention for the Safety of Life at Sea, (SOLAS), 1974.

European Convention on the Legal Status of Migrant Workers CETS No 093 of 24 November 1977.

Convention on the Elimination of All Forms of Discrimination against Women (CEDAW) 1979.

Search and Rescue Convention (SAR), 1979.

Convention against Torture and Other Cruel, Inhuman or Degrading Treatment or Punishment (CAT)1984.

Convention on the Rights of the Child (CRC) 1989.

International Convention on Protection of the Rights of All Migrant Workers and Members of Their Families (ICMRW) 1990.

United Nations Convention on the Law of the Sea, (LOSC) 1982.

Protocol against the Smuggling of Migrants by Land, Sea and Air, supplementing the United Nations Convention against Transnational Organized Crime, United Nation, New York 2004.

Charter of Fundamental Rights of the European Union, legally binding 2009.

Communications

European Commission Communication, COM(2002) 564, 14 October 2002.

COM(2015)0453 final, on EU action plan on return, on 9 September 2015.

European Commission Communication, COM(2006) 402, 19 July2006.

COM(2008) 611, on Strengthening the global approach to migration: increase co-ordination, consistency and synergies, 8 October 2008.

COM/2011/743 final, the Commission Communication, The Global Approach to Migration and Mobility.

COM/11(76) final, Communication of the Commission on the evaluation of EU Readmission Agreement, on 23 February 2011.

COM(2013)292 final, Commission Communication Maximising the Development Impact of Migration.

COM(2013)869 final. On the work of the Task Force Mediterranean.

COM(2014)199 final, Communication from the Commission to the Council and the European Parliament on EU Return Policy.

COM(2015)0510 final, Managing the refugee crisis: State of Play of the Implementation of the Priority Actions under the European Agenda on Migration.

COM (2015) 240 final, on European Agenda on Migration, 13 May 2015.

COM/2015/0285 final, EU Action Plan against migrant smuggling (2015 – 2020).

COM(2015) 185 final on the European Agenda on Security, on 28 April 2015.

COM(2015) 240 final, on European Agenda on Migration, on 13 May 2015.

COM/2016/031 final, First Report on the progress made in the implementation of the EU-Turkey Statement.

COM/2017/0201 final, on the operationalisation of the European Border and Coast Guard, on 2 March 2017.

COM/2017/0350 final, Fourth Progress Report on the Partnership Framework with third countries under the European Agenda on Migration, on 3 February 2017.

COM (2017) 200 final on a more effective return policy in the European Union, on 2 March 2017.

Decisions

Framework Decision 2002/946/JHA on the strengthening of the penal framework to prevent the facilitation of unauthorised entry, transit and residence, OJ L 328, 5.12.2002, p. 1.

Council Decision (CFSP) 2015/972 of 22 June 2015 launching the European Union military operation in the southern Central Mediterranean (EUNAVFOR MED), Official Journal L 157, 23.6.2015, p. 51.

Council Decision (EU) 2015/1601 of 22 September 2015 establishing provisional measures in the area of international protection for the benefit of Italy and Greece No longer in force, Date of end of validity: 26/09/2017 OJ L 248, 24.9.2015, p. 80–94.

Political and Security Committee Decision (CFSP) 2016/118 of 20 January 2016 concerning the implementation by EUNAVFOR MED operation SOPHIA of United Nations Security Council Resolution 2240 (2015) (EUNAVFOR MED operation SOPHIA/1/2016), Official Journal L 23, 29.1.2016, p. 63–64.

Council Decision (CFSP) 2016/2314 of 19 December 2016 amending Decision (CFSP) 2015/778 on a European Union military operation in the Southern Central Mediterranean (EUNAVFOR MED operation SOPHIA), OJ L 345, 20.12.2016, p. 62–64.

Directives

Directive 2002/90/EC establishing a common definition of the offense of facilitation of unauthorised entry, transit and residence, OJ L 328, 5.12.2002, p. 17.

Council Directive 2003/9/EC of 27 January 2003 laying down minimum standards for the reception of asylum seekers in the Member States, Official Journal L 31, 6 February 2003, p. 18–25.

Directive 2005/85/EC of 1 December 2005, Official Journal L326/13 of 13 December 2005.

Directive 2008/115/EC, of 16 December 2008, on common standards and procedures in Member States for returning illegally staying third-country nationals, OJ L 348 98, 24.12.2008, p. 98–107.

Directive 2009/50/EC of 25 May 2009 on the conditions of entry and residence of third-country nationals for the purposes of highly qualified employment, OJ L 155, 18.6.2009, p. 17–29.

Directive 2009/52/EC of the European Parliament and of the Council of 18 June 2009 providing for minimum standards on sanctions and measures against employers of illegally staying third-country nationals, OJ L 168, 30.6.2009, p. 24–32.

Directive 2011/36/EU of the European Parliament and of the Council of 5 April 2011 on preventing and combating trafficking in human beings and protecting its victims, and replacing Council Framework Decision 2002/629/JHA, OJ L 101, 15.4.2011, p. 1–11.

Directive 2011/95/EU of the European Parliament and of the Council of 13 December 2011 on standards for the qualification of third-country nationals or stateless persons as beneficiaries of international protection, for a uniform status for refugees or for persons eligible for subsidiary protection, and for the content of the protection granted, OJ L 337, 20.12.2011, p. 9–26.

Directive 2011/98/EU of the European Parliament and of the Council of 13 December 2011 on a single application procedure for a single permit for third-country nationals to reside and work in the territory of a Member State and on a common set of rights for third-country workers legally residing in a Member State, OJ L 343, 23.12.2011, p. 1–9.

Directive 2013/32/EU of the European Parliament and of the Council of 26 June 2013 on common procedures for granting and withdrawing international protection, Official Journal L 180, 29.6.2013, p. 60–95.

Directive 2013/33/EU of the European Parliament and of the Council of 26 June 2013 laying down standards for the reception of applicants for international protection, Official Journal L 180, 29.6.2013, p. 96–116.

Regulations

Council Regulation (EC) No 377/2004 of 19 February 2004 on the creation of immigration liaison officer's network.

Council Regulation (EC) No 2007/2004 of 26 October 2004 establishing a European Agency for the Management of Operational Cooperation at the External Borders of the Member States of the European Union.

Regulation (EC) No 1987/2006 of the European Parliament and of the Council of 20 December 2006 on the establishment, operation and use of the second generation Schengen Information System (SIS II). OJ L 381, 28.12.2006, p. 4.

Regulation (EU) No 265/2010 of the European Parliament and of the Council of 25 March 2010 amending the Convention Implementing the Schengen Agreement and Regulation (EC) No 562/2006 as regards movement of persons with a long-stay visa, Official Journal L 85, 31.3.2010, p. 1–4.

Regulation (EU) No 603/2013 of the European Parliament and of the Council, of 26 June 2013, establishing "Eurodac" for the comparison of fingerprints for the effective application of Regulation (EU) no. 604/2013 which establishes the criteria and mechanisms for determining the Member State responsible for examining an application for international protection, Official Journal L 180, 29 June 2013, p. 1-30.

Regulation (EU) No 656/2014 of the European Parliament and of the Council of 15 May 2014 establishing rules for the surveillance of the external sea borders in the context of operational cooperation coordinated by the European Agency for the Management of Operational Cooperation at the External Borders of the Member States of the European Union. (Official Journal L 189, 27.6.2014, p. 93–107).

Regulation (EU) No 1052/2013 of the European Parliament and of the Council of 22 October 2013 establishing the European Border Surveillance System (Eurosur), Official Journal L 295, 6.11.2013, p. 11–26.

Regulation (EU) No 1301/2013 of the European Parliament and of the Council of 17 December 2013 on the European Regional Development Fund and on specific provisions concerning the Investment for growth and jobs goal and repealing Regulation (EC) No 1080/2006 laying down tasks, scope, aims, thematic and investment priorities and output indicators for regional development.

Regulation (EU) No 1304/2013 of the European Parliament and of the Council of 17 December 2013 on the European Social Fund and repealing Council Regulation (EC) No 1081/2006.

Regulation (EU) No 516/2014 of the European Parliament and of the Council of 16 April 2014 establishing the Asylum, Migration and Integration Fund, amending Council Decision 2008/381/EC and repealing Decisions No 573/2007/EC and No 575/2007/EC of the European Parliament and of the Council and Council Decision 2007/435/EC.

Regulation (EU) No 656/2014 of the European Parliament and of the Council of 15 May 2014 establishing rules for the surveillance of the external sea borders in the context of operational cooperation coordinated by the European Agency for the Management of Operational Cooperation at the External Borders of the Member States of the European Union, Official Journal L 189, 27.6.2014, p. 93–107.

Regulation (EU) 2016/399 of the European Parliament and of the Council of 9 March 2016 on a Union Code on the Rules governing the movement of persons across borders (Schengen Borders Code). OJ L 77, 23.3.2016, p. 1–52 (which repealed and replaced the Regulation (EC) No 562/2006).

Regulation (EU) 2016/1624 of the European Parliament and of the Council of 14 September 2016 on the European Border and Coast Guard and amending Regulation (EU) 2016/399 of the European Parliament and of the Council and repealing Regulation (EC) No 863/2007 of the European Parliament and of the Council, Council Regulation (EC) No 2007/2004 and Council Decision 2005/267/EC.

Resolutions

UN General Assembly Resolution 2200A (XXI) of 16 December 1966.

Commission on Human Rights Resolution 1999/44 on the Human Rights of Migrants of 26 April 1999, 55th session.

Parliamentary Assembly of the Council of Europe, Resolution 1509 (2006) on Human rights of irregular migrants.

UN General Assembley Resolution A/RES/45/158 on International Convention on the Protection of the Rights of all Migrant Workers and Members of Their Families of 18 December 2006, 69th Plenary Meeting.

European Parliament resolution of 17 December 2014 on the situation in the Mediterranean and the need for a holistic EU approach to migration (2014/2907(RSP).

UN Security Council Resolution No 2240 (2015).

Italian Legislation

Italian Law ratified Geneva convention, 24 July 1954, No. 722, Official Journal No 196 of 27 August 1954.

Law No 147 of 3 April 1989, Official Journal No. 97 of 27 April 1989, Ordinary Supplement 31.

Martelli Law 28 February 1990, No. 40, Official Journal No 49 of 28 February 1990.

D.P.R. No. 662 of 28 September 1994, Official journal No. 281 f 1 December 1994.

Regional Law (Legge Puglia) 24 March 1995, No 8, Official Journal 3 Special Series, No 51, 23 December 1995.

Law of 29 December 1995, n. 563, Official Journal No 303 of 30-12-1995.

Turco–Napolitano Law No. 40, 6 March 1998, Official Journal No 59 of 12 March 1998, Ordinary Supplement 40.

Legislative Decree, coordinated text, 25/07/1998 No 286, Official Journal No 191, 18 August 1998.

Decree of the President of the Republic August 31st 1999, No. 394 Official Journal n.258 of 03-11-1999 – Ordinary Supplement No. 190.

Police agreement signed on 06/18/2000 and entered into force 09/01/2007. Source Italian Ministry of Interior.

Bossi-Fini Law 30 July 2002, No. 189, Official Journal No 199, 26 August 2002, Ordinary Supplement No. 173.

Legislative Decree No. 85, 7 April 2003, Official Journal, No 93, 22 April 2003.

Legislative Decree 30 May 2005, n. 140, Official Journal No.168 of 21 July 2005.

Decree 19 November 2007 No 251, Implementation of Directive 2004/83 / EC laying down minimum rules on the assignment, to third-country nationals or stateless persons, of the status of refugees or persons otherwise in need of international protection, as well as minimum standards on the content of recognized protection, Official Journal No 3 of 04-01-2008.

Legislative Decree January 28, 2008, No. 25, Official Journal No. 40 of 16 February 2008.

Law No 125 of 6 August 2008, Official Journal No. 188 of 14 August 2015, Ordinary Supplement 49.

Law 6 February 2009, No 7 Ratification and implementation of the Treaty of friendship, partnership and cooperation between the Italian Republic and the great Arab Jamamatic People's Socialist Republic, made in Benghazi on 30 August 2008. Official Journal General Series n.40 of 18-02-2009.

Law No 94 of 15 July 2009, Official Journal No 170 of 24 July 2009, Ordinary Supplement 128.

Legislative Decree of 1 September 2011 No. 150, Official Journal No. 220 of 21 September 2011.

Legislative Decree of 21 February 2014, No. 18 which came into force on 22 March 2014, Official Journal No 55 of 7 March 2014.

Law 28 April 2014, No. 67, Official Journal No 100 del 02 May 2014.

Legislative Decree No 142 of 18 August 2015, Official Journal No 214 of 15 September 2015.

Decree Law 17 February 2017, No. 13, Official Journal No.40 del 17 February 2017.

German Legislation

Agreement signed in Ankara on 12 September 1963, which created an association between the European Economic Community and Turkey (BGBl. 1963 II, p. 509) Of the Additional Protocol of 23 November 1970 (BGBl. 1972 II, p. 385) and the subsequent resolutions of the Association Council (ARB) Nos. 1/80 and 2/76.

Statue of 30 July 2004, Federal Law Gazette (BGBI) 2004 I, p. 1950.

Gesetz zur Zuwanderung und zur Regelung des Aufenthalts und der Integration von Unionsbürgern und Ausländer, 30 July 2004, BGB 1, 41, 05/08/2004, 01950-02011.

Residence Act as amended on 25 February 2008, (BGBl) Federal Law Gazette I p. 162. Federal Law Gazette (BGBI) 2004 I, p. 1950.

Gesetz über den Aufenthalt, die Erwerbstätigkeit und die Integration von Ausländern im Bundesgebiet (Aufenthaltsgesetz – AufenthG) Inhaltsübersicht) Resident Act, Geographical Restriction Art. 61, 1. Residence Act in the version promulgated on 25 February 2008 (Federal Law Gazette I p. 162), last amended Article 10 (4) of the Act of 30.10.2017 (Federal Law Gazette I p. 3618).

Asylbewerberleistungsgesetz – AsylbLG Law and the Social Security Law (Sozialgerichtsgesetz), introduced by the Law of 10 December 2014, Federal Law Gazette I p. 2438.

Gesetz zur Verbesserung der Rechtsstellung von asylsuchenden und geduldeten Ausländern of 23 December 2014, BGBI 2014.

Research Reports/Conference Presentations (chronological order)

U.N. Doc. A/CONF. 32/41 at 3 (1968).

OECD, 1977, SOPEMI. Trends in International Migration. Annual Report 1976. Paris: OECD.

L. MARTIN, L. PHILIP, Illegal Immigration and the Colonization of the American Labour Market, CIS Paper, No.1, Washington DC: Center for Immigration Studies, 1986.

OECD, 1989: SOPEMI. Trends in International Migration, Annual Report 1988, 20.

OECD, 1990, SOEPEMI. Trends in International Migration. Annual Report 1989, Paris: OECD.

Hugo van Alphen v. The Netherlands, UNHRC Comm. No. 305/1988, UN Doc. CCPR/C/39/D/305/1988, Aug. 15, 1990, decided July 23, 1990, at para. 5.8.

A. v. Australia, UNHCR Comm. No. 560/1993, UN Doc. CCPR/C/59/D/560/1993, Apr. 30, 1997, decided Apr. 3, 1997, at para. 9.3:"There is no basis for the claim that it is per se arbitrary to detain individuals requesting asylum."Article 9 (1) ICCPR.

G. TAPINOS, Irregular Immigration: Economic and Political Issues,, in OECD, Comating the Illegal Employment of Foreign Workers. Paris: OECD, pp. 13-43, 2000.

Report on the activities of the police forces and on the state of public order and security in the national territory (year 1999), Doc. XXXVIII n. 5, filed by the Minister of the Interior, Senate of the Republic, Chamber of Deputies, XIII Legislature, Bill of Rights and Relations, Rome 2000, p. 176.

UN Sub-Commission on the Promotion and Protection of Human Rights, rights of non-citizens: final report of the Special Rapporteur, Mr. David Weissbrodt, submitted in accordance with Sub-Commission decision 2000/103,Commission resolution 2000/104 and Economic and SocialCouncil decision 2000/283AddendumExamples of practices in regard to non-citizens, 26 May 2003, E/CN.4/Sub.2/2003/23/Add.3.

F. DÜVELL, Illegal immigration in Europe: beyond control?, Palgrave Macmillan, 2006; G. ENGBERSEN, Panopticum Europe and Criminalisation of Undocumented Immigrants. Paper presented to the 6th International Metropolis Conference, Rotterdam, 26-30 November 2001.

United Nations, 2002, Specific Groups and Individuals: Migrant Worker. Report of the Special Rapporteur, Gabriela Rodriguez Pizarro, submitted pursuant to Commission on Human Rights resolution 2002/62. E/CN.4/2003/85. Geneva: UN.

G. ENGBERSEN, J. V.D. LEUN and R. STARING, Illegal immigrants in the Netherlands, Sopemi-Report 2002, Paris, OECD.

V. GUIRADON, Controlling the EU Border by Proxy? The Delegation of Migration Control in Practice, Paper presented at the 13th International Conference of Europeanists, 14-16 March, 2002, Chicago.

UN High Commissioner for refugees Executive Committee, Conclusion on protection Safeguards in Interception Measures, Doc. No. 97 (LIV) – 2003, Oct. 10, 2003, at para. (a)(iv).

P. SCHOUKENS, Exploratory report on the access to social protection for illegal labour migrants, International Social Security Association – European Regional Meeting: Migrants and Social Protection, Oslo, 21–23 April 2004, ISSA/EUR/OSLO/04.

Council of the European Union: "The Hague Programme: strengthening freedom, security and justice in the European Union", document number 16054/04 JAI 559 of 13 December 2004.

P. MONZINI, Il traffico di Migranti per via marittima: il caso dell'Italia, in P.MONZINI, F.PASTORE, G.SCIORTINO, L'Italia Promessa. Geopolitiche e dinamiche organizzative del traffico di migranti verso l'Italia. Studies Centre of International Policy, Roma 2004, p.48.

European Economic and Social Committee, Opinion of the European Economic and Social Committee on the International Convention on Migrants, Brussels, 30 June 2004, OJ C 302, 7.12.2004, p. 49–52.

M. NOWAK, U.N. Covenant on Civil and Political Rights – CCPR Commentary, 2nd revised ed. 2005, Novak, CCPR Commentary, at 122-124.

K. KOSER, Irregular Migration, State Security and Human Security. A paper prepared for the Policy

Analysis and Research Programme of the Global Commission on International Migration. Global Commission on International Migration, available, 2005.

S. GRANT, International Migration and Human Rights, Global Commission on International Migration, 2005, p. 16.

U.N. Doc. CERD/C/64/Misc.11/rev.3 (2005), para. 26.

D. SRISKANDARAJAH, F. H. ROAD, Road, United Kingdom: Rising numbers, rising anxieties. Migration Information Source. Retrieved February 9, 2006.

K. ANNAN, UN Secretary-General Report on International Migration and Development, UN/GA A/60/871 of 18 May 2006, para 77.

J. SOMAVIA, Statement of the Director-General of the International Labour Office, ECOSOC High-Level Segment, Geneva, 5 July 2006.

ILO Multilateral Framework on Labour Migration: Non-binding Principles and Guidelines for a Rights-Based Approach to Labour Migration (International Labour Office, Geneva 2006), pp. 15 and 29.

A. GUILBERT, R. PLAETEVOET, The U.N. Migrant Workers Convention: Steps towards Ratification in Europe, European Platform for Migrant Workers' Rights, March 2007.

The discussion of terminology is based on the CLANDESTINO Project Research: Report on Methodological Issues, edited by A. KRALER and D. VOGEL and prepared by M. JANDL, D. VOGEL and K. IGLICKA, in November 2008.

U.N. Doc. A/62/10, para. 239.

Report of the United Nations High Commissioner for Human Rights, UN Doc E/201/89, 1 June 2010.

Reports on the state of military discipline and on the state of the organization of the armed forces (year 2008), Doc. XXXVI No 2, presented by the minister for relations with Parliament, Senate of the Republic, Chamber of Deputies, XVI Legislature, Drawings of the law and reports, Rome 2010, p. 124.

Plaintiff M70/2011 and Plaintiff M106/2011 v. Minister for Immigration and citizenship (2011) 244 CLR 144 (Aus. HC, Aug 31, 2011), at para. 249.).

Working Group on Arbitrary Detention, Report of the Working Group on Arbitrary Detention: Addendum: Mission to Germany, A/HRC/19/57/Add.3, 23 February 2012.

Response of the Federal Government to the major interpellation of the deputies Ulla Jelpke, Jan Korte, Agnes Alpers, other MPs and the DIE LINKE: printed matter 17/10597: implementation of the deportation policy of the European Union and the practice of detention, Ministry of Interior, 4 September 2012.

Majcher, Izabella, 2014, "The EU Returns Directive and the Use of Prisons for Detaining Migrants in Europe." EU Law Analysis. July. Court of Justice of the European Union (CJEU). 2014B. Pham. C-474/13.CJEU.

D. ANGELI, A. TRIANDAFYLLIDOU, A. DIMITRIADI, Assessing the Cost-effectiveness of Irregular Migration Control Policies in Greece, MIDAS Policy Paper, ELIAMEP, 2014.

V. T. REITANO, L. ADAL, M. SHAW, Smuggled Futures: The Dangerous Path of the Migrant from Africa to Europe, The Global Initiative against Transnational Organized Crime, Geneva, 2014.

UNHCR, Smuggling and Trafficking from the East and Horn of Africa, Progress Report, October 2014, p. 2.

F. PASTORE, E. ROMANO, Implementing selective Protection: Comparative Review of the Implementation of Asylum Policies at National Level Focusing on the Treatment of Mixed Migration Flows at EU's Southern Maritime Borders, FIERI working paper commissioned by the Sachverständigenrat deutscher Stiftungen für Integration und Migration, 2014.

K. HAILBRONNER and D. THYM, Completed Questionnaire for the project Contention: National Report – Germany, 2014.

S. CARRERA, L. den HERTOG, *Whose Mare?*, CESP paper in Liberty and Security in Europe, January 2015, No 79 cit. p. 4.

A. NOURAN, P. MONZINI, F. PASTORE, The Changing Dynamics of Cross-border Human Smuggling and Trafficking in the Mediterranean, Istituto Affari Internazionali, Roma, 2015, p. 20.

Reports on the activities of the police, on the state of order and on public security and on organized crime (year 2014), item I, Doc. XXXVIII n. 3, presented by the Minister of the Interior, Senate of the Republic, Chamber of Deputies, XIII Legislature, Bill of Rights and Relations, Rome 2015, p. 1301.

Report on the activities of the police, on the state of order and on public security and organized crime (year 2014), Volume II, Doc. XXXVIII n.3, presented by the Minister of the Interior, Senate of the Republic, Chamber of Deputies, XIII Legislature, Bill of Rights and Relations, Rome 2015, p. 1308.

Federal government, Antwort der Bundesregierung auf die Große Anfrage der Abgeordneten Ulla Jelpke, Jan Korte, Sevim Dağdelen, weiterer Abgeordneter und der Fraktion DIE LINKE: Drucksache 18/3769, Drucksache 18/7196, 6 January 2016.

European Commission, on 12 April 2016, Managing the Refugee Crisis: EU Financial Support to Greece, Fact Sheet, Migration and Home Affairs.

L. GAZZOTTI, German plans to send migrant children to reception centres in Morocco ignore lessons from history, The Conversation, 29 June 2017.

GDP and Jesuit Refugee Service Germany, Submission to the Universal Periodic Review (UPR): Germany, 21 September 2017, Global Detention Project.

Cases Law (chronological order)

Case 6/64 *Costa v. ENEL*, 1964, ECR 585.

Case 4/73 *Nold* (1974) ECR 491.

Case 36/75 *Rutili* (1975) ECR 1291.

Case 199/77 *Defrenne* (1978) ECR 1365.

Case 199/77 *Defrenne* (1978) ECR 1365.

Case 44/79 *Hauer* (1979) ECR 3727.

Case 222/84 *Jhonston* (1986) ECHR 1651.

Case C-374/87 *Orken* (1989) ECR 3283.

Case C-63/93 *Duff and Others*, 1996, ECR I-569

Van Raalte v. The Netherlands, Application No. 20060/92, Judgment of 2 February 1997, 24 EHRR 503, para 33.

Italian Constitutional Court, Decision No. 353/1997, Official Journal, first special serie 1997.

Case C-299/95 *Kremzow* (1997) ECR I-2629, para. 14.

Case C-249/96 *Grant* (1998) ECR I-621.

Chassagnou and Others v. France, Application Nos. 25088/94; 28331/95; 28443/95, Judgment of 29 April 1999, 29 EHRR 615, para.89.

C-180/99 *Addou* (2001) ECR I-7413

ECtHR *Čonka v Belgium*, Application No. 51564/99, 5 February 2002.

Opinion of AG Stix-Hackl in Case C-459/99 MRAX (2002) ECR I-6591.

Case T-77/01 *Territorio Historico de Alava* (2002) ECR II-81, para. 35.

Case T-54/99 *max.mobil Telecommunication* (2002) ECR II-313, para. 48.

European Court of Human Rights, *Seferovic c. Italia*, 8 February 2011, 12921/04.

ECtHR *Gebremedhin (Gaberamadhien) v France*, Application No. 25389/05.

Case T-315/01 *Kadi* (2005) ECR II-3649.

Issa and Others v. Turkey, 41 EHRR 27, ECHR, Mar. 30 2005, at para. 71.

Ilascu and Others v. Moldova and Russia, 2005, 40 EHRR 46, ECHR, July 8, 2004, at paras. 312, 314.

Case C-540/03 *EP v. Council* (2006) I-5769, para. 58.

Bankovic and Others v. Belgium and Others, (2007) 44 EHRR SE5 (ECHR, Dec. 12, 2001)

Case C-438/05 *Viking* (2007) ECR I-10779, paras. 43-44.

ECtHR, *De Souza Ribeiro v France* [GC], Application No. 22689/07.

Italian Judgment of the Cassazione Penale Court, Third section, of 23 January 2003, No. 3162, Official Journal No 298 of 22 December 2003.

European Court of Human Rights, *Mikolenko v. Estonia*, 8 September 2009, n. 10664/05.

Court of Justice (2009) C-357/09PPU, *Kadzoev, EC Rep*. 30 November 2009, p. I-11189.

ECtHR, *Hirsi Jamaa and Others v Italy* [GC], Application No. 27765/09.

ECtHR, *Sharifi and Others v Italy and Greece*, Application No. 16643/09.

Judgment of Constitutional Court No 249 of 8 July 2010, Official Journal 14/07/2010 No. 28.

Italian Judgment No 250, Constitutional Court, 5 July 2010, Official Journal No 28, 14 July 2010.

Case C-555/07 *Kücükdecevi* (2010) ECR I-00365, para. 22.

Case C-578/08 *Chrackoun* (2010) ECR I-01839, para. 44.

Case C-571/07 *Blanco Perez* (2010) ECR I-04629, para. 65.

C-400/10 *PPU McB* (2010) ECR I-08965, para. 51.

O′ Donoghue and Others v. the United Kingdom, ECHR (2010) Appl. No. 34848/07, judgment of 14 December 2010.

Court of Justice C-61/11 PPU, *EL Dridi, EC Rep*. 28, April 2011, p. I-0000

Italian Constitutional Court, Judgment of 25 July 2011 No 245, Official Journal No 32 27/07/2011.

Al-Skeini and Others v. United Kingdom, 2011, 53 EHRR 18 ECHR, July 7, 2011.

Al-Jedda v. United Kingdom, 2011, 53 EHRR 23, ECHR, July 7, 2011.

Case C-265/11 *Dereci and Others* (2011) Judgment of 15 November 2011.

Court of Justice C-329/11, *Achghbabian, EC Rep*, 6 December 2011, p. I-0000.

European Court of Human Rights, *Yoh-Ekale Mwanje v. Belgium* 20 Dicember 2011, n. 10486/10.

European Court of Human Rights, *Popov v. France* 19 January 2012, no. 39472/07 and 39474/07.

Case C-430/11, *Md Sagor*, judgment of 6 December 2012.

CJEU – Joined Cases C-473/13 and C-514/13 *Adala Bero v Regierungspräsidium Kassel and Ettayebi Bouzalmate v Kreisverwaltung Kleve.*

CJEU – C-474/13, *Thi Ly Pham v Stadt Schweinfurt.*

C-473/13, *Bero and Bouzalmate*, 17 July 2014.

ECtHR, sez. II, *Khaifia and others v Italy*, 16483/12, 1 September 2015.

ECtHR, *N.D. and N.T. v. Spain*, Application No 8675/15 and 8697/15, 3 October 2017.

Court of Justice C-430/11 *Md Sagor, EC Rep.*, 6 December 2012, p. I-0000.

Case C-290/14 *Skerdhan Celaj*, Fourth Chamber of the Court of Justice of the European Union, 01-10-2015.

Bibliography

C. AMALFITANO, *The European Union and protection of victims of trafficking in human beings*, in G. CAGGIANO (eds), The legal pathways for integration. Migrants and beneficiaries of international protection between EU law and Italian law, Turin, 2014, p. 753 ss.

B. ANDERSON, M. RUSH, *Guest editorial: researching illegality and lobour migration*, in *Population, Space and Place*, 2010, vol. 16, no. 3, pp. 175-9.

K. BADE, *Migration in European History, Blackwell Publishing*, Oxford 2003, p. 228.

D.E. BAINES, *Emigration from Europe*, 1815-1930. Cambridge, UK: Cambridge University, 1995, pp. 33-38.

M. BARBAGLI (ed.), *Rapporto sulla criminalita´ in Italia*, 2007.

T. BASARAN, *Security, Law, Borders. Spaces of Exclusion*, in International Political Sociology, 2(1), 2008, pp. 339-354.

L. BIALASIEWICZ, Off-shoring and Out-sourcing the Borders of Europe: Libya and EU Border Work in the Mediterranean, in Geopolitics, 17, 2012, p. 854.

A. BLOCH, *Irregular Migrants: Policy, Politics, Motives and Everyday Lives*, London, Routledge, 2012.

R. BOHNING, *The ILO and the New UN Convention on Migrant Workers: The Past and Future*, in *International Migration Review*, 1991, 698.

M. BORRACCETTI, *The EU, Migration and the Politcs of Administrative Detention*, 2014, Routledge.

M. BORRACCETTI, *La prima assistenza ai migranti in arrivo tra diritti fondamentali e zone franche*, in Dir. Imm. Citt., 2014, No 2, 13.

G. BORJAS, *Economic theory and international migration*, in International Migration Review, 1989, 23(3), 457-485.

G. BORJAS, *Friends or strangers: the impact of immigrants on the U.S. economy*. New York: Basic Books, 1990.

L.S. BOSNIAK, *Human Rights, State Sovereignty and the Protection of Undocumented Migrants under the International Migrant Workers convention, 25 International Migration Review*, 1991, 737, p. 740.

F. CAESTECKER, *Alien policy in Belgium, 1840-1940: the creation of guest workers, refugees and illegal aliens,* New York, Berghah, 2000.

G. CAMPESI, *L´Italia e il controllo delle frontiere marittime*, in M. SAVINO, La crisi migratoria tra Italia e Unione Europea: diagnosi e prospettive, Editoriale Scientifica, Napoli, 2017.

J. CAPLAN, J. TORPEY, (eds), *Documenting Individual Identities*, Princeton University Press, 2000.

T. CAPONIA, *(Im)Migration research in Italy: A European comparative perspective*, in *The Sociological Quarterly*, 2008, 49(3) 445-464.

F. CASOLARI, *The EU's Hotspot Approach to Managing the Migration Crisis: A Blind Spot for International Responsibility?*, in The Italian Yearbook of International Law, 2015, Vol. 25.

S. CASTELS, *Why migration policies fail, ethnic and racial studies*, 2004, vol. 27, no.2

S. CASTELS & M.J. MILLER, *The age of migration: international population movements in the modern world* (4th ed.) New York: Guilford Press, 2004.

M. CECCORULLI, N. LABANCA, *The EU, Migration and Politics of Administrative Detention*, Routledge London, 2014.

V. CHETAIL and G. GIACCA, Who care? The right to Health of migrants, in A.CLAPHAM and M. ROBINSON (eds), Realizing the Right to Health (2009) 244.

R. CHOLEWINSKY, *Migrant workers in International Human Rights Law: Their Protection Countries of employment*, Clarendon Press, Oxford 1997, p. 96.

A. CHOMSKY, *Undocumented: how immigration became illegal*, Boston, Beacon Press, 2015.

B. CONFORTI, *I. Carta, Immigrazione, Frontiere Esterne e Diritti Umani* , Teseo Editore, Roma, 2009

W. A. CORNELIUS, *Controlling "unwanted" immigration: lessons from the United States 1993-2004*, in *Journal of Ethnic and Migration Studies*, 2005, vol. 31, no. 4, pp. 775-94.

F. CORTESE, *La difficile classificazione dei migranti*, in M. SAVINO La crisi migratoria tra Italia e Unione Europea: diagnosi e prospettive, Editoriale Scientifica, 2017.

K. COUPER, U. SANTAMARIA, *An Elusive Concept: the Changing Definition of Illegal Immigrant in the Practice of Immigration Control in the United Kingdom*, in *International Migration Review*, 1984, 18 (3): 437-52.

P. CRAIG, G. DE BURCA, *EU Law: Text, Cases, and Materials*, 4th eds. Oxford University Press, Oxford 2008.

P. CUTTITTA, *Readmission in the Relations between Italy and North African Mediterranean Countries*, in J.P. CASSARINO(ed), Unbalanced Reprocities: Cooperation on Readmission in the Euro-Mediterranean Area., Middle East Institute, 2011, p. 40.

M. CVAJNER, G. SCIORTINO, *Theorizing irregular migration: the control of spatial mobility in differentiated societies*, in *European Journal of Social Theory*, 2010, vol. 13, no. 3, pp. 389-404.

N. CYRUS, D. VOGEL, *Immigration as a side-effect of other policies: principles and consequences of the German non-immigration policy.* IAPASIS, first report. Oldenburg: University of Oldenburg, 2000.

N. CYRUS, D. VOEGEL, *Ausländerdiskriminierung durch Außenkontrollen im Arbeitsmarkt?* Fallstudienbefunde – Herausforderungen – Gestaltungsoptionen, Mitteilungen aus der Arbeitsmarkt und Gerusforschung, 2000, 35(2), 254-70.

N. CYRUS, *Schattenwirtschaft und Migration in Berlin. Ethnologische Annäherungen an ein offenes Geheimnis*, in Frank Gesemann (ed), Migration und Integration in Berlin, Wissenschaftliche und Politische Perspektiven. Opladen, Leske und Budrich, 2001, pp. 209-32.

P. DE BRUYCKER, A. DI BARTOLOMEO, Migrants smuggled by sea to the EU: facts, laws and policy options, MPC Research Report 2013/09.

H. DE HASS, *Engaging diasporas: How governments and development agencies can support diaspora involvement in the development of origin countries*, A study for Oxfam Novib, Oxford: International Migration Institute, James Martin 21st Century School. New York: University of Oxford, 2006, p. 9.

M. DIAMANT, *Die Illegalen, Der Gewerkschafter*, 1973, 12: 474-5; B. HUBER, *Illegal Ausländerbeschäftigung und ökonomische Krise*, in *Demokratie und Recht*, 1993, vol. 4, 370-3.

A. DI PASCALE, *Italy and Unauthorized Migration: Between State Sovereignty and Human Rights Obligations*, Oxford Scholarship Online, 2014.

A. DRZEMCEWSKI, *The Position of Aliens in Relation to the European Convention of Human Rights: a General Survey*, in: Council of Europe (ed.), *Human Rights of Aliens in Europe*, Martinus Nijhoff Publishers, Dordrecht 1985, pp. 351-399.

F. DÜVELL, *Illegal immigration in Europe beyond control?*, Palgrave Macmillan, 2006.

F. DÜVELL, *Clandestine migration in Europe*, in *Social Science Information*, 2008, vol. 47, No. 4, pp. 479-97.

L. EINAUDI, *Le Politiche dell' Immigrazione in Italia dall'Unita' ad oggi* , Laterza, 2007.

K. EISELE, *The External Dimention of the EU's Migration Policy. Different Legal Position of Third-Country Nationals*, in the EU: A Comparative Perspective, in Immigration and Asylum Law and Policy in Europe, 2014, Vol. 34, Jan Niessen and Espelth Guild.

T. FAIST, P. KIVISTO, *Beyond a Border: The Causes and Consequences of Contemporary Immigration,* Thousand Oaks, CA: SAGE/Pine Forge Press, 2010.

P. FARGUE, S. BONFANTI, *When the best option is a leaky boat: why migrants risk their lifes crossing the Mediterranean and what Europe is doing about it*, Migration Policy Center, EUI, 2014, Italy.

N. FENNELLY, *Pillar Talk: Fundamental Rights Protection in the European Union*, in *Judicial Studies Institute Journal*, 2008, 95, p. 100.

A. FISCHER-LESCANO, L. TILLMAN, T. TOHIDIPUR, *Border Controls at Sea: Requirements under International Human Rights and Refugee Law*, in *International Journal of Refugee Law*, 21, 2009, p. 290.

J. FITZPATRICK, *The Human Rights of Migrants*, in T.A. ALEINIKOFF and V. CHETAIL (eds.), Migration and International Legal Norms ,T.M.C. Asser Press, The Hague 2003, pp. 171-172.

A. T. GALLAGHER, F. DAVID, *The international law of migrant smuggling,* Cambridge University Press, 2014.

T. GARDEN BARNES, *Shaping the Common Law: from Glanvill to Hale*, 1188-1688, Standford University Press, 2008, 27.

L. GIACOMO, *Migration Policies in Europe and the United States*, Dordrecht, Klumer Academic Publishers, 1993.

M. GIUFFRE', *Watered-Down Rights on the High Seas: Hirsi Jamaa and Others v. Italy*, in International and Comperative Law Quartely, 2012, No 61, pp. 728-750.

M. GONDEK, *Extraterritorial Application of The European Convention on Human Rights: Territorial Focus in the Age of Globalization?*, 52 Netherlands International Law Review, 2005, 3.

G. GOODWIN-GILL, J. MCADAMAT, *The Refugee in International Law*, Oxford University Press, 2007.

H. GOULBOURNE, *Race relations in Britain since 1945*, London: Macmillian, 1988.

C. GRAEBSCH, B. SELDERS, *Der Zugang zum Bundesgerichtshof ist das geringste Problem: Interview mit Christine Graebsch von Beate Selders, In Haft ohne Straftat. Fakten und Argumente gegen Abschiebungshaft*, Edited by Flüchtlingsrat Brandenburg, Flüchtlingsrat Schleswig-Holstein and Humanistische Union, Berlin, 2013, quoted in Federal Office for Migration and Refugees, 2014, op. cit.

E. GUILD, P. MINDERHOUD, *Immigration and criminal law in the European Union: the legal measures and social consequences of criminal law in Member States on trafficking and smuggling in human beings*, Martinus Nijhoff Publishers, 2006.

J. GUIRAUDON, *De-nationalizing control: analysis state responses to restraints on migration control*, in V. GUIRAUDON and C. JOPPKE (eds), Controlling a new migration world, London, Routledge, 2001

K. HAMITON, P. SIMON & C: VENIARD, *The challenge of French diversity*, Migration Information Source. Retrieved February 8, 2006.

S. HAMOOD, *Eu-Libya Cooperation on Migration: A Raw Deal For Refugees and Migrants?*, in Journal of Refugee Studies, 21, 2008, p. 33

B. HAPPLE, *European Social Charter*, *17 Industrial Law Journal* 1988, 124, p. 125.

A. HARGREAVES, *Immigration, "race", and ethnicity in contemporary France*. London: Routledge, 1995, p. 79.

D. HARRIS, *A Fresh Impetus for the European Social Charter, 41 International and Comparative Law Quarterly*, 1992, 659.

J.R. HARRIS & M.P. TODARO, *Migration , unemployment, and development: A two-sector analysis*, in American Economic Review, 1970, 60(2), 126-142.

M. HASENAU, *ILO Standards on Migrant Workers: The Fundamentals of the UN Convention and their Genesis*, 25 International Migration Review, 1991, 687, p. 695.

T.J. HATTON & J.G. WILLIAMSON, *The age of mass migration: causes and economic impact*. New York: Oxford University Press, 1998, p. 14.

D. HOERDER, *Cultures in contact: World Migrations in the Second Millennium*, Durham and London, Duke University Press 2002.

J.F. HOLLIFIELD, *Immigrants, market and states: the political economy of postwar Europe*, Cambridge, MA: Harvard University Press, 1992.

U. HOLM, *The Implication of the Concept of the French State-Nation and "Patrei" for French Discourses on (Algerian) Immigration*. Columbia International Affairs Online (CIAO). Working Paper, New York, Columbia University Press, 2003.

M. W. JANIS, R.S. KAY, A.W. BRADLEY, *European Rights Law, Text and Materials*, Third Edition, Oxford.

S. JOHNSON, S.J. FITZGERALD, *The United States and Mexico: Partners in Reforms*, Backgrounder, 2003.

C. JOPPKE, *Why liberal states accept unwanted immigration*, in *World Politics*, 1998, vol. 50, no.2, pp.266-93.

B. JORDAN, D. VOGEL, *Which policies influence migration decisions: a comparative analysis of qualitative interviews with undocumented Brazilian immigrants in London and Berlin as a contribution to economic reasoning*, 1997, ZeS Arbeitspapier No.14. Bremen: Zentrum für Socialpolitik.

B. JORDAN, F. DÜVELL, *Irregular migration: the dilemmas of transnational mobility*, Cheltenham: Edward Elgar, 2002.

P. KIVISTO & T: FAIST, *Citizenship: Discourses, theory, and transnational prospects, Malden*, MA: Blackwell, 2007.

N. KLEIN, *Maritime Security and the Law of the Sea*, Oxford University Press, Oxford, 2011, p. 75.

H. KLEINSCHMITT, *Menschen in Bewegung. Inhalte und Ziele historischer Migrationsforschung, Gottingen*, Vandenhoeck und Ruprecht, 2002.

S. KLEPP, *A contested asylum system: The European Union between refugee protection and border control in the Mediterranean Sea*, in European Journal of Migration and Law, 12, 2010, p. 4.

A. KREIENBRINK, *Spanische Einwanderungspolitik im Spannungsfeld von europaischen Anforderungen und nationalem Interessen*, in *Materialen zur Bevolkerungswissenschaft*, 2003, 107: 49-76.

E. LAUTERPACHT, D. BETHLEHEM, *The scope and content of the principle of non refoulment*, in E. FELLER, V. TÜRK, F. NICHOLSON (eds), Refugee Protection in International Law: UNHCR´s global consultations on international protection, Cambridge University Press, Cambridge 2003, p. 89-177.

S. LAVENEX, N. WICHMANN, *The External Governance of EU Internal Security*, in Journal of European Integration, 31, 2009, pp. 83-02.

E. LEE, *A Theory of migration. Demography*, 1966, 3(1), 47-57; H. DE HASS, (2006). Engaging diasporas: How governments and development agencies can support diaspora involvement in the development of origin countries, A study for Oxfam Novib, Oxford: International Migration Institute, James Martin 21st Century School. New York, University of Oxford, 2006.

D. LUTTERBECK, *Migrants weapons and oil: Europe and Libya after the sanctions*, in The Journal of North Africa Studies, 2009, No 14, p. 172.

M. MARRUS, *The unwanted: European refugees in the twentieth century*, Oxford University Press,1985.

L. MASERA, *La Corte di giustizia Ue dichiara il delitto di illecito reingresso dello straniero espulso (art. 13 comma 13 TUIMM) conforme alla direttiva rimpatri (2008/115/CE)*, in Contemporary Criminal Law, October 5, 2015.

L. MASERA, G. SAVIO, *La "prima" accoglienza*, in M., Savino, *La crisi migratoria tra Italia e Unione Europea: diagnosi e prospettive*, Editoriale Scientifica, Napoli, 2017.

E. MASSA, *Human Rights Law*, Fourth Edition, Oxford University Press, 2011.

D. MASSEY, S. ARANGO, J. HUGO, G. KOUAOUCI, A. PELLEGRINO & T. J. EDWARD, *Theories of international migration: a review and appraisal*, in *Population and Development Review*, 1993, 19(3), 431-466, p. 448.

D. MASSEY, S. ARANGO, J. HUGO, G. KOUAOUCI, A. PELLEGRINO & T.J. EDWARD, *An evaluation of international migration theory: The North American case*, in *Population and Development Review*, 1994, 20(4), 699-751.

D. MASSEY, J.E. TAYLOR, (Eds), *International migration: prospects and policies in a global market*. New York: Oxford University Press, 2004.

C. MAZZUCATO, *Il reato di ingresso e soggiorno illegale nel territorio dello stato. La posizione della Corte Costituzionale e i persistenti dubbi di legittimita´ riguardo ad una norma lucidamente incoerente, in Gli Stranieri*, Review of Studies and Four-Monthly Jurisprudence, No 2, 2010.

E. MITZMAN, *Il rimpatrio dei migranti irregolari*, in M. SAVINO, La crisi migratoria tra Italia e Unione Europea: diagnosi e prospettive, Editoriale Scientifica, Napoli, 2017.

P. MONZINI, *Il Traffico di Migranti per via marittima*, cit, p. 45.

G. MOON, *The Draft Discrimination Protocol to the European Convention on Human Rights: A progress Report*, in European Human Rights Law Review, 2000, 49, pp. 51-52.

V. MORENO-LAX, *Seeking Asylum in the Mediterranean: Against a Fragmentary Reading of EU Member States´ Obligation Accruing at Sea*, in International Journal of Refugee Law, 2011, 23, p. 199.

A. NATALE, *I migranti e l´ habeas corpus alla prova delle emergenze: il caso Lampedusa*, in Ques. Giust., 2013, No 5, 181.

J.L. MURRAY, *Fundamental Rights in the European Communuty Legal Order*, 32 *Fordham International Law Journal*, 2008, p. 531,

B. NASCIMBENE, *Nuove norme in materia di immigrazione. La legge Bossi-Fini: perplessita´ e critiche*, Corriere Giuridico, 2003.

M. NGAI, *The strange career of the illegal alien: immigration restriction and deportation policy in the US*, 1921-1965, in *Law and History Review*, 2003, 21(1) , 69-107.

M. NGAI, *Impossible subject: illegal aliens and the making of modern America, Princeton*, NJ, and Oxford, Princeton University Press, 2004.

J. NICKLESS, *European Code of Social Security: A Short Guide, Council of Europe Publishing*, Strasbourg 2003, p. 11.

G. NORIEL, *The French melting pot: immigration, citizenschip, and national identity*, Minneapolis: University of Minnesota Press, 1996, p. 64.

J. O′ CONNEL DAVIDSON, *Troubling freedom: Migration, debt, and modern slavery*, in Migration Studies, 1 July 2013, Vol. 1, Issue 2, Pages 176–195.

P. ODMALM, *Migration policies and political participation, Basingstoke*, UK: Palgrave Macmillian, 2005, p. 29.

V. ONIDA, *Efficacia non scontata per il ricorso al penale*, Il Sole 24 Ore, 22 May 2008.

R. C. OSTERGREN, *A community transplanted: The trans-Atlantic experience of a Swedish immigrant settlement in the Upper Middle West*, 1835-1915, Madison: University of Wisconsin Press, 1988.

C.OVEY, R.A.W. HITE, *The European Convention on Human Rights*, 4th end. Oxford University Press, Oxford 2006, pp. 419-429.

A. PALLISTER, *Magna Carta: the Heritage of Liberty*, Oxford: Oxford University Press, 1971.

E. PAPASTAVRIDIS, *The Interception of Vessels on the High Seas: Contemporary Challenges to the Legal Order of the Oceans, Hart Publishing*, Oxford and Portland 2013, p. 278.

S. PASQUETTI, *L′azione della UE nel campo della immigrazione legale: principi e obiettivi*, in *Le Migrazioni*, U. Leanza.

S. PEERS, *Human Rights, Asylum and European Community Law*, 24 Refugee Survey Quartely, 2005, 24, p. 29.

S. PEERS, *EU Justice and Home Affairs Law 3rd end*, Oxford University Press, Oxford, 2011.

W. PETERSEN, *A General Typology of migration*, in American Sociological Review, 1958, 23(3), 256-266.

A. PORTES, *Illegal immigration and the international system: lessons from recent legal Mexican immigrants to the United States*, in *Social Problems*, 1979, 26 (4), p. 425-443.

M.C. PUGH, *Europe′s boat people: maritime cooperation in the Mediterranean*, Institute for Security Studies, Western European Union 2000, p. 36.

N. O. PEREZ, *Spain: forging an immigration policy, Migration Information Source*, retrieved April 10, 2005.

J. RAITIO, *The General Principle of Legal Certainty as a General Principle of EU Law*, in U. BERNITZ, J. NERGELIUS and C. CARDNER (eds), General Principles of EC Law in a Process of Development, Kluwer Law International, Alphen aan den Rijn, 2008, pp. 47-73.

V. T. REITANO, L. ADAL, M. SHAW, *Smuggled Futures: The Dangerous Path of the Migrant from Africa to Europe*, The Global Initiative against Transnational Organized Crime, Geneva, 2014.

J. RIJPMA, M. CREMONA, *The Extra-Territorialisation of EU Migration Policies and the Rule of Law*, EUI Working Papers, Law 2007/1, Fiesole 2007; V. MITSILEGAS, Extra-territorial Immigration Control in the 21st Century: The Individual And The State Transformed, in B. RYAN, V. MITSILEGAS (eds), Extraterritorial Immigration Control, cit., pp. 38-64.

N. ROGERS, *Immigration and the Convention on Human Rights: Are New Principles Emerging?*, in *European Human Rights Law Review*, 2003, 53, p. 54.

B. RYAN, *Extraterritorial Immigration Control: What Role for Legal Guarantees?*, in B. RYAN and V. MITSLEAGAS eds., Extraterritorial Immigration Control: Legal Challenges 1, 2010.

M. SAVINO, *L'amministrativizzazione della liberta' personale e del due process dei migrant: il caso Khaifia*, in Dir. imm. citt., 2015, No 3-4, p.50.

M. SAVINO, *La crisi migratoria tra Italia e Unione Europea: diagnosi e prospettive*, Editoriale Scientifica, 2017.

L. SCHUSTER, *The exclusion of asylum seekers in Europe*, Center on Migration, Policy, and Society Working Paper No. 1, Wp-04-01. Oxford: University of Oxford, 2004

G. SCIORTINO, A. COLOMBO, *The Flows and the Flood: Public Discourse on Immigration in* Italy, 1969-2001, in *Journal of Modern Italian Studies*, 2004, 9(1): 94-113.

G. SCIORTINO, *Between phantoms and necessary evils. Some critical points in the study of irregular migrations to Western Europe,* IMIS-Beitrage, 2004, 24, p. 17-43.

J. SIMEANT, *La cause de sans papiers*, Paris, Presses de Sciences Po, 1998.

G. SIMMEL, *Exkurs über den Fremend*, in G. SIMMEL, *Soziologie: Untersuchungen über die Formen der Vergesellschaftung,* 1908/1992, vol. 11, Frankfurt, Suhrkamp.

G. SLAPPER & D. KLLY, *Sourcebook on the English Legal System,* London: Cavendish Publishing Limited, 2001, 487.

O. STARK, *The Migration of Labour*, Oxford, Blackwell, 1991.

Y. TANAKA, *The International Law of the Sea*, Cambridge University Press, Cambridge, 2012, p. 85.

P. TARAN, *Migration Today: the Global Challenge*, in *People and the Planet*, 1994, vol. 3. no. 4.

P.A. TARAN, *Human Rights of Migrants: Challenges of the New Decade*, 38 International Migration, 2001, 7, pp. 18-19.

C. TILLY, *Transplanted networks*, in V. YANS-MCLAUGHLIN (Ed.), Immigration reconsidered: history, sociology and politics, 1990, New York: Oxford University Press, p. 84.

M.P. TODARO, *A model of labor migration and urban unemployment in low-developed countries,* in American Economic Review, 1969, 59(1), 138-148.

M.P. TODARO, *Internal Migration in developing countries*, Geneva: International Labor Office, 1976.

M.P. TODARO, & L. MARUSZKU, *Illegal immigration and U.S. immigration reform: a conceptual framework,* in *Population and Development Review*, 1987, 13(1), 104-114.

M. TONDINI, *The use of force in the course of maritime law enforcement operations*, in Journal on the Use of Force and International Law, 4:2, 2017, 253-272.

M. TODINO, *The Legality of Intercepting Boat People Under Search and Rescue and Border Control Operations with Reference to Recent Italian Interventions in the Mediterranean Sea and the ECtHR Decision in the Hirsi Case*, in *Journal of International Maritime Law*, April 2012, Vol. 18, No. 1, pp. 59-74. at 62: "In the case of active resistance, the interception cannot fall within the SAR legal regime".

K. TOUZENIS, *Migration and Human Rights in Italy: Prospects for the ICRMW* in R. CHOLEWINSKY, P. DE GUCHTENEIRE, and A. PECOUD (eds), Migration and Human Rights: The United Nations Convention on Migrant Workers' Rights, 2009, 343.

F. TRAUNER, I. KRUSE, *EC visa facilitation and readmission agreements: A new standard EU foreign policy tool?*, in European Journal of Migration and Law, 10(4), 2008, pp. 411-438.

A. TRIANDAFYLLIDOU, *The political discourse on immigration in Southern Europe: a critical analysis*, in *Journal of Community and Applied Social Psychology*, 2000, 10 (5): 373-89.

A. TRIANDAFYLLIDOU, *Irregular Migration in Europe: Myths and Realities*, Farnham, Surrey, Ashgate, 2010.

T. TRIDIMAS, *The General Principles of EU Law*, 2nd eds. Oxford University Press, Oxford, 2006

I. VAN LIEMPT, *Navigating Borders: Inside Perspectives on the Process of Human Smuggling into the Netherlands*, Amsterdam: Amsterdam University Press, 2007.

M. VAN REISEN, C. RIJKEN, *Sinai Trafficking: Origin and Definition of a New Form of Human Trafficking*, in *Social Inclusion*, 2015, p. 113 ss.

G. VERMEULEN, E. DESMET, *Essential text on European and International Asylum and Migration Law and Policy*, Maklu, Antwerpen-Apeldoorn-Portland, 2017.

F. VIGANO', *Diritto penale e immigrazione: qualche riflessione sui limiti alla discrezionalita' del legislatore*, 12 Diritto, Immigrazione e Cittadinanza, 2010, 65.

A. VON BOGDANDY, *The European Union as a Human Rights Organization? Human Rights and the Core of the European Union*, 37 Common Market Law Review, 2000, 1307, p. 1338.

D. WEISSRODT, *The Protection of Non-Citizens in International Human Rights Law* in R. CHOLEWINSKY, R. PERRUCHOUD and E. MACDONALD (eds.), International Migration Law: Developing Paradigms and Key Challenges, T.C.M. Asser Press.,The Hague 2007, pp. 228-232.

A. WIESBROK, *Legal Migration to the European Union*, Martinus Nijhoff Publishers, Leiden, 2010, pp. 209-210

J. G. WILLIAMSON, *Migration to the new world: long term influences and impact.* Explorations in Economic History, 1974, II, 357-390.